FLY AWAY

FLY AWAY

The Great African American Cultural Migrations

• • •

PETER M. RUTKOFF AND WILLIAM B. SCOTT

JOHNS HOPKINS UNIVERSITY PRESS
Baltimore

Johns Hopkins Paperback edition, 2015
2 4 6 8 9 7 5 3 1

Johns Hopkins University Press
2715 North Charles Street
Baltimore, Maryland 21218-4363
www.press.jhu.edu

The Library of Congress has cataloged the hardcover edition of this book as follows:
Rutkoff, Peter M., 1942–
Fly away : the great African American cultural migrations /
Peter M. Rutkoff and William B. Scott.
p. cm.
Includes bibliographical references and index.
ISBN-13: 978-0-8018-9477-0 (hardcover : alk. paper)
ISBN-10: 0-8018-9477-8 (hardcover : alk. paper)
1. African Americans—Migrations—History—20th century. 2. African
Americans—History—1877–1964. 3. Migration, Internal—United
States—History—20th century. 4. Rural-urban migration—United
States—History—20th century. 5. African Americans—Social life and
customs. 6. United States—Civilization—African American influences.
7. United States—Emigration and immigration—History—20th century.
1. Scott, William B., 1945– 11. Title.
E185.6.R87 2010
973'.0496073—dc22   2009033384

A catalog record for this book is available from the British Library.

ISBN-13: 978-1-4214-1847-6
ISBN-10: 1-4214-1847-9

Frontispiece: "Sweeping the Sidewalk in the Morning," by Wayne Miller
(used with artist's permission)

The maps used in this book were created by Gordon Thompson.

*Special discounts are available for bulk purchases of this book. For more
information, please contact Special Sales at 410-516-6936 or
specialsales@press.jhu.edu.*

The Johns Hopkins University Press uses environmentally friendly
book materials, including recycled text paper that is composed of at least
30 percent post-consumer waste, whenever possible.

*To the Rothenbergs Sara, Susan, and Alan and
to Bill and Terry Lowry and Allen B. Ballard, Jr.,
and to our Kenyon students in North By South*

CONTENTS

MAPS AND ILLUSTRATIONS

ACKNOWLEDGMENTS

Our thanks to Alphonso Brown, Herb Frazier, the late Virginia Geraty, the late Philip Simmons, and Joseph Foreman, as well as to Alfreda Thompson and Joseph Legree of St. Helena and the staff at Penn Center. The staff at the Avery Center of the College of Charleston provided us enormous help and friendship, including Sherman Pyatt (now at South Carolina State University), Deborah Wright, Harlan Greene, Curtis Franks, Daman Fordham, and Georgette Mayor. Elain Boswell and Bob McIntyre at the Charleston County Register Mesne Conveyance, and the staffs at the Charleston County Public Library, the Charleston Museum, and the South Carolina State Archives gave us generous access to critical materials. In Mount Pleasant and North Charleston, we received generous help from Janette Lee, the late Mary and Jesse Bennett, Joyce Coakley, Ted Freeman, Elizabeth Hamlin, Dr. James Ward, the Reverend Alfred and Eva Jefferson, Fred and Pat Scott, Ruth Hurt, Sharon Crews, Mazie Coaxum Brown, Edward Coaxum, Isaac Coaxum, Michael Allen, Charlotte and Frank Simons, Thomasina Stokes-Marshall, and John Russell.

This project began at the Harlem home of Olive Adams. We thank her, along with her daughters Julie Adams Strandberg and Carolyn Adams. Also in Harlem, the Schomburg Center for Research in Black Culture of the New York Public Library proved indispensable, as did the hospitality of David Whitbeck.

Our Great Migration colleagues in Cleveland, especially Portia Morgan, Allan Keller, Rita Bigham, Jim Templeman, Linda Robinson, Barbara Irvin, Renee Gorham, Pam Craig, Milton Profit, James Heffernan, Marlana Hamer, and Paul Finucan, helped us every step of the way. Bill Lipscomb, Jim Lubetkin, and Bill McKersie, then of the Cleveland Foundation, and Terry Bishop of Dominion East Ohio Gas in Cleveland helped us find the funding to complete the project.

We are grateful to Michael Flug, librarian at the Vivian Harsh collection at the Chicago Public Library; the Reverend Christopher Allan Bullock; and the Chicago Art Institute. Also, the staff and congregation at Progressive Baptist Church in Chicago, including Ann Smith, Lillian Qualls, Emma Jean Miller, and Ruby Banks; Judith Sensibar and David Sensibar, who hosted us in Hyde Park; Celia Leventhal, a member of the Greenville Mississippi Club of Chicago; Suzanne Flandreau at the Black Music Research Center of Columbia College in Chicago; and John Weber all contributed in quite personal ways to the book, while Wayne Miller allowed us to use his photographs, and the late Archie Motley and his wife Valerie Brown gave permission to reproduce *The Liar* by Archibald Motley. We thank Gordon Thompson for producing the maps for this book.

We received extensive help from Miki Goral at the UCLA Library and the staffs at the Library of Congress, the National Archives, the Special Collections at UCLA, the Los Angeles Public Library, the Charleston County Library, the Houston Public Library, the Texas Southern University Library, the University of Houston Library, the Schomberg Library in Harlem and the New York Public Library, the Butler Library at Columbia University, and the Yale University libraries.

In Mississippi, we received help from the Reverend Earl Hall of Mound Bayou; the late Reverend Willie Morganfield of Clarksdale; Norva Lee Harris; the late Milburn Crowe of Mound Bayou; our host in Oxford, Dean Ron Vernon at the University of Mississippi; Arlene Dowd; Bruce Iglauer of Alligator Records; the staff at the Center for the Study of Southern Culture and the Blues Archive at the University of Mississippi; and Lisa Howorth of Square Books in Oxford.

Others who helped include Curley Comier, owner of the Silver Slipper in Houston; Rob Ruck at the University of Pittsburgh; John Brewer at the Trolley Museum in Pittsburgh; Sam Black, archivist at the Western Pennsylvania Historical Society; the Reverend Victor Grigsby in Pittsburgh; Nancy Boxill; Ken and Andrea Thompson, who introduced us to the Hill; and Karen Thompson at the Du Bois Institute.

We also thank James Baggett, head archivist, and his colleague Yvonne Crumpler at the Birmingham Public Library; Karen Utz, archivist at Sloss Furnaces; and the Reverend William Greason of the Birmingham Black Barons.

At Kenyon, we owe a debt to our "Crossroads" colleagues—especially Glenn McNair, Jon Tazewell, Sylvie Coulibaly, and Chris Kennerly, as well as David Lynn, George McCarthy, Vivian Conger (now at Ithaca College), Joan Cadden (now at University of California, Davis), Robert Hinton (now at New York University), Suzanne Wright, Jean Scott (now at Ohio State University), Carmen King, Nina Clement, Jami Peele, and Liz Forman.

Funding for this project came from the National Endowment for the Humanities, the American Philosophical Society, and the Faculty Development program at Kenyon College. The Cleveland Foundation, Dominion East Ohio Gas, and the Woodrow Wilson Foundation provided additional support.

Portions of chapter 4 appeared in the *Kenyon Review*, N.S. vol. 27, no. 2, Spring 2005. Parts of chapter 5 appeared in the *Journal of African American History*, vol. 89, no. 4, 2004.

Friends and scholars who had a powerful influence on our work include Bernard Powers at the College of Charleston, the late George Roeder at the Chicago Art Institute, the late Herbert Gutman at CUNY, Jannette Greenwood at Clark University, Paul Conkin at Vanderbilt University, Larry Ingle at the University of Tennesse at Chattanooga, Andrew Kahrl at Marquette University, Dale Rosengarten at the College of Charleston, Will Hustwit and Charles Eagles at the University of Mississippi, Berky Nelson and Joan Nelson at UCLA, and James Grossman at the Newberry Library.

We are especially grateful to Marlene O'Bryant-Seabrook, who allowed us to use a photograph of her story quilt "Roots and Wings" for the cover of *Fly Away*, and to our "flash of the spirit," Yale art historian Robert Farris Thompson, a colleague and friend.

Joshua Stewart crafted the index and Rebekah Rutkoff lent a keen eye.

Finally, we appreciate the endless help of the members of our families: Donna, DE, Joshua, Ansley, Laine, and Scott.

In the end, this book came about through the direct help of our colleagues at the Johns Hopkins University Press: our editor, Henry Tom, wielder of a laser pen, Deborah Bors, who guided the production, and Suzanne Flinchbaugh, who patiently guided us through thick and thin, again and again.

FLY AWAY

OUT OF AFRICA

•1•

West African Origins

In the nineteenth century, an American missionary, R. H. Strong, entered Abeokuta, a Yoruba city in present-day Nigeria. Strong saw firsthand a sprawling and vibrant industrial city that undermined his notion of Africa as a "dark" continent, peopled by "lazy, naked savages, living on the spontaneous productions of the earth." Instead, he found a large and complex city comparable to the industrial, midland cities of England. "What I saw disabused my mind of many errors in regard to . . . Africa," he wrote. The city extends along the bank of the Ogun for nearly six miles and has a population approximately [of] 200,000. . . . the men are builders, blacksmiths, iron-smelters, carpenters, calabash-carvers, hat makers, traders, barbers, tanners, tailors, farmers, and workers in leather . . . they make razors, swords, knives, hoes, bill-hooks, axes, arrow-heads."[1]

For reasons more to do with Western imperial ambition than West African reality, Strong's epiphany failed to open the eyes of westerners to the cultural wealth and complexity of West Africa. Not until 1984, when Yale art historian Robert Farris Thompson published his landmark study, *Flash of the Spirit: African and Afro-American Art and Philosophy,* did Strong's insight become familiar to Western scholars. Thompson's *Flash of the Spirit* exhaustively documented the historical depth and richness of West African art, dance, and religion, especially the Yoruba and Kongo cultures that West African slaves brought to the New World. In Brazil, Haiti, and New York City, Thompson found dynamic expressions of ancient West African, Yoruba, Ewe, Kongo, and Wolof cultures, evidence of what he termed the "flash of the spirit."[2]

FLASHES OF THE SPIRIT

Thompson found flashes of ancient West Africa in unexpected places, even in non–West Africans among whom the descendants of West Africans lived. In

2001 Thompson gave a lecture on West African culture at Kenyon College. In it, he juxtaposed two images—one of a University of Alabama cheerleader and the other of a statue of an equally young and fecund eighteenth-century Kongo woman. Both stood in a stylized pose with one arm held straight above their head and the palm of the hand open. They each propped their other arm coquettishly on their corresponding hip, and each arched their back thrusting their pelvis forward suggestively. Except for the color of the young women's skin, their hairdos, and ritual clothing, the two were startlingly identical. Next, Thompson showed another set of images, one of a West African dancer and the other a white drum major in the University of Alabama's "Million Dollar Band." Both raised one knee almost to eye-level in what an American audience would recognize as a "cake walk." Both held a staff in one hand that they carried above their shoulders. Each wore a feathered headgear, and both had bent their back so that the feather in the headgear almost touched the ground.[3] Without being told, the audience knew that after the game the white cheerleaders, drum major, football players, band members, and student fans would celebrate the University of Alabama's almost-certain victory over Auburn by dancing in a West African manner to music inspired by West African musicians. While much distinguished Alabama from Kongo, much connected them.

Similarly, on Christmas Day 2006, the famed "godfather of soul," James Brown, lay in state. The Carolina Funeral Home in Harlem had dressed the North Augusta, South Carolina, native son in an iridescent blue suit, permed his shiny hair, and placed him in a gold coffin in preparation for a royal funeral procession led by a horse-drawn white hearse down 125th Street to the Apollo Theater. Tens of thousands of Brown's adoring and tearful fans watched the man, "more influential than Elvis," pass. After the service, the funeral home flew his body to North Augusta and interred it in a Sanctified burial ground near other members of his family much as generations of his ancestors had been buried before him. Only then did the spirit of James Brown rest in peace.[4]

Brown's West African forbears had endured the "Middle Passage" only to find themselves auctioned off as slaves in Charleston harbor. In Africa's Cape Coast (in present-day Ghana), hundreds of thousands of other newly enslaved West Africans passed through the gates of its white "castle." In underground dungeons, the frightened men and women etched symbols into the stone walls, bearing witness to the horror and struggle of forced captivity. Above the dungeons, English governors, slave traders, and visiting dignitaries gathered in graciously furnished rooms to "palaver," complete the paperwork, and make the payments that converted the people incarcerated below from prisoners of war into

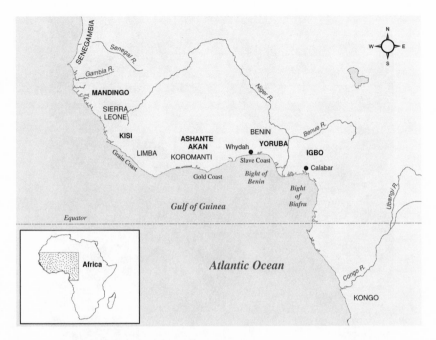

West African Slave Coast

chattel property. Here slave ship captains ordered their crews to row the newly enslaved Ewe, Igbo, Fon, and Yoruba to the dark ships anchored beyond the breakwater. The ironclad wooden door that opened onto the beach was known as "the door of no return."[5]

African Americans have always sought a return by "sweet chariot" to their spiritual homes. Since forced departure, many have yearned to fly away to their ancestral homelands so their spirits could reside with the spirits of their ancestors, their gods, and their people. Stripped, enslaved, and disrespected, they nonetheless carried to the New World the complex ways of West Africa. Their children, Americans to the core, refused to give up their West African souls that formed the core of their identity and enabled them to survive slavery and racism. It also became their gift to American civilization.[6]

A young black woman in Cleveland, Ohio, glides down Euclid Avenue, head held high, shoulders back, hips slightly forward. She bears a look of superiority, as if the mundane concerns of the world could not affect her. In Ghana, along dirt roads and paved highways, West African women walk in same manner. With their necks held straight, they balance pots and pans, fabric, freshly picked bananas, and pineapples atop their heads. Daily, Ghanaian women walk past countless

Mazie Coaxum selling baskets on U.S. Highway 17 (AME Highway),
Mount Pleasant, South Carolina (Peter Rutkoff)

open-framed wood shacks with tiers of shelves and thatched or tin roofs. At these
roadside stalls, women sell a variety of goods, mostly plastic items made in China
and phone cards. A few sell traditional goods, such as their "talking" drums, batik
and kente cloth, cowry shells, and woodcarvings. Similarly, in South Carolina,
along U.S. Highway 17, north of Charleston, not far from James Brown's birthplace, "Gullah" women, shaded from the sun by handmade wood stalls with
shelves and thatched or tin roofs, sell sweet-grass baskets similar to the coiled
baskets available in West African roadside stalls. Sweet-grass baskets came to the
Carolina Low Country from the Senegambia region of West Africa along with the
rice culture. In Low Country Carolina and Georgia, Gullah people created a creolized, West African culture and language adapted to the New World. Until quite
recently, the Gullah spoke a West African–English Creole, lived in houses struc-
turally similar to those in Ghana, sewed baskets and fishing nets like those found

Chariot coffin by Francis Dzormeku, Ho, Ghana (Peter Rutkoff)

on the Rice Coast of West Africa, worshiped a Sanctified Christianity similar to many West African religions and present-day Pentecostalism, and, like James Brown, buried their dead in conformity to West African traditions.[7]

In Ho, about 150 miles north of Accra, the capital of Ghana, Francis Dzormeku walks daily to his shop. A master drummer, his music contains Ewe-inspired polyrhythms and the call-and-response chants that characterized James Brown's Funk style. "Big" Francis Dzormeku makes his living as a coffin maker. He builds his favorite and most popular coffin in the shape of an automobile. His shop sits only ten feet from his house, a jumble of small rooms measuring twelve by fifteen feet, built of rough and unfinished wood. Dzormeku expanded his house, room by room, as his family grew. Today, the compound includes seven brothers and sisters and a handful of cousins. In the middle of the small, packed-earth court-yard, a family member tends a fire. Three teenage boys sit on the nearby porch. One boy works at a desk in the shade, completing his math homework with a Texas Instruments calculator. In the Carolina Low Country, such family com-pounds are called "growing houses." Most Gullah growing houses also have covered porches attached to the back and front of the house, much like the one Dzormeku's nephews sat on in Ho.[8]

Dzormeku makes coffins for important people. He builds them in the shape of

Preston Smith's Magic Chevy, Mississippi (Peter Rutkoff)

cars—a Mercedes or a BMW. "Big" Francis belongs to a tradition of carpenters who make coffins for the families of the deceased to carry their loved ones home to their spiritual ancestors.[9] Dzormeku designs his coffins to fit the person, suitable to his or her achievements and with space to include personal items. In Tutwiler, Mississippi, a small farm town in the Mississippi Delta, Preston Smith owns a brilliantly colored and decorated Chevrolet. Smith works in a local granary. In his spare time, he elaborately ornaments his car. Smith solders to the body of the car hood hundreds of gold and white spray-painted spam cans, whirligigs, cowry shells, and religious and profane plastic figurines. Fully operational, when Smith turns the ignition key, the car sounds like rolling thunder. Occasionally, Preston Smith drives his car at a ceremonial pace around Tutwiler. Asked why he built it, Smith replies, "because I like to."[10] Preston Smith, "Big" Francis Dzormeku, and James Brown each shared an ancient West African custom of elaborately prepared vehicles that transport the dead to a better, spiritual realm. Smith and Dzormeku recast the quintessential American icon into a holy chariot. A part of the sacred circle of life and death, the West African burial custom, while adapting to change, remains unbroken.

In Mount Pleasant, South Carolina, Joyce Coakley, a historian of the Low Country basket makers and herself a descendant of Low Country Gullah, partici-

Ghanaian net maker, Cape Coast, Ghana (Peter Rutkoff)

pated as a young girl in the ritual of "seeking." Her parents' African Methodist Episcopal (AME) church practiced seeking as an initiation rite. When she was twelve, elders in Coakley's church sent her into the woods to receive a "vision" to qualify for admission to the congregation.[11] The Ewe in West Africa also practice seeking in the forest. Before the start of planting season the Ewe cleanse themselves and their villages and then send supplicants to the forest to receive a vision on behalf of the community. On Watch Night, just before New Year, many Low Country Gullah perform a similar ritual of community purification. Before midnight on December 31, male elders cleanse their churches and houses of all evidence of Christmas, in effect restoring the primacy and purity of West Africa. In Chicago, on New Year's Day, other African American families also clean their houses from top to bottom, store money in their freezer chests, and eat "Hoppin' John," a Gullah dish that consists of pork, black-eyed peas, and rice—all "lucky" West African foods. As in Ghana, many African American families in Chicago will not return to their houses until they have been cleansed.[12]

The Mask

The poet Paul Lawrence Dunbar wrote, "We wear the mask that grins and lies. It hides our cheeks and shades our eyes."[13] Dunbar connected African Americans' strategy of hiding their identities from outsiders to West Africa. "Nay, let them only see us / while we wear the mask." Masks in Yoruba, Ewe, and Ashanti cultures mediated the sacred and secular. West Africans wear ceremonial masks to mark important events—birth, death, and initiations. Masks conceal the identity of the individual and protect society from the wrath of the gods.[14] The mask also alludes to the magic of transformation. To don a mask, the ordinary individual becomes something else, a magician or a shaman. In a masking ceremony, observers see the transformation from an ordinary person into a supranatural being. Masks, whether a literal mask or a facial attitude, enabled West Africans to survive slavery and preserve their beliefs. In North America, slave masters forbade slaves to use masks. In their place, slaves wore facial expressions of composure, or "cool," and during their worship services called to their West African spirits in Creole languages. Masking, through language and gesture, enabled African Americans to preserve their West African spirits even as they magically transformed themselves into New World people.[15]

The Circle

To West Africans, the unbroken circle symbolized the motion of the cosmos. In ring shouts, the dancers moved from left to right. In the Yoruba and Fon cultures, the beat of the drum announced the possession of the body by *orisha*, the spirit of the gods. Each *orisha* possessed its own cultural personality, as manifested in particular songs and dances. For the Bakongo people of Central Africa and Angola, the circle imitated the sun's motion, from east in the morning to the west in the evening. It moved between day and night, life and death, profane and sacred. Arranged as pinwheels, diamonds, or circled crosses, the circles of the "Four Movements of the Sun" in Kongo civilization alluded to eternal movement and completion. Water separated the spiritual and secular worlds, a fluid barrier to renewal.[16]

African American religious practices, particularly baptism and burial, embraced such ancient West African beliefs. During baptism, religious leaders immersed initiates in the water, a place where, according to Yoruba belief, Yemoja and Oshun dwelled, the god-spirits of sexuality, fertility, wisdom, and peace. The two *orisha*, identified with Saturday, the color blue, and coolness or composure—all attributes of Mississippi Delta blues. In rural parts of Ewe-land, between Ghana and Togo, people still bury the dead with their feet toward the nearest river. The ritual includes a ceremony performed on the riverbank in a "blind" of bent saplings covered with blue-indigo cloth.[17]

Historian Sterling Stuckey identified the ring shout as the primary means for the transmission of Kongo culture to the New World. West Africans perform ring dances in a variety of religious ceremonies. They accompany sacred singing and spirit possession.[18] Slaves in Brazil, the Caribbean, and the American South danced in sacred circles as they sang out or "shouted." Today, such dancing and shouting is central to Sanctified Baptist and Pentecostal services. Founded by a black Houston minister during a Los Angeles Holiness revival, in 1907, Pentecostalism is the fastest-growing Christian religion in Brazil, Jamaica, and West Africa. In Ghana, even rural Presbyterians dance and shout. In North America, the descendants of West African slaves created this "Africanized" Christianity that is the most powerful force in Christianity today.[19]

The Drum

Use of the ring shout in North America preserved West African sacred music and dance. It also preserved the percussive qualities of West African drumming.[20] West African dancers respond to drum rhythms with different parts of their body. As a percussive culture, West African dancers speak with their bodies as if they were drums. They beat their feet against the ground, slap their bodies, and knock together animal bones and sticks to create complex aural messages. Dances can affirm social values, satirize destructive behavior, or reinforce the interconnectedness between the dead and the living, past and present. West African dance emphasizes the angles of the body. To jut a hip or to bend at the knee creates a life-affirming shape. Only the spiritless dead lay rigid.

Master drummers also "talk" with their drums.[21] They vary the rhythm and create subtle differences in pitch by tightening and loosening the rigging on a set of "talking" drums. High pitches call for extraordinary leaps by the dancer. The dancer, in turn, will improvise, to which the drummer responds. Such improvisation assures that each performance is new and distinct in sound and motion. Because West African music is polyrhythmic, drums or sets of drums and bells and "clackers" form layers of rhythms. Yoruba and Ewe master drummers often set the beat without keeping time. They follow an internal metronome shared by the other musicians and dancers. In the 1940s bebop drummers in New York, Max Roach and Kenny Clarke, revolutionized jazz drumming by abandoning the drum's time-keeping function. They insisted that the drummers be musicians. Like other jazz musicians, drummers should be rhythmic and melodic improvisers and soloists. The central beat did not disappear. Though it went unheard, it was felt by other highly practiced jazz musicians.[22]

In North America, the ring shout also infused New World Christianity with an African spiritual fervor. African American worshipers even danced in their seats, swaying their bodies, raising their hands above their heads, and stamping their feet. Slavery often made secrecy a necessity. By concealing West African practices within Christianity, they preserved many traditional West African ways even as they formulated a new Africanized Christianity. Attendance at the masters' Sunday services acknowledged formal acceptance of Christianity by slaves, but spiritually they remained West African. On Saturday evenings, slaves sat or stood in circles in their cabins or gathered in the woods around a fire or in the sanctuary of a brush ("hush") arbor where they blended West African spiritualism into New World Protestantism.[23]

The juke, or jook joint, also came from West Africa. The word "jook" derived from the Baramba word *dzugu*, which means wicked or bad. At the end of the nineteenth century, in bad houses or the juke joints of the Mississippi Delta, black musicians created the blues. On Saturday night, black sharecroppers went to juke joints to listen and dance, performing steps drawn from their Africanized Christianity. For slaves, the passing of Saturday night into Sunday morning had marked a time-off from work. For later tenant farmers and sharecroppers, Saturday night remained sacred. The blues originated in the Saturday-Sunday continuum.[24] In freedom, Saturday remained a time for celebration and spiritual renewal. On Saturday night, African Americans went to the juke joint, danced to the blues, and found joy. Inside a Delta juke joint, the brutal world of southern sharecropping and segregation disappeared.[25]

Such Saturday carnal worship could last all night until the sun reappeared. Junior Kimbrough's "All Night Long" referred to Saturday night at his juke joint. Kimbrough's guitar evoked the drone of the Senegambian nyanyaur, a single-stringed instrument made from a calabash shell and lizard skin. Kimbrough played the guitar as a chorus for the song's chantlike, repetitive lyrics. He even located his juke joint in an abandoned Holiness church and kept religious images painted on the walls of the dance floor.[26] In the 1930s Mississippi Delta bluesman Robert Johnson explained his amazing virtuosity as a satanic gift that he received at a Delta crossroads in a midnight bargain with the devil. Johnson echoed the legendary behavior of Elegba, the Yoruba trickster-god who mediated between the divine and the human. As a messenger of the gods, like a Delta bluesman, Elegba embodied *ashe*, the source of cool, the energy in the universe, a combination of balance and generosity. As divine trickster, Elegba disrupted the existing order. If they were cool in demeanor, penitents could find Elegba at midnight at a cross-roads, where travelers continued their charted course or changed direction entirely. The juke joint became a crossroads where Sanctified Christianity's and the devil's music converged.[27]

FOUR PATHWAYS

Fly Away recounts four pathways of African American culture during the Great Migration of the twentieth century. The collective passing from South to North, this historical crossroads, brought enormous change to African Americans. In the twentieth century, African Americans, a largely rural, southern people, returned to the urban life that R. H. Strong had seen in Abeokuta. They had once again become a city people. Demographers estimate that as many as seven million African Americans, in two phases, spurred by World Wars, migrated from the rural South to the urban North. Epic and unprecedented, the Great Migration "to the Promised Land" of American cities profoundly changed African American life. Transformed in a thousand ways, African Americans, in all their variety, preserved important aspects of their ancient West Africa culture. Indeed, the eclectic nature of West African culture and its improvisational character proved invaluable in twentieth-century America's diverse and dynamic cities.

African American culture sheltered and guided migrants as they moved from the rural South to the urban North and West. Like the cultures of other migrants and immigrants, African American culture reshaped American cities. African

Americans challenged the deference of Americans toward European civilization and enabled them to take the first steps toward a multiracial, culturally eclectic society, open to a globalized world. The music, behavior, dress, sexuality, and religion of modern America owed much to the Great Migration. The various forms and cultural expressions of Sanctified Christianity unified African Americans as much as their racial identity. What in the rural South had been a "hidden" or "invisible" religion became in twentieth-century American cities a powerful, outgoing, and integrating force that transcended racial and class difference.

In the North, European Americans rarely welcomed African Americans with open arms. Not until after World War II, did northern cities begin to dismantle the system of racial apartheid they had borrowed from the Jim Crow South. Familiar with such behavior, in the nation's central cities African American migrants, determined to take full advantage of the freedom and resources of their new homes, set about creating a vibrant African American world. It included jazz clubs and dance halls, union halls and newspapers, gospel quartets and blues joints, baseball parks and revival tents, churches and funeral homes. After World War I, no visitor to an American city would describe it as a "white city." Commentators and writers, appropriately named the momentous time "the Jazz Age," heralded by the authentic, musical genius Louis "Satchmo" Armstrong in Chicago, not the contrived Gatsby on Long Island.

In short, this study rejects the assertion that Africans lost their culture during the traumatic Middle Passage, from West Africa to North America. We contradict the idea that, in the face of Protestant missionaries and despotic planters, the diverse array of Africans who came to North America lacked the institutions, cultural leaders, and unity necessary to transplant African ways; that African Americans lacked West African roots; or that slavery reduced them to impoverished and passive peasants. Anthropologists Melville Herskovits and Alonzo Turner disputed such claims, pointing to numerous West African "cultural remnants" found among southern blacks, including the Gullah language of Low Country South Carolina and Georgia. Not until Philip Curtin's publication of *The Atlantic Slave Trade: A Census,* however, did it become clear that scholars had profoundly misjudged southern slavery and, with it, African Americans and their slave culture.[28]

Curtin, with the help of his research assistant George Roeder, calculated that of the ten million or so slaves exported from West Africa to the New World, only about 5 percent had come to North America. Yet by 1870, when New World slavery ended, nearly one-third of New World people of African ancestry lived in

North America. One in twenty refugees of the Middle Passage had multiplied into one in three emancipated from slavery. In North America, within two generations of arrival, slaves formed viable biological communities that reproduced themselves at a rate just below the rate of increase for all North American people. Balanced in age as well as gender, North American slaves formed an African American culture that drew on West African cultures, the English- and French-based cultures of their owners, and their experiences in the New World.[29]

All other New World slave regimes failed to sustain their slave populations. Slave owners outside North America continuously imported millions of additional African slaves. Individuals in these largely African-born New World slave plantations retained their West African ethnic identities and failed to become a New World people. Not until the cessation of the international slave trade and the end of New World slavery did non–North American Africans form a New World culture and become a New World people. From a demographic point of view, New World slavery, outside North America, was an unmitigated tragedy comparable to the demise of Native American populations after 1492.

Within a single generation, North American slaves patched together Creole languages understandable only to other speakers of the language. Religiously, they melded West African religious ideas with the Christian beliefs of Roman Catholicism and Reformed Protestantism. They established family relations and social structures that withstood the worst features of plantation slavery, enabling African American women to bear and nurture children. Equally important, they created an African American culture that confirmed and fostered their identity as a New World people.

Each of the four southern communities that we studied evolved a distinct African American culture. African Americans in the Carolina Low Country, miners and mill workers in northern Alabama, cotton sharecroppers in the Mississippi Delta, and the African American migrants who lived in Houston's Third, Fourth, and Fifth wards shared a rich West African heritage. Still, each of these African American communities differed from one another. When southern African Americans left the land and moved to New York, Pittsburgh, Chicago, and Los Angeles, they all carried with them an African American outlook. But they did not each take an identical African American culture. They differed as individuals, by social class, by religion, and by region. Like every other people who have made North America their home, these diverse descendants of West Africa brought to America's cities their own particular ways and their shared ethnic culture. This was their gift to other Americans, to the world at large, and even to West Africa. In moving from the rural South into modern, American cities, African Americans became city people, like many of their West African ancestors. Their diaspora, while of long duration, from an American perspective, was but a link to West Africans' urban cultures. *Fly Away* is an account of the African American journey from the rural South and their spiritual return to the urban world of Abeokuta.

NEW AFRICA

•2•

South Carolina Low Country

CAROLINA LOW COUNTRY

Africans did not arrive in the Carolina Low Country until after 1670, fifty years after their appearance in Virginia. Still, the Carolina Low Country became the ancestral home of African Americans. More than two of every five African slaves who came to British North America entered through Charleston Harbor, ensuring that virtually every African American has Low Country roots.[1] Here, while enslaved, West Africans formed a Creole "Gullah" culture that established the foundation for African American culture throughout the Cotton Belt of the Lower South. By the nineteenth century, West African words, sayings, cuisine, music, dance, religion, and attitudes permeated every aspect of Low Country life. In Carolina, Igbo religions were as important as Anglican Christianity. On July 4, 1776, more than two out of three South Carolinians were descendants of West Africans. Until the 1920s, a majority of South Carolinians traced their ancestry to West Africa. In the Carolina Low Country, in New Africa, African American civilization began.[2]

The Carolina Low Country lies on the western edge of the Atlantic Ocean, a thousand miles northwest of Barbados and three thousand miles west of Africa. The sandy soil of the Carolina Low Country is virtually free of rock. For tools, the Neolithic Santee, Edisto, Sewee, and Combahee people resorted to seashell, bone, wood, shark teeth, and low-grade upcountry flint. Like later European and African settlers, Low Country Native Americans found themselves isolated from the main currents of North American life. The region's eastward flowing rivers, which originated in the Appalachian Mountains, rarely emptied directly into the ocean. Instead, the Pee Dee, Santee, Congaree, and Edisto rivers fed a series of black water swamps that formed a nearly continuous, almost impenetrable, twenty-five

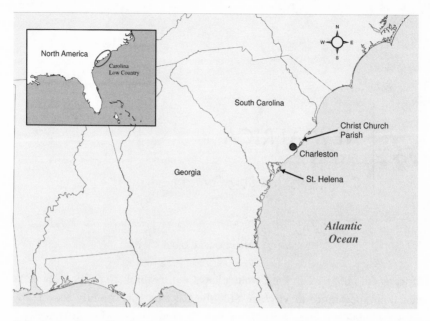

Georgia–South Carolina Low Country

to fifty-mile-wide barrier that began about twenty miles inland from the coast and stretched from present-day Savannah, Georgia, northward to Wilmington, North Carolina.[3]

The Carolina Low Country was an archipelago, 150 miles long and 30 miles wide, that ran southward from the Waccamaw River to Port Royal Sound, just north of Savannah. A saltwater marshland separated the region's ocean-bound barrier islands from its coastlands. The Gulf Stream flowed just offshore, warming the Low Country. Its semitropical climate supported an abundance of wildlife, which included alligator, water moccasin, waterfowl, and mosquito. The flora included sweet grass, grape, palmetto, cypress, poison ivy, and pine, all overshadowed by majestic oaks, the oldest with trunks up to 30 feet in diameter, crowns 150 feet across, and limbs bearded with strands of ghostly Spanish moss. Tidal creeks, marshes, and rivers cut up the coastal land into hundreds of islands. It was often easier to travel by water than by roads, ferries, or bridges. Until the twentieth century, most traffic was waterborne. No place in the Carolina Low Country was more than a mile or two from navigable water, although navigation frequently required flat-bottomed craft to ply the shallow tidal creeks that rose and fell three to six feet with every six-hour, tidal ebb and flow. On foot, an individual was constantly aware of the water, the heat, the humidity, the natural fecundity, water moccasins, alligators, and mosquitoes. From May to September, the Low Country was more akin to the Caribbean and equatorial Africa than to the remainder of North America.[4]

In 1670 a new order intruded into this primordial world. At the confluence of the soon-to-be Ashley and Cooper rivers, the Lords Proprietors, a consort of English court favorites, founded the British colony of Carolina. Here they built a colonial capital named Charles Town in honor of Charles II, the reigning English monarch. At the start, Charles Town was more a creature of Barbadian sugar planters than the Lords Proprietors in London. Whites from Barbados, suffering from overpopulation and a brutal government, swarmed into Charles Town. They brought with them West African slaves who cut lumber and herded livestock to sell in the West Indies. By 1715, rice cultivation freed Charles Town from its West Indian dependency. Influenced by the African rice regimes of Madagascar and the Gold Coast, Charles Town planters remade the coastlands of the Low Country into the most productive rice-growing region in the West. In the eighteenth century, Low Country Carolina became the rice bowl for Europe's rapidly expanding urban working class.[5]

In Carolina, rice planters redefined the ancient Old World food crop into a global commodity. About five miles inland, Low Country streams changed from salt- to freshwater tidal rivers, ideal for rice cultivation. Carolina planters fashioned their labor system after West Indian sugar plantations, importing West African slaves from the West Indies or directly from the west coast of Africa. Carolina planters directed West African slaves to clear the deadly and unhealthy cypress swamps along the rivers and to construct a series of enclosed fields by surrounding them with earthen levies. Adopting techniques borrowed from the West African rice coast, rice planters opened gates of the levees at high tide during the growing season to flood and irrigate the rice fields. At planting and harvest time, they opened the levee gates at low tide to drain the fields.[6] On the high ground, above the rice fields, slaves tended indigo fields and processed the semitropical plant into a purple dye coveted by English textile manufacturers. To encourage Carolina indigo production, the English Parliament granted Carolina planters a generous bounty for indigo dye. Together, rice and indigo assured the prosperity of South Carolina planters, who quickly transformed the Low Country into the most slave-dependent colony in British North America.[7] At the outbreak of the American Revolution, South Carolina resembled the West Indian sugar islands more than it resembled the other British North American colonies.[8]

Almost from the start, Carolina was a slave and predominantly West African society. Carolina's Barbadian pioneers discovered that the semitropical climate

Children grinding rice in West African way near Charleston, South Carolina (From a copy in the collections of South Caroliniana Library, University of South Carolina, Columbia)

and marshy rivers of the Low Country were a death trap for Europeans. West Africans, in contrast, seemed unfazed by the heat, humidity, and mosquito-borne diseases. Many West Africans, having come from low-lying river and marshlands similar to the Low Country, enjoyed a limited immunity to yellow fever and malaria, which infested the Carolina lowlands. Working in the rice lands, West Africans suffered much lower mortality rates than West Europeans, who had no acquired immunity. Moreover, many West Africans came from rice economies and brought to Carolina their rice-growing skills. West Europeans could refuse to work in the deadly rice fields. Enslaved West Africans could not. Before the American Revolution, to meet the almost unquenchable demand for rice, Carolina planters imported tens of thousands of West African slaves.[9] By 1776 three in four Carolinians were black slaves. When South Carolina rice planters Edward Rutledge, Thomas Heyward, Thomas Lynch, and Arthur Middleton signed the

Declaration of Independence that asserted "all men are created equal," they did not apply the sentiments to enslaved black Carolinians.[10]

In the rice land that surrounded Charleston, African Carolinians found themselves in a world apart. Five hundred miles to the north lay the small port of Norfolk and a hundred miles to the south, Savannah, a smaller version of Charleston. To the west lay the virtually impassable black water swamps and to the east the apparently boundless Atlantic Ocean and their African homelands. Thousands of African Carolinians had embarked for Charleston from fortified West African slave factories that lay along the coasts of Angola, Guinea, Gambia, and Senegal. They came from a variety of places throughout West and Central Africa. Ethnically, Carolina slaves included Gambian, Mandingo, Senegambian, Limbo from Sierra Leone, Guinea, Koromantee, Whydah, and a dozen other ethnic groups. Some were Muslims, a few were Christians, but most observed a traditional West African faith and spoke either Wolof or Bantu and adhered to a form of either Kongo or Yoruba culture. In the slave pens, captives shared enslavement and degradation but rarely one another's faith, ethnicity, or language. At best, they understood a few words and phrases of the coastal pidgin that served as the lingua franca of the slave trade—a mixture of English, Portuguese, and West African words and phrases. At the outset, only a few shared a language or imagined themselves members of a single ethnic or racial group.[11]

In the first years of the colony, Carolina planters purchased most of their slaves from the Guinea Coast or Senegambia. These "Guinea" West Africans spoke a form of Wolof and affirmed a Yoruba-based culture. In the middle decades of the eighteenth century, most Carolina slaves came from farther south in the Angola region of West Central Africa. Carolina planters preferred Mande or Yoruba slaves as house servants. As such, the Mande introduced many Yoruba terms into Low Country speech. Angolan slaves spoke a form of Bantu and conformed to a variation of Kongo culture. Planters used Angolan slaves primarily as field workers in the rice lands and sea islands. Isolated from direct white contact, Angolan slaves formed a Bantu-Kongo Creole culture known as Gullah (pronounced like the sea bird). These Gullah slaves preserved many elements of Bantu culture, including the ring shout, in the rice lands—the foundation of the African American culture throughout the Lower South except in the French Creole regions of Louisiana.[12]

Aboard the crowded slave ships, West African slaves found that all whites possessed despotic power over them and that all blacks were subservient to all whites. While whites recognized the ethnic differences among Africans, for them, too, color and race became a slave's primary identification and status. During the

Middle Passage, from Africa to America, being Whydah, Koromantee, Angolan, Sierra Leonian, or Senegambian lost much of its meaning. West Africans' shared identity as blacks and slaves became more important than their particular ethnicity. Many died in African slave pens or "castles" that marked Africa's South Atlantic coast. Others died on the brutal Middle Passage, and some committed suicide, especially Igbo. None of the slaves knew where they were headed, none could fathom their fate, none knew who their master would be, and few knew others on board. Torn from their ancestral homelands, their people, and their families, they endured the Middle Passage as individuals shorn of their clothing as well as the consolation of friends, family, or coreligionists. When West Africans entered Charleston Harbor, no one welcomed them to Carolina or celebrated their new lives. The future offered no hope. Only memories of their West African homelands, their people, their ancestors, and the holy places of their gods provided solace and comfort. When they disembarked at Sullivan's Island, in Charleston Harbor, their hearts yearned eastward, across the great water, across what, in time, they called the "River Jordan," which might someday carry them back to their West African Zion.[13]

WE LAND

With their arrival in Charleston Harbor, West Africans once again stood on firm ground. The hot, humid air of the teeming, mosquito-plagued land, combined with Carolina's predominantly West African population, must have seemed comfortingly familiar—indeed, remarkably similar to the West African slave castles with their slave trade pidgin. By British law, slave ships unloaded their human cargo at Sullivan's Island, a fortified island at the mouth of Charleston Harbor. As the slaves stepped ashore, custom officials counted, appraised, and inspected them before their incarceration in slave barracks. Newly arrived slaves remained quarantined on Sullivan's Island until officials determined that they were disease free. Once certified as healthy, Charleston slave traders ferried their cargoes, most under the age of twenty and male, across the harbor for sale on the wharfs along East Bay Street. Customs officials ordered the burial of those who had died in a potter's field on Sullivan's Island. Those who lived accounted for 40 percent of the slave imports into North America, making Sullivan's Island the West Africans' Ellis Island—or, in Gullah, their passageway to Egypt. Long before emancipation and the later Great Migration, the Carolina children of West Africa made the Low Country their own.[14]

In Charleston, the new arrivals underwent intense inspection by auctioneers and prospective buyers, who examined males and females, adults and children, stripped of their clothing, for sound teeth, strength, breeding qualities, disease, disfigurement, physical beauty, literacy, age, and temperament. Householders looked for docile, pleasant, literate, and attractive slaves, while planters, interested in field hands, cared more about health, strength, age, breeding potential, and rice-growing experience or other prized skills such as carpentry, weaving, medicine, midwifery, and iron mongering. Only a handful remained in Charleston. Buyers marched or shipped most to the rice lands where slaves joined other West Africans who had already begun the adjustment to the Carolina Low Country.[15]

In the rice lands, West Africans outnumbered West Europeans by nineteen to one. On a rice plantation of two hundred people, the only whites were the overseer, the planter, and their families. During the "sickly" summer months, the white families fled to Charleston, Beaufort, Georgetown, Mount Pleasant, or Summerville, leaving the rice lands almost exclusively black. Outside these white sanctuaries, slaves created a West African Creole culture drawn from the various ethnic groups present in the rice lands, particularly those from Sierra Leone and Angola. By the early decades of the eighteenth century, the Carolina Low Country had become a new Africa.[16]

The words new and Africa were equally significant. Not only did the slave trade set in motion the African Atlantic diaspora, it also led to a short-lived African racial identity. The slave trade placed Igbo, Whydah, Senegambian, and dozens of other ethnic West African refugees in an almost unfathomable situation. In the New World, their traditional ethnic identities meant little while their shared condition of servitude and racial appearance signified almost everything. In the diaspora, slavery and race became the basis of an African identify. Until enslavement by Europeans, sub-Saharan people had heard the term "Africa" only from traders, who used it as a geographic term, not a racial or cultural one. But in Carolina and other West European slave colonies, "African" referred to all persons of color born in sub-Saharan Africa. In the rice lands of the Carolina Low Country, Igbo, Senegambian, and Angolan, for the first time, shared a common identity.[17]

In the eighteenth century, West Africans called the South Carolina Low Country "We Land." In the nineteenth century, transplanted African American slaves from "We Land" planted cotton and practiced West African ways throughout the Lower South. Gullah culture and slavery reinforced a sense of separateness from whites and a bond with other blacks. The Gullah identity expressed African Americans' shared identity as members of a "black community" regardless of where their diaspora cast them. Ironically, Gullah also provided much of the cultural unity that southerners in the Lower South felt toward one another—black and

Gullah carrying baskets on their heads, 1879 (Library of Congress)

white. In 1861, when the Confederate government opened fire on the Union-occupied Fort Sumter in Charleston Harbor, it declared its independence from the United States, on behalf of chattel slavery as well as the distinct southern culture that West Africans helped forge in the Carolina rice lands.[18]

In the Low Country, a singular African identity persisted for only one generation. In the rice lands, only slaves born in Africa were considered Africans.[19] The children of West Africans, born in Carolina, called themselves Gullah or "We People," the Low Country's first African Americans. The African identity and African pidgin of first-generation slaves prepared their children to perceive of themselves as African Americans, not ethnic Africans. Even first-generation slaves viewed themselves as Africans only conditionally. In their hearts, they remained Igbo, Mandingo, and Mande. Their homelands lay across the Atlantic Basin on the African continent in Igbo, Dahomey, Mende, and Senegambia. In their hearts, they knew that at death their spirits would pass over the water to where the bodies of their ancestors lay. Death freed African-born slaves to "fly away" to their ethnic homelands. Only circumstantially Africans, they were never African Americans. For eternity, they remained Igbo born, Igbo bred, Igbo dead, and Igbo resurrected. At death, they flew away to Igbo.[20]

This climactic moment of African passing, or flying away, remained in the memories of Georgia and Carolina Low Country African Americans into the twentieth century. In the 1930s, the federal government, through its Works Progress Administration (WPA), commissioned interviewers to record the memories of several thousand former slaves, most in their eighties. The WPA slave narratives contain some of the richest, firsthand information extant on American slavery. The South Carolina narratives provide accounts from across the state, including several dozen from the Low Country. The Georgia WPA undertook a separate Low Country project overseen by Guy Johnson from the University of North Carolina. Entitled *Drums and Shadows*, the coastal Georgia project interviewed dozens of Georgia, Gullah-speaking African Americans or Geechees (the Georgia term) who provided unparalleled access to Gullah culture.[21] Before the twentieth century people of African ancestry spoke a Creole language drawn from English, Bantu, and Wolof, which most non-Gullah speakers found incomprehensible. The Gullah-speaking region centered in the South Carolina Low Country but extended along the coast from Wilmington, North Carolina, to Jacksonville, Florida, and included the Georgia Sea Islands and adjoining coastal counties.[22]

The frequent accounts of "Flying Igbo" and other "flying Africans" in the Georgia and South Carolina WPA slave narratives suggest an African American origin myth. Gullah speakers made a clear distinction between African-born slaves and those born in the Low Country, in effect, between West Africans and African Americans. The myth drew on a variety of sources pieced together from older historical accounts as well as the 1930s South Carolina and Georgia WPA slave narratives. In 1804 a Georgia planter purchased a group of Igbo from a slave dealer in Savannah. He took them to St. Simons Island to work sea island cotton. On arrival, the Igbo were noticeably dispirited. They did not understand the overseer's directions, and they adjusted poorly to the mindless work of hoeing cotton.[23] The WPA interviewer roughly quoted a Gullah-speaking informant, "The slaves were out in the field working. All of a sudden they get together and start to move round in a ring. Round they go faster and faster. Then one by one they rise up and take wing and fly like a bird."[24] According to another informant, "When they find out they was slaves and got treat so hard, they just fret and fret. One day they was standing with some other slaves an all of a sudden they say, 'We going back to Africa. So goodie bye, goodie bye.' Then they flied right out of sight."[25] Wallace Quarterman of Darien, Georgia, remembered a similar incident on Skidaway Island near Savannah. "Mr. Blue put them in the field, but he couldn't do nothing with them. They gabble, gabble, gabble, and nobody could understand them and they didn't know how to work right. . . . They's foolish acting. He got to whip them. Mr. Blue, he ain't had no choice. Anyways, he whip them good and they gets together and stick the hoe in the field and say, 'quack, quack, quack,' and they rise up in the sky and turn them self into buzzuds an fly right back to Africa."[26]

Shad Hall recounted another "flying" episode on Butler Island: "The massa was fixing to tie them up and whip them. They say, 'Massa you ain't going to lick me,' and with that they runs down to the river. The Overseer he sure thought he catch them when they get to the river. But before he could get to them, they rise up in the air and fly away. They fly right back to Africa."[27] The overseer failed to catch the Igbo after they had danced in a ring and began to "quack" and before they flew to Africa. He did, however, find their drowned bodies.[28] In an incident in North Carolina, a planter forced a group of newly arrived West Africans to work on a canal. Exhausted by the work, several collapsed on the bank where they remained overnight. The following morning, the overseer found them drowned in the canal. In the evenings afterward, the remaining West Africans broke out in song and dance, became ecstatic, picked up their personal belongings, faced eastward, and waded into the water. Many drowned before being stopped, having already flown away.[29]

Such accounts, along with a dozen others from Low Country Georgia and South Carolina, offer eyewitness accounts of the capacity of native West Africans to fly away. Several things stand out. First, of the West Africans taken to the Low Country, the Igbo were the most distraught and the most likely to fly away. Additionally, only native-born West Africans possessed the ability to fly away. Before passing, the Igbo formed a circle, sang, and became ecstatic. At the height of their ecstasy, they entered the nearest water as one and passed over to Africa. Flying referred to the Igbo's spirit, not their bodies. As Igbo, their ancestors were buried in Igbo near the Niger Delta in West Africa. After immersion in water, according to Igbo religion, their spirits returned to the burial ground of their ancestors, to their homeland. Before immersion and passing, Igbo summoned their spirits to the sacred ring through the invocation of sacred song—a ring shout. To non-Igbo and to the Low Country–born children of West Africans, the ritual song sounded like nonsense or quacking. To other Igbo, they spoke in a holy language understandable to their ancestors' spirits.[30]

In less dramatic ways, other West African–born slaves in the Low Country also appealed to their ancestral spirits in ring shouts and seemingly incomprehensible chants, faced eastward, immersed themselves in water, and passed over or flew away. According to Low Country lore, only West Africans could fly away. The bodies of the parents of those born in the Low Country lay in America. On their passing, the spirits of the American-born children of West Africans, these first African Americans, found spiritual peace in their new ancestral land, in New Africa. Their parents' deaths and their ritualized burials sanctified the Low Country. It became the burial ground of their parents and, thereby, their homeland. Flying away poetically captured the traumatic struggle for identity that enslaved West Africans faced. It also enabled their American-born children to come to terms with the loss of ethnic identity, ethnic speech, ethnic religion, and ancestral land. To speak Gullah was to know "who you were," and references to "We People" and "We Land" served as an expression of this communal bonding and an affirmation of the adoption of the Low Country as the new homeland. Long before emancipation, Gullah and Geechee were cognizant of their ancestral roots and their communal bond with other African Americans.[31]

GULLAH

Gullah language supplied Low Country slaves a verbal shield. In the presence of English speakers, Gullah speakers often resorted to Bantu or Wolof pronunciations, tempo, and intonation, making themselves selectively incomprehensible to whites. When addressed by whites, Gullah speakers often acted as if they could not understand what was said to them, shaking their heads, turning their palms upward, and crossing their arms over their chests. The Bantu or Wolof components of Gullah conferred membership in a language and cultural community that, at their choosing, excluded non-Gullah speakers. A Low Country visitor complained, "The lowland negro of South Carolina has a barbaric dialect. The English words seem to tumble out of his mouth, and to get sadly mixed up when he endeavors to speak."[32] It is impossible to overstate the importance of Gullah. It restored the speech of these uprooted West Africans. Before Gullah, they either had to remain silent, speak in their native tongue (which most other slaves did not understand), or use the crude slave pidgin that demeaned them as "niggers."

Drawing on the English of their masters and their own West African languages, ethnic West Africans created their own language—a legacy to their children.

Interviewers frequently complained about the difficulty in conversing with Gullah speakers. In Gullah parlance, they remained "closed teethed." Silence in the face of white authority became the first line of defense. Carolina rice planters may have owned their slaves and exercised absolute power over them, but the Gullah language radically limited the intrusion of whites into the affairs of slaves and preserved important aspects of West African cultures. In 1850 a European visitor to the Low Country, Fredrika Bremer, recounted hearing an elderly slave sing an African death song that consisted of a "monotone vibration upon three semitones."[33] Bremer also reported a young slave, accompanied by a banjo, who sang a ballad in which the first song line was repeated, followed by rhymed third and fourth lines with the last line also rhyming, but not repeating the first line. Bremer described an early form of the blues, "The last syllable of the first and last verse is long and drawn out." She observed, "The banjo is an African instrument, made from the half of a fruit called the calabash, or gourd, which has a very hard rind. A thin skin or piece of bladder is stretched over the opening and over this, one or two strings are stretched, which are raised on a bridge. The banjo is the negroes' guitar, and certainly it is the first-born among stringed instruments."[34]

In the 1930s linguist Lorenzo Turner discovered an entire Mende funeral dirge that Amelia Dawley, a Low Country Gullah woman, had learned from her mother. It contained the refrain that served as the title of the camp song, "Kumbi Ya."

> A wohkoh, mu mohne, kambei ya le, li lee it tohmbe.
> Come quickly, let us work hard, the grave is not yet finished; his heart is not yet perfectly cool.
> A wohko, mu mohne, Kambei ya; li leei ka.
> Come quickly, let us work hard; the grave is not yet finished; let his heart be cool at once.[35]

For Low Country slaves, the Gullah language kept open a cultural passage to their West African homelands.[36]

Since Turner's ear-opening work, other linguists have concluded that Gullah also derived from the slave trade pidgin used by English slave traders along the Slave Coast of West Africa. Based on English, but drawn from a variety of West African languages, the slave pidgin formed the basis of several Creole languages, including Jamaican Creole, Guyana Creole, and Gullah.[37] According to African linguists, Sierra Leone and Angola contributed the most words and phrases to Gullah, especially the Mende, Vai, and Bantu languages.[38] Gullah speakers adopted many names, such as Bala, Sorie, Ja, Marah, Sesay, and Bangura from Sierra Leone as well as nouns such as *joso* (witchcraft), *gafa* (evil spirit), *wanga* (charm), *do* (child), and *defu* (rice flour).[39] Indeed, speakers of Sierra Leon Krio and Low Country Gullah can converse with one another without a translator. Seemingly, many slaves acquired from Sierra Leone slave dealers an English–Sierra Leone pidgin before their Middle Passage.[40]

Gullah, like other West African–derived languages, uses the same pronouns for men and women. Gullah speakers Anglicize *e to he or em* but continue to use it as an all-purpose pronoun. Gullah use either *Yinna* or *unna* when speaking to more than one person and to acknowledge possession. The word's position in the sentence determines whether *unna* means possession or refers to persons spoken to. The most interesting and revealingly West African aspect of Gullah is its failure to distinguish between present and past. "John be here" may mean that John "was here" or that John "is here." Not only can this confuse and mislead a non-Gullah speaker, but linguistically it expresses the Gullah belief that past and present are intimately, even spiritually related. For Gullah, and many other southerners, the past is never dead; it is not even past.[41]

Nothing was ever past. To Gullah, past and present were virtually one and the same. Time lacked the sense of progression that post-Enlightenment Europeans took for granted. Equating past and present was tied to the West African belief in the interrelatedness of the living and the dead, the profane with the sacred. West Africans and Gullah, as well as many other southerners, view reality as a unified whole, not an analyzable system made up of discrete, separable parts. The "dead hand" of the past is always present. There is never getting beyond or away from the past or the dead. This sense of oneness gives great power to Gullah religious and artistic expression.

Low Country Gullah adopted from West Europeans what they found useful or valuable, but spiritually they remained West Africans. They used Protestant Christianity, much as they used English, to transport and preserve their traditional religious and magical beliefs. In the rice lands most West African slaves converted to Christianity, and in planter-sponsored services they worshiped like Anglicans or Methodists. But in their secluded slave cabins and praise houses, they infused Anglicanism and Methodism with West African ideas and continued to worship in West African ways. The Anglican, Methodist, and West African creolization enabled Gullah people to rework their West African beliefs into a new vessel of African Christianity.[42]

A Low Country planter, Henry William Ravenel, lived for more than seventy years with more than two hundred slaves on his thousand-acre Pooshee Plantation just west of Charleston. In 1876 Ravenel penned his recollections of slave life on the plantation.[43] He found the Gullah interesting and exotic—a people apart, a people that, at best, he had only glimpsed, despite long residence among them and his overarching power over them. Ravenel's slaves lived in small, two-room houses, about eighteen by thirty-six feet, "arranged in rows or streets about fifty yards apart—whitewashed every year or two." At a distance, they "presented a neat village-like appearance." As for religion, "They had a form of their own mixed up with much of their own native superstitions." Many slaves "believed more or less in witchcraft—and some of the more knowing ones practiced the healing art with decorations of native plants and other potent ingredients. Old March . . . besides being a Root Doctor . . . believed firmly in witchcraft." On Pooshee Plantation, a few couples underwent the ritual of Christian marriage that proscribed monogamy. For others, "This ceremony was left with the colored preachers, who used their own forms, and separation was permitted." Older, West African–born women admonished the mothers of Pooshee's newborns to "call the name of the child . . . to attract the spirit of the child" when they carried their infants to the fields. Ravenel explained that Low Country slaves believed that "every spring or fountain of water had a presiding Genius or guardian spirit" called "Cymbee." Pooshee slaves buried their dead at night, marching to the gravesite in torchlight processions. Before interment, they performed a ring shout around the grave. After the burial, in their cabins, they shared food.[44]

Nominally Christian, Pooshee slaves organized their own services in their own churches, conducted by slave preachers, who interrupted sermons with joyful singing and shouting. In the South Carolina WPA narratives, Agnes James of Claussen described her praise house meetings as "roaring and rocking."[45] As at Pooshee, most Low Country slave worship occurred in small, slave-built praise houses allowed by the planters or in secret "brush" or "hush arbors" hidden in the woods, marked by upside-down pots. Slaves spoke of "stealing away" in the night to their clandestine meetings. Augustus Ladson of Wadamalaw Island explained that "we could have ours [meeting] any night we want even without his consent."[46] Wallace Quarterman remembered church on Skidaway Island, "We sure have big time going to church in those days . . . you need a drum for shouting. . . . We beat a drum at the church and we beat a drum to the way to the graveyard to bury them. We walks in a long line moaning and we beats a drum all the way."[47]

The praise house and brush arbor served as centers of Gullah slave communities. Most plantations included a small, whitewashed clapboard praise house in which plantation slaves met, worshiped, and governed themselves. When slaves also maintained a brush or hush arbor in the woods or swamps, they would

A typical praise house on Saint Helena Island, South Carolina (Peter Rutkoff)

resolve personal issues here, under the leadership of a minister or "watchman," that had little to do with the planter's well-being or civil law. Planters and civil authorities concerned themselves more with property rights, profits, and public order.[48] An example of Gullah law took place on Edisto Island. After the master executed a male slave for murdering another male slave over a dispute involving a female slave, he used the execution of the murderer to warn other males not to kill another male in a dispute over a woman because it destroyed the master's property. After the execution and before burial, the slaves threw the woman who had provoked the conflict into the grave with her executed lover and proceeded to bury her alive. "But wiser [white] counsels prevailed and she was released." The slaves cared about justice, not the master's property, directing their outrage at the female seductress as well as the male murderer.[49]

Gullah praise houses litigated issues of theft, slander, disrespect, and violence against members of the community by other members, the care of orphaned children, witchcraft, and communal betrayal. In 1834 a Methodist missionary, Thomas Turpin, described the proceedings in a praise house on Bulls Island, off Cape Romaine:

> They had three degrees of punishment, and . . . the punishment was inflicted agreeably to the magnitude of the crime. If the crime was of the first magnitude, the

perpetrator had to pick up a quart of benne [sesame] seed . . . poured on the ground by the priest; and if of the second, a quart of rice, and if of the third, a quart of corn. . . . [T]hey also had high seats and low seats. . . . [I]t was also a rule among them never to divulge the secret of stealing, and if it should be divulged [to the master] that one had to go to the low seat or pick up the benne seed.[50]

To inform the master of the theft of the master's property by another slave was the most serious offense. Those who chose the planter over the slave community suffered public humiliation. The community reserved its high seats for its most respected and loyal members, a practice that conformed to rules of the secret Poro and Sande societies of Sierra Leone and of secret societies established after emancipation.[51]

Gullah Christianity revolved around several rituals—the worship service that included the ring shout; the nighttime, largely secret, burials; river baptism; and "seeking." English geologist Charles Lyell, on an 1845 visit to Charleston, described the ring shout. "At the Methodist prayer meetings, they are permitted to move round rapidly in a ring, joining hands in token of brotherly love, presenting first the right hand and then the left, in which maneuver, I am told, they sometimes contrive to take enough exercise to serve as a substitute for the dance."[52] Other accounts described the slave minister and congregation calling back and forth to one another. Spontaneously, the congregation formed a circle and slowly shuffled in a counterclockwise ring. The dancers moved their feet rhythmically along the floor, but their legs never crossed, as worshipers moved faster and faster and shouted louder and louder until they had achieved an ecstatic trance that signified the presence of the Holy Spirit. Then, everything stopped suddenly. The worshipers collapsed, exhausted but joyful, praising Jesus.[53] The planters' services, which slaves periodically attended, meant little to Gullah worshipers. They judged a service by the intensity of its ring shout, not by the decorum of the service or the eloquence of the minister.

Because of their secrecy, little information exists on Gullah burial practices, but even the fragmentary evidence is tantalizing. Burials took place on the night after the death. In Possum Point, Georgia, according to Susan Maxwell, "They beat the drum to tell everybody about the sitting up. . . . Everybody place their hand very light on the eyes and on the nose and then they say, 'Don't call me. I ain't ready for to go yet.' We bury them by torch light after dark. Everybody march round the grave in a circle. Every night after the funeral I put food on the porch for the spirit to come get it."[54] Slaves buried their dead with their faces toward the east, placed deliberately broken personal items in the grave, and performed secret rituals. This was done to appease the spirits of the recently departed to gain their goodwill. But the details are vague.[55]

Slave baptisms also conformed to West African–derived belief. Regardless of the masters' faith, slaves insisted on full immersion for their passage across the Jordan. Maxwell's account included a description of Gullah baptisms. "They baptize in the water down at the landing. All the candidates is dressed in white. They all confess their sins and say they want to be saved. We all march long in a line and sing and pray. When we get to the river bank, we stop and the preacher take the candidates one by one and they go down into the river. The preacher he say a prayer to the river. They always baptize on the ebb tide because the river is suppose to wash the sins away."[56] Much as in West Africa, Low Country Gullah, except for those who affiliated with a Methodist church, insisted on full-immersion baptism. Candidates dressed in white robes, which in West Africa signified purity. The service included processional singing that summoned the Holy Spirit, after which the minister offered a prayer to the river, where in West Africa the river god resided. The river would purify the supplicants as it flowed into the Atlantic, back to Africa.[57] Low Country Gullah considered themselves to be devout Christians but Christians who embraced the joy and cleansing spirituality of West Africa.[58]

Gullah spirituals proved so moving that, by the Civil War, most white, American Protestant churches included many in their own hymnals. These spirituals, often translated by whites into a "Negro dialect," drew on West African and Gullah phrases such as "fly away," "carry me off to heaven," "roll Jordan roll," "steal away," and "row the boat ashore." The spirituals expressed the longing of slaves for a free life that they imagined existed in Africa.[59] In their brush arbor services, Gullah gave West African spirituality free reign. During the ring shout, in the throes of ecstasy, Gullah spoke in tongues, comprehensible only to the Holy Spirit or, perhaps, to their ethnic forebears. In Gullah congregations influenced by Methodist missionaries, Gullah elders taught the young religious doctrine and required them to memorize key passages from the Bible. After their training, candidates underwent an oral exam. If successful, the candidates or "seekers" stayed alone in the woods until they had experienced a religious dream. Only after a successful dream could the seeker leave the woods. Following a successful seeking, Gullah watchmen baptized the young Gullah believer. Such an Africanized Christianity enabled Low Country slaves to shape their own lives, build viable communities, and sustain their spiritual ties to West Africa.[60] It gave their otherwise fractured lives unity and meaning. It also led to the formation of a new, highly spiritual form of Christianity, which, in time, exerted a profound impact on all southern Protestants, especially Methodist, Baptist, and, later, Holiness believers. Indeed, the brush arbors and praise houses of the Carolina and Georgia Low Country were the wellsprings of much of the South's religious distinctiveness.[61]

These rituals assured that the spirits of Gullah believers secured safe passage from the profane world of slavery to the sanctified world of freedom. "We People" "overcame" as they "flew away," "free at last, free at last." When Low Country Gullah watched Africans fly away and acknowledged their own inability to fly, they affirmed their American identity. They had become We People in We Land. By virtue of their parents' burials and their own tidal baptisms, they had become Americans. In her memoir, *Lemon Swamp,* Mamie Fields, the child of slave parents, explained to her northern-born granddaughter why the granddaughter was a Charlestonian. According to Fields, if a person had at least one set of grandparents buried in a Charleston cemetery, they were Charlestonians "by birth" even if they had been born in New Jersey. The ancestors of Mamie Fields's granddaughter lay buried in Charleston where, like the Igbo, their spirits resided, making Charleston, forever, their descendants' homeland.[62] Once native-born Africans had flown away, the Low Country became New Africa, the land of their ancestors, the home of their spirits, and the cultural cradle of the Lower South.

THE SEAT OF SLAVERY

Arriving by ship in Charleston from Boston in 1849, Fredrika Bremer, on stepping off Adger's Wharf, noted the large number of blacks that filled the city's docks and streets. "Negroes swarm in the streets. Two-thirds of the people whom one sees out in the town are negroes or mulattoes."[63] The poverty and illiteracy of the slaves highlighted the wealth and power of the white population. Behind the princely mansions that crowded South Battery, East Bay, and Meeting Streets lay crowded hovels of Charleston slaves and free blacks. The graciously appointed Dock Street Theater presented fashionable dramatic fare while French dance and music teachers instructed the children of the rice planters. Blacksmiths, painters, tailors, and dress, carriage, furniture, and candle makers abounded, crafting for their wealthy and demanding patrons fine wear and furnishings, often with slave labor.[64]

Charleston was not simply the seat of slavery. It was a city of slaves and slave owners. In 1820 more than half the city's residents were enslaved and nearly a half of the remainder owned slaves. In 1860 the percentage of slaves declined to about a third, although the number of slaves in the city remained constant at about thirteen thousand. Many worked in planter households, tending their masters' children, preparing their food, maintaining the mansion, receiving guests, driving the carriage, shopping for food and fuel, and looking after the horses, stables, and gardens. A fashionable Charleston home easily commanded twenty or more house servants, most of whom lived in the garret of the owner's home or in slave quarters at the rear of the house.[65] In the city, no quarter was free of slaves. Slaves performed almost all the dockside labor of the port, not only preparing cotton, rice, and indigo for shipment but also loading and unloading vessels, repairing and building ships on the dry docks, making rigging and sails, and hauling goods from dockside to warehouses along East Bay and Meeting streets. Slaves cleaned and repaired the streets, barbered, and worked as carpenters, masons, and barrel makers.[66] From the planters' point of view, Charleston could no more function without slaves than could their rice plantations.[67]

In Charleston, most slaves, except for house servants, lived in single households, mixed freely with free blacks and whites, and often lacked direct supervision. Masters rented out slaves and many Charleston slaves could read and write. Much to the discomfort of some whites, slaves appeared to have the run of the city, freely moving about without passes or permission. To ensure control, city authorities organized a large municipal police force of 250 men, maintained a regular slave patrol, and in 1842 established the Citadel Military College to provide the city with a home guard.[68] Charleston authorities punished all hint of insurrectionary activity swiftly and ruthlessly. The city suffered its only slave rebellion in 1739 and detected another alleged slave conspiracy in 1822, purportedly led by Denmark Vesey.[69]

The 1822 conspiracy trial centered on the role of the African Church in which Denmark Vesey taught Sunday school. From the accounts in the trial record, the African Church resembled the urban equivalent of rice plantation Gullah praise houses and brush arbors.[70] Its minister, Morris Brown, fearing prosecution, left Charleston for Philadelphia, where the African Methodist Episcopal Church (AME) ordained him as a minister. Daniel Payne, who conducted a school for free black children in Charleston, also fled to Philadelphia, where he became a bishop in the Philadelphia AME church.[71] Much of Vesey's prestige rested on his role as a teacher of the Christian Bible. The planter-dominated court found the unsupervised conjunction of West African magic and Christianity a volatile combination. Fearing such a radicalized Christianity, Charleston authorities executed and deported the African Christian conspirators, tore down the African Church and its two branches, banned within the city any independent black church, and prohibited teaching slaves to read and write.

In 1850 Charleston contained nearly 20,000 slaves, 3,500 other persons of mixed race, and 20,000 whites.[72] Many of these free blacks were either manumitted slave mistresses or the illegitimate, mixed-race children of white planters. Many white masters, on the death of their white wives, never remarried, preferring the companionship of slave mistresses, whom they often manumitted in their wills.[73] Charleston's free black population continued to grow throughout the antebellum period despite the passage of legislation that required the removal of manumitted slaves from the state. In Charleston, while the law dictated racial apartheid, passion dictated human intercourse.[74]

The assimilation of Charleston's mulattoes went more than skin deep. Culturally, most mulattoes viewed themselves as Europeans, not Africans. Like whites, they considered Europe the center of civilization and Africa a place of unmitigated savagery. Charleston mulattoes spoke the "Queen's English," dressed in Paris, London, and New York styles, gave their children European names, ate English and French cuisine, modeled their homes and lives after rice planter families, and worshiped in Episcopal, Presbyterian, and Methodist churches. By choice, they shared little with Low Country Gullah slaves. Like their white kin, before the Civil War many Charleston mulattoes supported slavery with its inherent color consciousness.[75]

During the Civil War, in August 1862, Congress authorized the enlistment of five thousand black soldiers into the Union Army. Most of the black recruits had stolen away from the rice and sea island plantations of the Carolina Low Country, crossing the Union lines at Beaufort. In January 1863 Colonel Thomas Wentworth Higginson formed the first black Union regiment, the First South Carolina Volunteer Regiment, which, except for its white officers, consisted almost entirely of Gullah soldiers. During the war, Beaufort served as headquarters of the Union South Atlantic Command that included a naval hospital on Hilton Head Island, a training camp for Gullah recruits, a supply depot, barracks, and two Union weekly newspapers. The South Atlantic Command interred most of its dead, many of them Gullah, in the United States Military Cemetery at Beaufort.[76] Boasting the largest number of "colored" soldiers, it was the Arlington Cemetery of black Civil War veterans.

By the end of 1863, the Union army had organized four more black regiments —the Second, Third, Fourth, and Fifth South Carolina Volunteers that together totaled about five thousand men. The army later consolidated these five units into the Twenty-first, Thirty-third, and Thirty-fourth United States Colored Troops. Low Country Gullah also enlisted in the famous Fifty-fourth and Fifty-fifth Massachusetts Colored Regiments that suffered enormous casualties during the assault on Battery Wagoner in Charleston Harbor. In the final year of the war, the Union

African American Fourth of July celebration on Saint Helena Island, South Carolina, in
1930s (Library of Congress)

army recruited Low Country Gullah blacks for the 103rd, 104th, 105th, and 128th
United States Colored Troops, but the war ended before they saw combat.[77]

Altogether, about seven thousand Low Country Gullah served in the Union
army in the war against slavery. On February 19, 1865, after General William
Sherman's Union army cut off supplies to Charleston, Gullah troops entered
Mount Pleasant, on the eastern bank of the Cooper River that overlooked the city.
Colonel Charles Fox, the white commander of the Fifty-fifth Massachusetts,
described the entry into Mount Pleasant: "Shouts, prayers, and blessings resounded. . . . Their [Gullah] people . . . all felt that the hardships and dangers of the
siege were fully repaid."[78] Two days later, when the Fifty-fifth crossed the harbor
and occupied Charleston, Fox declared, "It was one of those occasions which
happen but once in a life-time, to be lived over in memory forever."[79]

A month later, in a show of racial solidarity, Charleston blacks and browns
celebrated the city's liberation with a parade that included the black Union regiments and a company of school boys followed by thirteen young girls "dressed in
white," riding in the Car of Liberty. Zion AME Church marched as a body, including men, women, and children, followed by the city's black fire companies, a black

band, dockworkers, Gullah farmers, and members of the city's skilled trades—carpenters, coopers, wheelwrights, blacksmiths, masons, barbers, painters, and wagon drivers.[80] On April 14, Secretary of War Edwin Stanton announced a national memorial day to celebrate the fall of Charleston. In the heart of the city, at Citadel Square, the platform party included the former Union commander of Fort Sumter, Robert Anderson; Henry Ward Beecher, the brother of Harriet Beecher Stowe; abolitionist William Lloyd Garrison; Gullah U.S. naval commander Robert Smalls; and Robert Vesey. For the next century, on New Year's Day, in commemoration of the Emancipation Proclamation, African Americans marched out of Charleston's black neighborhoods, and paraded down the city's main street through the white downtown to the Battery where they celebrated the defeat of the Confederacy and the end of slavery.[81]

FORTY ACRES AND A MULE

In the summer of 1866, white mobs assaulted blacks in Charleston and in several other southern cities. These actions provoked Congress to demand that the army enforce civil rights laws in the occupied South. In the congressional elections of 1866, northern voters gave Republicans a sweeping victory and uncontested control of Congress. Immediately, Congress declared martial law throughout the former Confederacy and ordered military commanders to curb white violence against blacks and suspend civil government. The resurgence of the Republican Party in 1866 marked the start of the ten-year-long effort to reconstruct the South. For nearly a decade, it looked as if emancipation might mean full legal and civil equality for Low Country African Americans.[82]

By 1872, however, northern voters had tired of Reconstruction. Northern whites associated Reconstruction with black political ineptitude and civil disorder in the South. In the presidential election of 1876, anxious to put the Civil War behind them, northern voters elected Kenyon graduate Rutherford B. Hayes as president. Once in office, Hayes withdrew Union troops from the South and abandoned black freedmen. Despite Republican defeat in South Carolina, the state's white-only Democratic Party moved cautiously against blacks. Educational reform slowed, segregation of public accommodations and transportation increased, and upstate racial violence became commonplace. Not until 1888, however, with the election of "Pitchfork" Ben Tillman to the governorship, did the South Carolina legislature impose a statewide system of racial segregation.[83]

In 1889 the South Carolina legislature repealed the state's Reconstruction-era civil rights law that had prohibited segregation in public accommodations. By

1900, South Carolina enforced a comprehensive system of racial apartheid that required separate cars for whites and blacks on railroads and trams, separate schools for whites and blacks, and separate restaurants, theaters, barbershops, and hotels, and it barred blacks from public parks and playgrounds when in use by whites. In many instances, this meant that the state's meager public facilities were reserved exclusively for whites, leaving blacks to their own resources.[84]

Even so, for the remainder of the century, the Low Country avoided much of the racial violence that plagued the remainder of the state. Until the 1890s, the Republican Party won local elections in the Low Country, and in 1900 Beaufort County voters elected black candidates to county, state, and national offices. The overwhelming numerical superiority of blacks in the Low Country kept the Ku Klux Klan and its ilk at bay. A 1940 University of North Carolina study reported that after 1880 no lynchings had taken place in the five Low Country counties of Berkeley, Beaufort, Charleston, Colleton, and Georgetown.[85] Because of the relative safety of Charleston County, until World War I, it attracted a steady stream of black migrants from the remainder of the state.[86]

The well-being of Low Country blacks went beyond the absence of overt violence. With emancipation, Low Country Gullah proved remarkably successful in acquiring land. In 1940 79 percent of Beaufort County's black farmers owned their own farms, 55 percent in Berkeley County, 48 percent in Charleston County, and 59 percent in Georgetown County.[87] Regionally, about six in ten Low Country black farmers owned land. This exceeded the percentage of white landownership in the region. In 1866 Congress had created the Freedmen's Bureau to oversee the transition of freedmen from slavery. In the Low Country, the bureau oversaw legal contracts, served as a savings bank, and arbitrated disputes between ex-slaves and ex-masters. Many conflicts arose over labor obligations and the wage-labor system. The most important issues, however, involved landownership.[88] Former masters considered their plantations their exclusive property. They believed that emancipation had freed slaves to leave the plantation, but it had given freedmen no claim to the land, not even to their ramshackle homesteads. Former slaves believed that generations of unpaid labor had earned them title to their plantations. Across the South, emancipation raised the issue of landownership, but no other former slaves pursued landownership with the intensity and success of Low Country Gullah.[89]

Before emancipation, when planters had referred to "their" plantations, Gullah understood them to mean "We Land." With the Union occupation of Beaufort and Port Royal Sound in 1861, the federal government encouraged Low Country Gullah to occupy and work their former plantations. The most concerted effort by the federal government to transfer land from planters to freedmen occurred on Saint Helena Island, near Beaufort. In June 1862 Congress imposed a land tax on all areas in rebellion, including Union-occupied Beaufort County. With the arrival of Union gunboats in the fall of 1861, most Beaufort plantation owners fled to Confederate lines, making it impossible for them to pay the federal land tax. These tax delinquent plantations fell to the Treasury Department. General Rufus Saxton, the military governor of occupied South Carolina, argued that these lands should be sold to former slaves—twenty acres for an individual, forty acres for a family. The Treasury Department preferred to sell the plantations at auction to northern land speculators. Saxton, with the help of Boston businessman E. S. Philbrick, secured sixteen of the plantations on Saint Helena Island for its former slaves. Saxton offered former slaves the land for a dollar an acre. Although whites acquired most of Beaufort County's confiscated land, by the end of the war most of Saint Helena Island former slaves owned farmsteads of ten to forty acres, making Saint Helena an almost exclusively black island of landowning Gullah.[90] Separated from the remainder of South Carolina by open water, after 1865 Saint Helena became a virtually self-governing African American community almost entirely independent from Beaufort County and state officials. Only a handful of white-owned plantations, including the Trask family estate "Orange Grove," remained on Saint Helena along with Penn Center, a vocational school founded during Union occupation and staffed by northern missionaries.[91]

Elsewhere in the Low Country, large numbers of freedmen also acquired farmsteads. On January 16, 1865, General William Sherman, in consultation with Secretary of War Edwin Stanton, issued Special Field Order Fifteen, which set aside for freedmen "the islands from Charleston south, the abandoned rice fields along the rivers for thirty miles back from the sea and the country bordering the St. Johns River, Florida."[92] Sherman's order allowed black heads of family to preempt up to forty acres of tillable land. The military issued a "possessory" title that established ownership and boundaries. The order also allowed a black enlistee to use his $300 enlistment bounty "to assist his family and settlement in procuring agricultural implements, seed, tools, boats, clothing, and other articles necessary for their livelihood." Order Fifteen declared that "no white person, whatever, unless military officers and soldiers detailed for duty, will be permitted to reside; and the sole and exclusive management of affairs will be left to the freed people themselves, subject only to the United States Military and the acts of Congress." Had Special Order Fifteen remained in force, the Carolina Low Country would have become a self-governing, Gullah region. By late summer 1865, under Saxton's direction, the army resettled nearly forty thousand Low Country Gullah on their former plantations.[93]

With their backs to the wall, many Low Country planters negotiated private sales with Gullah freedmen. Informal and unrecorded, these sales were either oral or written bills of sale often on scraps of paper. Few were filed in county land registries because the filing fees often exceeded the price paid for the land.[94] Even so, Low Country courts rarely challenged the oral claims based on occupation or the bills of sale that freedmen kept in their family papers. Few planters reneged on the informal sales, perhaps out of compassion toward their former slaves, or out of economic necessity because they depended on their former slaves for labor, or perhaps, out of fear, remembering that their Gullah slaves had borne arms against them during the Civil War.[95] Whatever the motive, an analysis of the records for the 1880, 1890, and 1900 census of Christ Church Parish, a rural district to the north of Charleston, make it clear that most Low Country freedmen secured title to land after the Civil War.[96]

Within ten years of emancipation, two in five of these illiterate and impoverished former Christ Church Parish slaves had acquired their own homesteads, a higher percentage of landownership than in the United States as a whole.[97] Most lived on land purchased from their former owners. But they did not live in former slave cabins in the old plantation slave quarter. Nor did they scatter themselves across Christ Church Parish as independent farmers. Instead, former slaves from contiguous plantations formed independent Gullah villages on the basis of the communal and family ties fashioned during slavery. Each family in these villages owned a five- to twenty-acre family lot. Gullah villages contained twenty-five to fifty homesteads and encompassed one hundred to two hundred acres of land. Like other Low Country parishes, Christ Church contained about a dozen of these Gullah communities, including Remley's Point, which overlooked Charleston Harbor; Snowden, on Long Point Road near the Wando River; Hamlin community, located seven miles from the Charleston ferry; and Phillips, on the Cainhoy Road to Mount Pleasant. Ninety percent of Christ Church blacks lived in these tightly clustered communities that contained churches, general stores, taverns, praise houses, one-room schoolhouses, and sweet shops. The remaining 10 percent lived in the fishing and farming village of Mount Pleasant. On their small parcels of land, Gullah families grew their food. In nearby tidal creeks, the men fished, shrimped, and gathered oysters, which the women sold in Mount Pleasant and Charleston, along with vegetables, flowers, and hand-sewn sweet-grass baskets. These sales enabled Gullah families to purchase cloth, tools, and kerosene.

Poor and largely illiterate, Low Country Gullah, nevertheless, were free and autonomous landowners.[98]

By 1890 many Gullah families in Christ Church had acquired tracts of marginal land from their old plantations. The white owners of Boon Hall, Hamlin, Phillips, and other Christ Church plantations hired surveyors to lay out subdivisions of two hundred to three hundred acres with fifty or so ten- to twenty-acre lots that they sold for a dollar an acre. Deed registration required a trip to Charleston, an attorney to draw up the form, and the payment of a title fee. Few Gullah registered their land.[99] Failure to register proved of little consequence. Outsiders did not challenge their occupancy, and few Gullah sold their land. At the marriage of a son, the family allowed him to build a house on its lot. At the death of the male head of family, by tradition the remaining family members shared in ownership of the unrecorded family lot. These "heirs," through mutual agreement, extended house and yard rights to fellow "heirs" as the need arose. This ensured that all heirs "possessed" a house lot and a small garden plot on the family's lot. Generation after generation transferred its land privately, innocent of legal forms or sanction. Each Gullah family—husband, wife, children, and related dependencies—lived in a separate house while the land remained the collective property of the heirs of the original owner. Each heir held a claim to his or her house and yard, but no individual possessed the right to sell the land.[100]

Such "heir's property" bound together Low Country Gullah villages. Much as during slavery, no matter who died, no matter what the price of rice or cotton, no matter when or where the boll weevils attacked, no matter who fought what war, no matter who voted or held office, no matter what the South Carolina legislature or U.S. Congress chose to do, the "We Land" of Greenhill, Beehive, Phillips, Hamlin, Ten Mile, and other Gullah communities assured that "We People" retained an unalienable claim to their homelands. No family claimed much land, no individuals exercised the right on their own accord to sell the family land, and landownership offered no path to riches or fame. Through hurricanes and earthquakes, hell and high water, these Gullah communities remained intact, islands of Gullah autonomy in an otherwise white-owned and white-dominated Low Country.[101]

Most Gullah homes were small shanties, raised off the ground by timbers. The dwellings had makeshift chimneys, no indoor plumbing, and only two or three shuttered windows and were lit by kerosene lamps. Built of rough-sawn lumber, the whitewashed houses had cypress-shingle roofs. Families maintained carefully painted blue or green window sashes and red doors to ward off bad spirits and haunts. Gullah scraped and swept their yards, leaving them free of grass, set off by

A typical Low Country growing house, Mount Pleasant, South Carolina (Will Scott)

pecan and chinaberry trees, small vegetable and flower gardens, and walks lined with sun-bleached white conch shells. Most homes contained two rooms about twelve by fifteen feet in dimension, a sleeping loft in each room, a fireplace, and a covered front and back porch. The front porch stretched across the front of the house and accommodated several roughly hewn chairs or benches. When the need arose, the families of these two-room Low Country cabins expanded their homes with twelve- by fifteen-foot additions to either side or to the back. Some- times they attached one addition onto a previous one. Such Low Country "grow- ing houses" were adapted to changing family needs, additional children, or the arrival of a dependent parent or a grandchild. Occasionally, when a son married, the family simply detached "his" room from the family's house and moved it a hundred or so feet away where he started his own "growing house." Low Country growing houses resembled West African houses in size, proportion, and yard, giving a West African feel to the Low Country.[102]

These houses and their autonomous communities served as a reward to the Gullah for their service in the Civil War. Emancipation enabled them to live their lives according to their beliefs. They no longer had to attend the planter's church service on Sundays, nor did they have to steal away to their brush arbors at night. Throughout the Low Country, Gullah freedmen built small praise houses and larger Baptist and Methodist sanctuaries. The small praise houses accommodated thirty to forty people on movable benches. The services included songs, a sermon, an offering, and, until recently, ring shouts.[103] In 1862 Colonel Thomas Wentworth Higginson, commander of the First South Carolina Volunteers stationed in Beaufort, left a description of his Gullah soldiers' ring shout around the camp fires. "These fires are usually enclosed in a little booth, made neatly of palm-leaves and covered in at top, a regular native African hut, in short," explained Higginson.

> This hut is crammed with men, singing at the top of their voices, in one of their quaint, monotonous, endless, negro-Methodist chants, with obscure syllables recurring constantly, and slight variations interwoven, all accompanied with a regular drumming of the feet and clapping of the hands, like castanets. Then the excitement spreads; inside and outside the enclosure men begin to quiver and dance, others join, a circle forms, winding monotonously round some one in the center; some "heel and toe" tumultuously, others merely tremble and stagger on, others stoop and rise, others whirl, others caper sideways, all keep steadily circling like dervishes; spectators applaud special strokes of skill . . . and still the ceaseless drumming and clapping, in perfect cadence, goes steadily on. Suddenly, there comes a sort of *snap*, and the spell breaks, and general sighing and laughter. And this, not rarely and occasionally, but night after night."[104]

Following emancipation, in addition to praise houses, Gullah also built formal Baptist and Methodist churches that included alters, choir rows, and fixed seats. The fixed seating made it difficult to perform a ring shout. Instead, congregants "shouted" and "jumped" in place. Possession by the Holy Spirit caused worshipers to run, jump, and even faint. Gullah Methodist and "Sanctified" Baptist services sustained the content of pre-emancipation African Christianity that included feeling the spirit, the shout, joyful singing, and, when possessed by the Holy Spirit, "speaking in tongues." Sunday services lasted several hours, followed by cover-dish dinners and group singing.[105] Most Low Country Gullah churches, built with the help of their local black Masonic lodges, appeared in the 1870s and 1880s, at the time of the formation of the Gullah villages. The Masonic lodges seem to have been the successors to secret slave societies that were themselves successors to West African secret societies.[106]

Methodism dominated black communities in the Gullah region, unlike in the remainder of the South. Gullah people called U.S. Highway 17, built in the 1920s, the "AME Highway," in recognition of the dozens of African Methodist Episcopal churches scattered along its way from North Carolina to Georgia. Following the

Vesey conspiracy, the South Carolina white Methodist Church launched a massive missionary effort directed at Low Country slaves. White Methodist missionaries encouraged Gullah singing and its "warm hearted," highly spiritual worship, including "seeking." In Philadelphia at the same time, Charleston refugees Morris Brown and Daniel Payne received ordination as ministers in the black African Methodist Episcopal Church.[107] In 1865, when Payne and Brown returned to Charleston to found the Emanuel and Morris Brown AME churches, they also proselytized in the rural Gullah rice lands. With emancipation, most Gullah churches affiliated with the African Methodist Episcopal Church.[108]

The Goodwill AME, along Highway 17 in Christ Church Parish, traces its origins to slavery. According to Goodwill church historians, slaves built the church in the 1820s with the approval of the owner of Boon Hall Plantation when Denmark Vesey formed his African Church in Charleston.[109] Local authorities did not close the Goodwill "Independent Church" after the Vesey conspiracy, as was done with the Charleston African churches. On Sundays, Gullah slaves, from the surrounding plantations—Boon Hall, Hamlin, Phillips, and Laurel Hill—attended services at the church.[110] With emancipation, the "Independent Church" joined Payne's AME to become Goodwill AME. In 1867 the church registered its title to the land it had occupied since the 1820s.[111]

Rural Low Country AME congregations retained many West African, Gullah ways. These Gullah AME churches anticipated later Pentecostal belief and worship.[112] The West African practices of rural Low Country AME congregations disturbed church officers in Charleston such as Bishop Daniel Payne. Historically, the AME followed the practices of the white Methodist Church. In the 1790s, Richard Allen, with the blessing of Francis Asbury, bishop of the American Methodist Episcopal Church, had formed the separate black African Methodist Episcopal Church in Philadelphia.[113] At the end of the Civil War, when the AME sent Bishop Payne back to Charleston to organize a South Carolina synod, Payne welcomed the Gullah churches into the AME fold. He soon discovered, however, that his Gullah parishioners had minds of their own and had no intention of giving up their West African ways. Founded by middle-class free blacks, the AME considered Gullah religious practices savage, pagan survivals. Payne sought to cleanse Gullah churches, such as Goodwill, of West African practices. In his autobiography, Payne recounted a visit to a Gullah "bush meeting": "After the sermon they [members of the congregation] formed a ring and with coats off sung, clapped their hands and stamped their feet in the most ridiculous and heathenish way. I requested the pastor to go and stop their dancing. At his request they stopped their dancing and clapping of hands, but remained singing and rocking their bodies to and fro. . . . In that instance they broke up their ring; but would not sit down and walked sullenly away." The local minister explained to Payne, "Sinners won't get converted unless there is a ring."[114] At Goodwill and other Gullah AME Churches, either ministers allowed the ring shout and other Gullah practices or they lost their congregation to Sanctified Baptist churches that openly encouraged dancing, shouting, jumping, and full-immersion baptism. Most rural Low Country AME ministers chose to allow the ring shout or its equivalent, the jump and shout.[115]

Goodwill, much as it had during slavery, served as a center for Gullah culture. Slaves from surrounding plantations attended their own praise houses or brush arbors during the week, but on Sunday they traveled to Goodwill for all-day services and socializing. Until recently, at burials mourners threw coins into the graves and passed young infants across the open coffins to appease departed spirits.[116] Family members also placed conk shells around graves, left food near the graves for the deceased, and put on the graves burial goods, such as broken pottery, water vessels, and miscellaneous personal items of the deceased. Gullah believed that the white conk shells pointed the way across the water that separated the living from the dead. The broken clocks and other broken grave goods severed the ties of the deceased to this world, freeing its spirit to pass.[117] In some Gullah burial grounds, relatives erected iron and wooden beds to ease the passage of the spirit. Until the 1970s, these practices remained common throughout the Low Country. Gullah graveyards oriented the dead to the east so that they looked toward the rising sun. Similarly, when individuals reached the edge of death but unaccountably lingered on, family members moved the deathbed so that the foot of the bed pointed east to make it easier for their spirits to pass.[118]

Under the influence of Christian missionaries, Gullah people distinguished between religious belief and superstition—associating religious belief with Christianity and superstition with African magic. When WPA interviewers asked former Gullah slaves whether they believed in magic, almost to a person they denied it, affirming their Christianity. Later in the interview, however, they offered detailed accounts of root doctors, conjurers, haunts, hags, and mojo bags. The conjurer or "root doctor" rivaled the minister as the most important individual in a Gullah community.[119] Until his death during World War II, Dr. Buzzard, reputed to be the most powerful and feared man in Beaufort Country, cast spells, healed the sick, and comforted the lovelorn. His agents sold Dr. Buzzard's famous "red" and "black" mojo bags in Beaufort, Charleston, Savannah, and Harlem, making him quite wealthy. Because many Low Country planters had denied their slaves proper burials, an unusually large number of "traveling spirits" were believed to haunt the region. Such haunts possessed people in their sleep, caused ill fortune, and brought on debilitating disease. The reluctance of white authorities to enforce public law in Gullah communities left many with no recourse except private justice, which included evil spells. Root doctors like Dr. Buzzard, Dr. Bug, Dr. Crow, and Dr. Snake enabled aggrieved parties to control wayward spirits or to harness them for their own purposes. Gullah believed infants born with a membrane or caul over their faces to be magically gifted and potential root doctors or witches. The ethnic diversity of the original Low Country slave population bequeathed to Gullah a variety of magical and religious beliefs. Gullah Christians often considered these beliefs magical and pagan but nonetheless practiced them.[120]

An example was the Gullah celebration of Watch Night. Watch Night took place on New Year's Eve. Traditionally, Low Country slaves had received nearly two weeks of freedom from plantation tasks at the end of December. On December 31, slaves gathered in their praise houses or brush arbors to sing and dance. A "Watchman" stood outside looking for the approach of the overseer, who at midnight entered the slave quarters to announce the end of the Christmas holiday and the return to work. When the Watchman spotted the overseer, he entered the praise house and halted its rituals. Following slavery, Watch Night services continued in Gullah churches on New Year's Eve, beginning in the early evening and ending at midnight.[121] In some communities, on New Year's Day, Gullah families ceremonially removed all decorations and manifestations of Christmas from their homes and churches. A male elder, often a member of the Masonic or other secret fraternal order, visited each house to ensure that no Christian symbols remained after Watch Night. On New Year's Day, Gullah ate only "lucky" African food—collards, okra, yams, and "Hoppin' John," a mixture of boiled rice, black-eyed peas, and pork.[122]

Because of their isolation, Gullah also retained a large number of West African skills and crafts. Most Gullah, especially the women, carried their bundles balanced on their heads.[123] Women sewed quilts with West African strip and patchwork designs that were deliberately asymmetrical in shape (one end slightly larger than the other).[124] Women wove their hair in traditional styles or wrapped it in red, white, or blue scarves. Gullah men wove cast-nets out of cotton cord, modeled after nets used on the rice coast of West Africa, to catch fish and shrimp in shallow tidal creeks.[125] Gullah women, and a few men, sewed coiled grass baskets also based on West African designs and techniques. Slaves used sweetgrass and bulrush baskets for a variety of functions. On the rice plantations, slaves placed milled rice on large, flat baskets or "fanners" which they used to throw milled rice into the air to separate the grain from the chaff. Made from sweet grass or bulrush and sewn in circular coils with strips of palmetto fronds, "sweet-grass" baskets survived in the Gullah communities affiliated with the Goodwill AME in Christ Church Parish. After slavery, the women of Goodwill sewed and sold baskets and flowers in Charleston. In the 1920s, with the construction of U.S. Highway 17, they built roadside stands to attract tourists, providing another cash crop even as they preserved the ancient West African craft.[126]

A large number of Gullah males, perhaps Bantu descendants, possessed iron-working skills. Gullah blacksmiths built plantation equipment, repaired iron-rimmed wheels, and constructed gates and other decorative ironwork for plantation and Charleston homes. After World War II, a young Gullah blacksmith, Philip Simmons, designed and built a commissioned wrought-iron gate for the historic home of the city's mayor. Born in the Gullah community on Daniels Island in Charleston Harbor, Simmons came to Charleston as a young boy in the 1920s and apprenticed himself to Peter Simmons, a master blacksmith. When automobiles replaced horses in Charleston, Philip Simmons took up wrought iron decorative work. By the 1940s the owners of mansions that rice planters had built turned to Simmons to repair the pre–Civil War wrought iron on their homes. An artist as much as a blacksmith, Simmons moved away from restoration work to design his own ironwork. Simmons's designs diverged from the German-inspired work of the city's pre–Civil War wrought iron. He drew explicitly on his Gullah culture. His stylized snakes, fish, birds, hearts, circles, and stars gave his gates and fences a distinct Low Country character, unmatched by the city's earlier European iron work. Art historians have traced many of his motifs and ideas to the Kongo culture of Angola.[127] Unconsciously, Simmons inherited his ideas from his Gullah fore-bears, who in turn had inherited them from their West African ancestors. Whether as Sanctified Christians, cooks, house servants, laborers, musicians, farmers, fishers, quilters, net makers, house builders, or basket makers, Gullah people fastened their West African ways on Low Country life.[128]

CATFISH ROW

After Reconstruction, Charleston's black population increased dramatically. Every day, it seemed, in every way, Charleston became blacker and blacker. On the eve of the Civil War only sixteen thousand blacks had lived in Charleston compared to twenty-three thousand whites. In 1900 the city's black population had doubled to thirty-two thousand, from about two in five of the city's total population to nearly three in five. The white population remained stable at about twenty-four thousand.[129] At the same time, none of Charleston's twelve census wards in 1900 were

Philip Simmons, Gullah ironworker, Charleston, South Carolina (Peter Rutkoff)

either overwhelmingly black or white. Ward 2 claimed the highest percentage of whites. Still, nearly two in five of its residents were black. Similarly, in the city's blackest ward about one-third of the residents were white. The remaining ten wards ranged from 45 percent to 55 percent of one race or the other. Charleston's residential integration went beyond the ward level. Virtually every block in the city housed some white and black families, and many of Charleston's three- and four-family "single houses," with front doors that opened onto full-length, multistory, side porches, were occupied by both black and white families.

Until 1890, most public facilities in Charleston and the remainder of the Low

Country, except for schools, were not formally segregated. In the 1890s, Governor Tillman changed this. After 1900, systematic segregation spread to the Low Country. Tillman's segregation did not simply separate blacks and whites. In most instances, it meant white-only public facilities and accommodations. Usually, there were no provisions for black public services and accommodations. Charleston city ordinances prohibited blacks from using Colonial Lake, Hampton Park, the Battery, or any other municipal park, including the local public beaches on Folly and Sullivan's Island. Out of necessity, black children used streets for playgrounds and stagnant ponds and river beaches for swimming. On Christmas Day, the police department closed off select streets so that black children could skate and ride their Christmas bikes and roller-skates safely. Only on specified days, such as New Years and the Fourth of July, did the city allow black use of otherwise white-only, public spaces.[130]

In celebration of Emancipation Day and Watch Night, Charleston's black Masons annually held a New Year's Day parade that marched down the city's main commercial street to the Battery. Black churches, lodges, labor unions, and schools decorated floats that carried stylishly dressed young girls while the Jenkins Orphanage Band marched and danced to the cheers of black and white spectators. On Independence Day, the city turned over the Battery to blacks for picnics and fireworks, while Charleston's pro-Confederate whites remained in their homes and closed the shutters, mourning the Yankee holiday.[131] On the weekends, black families could take the *Planter* or the *Sapho* ferryboats across the Cooper River to Remley's Point, a black-only river-beach with a nightclub, White's Paradise, which featured local dance bands and visiting national black show bands, such as Fats Domino or James Brown and the Flames. On select days, Mount Pleasant allowed blacks to use its municipal Alhambra Hall for lodge and church events.[132]

Despite such symbolic gestures, only the waterways remained unencumbered by racial apartheid. Almost every black family had access to a small fishing boat or fished and crabbed from the city wharfs and piers. Most black social life took place behind closed doors and curtained windows of Low Country black homes, churches, schools, and lodge halls, much like the brush arbors of slavery. "Tillmanism" brought together all segments of black society and encouraged black-owned businesses and professional services. In the face of education and cultural assimilation, segregation fostered black racial consciousness and important components of West African culture, especially in religion and music. Whether black and Gullah or brown and middle class, all Low Country African Americans belonged to a single persecuted people. Racial apartheid forced Low Country African Americans to work together. Middle-class African Americans from Charleston and Mount Pleasant, with missionary-like zeal, focused their uplift efforts on rural Gullah and working-class blacks. Working-class blacks and Gullah, in turn, demanded that middle-class blacks acknowledge and respect their shared West African heritage and blood. In the twentieth century, racial segregation assured that neither urbanization nor education nor upward mobility erased the Low Country's West African ways.[133]

After World War I, two white Charleston authors, Dubose Heyward and Julia Peterkin, won national recognition for their fiction portrayals of Low Country Gullah life in Charleston and in the surrounding rice lands. Descendants of rice planters, Heyward and Peterkin both understood that much of the distinctiveness of the Carolina Low Country derived from its Gullah people. The real-life equivalents of Heyward's fictional *Porgy* and Peterkin's *Scarlet Sister Mary* had shaped the Low Country as much as Heyward's and Peterkin's rice planter ancestors.[134] Cat Fish Row, the all-black tenement in which Porgy and Bess lived, adjoined Charleston's most prestigious neighborhood, within a block of where Dubose Heyward grew up. Poetically, Porgy, Bess, and Dubose had been neighbors, and as children they would have played together. Charleston's Mosquito Fleet, manned by Gullah fishermen, tied up along East Bay Street near Adger's Wharf within sight of Heyward's home and the Battery, Charleston's most coveted residential address. Gullah fishmongers and vegetable venders pushed their carts through the city's streets and alleys daily, singing out "porgy, crab, balled [boiled] peanuts, collards, and melon." Gullah farmers from Daniels Island, James Island, Johns Island, and Christ Church Parish rowed their flat-bottom boats to the foot of Market Street where they sold fresh produce and flowers, sugarcane, smoked and pickled meat, seafood, and sweet-grass baskets in the city's open-air market.[135] At night, when Gullah venders went home, the historic St. Michael's Episcopal Church, at Broad and Meeting streets, allowed them to store their carts in its gated graveyard.[136]

Much like pre–Civil War Charleston, African Americans and West African folkways penetrated every aspect of the city's life. The 1900 federal census takers recorded that 85 percent of Charleston domestics were black, almost all of its barbers and hairdressers, 90 percent of its wagon drivers, 90 percent of its peddlers, 60 percent of its blacksmiths, and 75 percent of its house painters, cobblers, butchers, and carpenters, 85 percent of the city's masons, and 97 percent of its fish and oyster men. More telling, twenty of the city's forty-four firemen and thirty-three of its seventy-eight policemen were black. No one in Charleston could step out of his door without meeting someone of the other race, and most did not even have to leave their homes. Not only did black domestics live in upper-class white homes, but working-class blacks and whites often lived on different floors of the same apartment house. Few other American cities enjoyed such an intimate, biracial existence.[137]

In response to the 1891 state statute that required all municipalities to establish and maintain racially segregated, public cemeteries, Mount Pleasant designated its Ocean Grove potter's field as the black municipal cemetery. Whites buried their dead in the adjoining St. Paul's Lutheran Cemetery. "Hallejulla Road," an unpaved service path used by burial parties, separated the graves of whites and blacks in Mount Pleasant.[138] The white St. Paul's Cemetery organized its graves into neat rows that conformed to Mount Pleasant's carefully surveyed, magnetic-north-determined street grid. In the white cemetery, gravestones stood at the south end of the graves with the head of the deceased facing north, perpendicular to the east-west cemetery rows and city streets. Families distinguished their plots from their neighbors with marble pavers or bricks. In the adjacent black Ocean Grove Cemetery, the burial rows also ran perpendicular to the town's north-south street grid. The individual graves in Ocean Grove, however, lay west to east, but not perpendicular to magnetic north. As in West Africa and Goodwill AME, the faces of the deceased looked eastward into the rising sun, slightly askew of the town's magnetic-north grid. In Mount Pleasant African Americans buried their dead much as premodern African and European people had buried theirs, oriented to the rising sun. Mourners scattered conk shells and other burial goods over individual graves. These included ceramic frogs, photographs, broken pottery, bottles, and flowers.

In the black section, military headstones marked a large number of graves, in proud acknowledgment of the deceased's service in the armed forces. One series of markers appeared to be a grandfather, a son, and a grandson—the first noting service in World War I, the second World War II, and the third the Vietnam War. Since the Civil War, the federal government has remained an ever-present, if distant, guardian of Low Country African Americans. The clear differences between the white and black sections of the two Mount Pleasant public burial grounds underline continuing Gullah influences, even on the educated and citified African Americans of Mount Pleasant.[139]

In 1900 South Carolina had allocated $1.30 for each black student, a situation that did not materially change until after World War II.[140] Black churches, lodges, and private individuals tried to fill the gap, but most of Charleston's black children were, at best, literate. In 1891 Rev. Daniel Jenkins, pastor of the Tabernacle Fourth Baptist Church, took on the even more daunting problem of homeless black children. In 1891 Jenkins organized the Orphan Aid Society for black Low Country orphans. Renamed the Jenkins Orphanage, in 1893 Jenkins moved the facility from its cramped quarters on King Street to the spacious, former Marine Hospital Building at 20 Franklin Street, on the city's west side near the city jail and next to the black Fielding Funeral Home. At its peak, Jenkins Orphanage housed about four hundred children. Between its founding and World War II, it cared for more than fifteen thousand orphans.[141]

Inspired by Booker T. Washington's gospel of self-help and manual labor, the orphanage maintained a 140-acre farm north of the city and, in Charleston, taught printing, shoe repair, clerical skills, home economics, and tailoring. While Jenkins received a modest annual appropriation from the city and contributions from Low Country Baptist churches and individual donors, the most important source of income for the orphanage derived from the Jenkins Orphanage Band. By 1900 the Jenkins Orphanage Marching Band scheduled regular tours through the North and also in England and continental Europe. The band combined formal music training with high-stepping, dance-like routines and lively, syncopated songs. During a march, with the band playing, individual players broke ranks and performed extemporaneous dances to the applause of onlookers. Often, crowds threw coins to reward spectacular performers.[142]

Many of the band's routines came from dances performed in juke joints, frequented by Gullah dockworkers in Charleston and New York. In 1913 at the Jungles Casino in Harlem, pianist James P. Johnson played and performed what in the 1920s became popularized as the "Charleston."[143] Drawn from minstrel clowning and Gullah ring shouts, the signifying step of the Charleston was no step at all. Instead, the dancer stopped, bent forward, and set his or her legs squarely apart. Dancers swung their knees in and out as their hands moved back and forth across their knees, creating an optical illusion of crossing legs. The move came directly from the ring shout and Gullah religion that prohibited the crossing of the legs while dancing. A number of Jenkins Orphanage graduates, including trumpeters Jabbo Smith, Gus Aikens, and Cat Anderson and drummer Tommy Benford, joined the Harlem jazz bands of James Europe, Chick Webb, Jelly Roll Morton, Fletcher Henderson, and Duke Ellington.[144]

Scores of Jenkins Orphanage graduates organized bands and music programs in black high schools and colleges throughout South Carolina, North Carolina, Georgia, and Florida. Jenkins graduates taught their students musical notation, proper technique, and the European concert tradition. They also taught jazz, blues, Gullah spirituals, and the rousing, high-stepping, cakewalk marches that the Jenkins Orphanage borrowed from minstrel shows and West African dance. Jenkins Orphanage spread Low Country music and dance across the Lower South and, after the outbreak of World War I, to northern East Coast cities.[145]

STEALING AWAY

Heightened racial tensions, a depressed local economy, and a high, wartime demand for labor in northern cities set off the black exodus from the Low Country. It took decades for South Carolina to recover from the Civil War.[146] With few employment opportunities, South Carolina became a reservoir of cheap, black labor for the remainder of the South. In 1880 the ratio of blacks to whites in South Carolina reached a historical high of three blacks for every two whites. Between 1870 and 1900, more than 275,000 blacks left South Carolina, nearly all migrating to other southern states—either to the prosperous Mississippi Delta or to the Cotton Belt that ran from Georgia and northern Florida to Arkansas and Texas. These migrants, many of whom were Gullah, took their culture with them. Elements of West African language, foodways, religious practice, and folkways, including naming practices, vocabulary and syntax, red-flannel mojo bags, the shout, brush arbors, and Hoppin' John appeared in African American communities across the Lower South. In the 1890s the booming New South cities of Atlanta, Birmingham, and Charlotte lured Carolina blacks, competing with lumber and railroad construction camps for their labor.[147] Lumber and railroad work, however, meant leaving home for months at a time or abandoning the Low Country altogether, a prospect that most Low Country African Americans resisted.

Between 1870 and 1900, the black population of Charleston County increased at twice the rate of any other South Carolina county. From 1890 to 1900, Charleston's black population grew 72 percent, three times the next highest rate of increase, even though Charleston County offered African Americans only meager employment opportunities.[148] After 1900, Charleston's appeal to African Americans dimmed. In 1900 the state's rising tide of white racial violence reached Charleston. Residential segregation increased, the state enforced the segregation of all public transportation, the city segregated public accommodations, black education stalled, and the growing black population depressed the labor market. No longer a black Mecca, black Charleston was crowded, impoverished, and crime ridden. From "bad to worse," became a Low Country cliché. In 1884 a hurricane slammed into the region and destroyed the rice land's complex system of irrigation canals, levees, and tidal gates. A massive earthquake shook the city in 1895, knocking down much of its housing. Especially hard hit were the city's black tenements. In 1914 boll weevils attacked the Low Country's sea island cotton and another killer hurricane struck the Low Country. Even phosphate mining, the one bright spot in the region's post–Civil War economy, faded with the opening of deposits near Tampa, Florida, that were richer and easier to mine.[149]

Before 1910, most Low Country black migrants had headed west but remained in the South. The 1900 census reported that in the previous decade fewer than 4,000 black South Carolinians had migrated to a northern state out of a total out-migration of more than 106,000. In 1910 the number of black migrants to the north jumped to 10,000, most to New York. In 1920, out of 164,000 black migrants who left the state in the previous decade, a third went to a northern city. The Census Bureau estimated that in 1924, for the first time since the seventeenth century, whites made up a majority of South Carolinians. Of the 312,000 black migrants who left the state during the 1920s, 122,000 traveled north. In the 1930s, three-quarters of South Carolina's black migrants went north, most to Harlem.[150]

Economic decline and World War I set in motion the Great African American Migration northward. The Low Country lost its primary agricultural crop, rice, to Louisiana and Texas. Not since the Civil War had its agriculture been so depressed, condemning the region's agricultural workers to deepening poverty. While cotton and phosphate mining declined, the region failed to build a manufacturing base, and it no longer served as a major southern port. The state's segregation policies ensured that, however broadly shared the Low Country's poverty, blacks suffered disproportionately. The state refused to provide a basic education to black children, exacerbating an already dire situation. Even the most optimistic became discouraged. In the North, things looked much better. With the outbreak of war in Europe, American factories became inundated with orders, especially for military materiel. Northern factories, anxious to expand production, faced an acute labor shortage caused by European belligerents' curtailment of immigration. Employers, who in the past had refused to hire women and blacks, now, eagerly offered both high wages. When the United States entered the war in 1917, the army also enlisted 25,000 South Carolina black males to join the fight "to make the world safe for Democracy." Many, on their return to the United States, chose not to return to South Carolina.[151]

With peace, Low Country blacks expected their military service to be repaid with respect and opportunity. Instead, southern whites greeted the demobilization of black troops with a wave of lynchings, seventy altogether, including the public murder of ten men in uniform. Southern whites made it clear that the war had not changed the region's race relations. Even in Charleston, for the first time since Reconstruction, blacks became the targets of vigilante violence. On May 11, 1919, several enlisted, off-duty navy "blue jackets" attacked a black soldier, Isaac Docktor. The attack sparked a citywide race riot during which white mobs beat dozens of blacks, vandalized black stores, and threatened black homes.[152] While mild compared to other race riots in East St. Louis and Chicago, the Blue Jacket Riot dispelled any illusion that Charleston or the Low Country was any longer an African American sanctuary.

Emboldened by World War I and heartened by stories of black Harlem, thousands of Low Country blacks gathered their belongings and purchased steamship tickets from the Clyde Line for passage to New York. Each day, when the New York steamer pulled away from Adger's Wharf, scores of Low Country blacks anxiously peered over the ship rail to wave goodbye to relatives and friends. Across the water, Harlem became their new Zion. And like other southern black migrants, Low Country migrants took their West African ways with them.[153] For these migrants, World War I marked a second emancipation. Adger's Wharf and the Clyde Steamship Line offered Low Country African Americans passage to Harlem, a place far more promising than the Middle Passage and the Sullivan's Island slave pens that their ancestors had endured. Harlem promised them the rights of American citizenship, racial dignity, and individual freedom. In Harlem, they could become Americans as well as African Americans. In the process, they made Harlem "We Land" much as their ancestors had made the Carolina Low Country.

NEGRO CAPITAL
OF THE WORLD

• **3** •

Harlem

Jamaican-born, Harlem writer Claude McKay proclaimed, "As the metropolis of New York attracts Americans and the rest of the world, so does Harlem
[attract] the Negro of America and the world. Harlem is the queen of the black
belts, drawing Aframericans together in a vast humming hive . . . from the
different states, from the islands of the Caribbean, and from Africa. . . . It is the
Negro capital of the world."[1] Before Harlem, white racism had blocked efforts of
most African Americans to escape poverty and enter the middle class. For many,
emancipation had encouraged whites to view African Americans only as an un-
differentiated mass of ignorant, immoral, and violent people. Many whites failed
to see that significant numbers of African Americans were, by white standards,
quite educated, moral, and law abiding. Some were even light skinned, often
sharing ancestors with the very whites who treated them as members of a racial
underclass. To the casual observer, such African Americans seemed in both com-
portment and appearance to be white people in light-brown skins.

By 1900 the resurgence of white racism in the South, combined with the
deepening crisis in southern agriculture, forced tens of thousands of African
American farm laborers to abandon the rural South and to seek work in the cities
of the South and North. Impoverished and desperate, black migrants crowded
into already congested urban slums, seeking any work available at any wage.
Working-class whites viewed the growing tide of impoverished black migrants as
a threat to their own precarious livelihoods. They treated all blacks as racial
inferiors who degraded their neighborhoods. Angry and afraid, in city after city,
white mobs vented their frustrations on any and all nonwhites who crossed their
paths, setting off a wave of urban race riots more violent and destructive than
rural lynchings. Realizing that accommodation had failed, in 1903 W. E. B. Du
Bois, professor of sociology at Atlanta University, published *Souls of Black Folk*, in
which he demanded that the broken promises of emancipation be honored and

that blacks, led by their "talented tenth," be admitted to full and unqualified membership in American life. He also declared that African Americans need not look to Europe for intellectual and moral leadership. They only needed to recover their African souls.[2]

Migrants to New York found three quite different Harlems—its Old Settlers and New Negro migrants, its rural southern blacks, and its black West Indians. By the 1920s, rural southern blacks made up the overwhelming majority of Harlem's African American residents. Above 135th Street, southern blacks, many from the Low Country counties of the Carolinas and Georgia, lived in crowded tenements, the most densely populated blocks in New York City. Harlem's poorest and least-educated residents, these rural southern blacks had little contact with whites and, at first, accepted the leadership of Harlem's other two black groups—its citywise Old Settlers and its politically militant and racially conscious West Indians. In the first three decades of the twentieth century, Harlem's Old Settlers dominated central Harlem and its major institutions. West Indians gravitated toward southeastern Harlem, just north and east of Central Park, and ran the *Amsterdam News*. Regardless of where they lived, all blacks came to Harlem for the same reason. It promised African Americans a new beginning, a chance to share in America's bounty, an opportunity to put racial segregation and slavery behind them. In Harlem, these very different African American groups worked out their differences. In the 1930s they formed an urban black united front, which, in the minds of most white Americans, spoke for black America, including its West Indian immigrants and southern migrants.[3]

NEW NEGRO HEAVEN

After World War I, black migrants and immigrants like Claude McKay viewed Harlem as the Negro Mecca, "the Negro capital of the world." In 1900 no one would have made that claim. Before 1900, except for a few dozen live-in servants, no African Americans lived in Harlem. Developers had built the community, just north of Central Park, as a new neighborhood for New York's upwardly mobile Jews, who had made good in Manhattan's Lower East Side slum. In 1900 a stylish neighborhood of broad avenues and brownstones, Harlem became mired in a housing glut because of a failed speculative building boom. Harlem developers, unable to sell their properties and on the verge of financial ruin, approached Philip A. Payton, a black real estate agent. In 1903 Payton, a graduate of Livingston College in North Carolina, organized the Afro-American Realty Company to broker leases between white landlords in Harlem and upwardly mobile black tenants.[4]

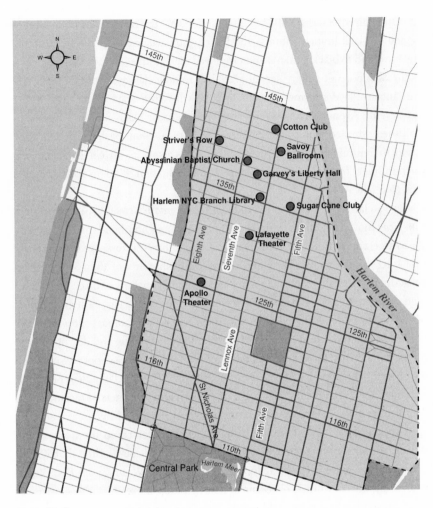

1920s Harlem

By 1908 Harlem had become New York's only racially mixed, middle-class neighborhood. At first, white residents kept African Americans north of 135th Street, but each year blacks expanded southward toward Central Park. In 1911 the most prestigious black church in New York, St. Philip's Protestant Episcopal Church, acquired a new building on West 133rd Street and purchased nearly a block of nearby apartment houses. Soon after, Manhattan's other socially prominent, African American churches moved to Harlem, accompanied by the New York Urban League, the editorial offices of *Crisis* and *Opportunity* magazines, and the city's two black weekly newspapers, the *Amsterdam News* and the *New York*

Age. On 135th Street, the YMCA built a "colored Y," the New York Public Library opened a "black branch" library, and the city constructed the Harlem Hospital, which catered to black patients and employed black nurses. James Van Der Zee's fashionable portrait gallery served Harlem's middle classes, while the Lafayette and Lincoln Players formed the core of a brown "white way" along 125th Street and Seventh Avenue. As a Sunday ritual, middle-class black couples "dressed to the nines" strolled along Lenox Avenue to Fifth Avenue, past the private Rice School to Central Park. Nowhere else did middle-class blacks live in such gracious surroundings, free from white violence and humiliation. Harlem had become a New Negro heaven.[5]

In 1909 James H. Anderson founded the *Amsterdam News.* In 1910 the *Amsterdam News* moved its offices from the San Juan Hill neighborhood in the West Side slums to Harlem. Both the *Amsterdam News* and the *New York Age* scrupulously kept track of the social affairs and the accomplishments of their middle-class subscribers. They also reported on the employment concerns of black longshoremen and Brooklyn Navy Yard workers, who purchased their papers at newsstands on the way to work. Harlem's two newspapers kept readers abreast of the activities of the Masons, Elks, and Knights of Pythian lodges, the ups and downs of local black sports teams, the academic success of Harlem's public school children, and the opening performance of *Hamlet* at the Lafayette Theater. They also constantly reminded their readers of lynchings in the South and other acts of racism across the country. Both papers supported American entry into World War I and encouraged young black males to enlist, although each underscored the irony of the Wilson administration's "war to save democracy" at the same time that Wilson systematically segregated the federal government and Washington, D.C. While addressing the communal concerns of its fifty thousand readers, the *Amsterdam News* did so from an upper middle-class, New Negro perspective.[6]

Middle-class migrants to Harlem traveled along social networks established at all-black colleges and schools. After the Civil War, throughout the South and in northern border states, black churches and white missionary societies had founded scores of black schools and colleges, usually staffed by whites and dependent on white philanthropy. These included Fisk in Tennessee, Howard in the District of Columbia, Lincoln in Pennsylvania, Wilberforce in Ohio, and Spellman and Morehouse in Georgia, Dillard in Louisiana, Tuskegee Institute in Alabama, and Hampton Institute in Virginia. On graduation, many of these young African Americans left the South and joined classmates and friends in the bourgeoning black communities of the North. They joined northern Old Settlers to form a New Negro middle class. In Harlem, such middle-class black-college graduates staffed

"Wedding Day," Harlem, 1920s (James Van Der Zee: Library of Congress)

the YMCA, YWCA, and the Urban League and worked for the *Crisis, Opportunity,* the *New York Age,* and the *Amsterdam News.* They founded funeral homes, opened small businesses, and joined Harlem's prestigious churches, especially AME, Episcopal, and Presbyterian, but also established Baptist congregations. Most lived in the brownstones and apartments south of 125th Street in Harlem's racially mixed neighborhoods, but the wealthiest purchased stylish homes in Harlem's all-black neighborhoods of Strivers' Row and Sugar Hill to the north.[7]

In 1917 when Congress debated war against Germany, Harlem's New Negro leadership saw the war as an opportunity to demonstrate the patriotism of African Americans and to secure civil equality. Congress approved the commissioning of black officers but insisted that all black troops serve in segregated units. The most famous of these was the 369th United States Infantry recruited largely from Harlem. The 369th served 191 days in the European trenches under French command, where it established a reputation as the most feared Allied combat unit. German troops nicknamed them the "Hell Fighters." The regiment won the Croix de Guerre and 171 of its officers and men received the French Legion of Honor. The 369th's regimental band, led by Harlem bandleader James Europe, created a furor when it introduced French audiences to black ragtime and jazz. At the end of the war, New York City gave the 369th a ticker-tape parade along Fifth Avenue. For a brief moment, the war seemed to mark a new day for Harlem's New Negroes.[8]

This ended quickly. In 1919 the number of lynchings in the nation escalated to seventy. Membership in the Ku Klux Klan grew dramatically during the war, and in East St. Louis a white mob, supported by white police, murdered forty African Americans. In July 1919 thirty-eight people died in a Chicago race riot. Two dozen other race riots broke out in cities across the country in the summer of 1919, including Charleston, but not in New York.[9] The wartime migration of southern African Americans from rural areas to cities and from southern cities to northern cities changed American urban life. In the 1920s, for the first time, every American city contained significant numbers of African Americans. Before 1900, African Americans had been primarily a rural and southern people. After 1920 they also became an urban and northern people.[10]

World War I placed Harlem's black middle class in a quandary. As the self-appointed leaders of black America, it felt obligated to help Harlem's poor; but doing so caused Harlem to be overrun by poor, uneducated, and unskilled southerners. Many of the problems that had driven middle-class New Negroes out of the West Side slums now followed them to Harlem. At the same time, the intensification of white racism after the war clarified their status. Regardless of education or cultural refinement, whites saw all African Americans as poor, ignorant, and black, no different from the thousands of poor, uneducated black migrants who arrived daily from the South. Du Bois and others learned that when whites such as Woodrow Wilson advocated democracy and equality, they meant whites only. In the eyes of most white Americans, neither migration nor military service nor cultural assimilation made a black person equal to a white person. No matter how much Harlem New Negroes resented it, white New Yorkers saw Harlem as "nigger heaven."[11]

Determined to demonstrate their gentility, Harlem's brown-skin elites announced the Harlem Renaissance.[12] In March 1925 the editors of the white-owned and white-edited *Survey Graphic* published a special edition on Harlem, edited by Howard University philosophy professor Alain Locke. Backed by Greenwich Village publishers Albert and Charles Boni, Locke expanded the *Survey Graphic* special edition into a book, *The New Negro*. Locke included African American writers from throughout the United States and added a section that highlighted developments and accomplishments of what Locke called the "New Negro," a term first coined by labor leader and socialist A. Philip Randolph in the *Messenger*. Locke described "New Negroes" as those African Americans who had transcended their backward peasant ways and become civilized. In short, New Negroes had freed themselves from their African cultural roots and, except for physical appearance, were no different than middle-class, European Americans.[13]

Published at the peak of the postwar wave of black migration to the North, Locke directed the essays in the *New Negro* to Harlem's poor blacks as much as to Manhattan's white elite. Laying claim to Randolph's term, Locke and the other contributors to the *New Negro* emphasized the necessity for blacks to integrate into American life by casting off their backward rural ways, rooted in segregation, slavery, and African superstition, and to adopt the civilized manners, speech, and culture exemplified by European and European American middle and upper classes. They argued that genteel whites would accept these gentrified New Negroes as equal citizens, in no significant way different from themselves. A central document of the Great Migration, the *New Negro* addressed few of the issues that affected most of Harlem's black residents. Instead, it became the rallying cry of what Du Bois described as the black "talented tenth."[14]

Disdainful of rural southern black culture, by 1925 Harlem's New Negroes understood their fate was intertwined with poor southern migrants. The Great Migration had redefined their status, from a small and isolated group of northern Negroes, who provided menial services to wealthy whites, into the leaders of a large and increasingly powerful racial class, answerable only to its own people. In the 1920s Harlem's Old Settlers formed migrant assistance organizations, recruited migrants to their churches, and provided newcomers legal, medical, dental, beauty, and funeral services. They advised migrants on appropriate dress and hygiene and served as their formal and informal teachers. Old Settlers, now New Negroes, became Harlem's leaders.[15]

Supported by downtown white patrons and black Harlem, in the 1920s, Harlem writers and artists thrived. They created a rich body of work that drew on black themes and utilized black images. New Negro writers centered their stories on African Americans and treated them as complex, tragic, and romantic figures, filled with emotions, disappointments, and contradictions. In Harlem, Langston Hughes, from Ohio and Fisk University, Zora Neale Hurston, from Florida and Howard University, and Claude McKay, from Jamaica and Tuskegee Institute, produced some of the most important American writing of the 1920s. Florida-born sculptor Augusta Savage and painter Aaron Douglas from Kansas laid the foundation of a vibrant Harlem art community, while singers Roland Hayes, Marian Anderson, and Paul Robeson gained international recognition. Ohio-trained composer William Grant Still was acclaimed for his *Afro-American Symphony, Dark America, From the Black Belt,* and *La Guiablesse.* Never before had black Americans produced so much first-rate work.[16]

Even so, Harlem's literary and artistic community found itself upstaged by Harlem's more successful and precocious popular entertainers. Before World War I, New York stages had hired African American entertainers either for comic relief or to perform degrading, racially typecast figures like the legendary black minstrel character Jim Crow, who clowned and danced in blackface to the delight of white audiences North and South. A few, such as composer Scott Joplin, conductor James Reese Europe, playwright Rosamond Johnson, and lyricist Will Marion Cook, secured footholds on Broadway but only as Negro writers or performers, only a step away from cakewalking minstrels. In 1917 Emily Hapgood broke with New York's black minstrel tradition by producing three plays with all-black casts in a near-Broadway theater. In 1920 the Provincetown Players cast African American actor Charles Gilpen in the starring role of Eugene O'Neill's *The Emperor Jones* that moved to Broadway after opening to full houses in Greenwich Village. In 1923 Paul Robeson starred in O'Neill's *All God's Chillun Got Wings,* followed by the Broadway revival of *The Emperor Jones,* again starring Gilpen. These small first steps opened the way for a number of more popular black productions during the 1920s, many that either played or premiered in Harlem.[17]

In the 1920s Harlem became New York's second most popular entertainment center and its primary center for adult entertainment. White New Yorkers first encountered many of the dance rages of the decade at Harlem clubs and dance palaces such as the Manhattan Casino, the Palace Casino, and the Savoy Ballroom. Harlem's famous nightclubs—the Cotton Club, Connie's Inn, Baron's, and Leroy's—featured black male orchestras and light-brown, scantily clad female chorus lines that often moved downtown to Broadway. The hit black musical reviews, *Shuffle Along, Chocolate Dandies, Black Birds,* and *Keep Shuffling,* all began in Harlem, with Harlem directors and performers. These Harlem productions made Ethel Waters, Bill "Bojangles" Robinson, and Florence Mills headline enter-tainers on Broadway.[18] Harlem's giants, however, were its female vocalists and jazz men. Blues singer Bessie Smith changed American popular music and dem-onstrated that a black singer, singing black music, could prosper by reaching a white audience. Harlem's great jazz orchestras followed Smith's lead. Fletcher Henderson's orchestra, the prototype of the big swing bands of the 1930s and 1940s, played in Harlem and downtown at the Roseland Ball Room, while Chick Webb, Count Basie, and Cab Calloway attracted more white fans to their Harlem shows than black. But at the Cotton Club, Duke Ellington reigned supreme.[19]

Born to a black middle-class, Washington, D.C., family, Ellington as a young man came to Harlem to play jazz. An admirer of Harlem Stride pianist James P. Johnson and his "Carolina Shout," Ellington's band secured its first professional gig at Baron's in Harlem and then quickly moved downtown to the Hollywood Café near Times Square. In 1927 Ellington accepted a contract as the house band of the Cotton Club, the hottest club in Harlem, which allowed the radio broadcast of its nightly shows. By 1930 Ellington was the best-known name in jazz, direct-ing the nation's top jazz orchestra and composing dozens of original pieces. Ellington exemplified New York's first wave of the Great Migration. Southern-born, he succeeded by pleasing white New Yorkers. Ellington's elegant manners and dress appealed to white audiences (the Cotton Club, owned by a white mob-ster, did not admit black patrons). Unquestionably African American in tone, nonetheless, Ellington's music meshed easily with white popular and European classical music. Harlem's status-conscious, black middle class claimed him as their own, the ideal race model. Ellington fulfilled the New Negro image—light-skinned, straight hair, formal English, urbane, and impeccable manners. Yet, he was self-confident and undeniably African American, and his music was dis-tinctly African American, if only marginally African.[20]

The members of the Duke Ellington Orchestra, however, were black and not middle class. Most members had no formal musical training, and several could not read music. The lead trumpet player, Bubber Miley, had grown up in South Carolina, migrating to Harlem with his family just before World War I. Under Ellington's guidance, Miley became a premier trumpet player and composer, giving the orchestra much of its earthy, "gut bucket" sound. Miley was also un-educated, crude, and undisciplined and an alcoholic—the very opposite of Elling-ton. Gifted and brilliant, Miley's music was rooted in southern black culture, and he embarrassed Harlem's New Negroes. He represented what they strove to overcome—African Americans' rural, and to their minds, subservient, unrefined, overly passionate, and ignorant ways.[21]

The desire to fit in, to accommodate to European American, middle-class culture, was not limited to Harlem's elite. Many, if not most, first-generation, working-class, southern migrants also desperately tried to assimilate to northern white culture. The wealthiest individual in Harlem, Madam C. J. Walker, made her fortune by selling her hair-straightening formula to black southerners. Madam Walker lived in a Harlem brownstone on West 136th Street, elbow to elbow with Harlem's poor, but she also owned a palatial mansion on the Hudson much like other Manhattan elites. Poor migrants and immigrants came to Harlem, not just to improve their economic circumstances; they also dreamed of becoming New Yorkers. The young, especially, dressed as New Yorkers, spoke in urban slang, adopted new foods, applied bleaches to their skin, and patronized beauty parlors and barbershops that promised to remake them into stylish, urban people. Jazz clarinetist Garvin Bushell observed that in the 1920s "most of the Negro population in New York then had either been born there or had been in the city so long that they were fully acclimated. They wanted you to forget the traditions of the South and were trying to emulate the whites. . . . You weren't allowed to play blues and boogie woogie in the average Negro middle class home. . . . You could only hear the blues and real jazz in the gutbucket cabarets where the lower class went. The term 'gutbucket' came from the chitterlings bucket."[22] Poor blacks wanted to dress like New Yorkers, sound like New Yorkers, and look like New Yorkers. Like European immigrants, many Harlem migrants shed their country ways and clothing to become New Yorkers.

CAROLINA SHOUT

The Clyde and Ward steamship lines maintained passenger service between Charleston and New York. Until the 1930s, most black Charlestonians chose the Clyde Line over the railroad. Low Country Gullah, in particular, viewed the Clyde Line as the primary passage to New York because many had family who worked on the piers of the Clyde Line in Charleston and New York. Passage on Clyde Line freighters cost less than the Atlantic Coast Rail Line. On boarding the steamer at Adger's Wharf, bound for Harlem, many Gullah passengers must have mouthed the Sea Island spiritual, "The Jordan is wide and deep, hallelujah!" On entering New York Harbor and glimpsing the Statue of Liberty, they must have sung out, "Michael row the boat ashore, hallelujah!" Determined to become New Yorkers, they were no less Gullah.[23]

Disembarking on the Clyde Line West Side piers, just below Houston Street, some found family members who greeted them warmly, while others timidly asked for directions to Harlem. Several blocks east, they found the subway entrance for the A Train that took them north to 135th Street, the gateway to Carolina Harlem. Black Harlem, however, was larger. In 1920 black Harlem started just north of Central Park and went westward to Amsterdam Avenue and northward to 145th Street. Harlem's best shops, the fashionable Theresa Hotel, and assorted movie houses lay along 125th Street, while Harlem's civic institutions—the Harlem Y, the Harlem Hospital, the Harlem Branch of the New York Public Library, the editorial offices of the *New York Age*, and the Harlem Police Station prominently lined 135th Street between Seventh and Lenox avenues. Harlem's best restaurants, its most prestigious churches, the offices of the *Amsterdam News*, the famed Lafayette Theater, Harlem's busy beauty shops, its countless grocery stores, barbecue joints, pool halls, candy shops, barber shops, and funeral homes lay along its two great avenues, Lenox and Seventh between 125th and 135th streets, the boundaries of central Harlem. Its smaller nightclubs and storefront churches nestled among brownstones, apartment houses, and tenements along the cross streets bounded by Lenox and Seventh.[24]

Harlem's poor, most from Virginia, North Carolina, Georgia, and South Carolina, lived north of 135th Street and east of Seventh Avenue up to the slopes of Edgecomb Avenue that bordered the Polo Grounds. A 1927 survey of 2,400 Harlem apartments north of 125th Street reported that households averaged six members, and almost all included two parents. About half the households had occupied their apartments one year or less and paid forty-two dollars a month for rent—about 10 percent higher than similar housing in Manhattan outside of Harlem. Most resided in a "railroad flat," five rooms, one behind the other with no hallway. Typically, two families shared a railroad flat, each occupying two rooms and sharing the central room that contained a sink and a stove or hot plate. A quarter of the apartments were cold-water flats and 10 percent contained no bathroom. Tenants frequently complained of rat and roach infestation, unlighted rooms, no hot water, poor ventilation, and generally filthy conditions.[25] While dismal, Harlem housing compared favorably to black housing in Savannah, Charleston, and Wilmington. And in Harlem, Carolina and Georgia blacks enjoyed freedom not only from white despotism but also to live as Gullah.

Ralph Ellison, in his novel *Invisible Man*, recounted an experience in the mid-1930s similar to his own when he arrived in Harlem, fresh from Tuskegee, filled with middle-class ambitions. Cut off from his past and unsure of his identity, Ellison's "invisible man" stepped out of the 135th Street YMCA and walked over to 136th Street, passing the brownstone of Madame Walker, the cosmetic magnate, and the St. Helena Funeral Home that faced it, directly just across the street. At

"The Most Crowded Block in New York," 136th Street, 1939 (Aaron Siskind: Library of Congress)

the corner, he stopped at a street vender and bought a buttered yam that he gobbled down. The taste triggered childhood memories. His college education notwithstanding, the invisible man realized that he remained "a shameless chitterling eater," who as a boy had lugged out "yards of them, with mustard greens, and racks of pigs ears, and pork chops and black-eyed peas." Puzzled by his reaction, Ellison's character believed that by eating the buttered yam he had lost caste and had "reverted to Field Niggerism!" Awakened to his essential identity, he asserted, "To hell with being ashamed of what you liked. No more of that for me. I am what I am. I wolfed down the yam and ran back to the old man and handed him twenty cents, 'Give me two more. . . . They're my birthmark. . . . I yam what I yam.' The old man replied, 'Then you must be from South Carolina. . . . Come back tomorrow if you can eat some more. . . . My old lady'll be out here with some hot sweet potato fried pies.' "[26]

Down the street, the invisible man came across an old couple who had lived in Harlem for twenty years. Unable to pay their rent, they found themselves on the sidewalk, evicted from their apartment. Bewildered amid their possessions, the old woman stood with a red bandana wrapped around her head, clasping to her breast a worn Bible. The invisible man turned aside and looked at the clutter of household objects. . . . My eyes fell upon a pair of crudely carved "knocking bones," used to accompany music at country dances, used in black-face minstrels; the flat ribs of a cow, a steer or sheep, flat bones that give off a sound, when struck, like heavy castanets . . . or the wooden block of a set of drums. Pots and pots of green plants were lined in the dirty snow . . . ivy, canna, a tomato plant. And in a basket I saw a straightening comb, switches of false hair, a curling iron, a card with silvery letters against a background of dark red velvet, reading "God Bless Our Home" and scattered across the top of a chiffonier were nuggets of High John the Conqueror, the luck stone . . . a whiskey bottle filled with rock candy and camphor, a small Ethiopian flag, a faded tintype of Abraham Lincoln, and the smiling image of a Hollywood star torn from a magazine.

In the poor woman's Harlem possessions, the invisible man had stumbled across the physical remnants of post-emancipation, black America. Turning away, he spied an old paper that read: *"Be it known to all men that my negro, Primus Provo, has been freed by me this sixth day of August 1858. Signed John Samuels Macon,"* a reminder of the cause of the African diaspora.[27]

For Low Country migrants, Harlem's congested tenements became home—an urban We Land. Beyond the bright lights and invisible to whites, above 135th Street, southern blacks, with their West African Creole culture, formed Sanctified Baptist, Pentecostal, and AME churches, entertained themselves at rent parties, sweet shops, and neighborhood juke joints that offered chitterlings, fried chicken, and moonshine. Their musicians played bluesy stomps derived from Gullah ring dances. Ohio-born clarinetist Garvin Bushell recalled that Charleston and Savannah dockworkers, who danced in Harlem's joints, demanded the band play "their music." "The Charleston was introduced in New York at Leroy's." According to Bushell, "Russell Brown came from Charleston and he did a Geechie dance from the Georgia Sea Islands . . . a cut dance. People began to say to Brown, 'Hey, Charleston, do your dance.' They finally called it the Charleston." They also revered Ethiopia, Abraham Lincoln, and Hollywood movie stars.[28]

Most of Harlem's poor came from the South Atlantic states of North Carolina, Georgia, Virginia, Florida, and South Carolina, and a majority of these from the Gullah counties of coastal Carolina and Georgia. Of the nearly 180,000 native-born African Americans who in the 1920s arrived in Harlem, all but about 10,000 came from these five South Atlantic states.[29] By most accounts, they came to find work.[30] They formed households of a husband and wife, several children, a relative or two and, frequently, a boarder from back home. Because most were either illiterate or, at best, semiliterate, these southerners settled for low-paying, menial jobs. About half of the wives worked, most in the needle trades, in laundries, or as domestics. A few found jobs in beauty shops or worked as clerks and cooks, and according to welfare agencies, several thousand resorted to prostitution. Males worked as janitors, day laborers, porters, and elevator operators, while a few, no more than 5 percent, acquired middle-class employment as undertakers, ministers, teachers, doctors, lawyers, and small shop owners. Another 5 percent worked in well-paid skill crafts as masons, carpenters, barbers, cabinetmakers, and plumbers. About 5 percent worked either for a railroad or as postal clerks, and another 5 percent worked in factories or at the Brooklyn Naval Yard. Ten percent of South Carolina and Georgia males, and about the same percentage of West Indian males, worked as longshoremen on the Westside and Brooklyn piers.[31]

The Scottish-owned Clyde Line specialized in the Carolina coastal trade of rice, cotton, tobacco, lumber, vegetables, and passengers from Charleston and Wilmington. The Mallory Line served Savannah and Jacksonville. In 1895, when the Clyde and Mallory lines, along with the Ward Line, faced labor strikes in New York, they recruited scab workers from the longshoremen who worked for them in their southern and West Indian ports. At the end of the strike, rather than fire their black workers, the Clyde, Mallory, and Ward lines retained their loyal Gullah and West Indian longshoremen, ending the stranglehold of Irish and Italians on the New York docks. By 1919 five thousand blacks worked on the New York docks, the largest group of black industrial workers in the United States outside the Birmingham steel mills and coal mines.[32]

In 1917 James P. Johnson, the dean of Harlem's Stride pianists, composed his famous "Carolina Shout," an allusion to the Gullah ring shout that had shaped Low Country African American religion. Born in Baltimore, Johnson had learned to play the piano in the city's African American dives and bordellos where he absorbed the rhythmic syncopations of ragtime. In New York, he acquired a formal music education and made his living in Harlem reformulating Tin Pan Alley tunes into ragtime dance songs. In the Harlem Stride tradition, the right hand carried the melody, while the left hand rocked between a "bass note and middle register chord," creating a heavy "oompah," the trade mark of Harlem Stride pianists who included Johnson, Willie "the Lion" Smith, Fats Waller, Luckey Roberts, and Duke Ellington. A participant in the pre–World War I migration to Harlem, Johnson took great pride in his urbanity and European musical sophistication, "I did double glissandos straight and backhand, glissandos in sixths and double tremolos.... I would learn concert effects and build them into blues and rags.... When playing a stomp, I'd soften it right down—then I'd make an abrupt change like I heard Beethoven do in a sonata."[33]

White New York audiences loved Johnson's melodic, Europeanized "Snowy Morning." In Harlem, however, his fame rested on the southern-inspired "Harlem Strut," "The Mule Walk," and his signature piece, "Carolina Shout." At the Jungles Casino on West Sixty-fourth Street in 1913, Johnson observed a group of Gullah dockworkers performing "wild and comical" dances. Like other Harlem musicians, Johnson found that Harlem's Gullah longshoremen were his most generous tippers and nothing loosened their purse strings quicker than a fast-paced, polyrhythmic, down-home southern stomp with seemingly endless, improvised verses. According to Johnson, Gullah dockworkers stomped the soles off their shoes dancing to his Carolina-inspired shouts. "The people who came to the Jungles Casino were mostly from around Charleston, South Carolina. . . . Most of them worked . . . as longshoremen or on ships that called at southern ports. . . . These Charleston people and the other Southerners had just come to New York. They were country people and they felt homesick. . . . They'd dance, hollering and screaming until they were cooked. The dances ran from fifteen to thirty minutes, but they kept up all night long or until their shoes wore out—most of them after a heavy day's work on the docks."[34]

By 1920 nearly twenty thousand South Carolina–born African Americans had migrated to New York. In the next decade, another forty thousand arrived. According to the 1930 federal census, more than 75 percent of Harlem's African American migrants had come from the five South Atlantic states of Virginia, Florida, Georgia, North and South Carolina. In the depression years of the 1930s, southern migration to Harlem slowed but then accelerated with the outbreak of World War II. From 1910 to 1920, nearly two-thirds of the African American migrants from the South Atlantic region settled in the Middle Atlantic States of New York, New Jersey, and Pennsylvania. From 1920 to 1930, the percentage of South Atlantic migrants who settled in the Middle Atlantic States rose to 69 percent. From 1940 to 1950, 71 percent of the migrants from the South Atlantic region migrated to the Middle Atlantic region.[35] Such statistics only bore out what most in Harlem already knew. By sheer force of numbers, Harlem exuded a strong Gullah flavor. Bushell observed that "our clientele at Leroy's were mainly Negroes from the South, who had migrated. They lived in the 130s, off Fifth Avenue—that was one of the toughest parts of Harlem."[36]

The Census Bureau did not compile figures specifically for Harlem. For New York City as a whole, however, it calculated that in the 1940s the African American population in the city increased by 300,000 and by another 300,000 in the 1950s. Almost all of the increase derived from the South Atlantic states or natural increase. In 1950 more than sixty percent of the more than 800,000 South

Atlantic migrants to New York came from South Carolina or Georgia. Even Harlem's natural increase had strong ties to Georgia and South Carolina because most New York–born Harlemites were the children of earlier migrants from Georgia and South Carolina. By 1960, New York City's African American population had increased from less than 2 percent in 1910 to about 15 percent. In these fifty years, New York became steadily more African American, while the culture of its African American residents became increasingly Gullah influenced.[37]

Harlem's ever-mounting Gullah presence voiced itself on Harlem's streets, especially above 135th Street. Newly arrived, southern men dressed in jeans or overalls with their hair clipped short. The women wore one-piece, short-sleeved cotton dresses, their hair either straightened, braided, or tied up in colorful head clothes. Both men and women frequently smoked corncob pipes or dipped snuff. Southern venders pushed handcarts up and down the streets, singing out to advertise their fish and vegetables just as they had done in Charleston, Savannah, Jacksonville, and Wilmington:

> Yeah yo' nice, fresh, tender
> String beans!
> An' Yo' young, 'Down Home'
> Colla'd greens;
> Five a pound, hyeah!
> String beans!
> Colla'd greens![38]

Small kitchen diners festooned Harlem's avenues and cross streets, featuring pork and chicken barbecue, fried chicken, chitterlings, steamed corn-on-the-cob, boiled collard, mustard and turnip greens, corn bread, grits, pickled pig feet and tails, yams, and sweet potato pie. Grocers sold rice, cornmeal, black-eyed peas, and grits in fifty- and hundred-pound printed cotton sacks and displayed piles of fresh okra, tomatoes, yellow squash, cucumbers, and sugarcane shipped up from Charleston and Savannah. Fish markets placed on crushed ice catfish, porgy, shrimp, and crab next to bottles of homemade hot pepper and Tabasco sauce.[39]

Harlem funeral homes, such as the Carolina Funeral Home on Lenox Avenue and the St. Helena Funeral Home on West 136th Street, specialized in southern burials, ensuring that the body of the deceased lay buried east to west and that family members had an opportunity to perform appropriate funeral rites. Southern funerals were highly emotional, involving singing, shouting, and all-night "sit bys." Relatives placed elaborate burial decorations on the graves, especially flowered funeral wreaths and broken vessels. Some insisted that, at death, their bodies

"Watermelon seller," Harlem, 1940 (Aaron Siskind: Library of Congress)

be sent home for a more traditional burial near the graves of their family and ancestors. The Carolina Funeral Home frequently sent bodies back to Charleston for burial by the Harleston Funeral Home, while the St. Helena Funeral Home sent the bodies of many of its Gullah patrons to the Sea Islands for interment. The reuniting of the spirit of the deceased migrant with its southern ancestors testified to the traditional ties that migrants sustained even as they adapted to New York City. The continuities were as important as the changes.[40]

Each Christmas, hundreds of Harlem African Americans boarded a steamship or train for home, some traveling alone and others with their spouses and children. During the Christmas and New Year season, they visited relatives and friends, attended church services, placed flowers and personal items on the graves of family members buried in their absence, feasted on home cooking, and celebrated Watch Night. Children met their southern grandparents, uncles, aunts, and cousins while young singles courted possible mates. Dressed in their most citified clothing, Harlem's migrants brought home gifts and endless tales of Harlem, where even the policemen were black. Harlem women taught their southern relatives the marvels of canned vegetables and meat, store-bought white bread, and Harlem's favorite dish, macaroni and cheese. They shared copies of the *Amsterdam News* and told stories about seeing Joe Louis on Lenox Avenue, their attendance at Adam Clayton Powell's Abyssinian Baptist Church, hearing the Duke Ellington Orchestra at the Savoy Ballroom, or brushing past W. E. B. Du Bois on Seventh Avenue. Anxious for visitors, they promised all who came to Harlem tickets to the Apollo and the Savoy and a shopping trip along 125th Street, which offered the latest in New York fashions and gadgets. Some Harlem parents, afraid of the city's influence, left children with grandparents to be raised southern.[41]

One of the strongest links, especially for Low Country, rural Gullah, was their "heirs" title to the family homestead. Even today, the titles to nearly 10 percent of the homesteads in the Gullah villages of rural Christ Church Parish are registered to individuals living in Harlem, Brooklyn, the Bronx, and New Jersey.[42] Just as southern-born African Americans failed to draw a rigid line between the living and the dead, so they refused to burn the cultural and family bridges between Harlem and their southern homelands. Afro-Carolina lay on every street of Harlem just as aspects of Harlem sprouted in every Afro-Carolina community. In the Sanctified Baptist, Methodist, and Holiness churches of coastal Georgia and South Carolina, young band members dreamed of playing at the Savoy Ballroom or the Apollo Theater.[43]

Southern migrants' longing for spiritual comfort provided eager recruits for Harlem's churches, including such radical organizations like the Church of the Living God. During World War I, George Baker Jr., who called himself the Messenger, moved to Brooklyn from Valdosta, Georgia. Known to his followers as the Reverend Major Jealous Divine or just Father Divine, Baker had been born in Rockville, Maryland, in 1879. His parents, both of whom had been slaves, raised Baker as a black Methodist. At age twenty, Baker left home for Baltimore where he settled in the African American neighborhood of "Pigtown." Unhappy with the formality of Baltimore's African American Presbyterian, Methodist, and Baptists churches, Baker visited a series of storefront Holiness and Sanctified churches, attracted by the lively music and the ministers' promises of "spiritual healing." In 1906 Baker left for Los Angeles to join the interracial Azusa Street Revival that gave rise to the Pentecostal movement. Pentecostals emphasized full-immersion baptism, lively music, faith healing, spiritual seizures, and speaking in tongues. In 1907, according to Baker, the Holy Ghost informed him that Jesus had come from the Holy Land of Ethiopia and was black. The Holy Spirit also instructed Baker that he was "the son of God" and that he should call himself the Messenger.[44]

From 1907 to 1917, the Messenger traveled throughout eastern Georgia, preaching his message of charity, chastity, faith healing, and communal living. The Messenger appealed especially to women, whom he told to leave their husbands and to live with him communally. Claiming to have come "from the Sea Islands," the Messenger insisted on celibacy, healed the sick, and placed curses on his enemies. At age thirty-eight, the Messenger left Georgia for Brooklyn where he formed a new collective that prohibited sex, smoking, profanity, illegal drugs, and alcohol.[45] In the Messenger's Brooklyn commune, men and women lived in separate apartments and refrained from social contact with one another, but shared their income with the church and ate together at Holy Communion Banquets. In Brooklyn, the Messenger married and changed his name to Father Divine, the Living God. In 1919 Father Divine moved his collective to Sayville, Long Island. On Sundays, up to a thousand people, black and white, motored to Sayville for worship with Father Divine. Like southern Sanctified churches, Divine's services featured boisterous music, singing, dancing, speaking in tongues, healing, and ecstatic seizures that concluded with a Holy Communion Banquet. In 1931 the Sayville town government charged Divine with disturbing the peace and ordered the commune closed. A local judge sentenced Divine to a year in prison. On appeal, a New York State court cited the presiding judge with prejudice and reversed the decision, but not before Father Divine had moved to Harlem and placed a curse on the judge who had sent him to jail. The night after being cursed, the judge died of a heart attack. When questioned by the press, Divine answered that he "hated to do it."[46]

On December 20, 1931, Divine announced his Harlem arrival at the Rockland Palace on 155th Street and Eighth Avenue, the largest public event in Harlem since the return of the Harlem Hell Fighters. With the Depression raging, Divine's message of peace, charity to the poor, self-help, and communal responsibility appealed to thousands of Harlem's poor, especially women. By 1932 his weekly services attracted twelve thousand worshipers, who, attired in white, danced, sang, and shouted. In 1933 Divine claimed more than two million members nationally. A critic of the New Deal and socialism, Divine expressly rejected as racial separatism a return to Africa. Equally important, Divine had a genius for business. Everything he touched prospered, including his followers. He acquired six brownstones on 126th Street for his collective where anyone in Harlem could secure inexpensive housing and food. He bought farmland in upstate New York

"Daddy Grace," Harlem, 1930s (Library of Congress)

to grow food for his urban communes and set up a rural commune in High Falls, New York. In the 1930s Divine supported a boycott of Harlem businesses that had refused to hire blacks, supported the Communist Party's efforts on behalf of the Scottsboro Boys, and campaigned for a federal antilynching law. Early on, Divine declared Hitler a moral outlaw. In 1942 he left Harlem and resettled in Phila-delphia, where, at his wife's death, he married a white woman. After World War II the church declined in membership but survived until Divine's death in the late fifties.[47]

Father Divine and the Church of the Living God were a curious mixture of personal creativity, cultural assimilation, and Sanctified black religion. Divine shared the puritanical concerns of black Sanctified and Holiness churches and their openness to white membership. He engaged in spirit healing, encouraged ecstatic seizures, spoke in tongues, and used a variety of musical instruments in his services. His claim to have "come from the Sea Islands " enhanced his moral authority and tied him to the region's rich West African traditions. At the same time, Divine eschewed the Baptist Gullah practice of full-immersion baptism even as he railed against the use of hair straighteners. Divine's claim to divinity was blasphemy to many southern Protestants but not to those influenced by West African notions of polytheism. Father Divine preached material well-being, racial assimilation, and an earthly Kingdom of God. He acquired many of his religious ideas from Sanctified churches in rural Georgia and South Carolina, but he found most of his converts in the black urban neighborhoods of Brooklyn, Harlem, Philadelphia, Chicago, and Los Angeles. Dressed in a dark, pinstriped business suit, a starched, immaculately pressed white shirt, and a stylish silk tie, Divine looked more like a banker than a southern preacher.[48]

WEST INDIANS

Working on the docks sustained the ties that Gullah and West Indian blacks maintained with their respective homelands. It made it easy to return home for visits and to refresh ties to their Creole cultures. It also allowed them to take home coveted city gifts and to display their newly acquired Harlem ways. Such travel made Harlem an extension of these West Indian and Gullah communities. Even in Harlem, water linked West Indians and Gullah to their Gods, to each other, to their ethnic homelands, and to their distant ancestral homelands in West Africa. British West Indians came to Harlem for many of the same reasons that motivated Carolina and Georgia Gullah. Before the 1890s only sporadic ties existed between New York and the British West Indies. In the 1890s when large growers introduced banana production throughout the West Indies, New York became the primary North American banana port, leading the Ward Steamship Line to establish regular steamship runs between the West Indies and New York. Much as Gullah traveled on the Clyde and Mallory Lines, so British West Indians, especially Jamaicans, traveled to New York on the Ward Line. With American construction of the Panama Canal in the early 1900s, many Jamaican laborers went first to Panama and then to New York. By World War I, Jamaicans formed one of the largest immigrant groups in New York and by far the city's largest nonwhite immigrant group. Many found work on the Ward Lines docks in Manhattan and Brooklyn.[49]

Gullah and Jamaican similarities ran well beyond the water's edge. Both groups derived from common West African ancestors—largely Yoruba and Ashante, but also an assortment of other West and Central African peoples, including Igbo and even followers of Islam and Christianity. Many of the same ships that had transported slaves to Jamaica brought slaves to Charleston. In the face of declining sugar production and slave rebellion, in 1834 the English Parliament emancipated all Jamaican slaves. Like Low Country Gullah, Jamaica's newly freed slaves acquired small homesteads of ten to twenty-five acres and formed small neo–West African villages scattered throughout rural Jamaica. A typical Jamaican cottage measured seventeen by thirteen feet, faced precisely west with its back to the sunrise, contained two rooms divided by a central hall, and was situated in a fenced yard surrounded by fruit trees and vegetable gardens. Jamaican villagers ate pork, chicken, fish, mango, avocado, coconut, and limes as well as tomatoes, okra, peppers, and yams. On Saturday, the women carried their extra produce to local markets in hand-woven baskets securely balanced on their heads, much as women did in West Africa and the Carolina and Georgia Low Country.[50]

In the 1850s a religious revival convulsed these transplanted West Africans. Jamaican Revivalism fused West African with Christian belief and practice. Zion Revivalists accepted Jesus as the son of God, adopted the Bible as their primary religious guide, and affirmed Protestant notions of redemption, salvation, and resurrection of the spirit. Formally rejecting specific Yoruba deities, nonetheless, Revivalist Zion retained much of West African religion. Like Gullah, Jamaican Revivalists drew no distinction between sacred and secular. God was an imminent presence that pervaded all aspects of life, not a transcendent and distant being. Revivalists believed in the presence of spirits, not just the Holy Spirit. Spirits of the dead looked after living individuals and the community. Evil spirits also existed, directed by conjurers or Obeah men. Revivalists believed that each individual possessed two spirits and that at death one departed the earth while the other remained to ensure that the living respected those who had passed. Jamaicans went to great lengths to appease such spirits so they would not turn against them. Much more than European forms of Christianity, Jamaican Revivalists believed in spirit possession, attributed great spiritual significance to water, and understood worship services as a means for worshipers to call forth benign spirits through rhythmic music, ritual ring dancing, drums, and singing. Spirits manifested themselves by causing worshipers to speak in tongues, to fall into ecstatic trances, and become healed.[51]

Much as in Gullah culture, these West African–derived beliefs shaped Jamaican burial and birth rituals. Soon after birth, mothers buried their infants' umbilical cords near special "natal trees" to bring the child good fortune. Mothers kept infants indoors for nine days after birth to prevent Obeah men from seizing their spirits. After nine days the infants were christened. If an infant died before its ninth day, its spirit or dupy would not recognize its family and could be directed to malicious ends by Obeah men. Jamaicans also believed that infants born with cauls over their faces possessed special access to spirits. Such people could fore-see the future, see dupys, and cast or remove spells. Obeah men had been born with cauls. Like Gullah, Jamaicans who feared the presence of malevolent spirits left a Bible on a chair near the front door of their houses to ward off bad spirits. Individuals also paid Obeah men to cast a spell on an enemy or to remove a spell cast by a rival Obeah man.[52]

After the death of a family member, Jamaican behavior was similar to that in the Low Country. Jamaicans covered the mirrors in the home and ritually washed the deceased. They then poured the death water over the grave. The burial party ate food before and after the burial and left food and personal possessions at the grave for the deceased. Friends and family passed infants over the open grave of the deceased so that its spirit would know the infant and look after it. Before interment, the burial party sang songs, accompanied by drums and horns, and danced in a counterclockwise circle around the grave. Families positioned the body in the grave east to west, with the face looking eastward to the sunrise. They located the grave near the family home to ensure that the spirit of the deceased looked after the family. After the funeral, Jamaican families ritually "swept the house clean" of spir-its. At midnight on subsequent Christmases, a family member poured a glass of rum punch on the ground outside the home for the spirit of the departed, main-taining the ties between the living and the dead. Distinctly Jamaican, Zion Revival-ism shared much with the Gullah communities of the Carolina Low Country.[53]

Jamaicans' attitude toward politics, however, differed dramatically from Gul-lah practice. West Africans had largely peopled Jamaica. Unlike in the Carolinas and Georgia, imperial outsiders in London ruled Jamaica, not local, white elites. After 1834, English authorities agreed to emancipate Jamaican slaves and to inte-grate them into the mainstream of Anglo-Jamaican life. This meant political enfranchisement and a comprehensive public school system. Because almost all Jamaicans claimed West African ancestry, blacks constituted much of the Jamai-can middle class, especially in the capital of Kingston. In the 1890s, when Jamai-cans first arrived in New York, most came from the Jamaican middle class. They were literate, spoke British public school English, formally belonged to the Angli-can state church, and included large numbers of professionals and merchants. Jamaicans also brought with them a highly developed political consciousness and extensive experience with democratic politics. Poor and uneducated Jamaicans, who worked on the docks, came from the island's impoverished rural areas and, like the Gullah, brought with them much of their West African culture.[54]

On the whole, Jamaicans were remarkably well traveled, especially its poor, uneducated rural working class. Many had worked on the banana boats that shipped out to London, Europe, and other parts of the Caribbean and Panama, as well as to Philadelphia, Boston, Baltimore, and New York. No other New York immigrant group had traveled so extensively or brought with it such cosmopolitan outlooks. In their travels in Europe and America, working-class Jamaicans found that white people everywhere treated black people as inherently inferior without regard to class, education, or nationality. In New York, educated and racially sensitized middle-class Jamaicans, accustomed to civil equality in Jamaica, considered themselves Harlem's natural leaders—indeed, the natural leaders of all persons of African ancestry, including Africans. This led to tension between middle-class Jamaicans and Harlem's New Negroes.[55]

By 1930 nearly 100,000 Jamaicans lived in New York, most in Harlem north of Central Park and south and east of Lenox Avenue. Nominally Anglican, most middle-class Jamaicans joined Episcopal or Catholic parishes in Harlem. Working-class Jamaicans, in contrast, tended to join storefront Revivalist churches that resembled Low Country Sanctified congregations. The two largest middle-class West Indian churches were St. Philip's Episcopal Church on West 135th Street and St. Martin's Episcopal Church on Lenox Avenue. Like other unskilled blacks in New York, working-class Jamaicans worked menial, low-paying jobs that whites shunned. Women gained employment as maids and dressmakers, while men became elevator operators, cooks, clerks, porters, waiters, factory workers, and longshoremen.[56] Their lodges included the Ancient Order of the Shepherd, the Scottish and English Mechanics, the Free Gardeners, and the Odd Fellows. When not working, women dressed in bright, colorful dresses and the men wore Panama hats and white linen suits. Jamaicans ate many of the same foods as Carolina blacks but cooked with different spices and with a heavier reliance on fish, mango, and limes. Jamaican music exhibited more complex rhythms as dancers swayed and moved their bodies suggestively. In the 1920s New Yorkers encountered Jamaican music in the popular Lindy Hop.[57]

Harlem's New Negroes harbored resentments toward their West Indian neighbors. New Negroes considered Jamaicans foreign upstarts and pointed out the national differences between American blacks and Jamaicans. Derisively, they called West Indians "monkey chasers," "King mon," and "black Jews" and criticized them for flying the British flag on Independence Day. Common Harlem taunts were that West Indians had come to New York "to teach, open a church, or start trouble" and that "when a monkey-chaser dies, you don't need an undertaker; just throw him in the Harlem River; and he'll float back to Jamaica." The percentage of married women who worked was much smaller for Jamaicans than for black southerners. Most commentators described southern women as more assertive and outgoing than Jamaican women, and southern women exercised more influence in their families than Jamaican women did.[58] The question of social status was equally galling to southern African Americans: many more Jamaicans were literate, and Jamaican migrants boasted a higher percentage of businesses owners and professionals than did southern migrants. New Negroes resented the assertiveness of middle-class Jamaicans, while poor southern migrants saw the Jamaican poor as economic rivals. In a Harlem census district, which included large numbers of southern and Jamaican households, five Jamaicans were engineers and twelve were self-employed. The list contained no southern engineers and only two self-employed southerners. Jamaicans owned the *Amsterdam News*, Harlem's most important newspaper, and they supplied Harlem with many of its physicians, attorneys, ministers, and teachers. Most important, in the 1920s Jamaicans took charge of Harlem politics.[59]

In Jamaica, blacks participated actively in politics and held most of the public offices on the island. Because of the higher ratio of blacks to whites (about 19 to 1), Jamaican public life was racially integrated. In New York, Jamaicans resented the city's deeply entrenched pattern of racial segregation and blacks' exclusion from power. Refusing to accommodate themselves to such a humiliating and intolerable situation, Jamaicans protested and organized. But as a small immigrant group as well as members of a racial minority, they found themselves isolated in the city's democratic politics. When push came to shove, on election day Jamaicans could deliver only a few thousand votes, not even enough to determine elections in Harlem. Jamaican politicians responded by playing down their West Indian origins and emphasizing their racial identities. A migratory people, Jamaicans understood the pervasiveness of white racism outside their home island and the need for black people to transcend their ethnic differences and view themselves as racial brothers and sisters. Jamaicans insisted that whites would never accept blacks as anything other than racial inferiors and that only through militant politics would blacks gain their rightful deserts. Whites thought and acted racially; so must blacks.[60]

Thinking like a Jamaican but acting like a black Messiah, Marcus Garvey shook the political foundations of Harlem and ushered in modern black politics. Born in 1887, Garvey grew up in a society with a declining economy and an expanding population. While banana production replaced the sugar plantations, it employed fewer people. Like other Jamaicans, Garvey's father, a stonemason, scraped by with irregular work that he supplemented with subsistence farming. A printer by trade, Garvey left his parents' home at eighteen to find work in Kingston. In 1910 he left Jamaica and traveled to Costa Rica, Guatemala, Nicaragua, Ecuador, Chile, Peru, and Panama. In the Canal Zone, Garvey published a paper and rallied West Indian workers against their employers. Facing prosecution, he fled to England. In 1914, with the outbreak of war, Garvey returned to Jamaica. In Kingston, he formed the Universal Negro Improvement Association (UNIA) that advocated racial self-help, the liberation of Africa from European colonialism, and the return of all black people to Africa. Garvey saw his "Africa for Africans" as the black equivalent of Woodrow Wilson's notion of "national self-determination." Garvey read *Up from Slavery* by Booker T. Washington and left Jamaica to visit Tuskegee Institute. Before he arrived, Washington had died. Garvey shifted course and in 1916 landed in New York City. Fascinated by Washington's program of "separatism" and "self help," Garvey dismissed the NAACP's effort to gain entry into white America as futile. Instead, he insisted that blacks fend for themselves, form their own nation, charter their own corporations, and care for their own people. His newspaper, the *Negro World*, claimed a circulation of sixty thousand. At its peak, the UNIA listed more than seven hundred chapters in thirty-eight states— by far the largest national black organization in the United States. Garvey asserted that UNIA membership exceeded six million members. Its actual number was closer to a half million, with fifty thousand to a hundred thousand members in Harlem.[61]

In the early 1920s, a Garveyite parade down Seventh Avenue became a major Harlem spectacle. Garvey led the way in his military regalia. The female corps, decked out in sparkling white dresses, was followed closely by the male corps, which marched in military formation, wearing snappy military-parade uniforms. Anyone who viewed a Garvey UNIA rally in Harlem could have imagined it as an international movement, supported by millions. One of the great political impresarios of the early twentieth century, Garvey expressed the dreams of Harlem's southern and West Indian poor. Dressed in his extravagant, gold-embroidered uniform, with a plumed hat, gold sword, brightly colored sash, and flanked by his male and female legions, Marcus Garvey looked and acted like a head of state.[62]

Garvey thrilled black Harlem with his message of racial pride, black economic autonomy, and moral virtue. A nominal Christian, Garvey portrayed God as a creator without any physical or racial attributes and treated religion as a personal matter. He declared, "Religion is one's opinion and belief in some ethical truth . . .

Marcus Garvey honor guard marching in Harlem, 1924 (Library of Congress)

but there are so many religions that every man seems to be a religion unto himself." Influenced by Hegel, Garvey argued that blacks could realize their destiny as a modern people only by forming a nation. "Nationhood is the highest ideal of all people. . . . Let Africa be our guiding star—OUR STAR OF DESTINY." While emphasizing racial pride, Garvey had no place for racial hatred in his movement. He declared, "I have no time to hate anyone." The UNIA stood for "Justice, love, charity, mercy, and equality." Garvey neither smoked nor drank. Ostensibly faithful to his own wife, he asked other black men to marry black women and to form strong families. Most of all, he sought to "awaken the spirit" of the black race.[63]

Viewing capitalism as the wave of the future, Garvey invested in several ill-fated enterprises, including the disastrous Black Star Steamship Line. Garvey hoped to buy surplus ships left over from World War I to form a black-owned shipping line that employed African Americans and brought together the scattered children of the African diaspora. The Black Star Steamship Line would also provide an economic foundation for his envisioned African nation. Unfortunately, Garvey proved incompetent at business, trusting charlatans, buying overpriced ships, and embarking on business ventures without secure contractual commitments. When the Black Star Line foundered, the justice department, with flimsy evidence and urged on by Harlem's brown elite, indicted Garvey for stock fraud. A federal jury convicted Garvey and sentenced him to prison in Atlanta, ending his political career. Both W. E. B Du Bois and A. Philip Randolph applauded Garvey's fall. Randolph's magazine, the *Messenger*, characterized Garvey as the "supreme Negro Jamaican jackass."[64] In a follow-up editorial, the *Messenger* called Garvey "A Jamaican Negro of unmixed stock, squat, stocky, fat and sleek with protruding jaws and heavy jowls; small, bright pig-like eyes and rather full dog-like face . . . a sheer opportunist and demagogic charlatan."[65]

Garvey's white and black enemies tried to bury him with ridicule and reduce him to an incompetent clown and opportunistic crook. Other commentators have described him as a protofascist who anticipated the fascist movements that swept Europe and Latin America in the late 1920s and 1930s. Both were wrong. Coming from Jamaica, Garvey had extensive democratic experience and wanted to see black self-government in the United States and elsewhere. His proclivity for uniforms and parades derived from African American secret societies, such as the Masons, the Elks, and the Knights of the Pythias. These efforts appealed to West Indians as well as to poor, southern blacks.

Garvey mobilized Harlem's masses. He challenged white Americans' capacity to transcend their racism, and he accused Harlem's New Negroes of wishful thinking and callous indifference to the concerns of Harlem's poor. As a "race man," Marcus Garvey made the black residents of Harlem proud of their African ancestry, proud to be black. While impractical, his "back to Africa program" touched the perennial longing of many African Americans for their ancestral homeland—their desire to fly away to their West African ancestors. Garvey's charismatic leadership, the emotional power of his rallies, his use of white as the UNIA ceremonial color, his religiously infused rhetoric, his affirmation of racial pride, and his dream of African Americans' reunion with Africa appealed to both poor southern migrants and poor West Indian immigrants. Garvey emphasized the racial and class issues shared by both groups and looked beyond their ethnic and national differences. The political issues that Marcus Garvey raised and his declaration of black pride remained central to Harlem and African American politics long after he died an exile in 1940. In Harlem, Garvey let the genie of black mass politics out of the African American bottle of racial accommodation and deference to Anglo-European culture.[66]

E PLURIBUS UNUM

Garvey and other West Indians awakened Harlem's black masses and demonstrated the potential power of a racially based, mass political movement. With his departure, Harlem's leadership fell into the hands of its New Negro elite. Chastened by Garvey's success with southern migrants as well as poor West Indians, Harlem's New Negroes, no longer content with gaining white downtown approval, assumed leadership of black Harlem. Before World War I, most of New York's socially prestigious black churches had relocated to Harlem. The members of these churches filled the ranks of the NAACP, the Urban League, the Harlem Republican Party, and Harlem's exclusive Greek-letter fraternities and sororities. Their services emulated white Protestant practices and were decorous and staid. Well-dressed worshipers sang hymns from approved hymnals, listened attentively and quietly to formal sermons, and avoided displays of emotion associated with poor ignorant southerners. After World War I, Harlem's middle-class black churches realized their future lay with Harlem's swelling ranks of southerners. At first, Harlem's old-line churches tried to maintain the decorum and restraint characteristic of white Protestant denominations as they instructed southern worshipers in correct behavior and dress. The churches also offered migrants a wide variety of social services that included employment agents, adult education classes, recreational athletic leagues, church socials, soup kitchens, and instruction in homemaking and personal hygiene. They sponsored rummage sales of used clothing, furniture, and housewares. Harlem's *New York Age* and the *Amsterdam News* worked in consort with its established churches, informing migrants of church services and the activities of related civic organizations.[67]

With Franklin Roosevelt's landslide presidential victory in 1932, Harlem's previously Republican black churches energetically started to recruit migrants to the Democratic Party. Such efforts at outreach and uplift failed to attract many southerners to mainline churches. Migrants found the services cold and formal, even condescending. Undaunted, led by ambitious young ministers, Harlem's established churches, little by little, adopted southern ways. The grand churches along Seventh and Lenox avenues offered church breakfasts before the Sunday service that included grits and bacon as well as macaroni and cheese. They added more spirited songs to their hymnals and formed lively choirs. Ministers adopted aspects of southern preaching that combined folksy conversation at the start of the services with spirited preaching and dramatic call-and-response climaxes. Harlem's enlivened churches succeeded in recruiting southern migrants who organized South Carolina, North Carolina, Georgia, Florida, and Virginia clubs in their adopted northern churches. In time, southerners felt at ease and among friends even in Harlem's most prestigious churches, at times comfortable enough to exhort the minister with an, "Amen, brother," "Tell it," and "Amen," or "Blessed Jesus." During songs, Harlem worshipers stood, clapped, and swayed in unison. These services were not nearly as boisterous as southern services or nearby Holiness

Closing ranks: NAACP voter registration, Harlem
(Library of Congress)

and storefront Sanctified churches. Still, after World War I, Harlem's middle-class churches slowly adopted southern practices.[68]

Adam Clayton Powell, minister of the Abyssinian Baptist Church on 138th Street, set the pace. Just before World War I, the Abyssinian Baptist Church had moved from West Fortieth Street to Harlem. Born in Virginia and educated at

Howard University, after World War I Powell successfully brought together his northern and southern congregants. Charismatic and familiar with southern religion, Powell remade the Abyssinian Baptist Church into Harlem's most powerful institution. His formal education, personal magnetism, and political savvy attracted Harlem's New Negroes, while his stirring sermons and the church's magnificent choirs, colossal sanctuary, and enormous wealth attracted southern migrants. By 1930 the Abyssinian Baptist Church had become the most southern of Harlem's old line, premigration churches. It had also become the largest and wealthiest black Christian church in the world. No visit to Harlem was complete without a visit to an Abyssinian Baptist Sunday service. Powell, like Garvey and Father Divine, captured the imaginations of southern migrants and mobilized their energy by grounding his efforts in their culture. And like those of Garvey and Divine, most of Powell's followers were women, who on Sunday filed into the Abyssinian Church, many dressed in white, much as African American women did in the South, West Indian women did in Jamaica, and West African women did in West Africa. They also wore fancy, exuberant hats, like all New York women.[69]

The change in the Abyssinian Baptist Church mirrored similar changes throughout Harlem. When the Great Migration ended in the late 1960s, for most outsiders Harlem was the quintessential African American community. The Apollo Theater, the Abyssinian Baptist Church, the *Amsterdam News,* the Harlem Y, the Hotel Theresa, Lenox Avenue, and the Schomburg Library were racial icons, household names for most African Americans and many whites. In the 1960s the label *African American,* however, included a diverse black population. Harlem reflected a broad range of people, who, since World War I, had made it their home—Old Settlers, New Negro college graduates, middle-class and poor West Indians, southern migrants, and second- and third-generation Harlem-raised and Harlem-born blacks, as well as newly arrived Puerto Ricans. In its half century as "the Negro capital of the world," Harlem had become home to a broad spectrum of African Americans—doctors, lawyers, entrepreneurs, publishers, politicians, ministers, and civic leaders. From across the New World and Africa, black athletes, dancers, actors, artists, playwrights, and musicians came and made it their home as did many of the city's sanitation workers, longshoremen, postal clerks, nurses, elevator operators, janitors, doormen, and domestics. With rare exceptions, if you were black and lived in New York, you lived in Harlem or Bedford Stuyvesant in Brooklyn, no matter your education, vocation, religion, ethnicity, or income.

The hostility of white New Yorkers compelled the city's African Americans to close ranks as a people. Harlem became a black sanctuary in a sea of white people. Here blacks from across the Americas and Africa met one another, shared ideas,

Fats Waller's funeral procession at Abyssinian Baptist Church, December 20, 1943 (Library of Congress)

and borrowed music, cuisine, and behavior from one another. Always more than the sum of its parts, Harlem cast its magic on everyone who called it home. Almost as soon as they had arrived, immigrants and migrants emulated Harlem ways. In the public schools, the children of rural southerners learned the rules of formal English but also adopted Harlem lingo and accents. Harlem cooks used southern and West Indian food and recipes to concoct their own creolized cuisine. Harlem beauty shops offered women and men elaborate hairstyles that combined traditional ideas with ostentatious city hairdos, setting the pace of black fashion around the world. In the late 1930s, Harlem youth started to wear the "zoot suit" with broad, padded shoulders, pegged cuffs, and baggy legs. In the 1940s, these zoot suits, and the female equivalents, became the "black urban style."[70] In Harlem, African Americans became a city people. They worked at city jobs, not as farmers. They lived among neighbors, not family. The clock, not the calendar, governed their lives; and they answered to themselves, not to "The Man." The change occurred slowly, one person at a time, day by day. By the end of World War II, however, black Harlem's melting pot had produced a people and a culture in many ways as distinct as the Carolina Low Country.[71]

Two Harlem race riots framed the coming together of black Harlem. The first occurred in 1935 and the second in 1943. In both riots, Harlem's largely southern-born population refused to countenance the kind of white on black violence commonplace in southern cities. In Harlem, a black life, any black life, had become precious. Harlem's southern migrants, alongside other Harlem blacks, demanded respect and protection of the law. Such black, civic consciousness began almost at the moment migrants and immigrants arrived in Harlem. In account after account, migrants testified to the startling effect of seeing in Harlem their first black police officer. Black police possessed the authority to arrest whites as well as blacks. Union members, postal clerks, and male dock and railroad workers, along with women in the needle trades and in domestic service, participated in Harlem politics, following the leadership of their ministers and such labor leaders as A. Philip Randolph. The editors of the *New York Age* and the *Amsterdam News* repeatedly asked their readers to register and vote. In 1925, even as Marcus Garvey entered the Atlanta federal prison, the *Amsterdam News* launched its boycott of white-owned Harlem stores that refused to hire black employees. With the onset of the Depression, the "Don't Buy Where You Can't Work" campaign gained support from the NAACP, the Urban League, the New York State Employment Commission, A. Philip Randolph's Brotherhood of Sleeping Car Porters, the International Ladies' Garment Workers' Union, and Harlem's black churches, led by Adam Clayton Powell Jr.[72]

In 1944 Harlem's loyal support of the New Deal and its growing population resulted in a second, nearly all-black congressional district that elected Adam Clayton Powell Jr. to Congress.[73] Like his father, Adam Clayton Powell Jr. led the way in unifying Harlem's diverse black population. Articulate and defiant, Powell cut his political teeth by heading the poor-relief efforts of the Abyssinian Baptist Church. In 1931 he gained notoriety by protesting the Harlem Hospital's firing of three black doctors. Powell joined the Harlem committee to defend the Scottsboro Boys and participated in the "Don't Buy Where You Can't Work" campaign that forced white-owned stores along 125th Street to hire black employees. In the

Harlem celebrating Joe Louis victory, 1930s (Library of Congress)

1930s Powell seemed at the forefront of every Harlem protest movement. In 1941 he became New York's first black alderman, and in 1944 he left for Washington to embark on his career as the spokesman for black America. A child of Old Settlers, Powell was familiar with Harlem's poor and could work with New York's white elite. As an ordained Baptist minister and the leader of the largest black church in the United States, a notorious playboy, an unequaled showman, and a charismatic leader, the younger Powell embodied Harlem—its diversity, its changes, its freedom, its ambitions, and its North-South identity.

Powell's election marked the changes that had occurred in Harlem since Marcus Garvey. In Harlem, southern blacks realized that their votes mattered, but only if joined with the votes of other blacks in Harlem. Black unity meant black power. Whether West Indians, migrants from Louisiana or South Carolina, college graduates, or socially prominent Old Settlers, the black residents of Harlem saw themselves as members of a unified black community, a We People. Political participation validated their new city ways. Powell's election also demonstrated that Harlem's New Negroes had cast their fate with Harlem's southern migrants rather than New York's white elite. The sheer number of southern migrants became the source of New Negro political power. Harlem's black leaders no longer asked white power brokers for favors. As leaders of a powerful block of voters, they demanded public services for their constituents, just like every other leader in the city of an important interest group. Power became a source of respect.[74]

SHOWTIME

Entertainment also unified Harlem and engendered racial pride. In January 1934 the Apollo Theater opened on 253 West 125th Street as a black theater. The Apollo debut signaled change. Until 1934 most of Harlem's black entertainment lay north of 125th. The Odeon and the Roosevelt theaters lay along 145th Street, the Douglas Theater and the Cotton Club on 142nd, the Savoy Ballroom at 140th and 141st, the Lincoln Theater on 135th, and the Lafayette Theater on 132nd. Most whites, New Negroes, and West Indians lived below 125th. At 125th Street, the Apollo reached across Harlem's social divide. It gave black entertainers a stage of their own and quickly became the premier national showcase for black entertainment.[75]

In the three decades after its opening in 1935, the Apollo overshadowed all other Harlem institutions. Apollo appearances bolstered the careers of Ray Charles, Count Basie, Leslie Uggams, Ella Fitzgerald, and Dizzy Gillespie. It introduced white audiences to bebop, jump blues, rhythm and blues, black comedians, gospel quartets, and soul music. Structured as a variety show, the Apollo offered four shows a day, seven days a week, with eight to twelve acts per show. Even tickets for shows that featured headliners, such as Bessie Smith or Louis Armstrong, rarely cost more than two dollars and at most one dollar—not just for a single show but, if you wished, for the entire day's run.[76] From the start, the white owners of the Apollo understood that pleasing black audiences was the key to success in Harlem entertainment. Apollo headliners received only modest fees and everyone worked under trying conditions. Seating thirteen hundred people, the Apollo was notorious for its cramped third-floor dressing rooms, shabby facilities, and dirty backstage conditions that included drug dealers and prostitutes. Even so, few black entertainers could resist its lure. From 1935 to 1960, in the golden age of Jim Crow, there was no greater achievement for a black entertainer than to play at the Apollo and no greater thrill than receiving a standing ovation at the Apollo, the toughest audience in North America.[77]

The Apollo operated on the principle that the audience was king. If a newcomer, performing in a virtually no-pay, time-filler act, captured the heart of the Apollo crowd, overnight, he or she gained top billing on the Apollo marquee.

Fame at the Apollo translated into national fame. Booking agents and record producers attended every new act. If headliners failed to live up to the audience's expectations, they found themselves booed and pelted with vegetables and bottles, fearing for their lives and careers. By 1940 the Apollo had become the Carnegie Hall for black stage-entertainers. Performers and audiences maintained a constant give-and-take, similar to the "call and response" in Harlem's churches. Audiences did not come to be entertained; they came to be moved, to have their hard lives transformed and exhilarated. Successful Apollo entertainers reached the hearts of their audiences and poured out their souls, often driving themselves to exhaustion. And on Wednesday night, Amateur Night at the Apollo, anyone might gain the spotlight, please the audience, and become a star. Magically, right before the audience's eyes, unknown but talented black entertainers might fulfill their dream to become the next Ella Fitzgerald, Duke Ellington, or Bill "Bojangles" Robinson. A place of black magic, the Apollo featured its own version of the West African trickster deity, Elegba, in the person of Norman Miller. Dressed in comic clothes as "Porto Rico," Miller ruled Amateur Night at the Apollo. At any point in a performance, if he sensed audience dissatisfaction, Porto Rico rushed on stage, fired a cap pistol at the offending entertainers, and drove them off stage to their shame and the delight of the audience.[78]

Harlem's black working class reigned at the Apollo. Its will, as expressed by Porto Rico, made itself felt throughout black America. This was the Apollo's aura. On stage at the Apollo, black entertainers subjected themselves to the judgment of other black people, not to white management, not to white booking agents, not to white critics, and not to white audiences, but to black Harlem. Established stars such as Paul Robeson, Count Basie, and Aretha Franklin appeared gladly at the Apollo, not for its modest pay or its miserable working conditions, or to advance their careers, but to certify themselves as stars before the most powerful black audience in America, an audience respected by every other black audience in the world.

The Apollo audience represented Harlem. In the 1930s the Apollo's largely southern audience shared the seats with West Indians, upper- and middle-class New Negroes, and a surprisingly large number of whites, including Time Square booking and recording agents. By World War II, the number of West Indians had diminished significantly, and after the 1943 race riot, few whites ventured into Harlem, even to attend the Apollo. Ed Sullivan, Marilyn Monroe, and Elvis Presley were the rare exceptions. After World War II, the audience included a growing contingent of Puerto Ricans and Cubans. The biggest shift in Harlem and at the Apollo, however, took place during World War II.

During the Great Depression, African American migration to New York dropped 25 percent from 173,000 to 136,000. Then, with the outbreak of World War II, it nearly doubled in the 1940s to 243,000. Out-migration from Georgia, North Carolina, and South Carolina jumped to 477,000 in the 1940s. Harlem became steadily blacker, more southern, more Hispanic, and poorer, although the educational level increased by about a year and a half, reflecting improved public education in Harlem and the South. The emergence of bebop and a second Harlem Renaissance reflected these changes, as well as the growing maturity and self-confidence of Harlem as a black community.[79]

During World War II, Dizzy Gillespie from South Carolina and Charlie Parker from Kansas City formulated a revolutionary new jazz in Harlem clubs. Parker and Gillespie grew tired of the large swing band format that had dominated jazz since the mid-1920s. Patterned after the European symphonic orchestra, swing bands played set pieces that offered musicians little room for improvisation. Playing primarily for white dance audiences, according to Gillespie and Parker, big band jazz had lost touch with its blues roots and with much of black America. It succeeded as entertainment but at the expense of its artistic creativity and its capacity to speak with a black voice to black audiences. In Harlem, at Minton's Playhouse on 118th Street, Monroe's on 134th Street, and Dan Wall's Chili House on 140th Street, Gillespie and Parker, along with drummer Kenny Clarke and pianist Thelonious Monk, created bebop, a blues-based, highly dissonant, and musically demanding jazz. By 1945 Parker and Gillespie had become cult figures in Harlem. They performed in small clubs, dressed in black shirts and pants, wore berets and sunglasses, and spoke in a "cool, hip" jargon that called women "softs" and hundred dollar bills "cows." Earlier, Cab Calloway had fired Gillespie because of his innovative harmonics and contentious behavior—both trademarks of other Harlem beboppers. Much of the innovation, however, derived from traditional black music, especially the blues. Gillespie, a native of Cheraw, South Carolina, understood the connection.[80]

Gillespie's father had played the guitar, mandolin, bass fiddle, and piano for a local Cheraw black band. At his death, he instructed his family to bury him under a cedar tree, a carry-over from West African burial rites. Growing up, Dizzy followed his father's steps, playing a variety of instruments and listening to any jazz record that he could find. His most important musical influence, however, was the Sanctified churches around Cheraw, which practiced spirit possession and spoke in tongues. Gillespie described it as "akin to African religion." In the Sanctified churches of Cheraw, Gillespie "learned the meaning of rhythm" and "how music could transport people spiritually." He explained that, in addition to the different rhythms of the snare drum, bass drum, tambourine, and cymbal, the congregation contributed rhythms with "foot stomping and jumping up and down on the wooden floor which also resounded like a drum. . . . People like James Brown and Aretha Franklin owe everything to that Sanctified beat," declared Gillespie. "I received my first experience with rhythm and spiritual transport going down there to the well every Sunday, and I've just followed it ever since."[81]

In 1932 Gillespie left home for the Laurenberg Institute in Laurenberg, North Carolina, a black orphan home similar to the Jenkins Orphanage in Charleston. Here, he learned formal music and adopted the trumpet as his primary instrument. In the mid-1930s, Gillespie moved to Harlem and picked up work at the Savoy Ballroom, where he met Kenney Clarke and his future wife, Lorraine Willis, a dancer from Darlington, South Carolina. Gillespie and Clarke insinuated their music into the big band format while playing for Earl Hines at the Apollo, but they found that only "Charlie Parker played very syncopated and Sanctified" music. They also discovered that southern audiences, raised on the blues, did not like bebop at first. Determined to win them over, Gillespie, Parker, and Clarke played at the Apollo and other northern theaters on the "Chitterling Circuit" and took frequent southern tours. Gillespie recounted one southern patron asking him after a performance, "Can't you niggus play no blues." They took such comments to heart. According to Gillespie, modern jazz musicians had "to know the blues." By 1946, he reported, we had "conquered the South."[82]

Living in Harlem, Gillespie understood that the blues and Sanctified music were aspects of a much larger and more varied tradition of West African–inspired music. In the early 1950s, Gillespie recruited to his band Cuban drummer Chano Pozo. Gillespie believed that North American black music had lost the complex polyrhythms of West Africa because most slave plantations had prohibited the playing of drums. "The Afro-Cubans, the Central Americans, and the West Indians remained polyrhythmic. They didn't give up theirs [drums]. Our beat in the United States was so basic though that other blacks in the hemisphere could easily hear it. . . . Chano taught us all multi-rhythms. . . . Chano wasn't a writer but a stone African." Bass player Al McKibbon observed, "He belonged to that society Nanigo, you know. It's like being a Mason in this country. . . . He used to tell me about a lot of stuff he shouldn't have repeated." Fellow band member Mario Bauza commented, "When Dizzy organized his band with Chano . . . the Congo interrupted them, you know, until they found the right kind of approach between the two countries. It's two countries, but it's the same thing. Every rhythm comes from Africa, and all blacks come from there, regardless." Gillespie concluded, "Now, our music is universal. It shares the rhythmic content of African music,

music of the Western Hemisphere and various lands of the East, and has merged this rhythm with European harmonies, the soul of the slaves, the blues, and the spirituals to create jazz. Boy!"[83]

MOTHERS AND SONS

Most major figures of the Great Migration were men. Yet migration affected southern women even more than men. Most traveled as members of a family, but the trauma of migration often ended in the separation of fathers from their families and left children under the sole care of their mothers. In leaving the South, many young black women broke with their families and found themselves alone, except for their children. In the North, few uneducated black women enjoyed upward mobility. They gained the vote, but most found only menial employment, usually as domestics. Their children, however, especially their sons, became the justification for migration. They gained access to well-funded public schools and to opportunities unimaginable for black males in the South. In New York, three sons of poor migrant women found international fame, made possible by their mothers' decisions to migrate. Harlem painters William H. Johnson and Jacob Lawrence and dancer and composer Alvin Ailey were quite different men. Each followed a different artistic path, but without their mothers' help, none could have fulfilled their artistic dreams.

On March 18, 1901, a black midwife delivered Alice Smoot Johnson of her first child, William Henry Johnson. Alice Smoot and her husband Henry Johnson lived in Florence, South Carolina, the largest city between Wilmington, North Carolina, and Charleston. A booming county seat and farm-market town, Florence lay astride the Atlantic Coast Line Railroad that ran from Miami to New York City. About half the residents of the town of Florence were black and two-thirds of the county's rural residents. Most black males labored in the tobacco fields and warehouses or the railroad, while most black women served as domestics. Henry Johnson shoveled coal for the Atlantic Coastline and Alice Johnson worked as a maid. Light-skinned and with wavy hair, William was the Johnsons' only child for nine years. William, a loner, attended Florence's all-black public school, accompanied his mother to church, and imbibed her middle-class ambitions. Encouraged by Alice, William wanted to become a painter, but Florence, South Carolina, offered little training for artists of any color. Ambitious for her son, Alice Johnson approached her brother, Willie Smoot, who lived in Harlem and worked as a Pullman porter on the Atlantic Coast Line. In 1918, at age seventeen, William Johnson boarded the train to New York to become a painter. His mother accompanied him to the station. For the remainder of her life, Alice Johnson maintained a steady correspondence with her son.[84]

William Johnson lived with his uncle and aunt on 128th in Harlem. To pay his way, he worked at an assortment of jobs. In 1921 he enrolled at the National Academy of Design, a tuition-free art school that taught traditional, representational styles. Like many other young American painters, Johnson looked to Europe for artistic inspiration. From 1926 to 1930, he lived in Paris and then settled in Denmark, where he absorbed the ideas of European modernism. In 1938 Johnson returned to "paint his own people." He rented an apartment near Greenwich Village but commuted daily to Harlem where he taught and worked for the Harlem Community Art Center on Lenox Avenue. In Harlem, Johnson used African and Caribbean motifs to portray Harlem scenes. His paintings included Joe Louis boxing a white man as well as Carolina migrants adapting to and enjoying Harlem life. In 1940, encouraged by other Harlem painters, he undertook a series of South Carolina paintings that depicted rural blacks at work, at home, with their families, riding to church, and working on a chain gang. Using bold, primary colors, a flat perspective, and cubist-like figures, Johnson depicted the world of his mother.

In 1942 Johnson painted a series on American blacks in World War II. These wartime paintings included black soldiers in training, black Red Cross nurses aiding black sharecroppers, wounded black soldiers convalescing in a military hospital helped by black nurses, and slain black soldiers on a Pacific battlefield. Johnson also painted black couples fixing a broken down car, dancing a jitterbug in a country juke joint, and going on their honeymoon. No matter what the activity, Johnson painted only black people. The only exceptions were several dead Japanese infantrymen killed by black American soldiers in battle. Fathers, mothers, couples, male field hands, female nurses, and male soldiers populated Johnson's world. His strong, nurturing black women were especially noteworthy. They, like his mother Alice, held together their families and communities. They nursed their wounds, psychological and medical.[85]

Johnson painted the places, people, and consequences of the second wave of the Great Migration. Fellow Harlem painter, Jacob Lawrence, painted the migration itself. Few people experienced migration more profoundly than Jacob Lawrence. Before World War I, his mother, Rosa Lee Armistead, had migrated from Virginia to Atlantic City, New Jersey, where she met her husband, Jacob Lawrence, a cook from South Carolina. In 1917 Rosa Lee Lawrence bore her first child, whom the couple named Jacob. Two years later, they moved to Easton, a small Pennsylvania coal town. In 1924 Rosa Lee divorced Jacob and moved to Philadelphia. A domestic, Rosa Lee Lawrence had difficulty finding steady work. Desperate, she placed her three children in foster care so she could search for work in New York City. In 1930 she brought Jacob, his brother, and sister to New York. Arriving in Harlem, Jacob recalled "seeing big apartments" as "a completely new visual experience." Rosa enrolled Jacob in Public School 68 and, after school, placed him in Utopia House, a daycare center that included an intense painting program. Every Sunday Rosa Lawrence, with her three children, attended Sunday school and church services at Adam Clayton Powell's Abyssinian Baptist Church.[86]

Defining himself as a "Negro artist," Lawrence completed a series of paintings on Harriet Tubman and the Underground Railroad, another on abolitionist Frederick Douglass, and a third on the Haitian revolutionary Toussaint L'ouverture. In 1940 the Rosenwald Fund awarded Lawrence a fellowship to paint the Great Migration. Working with Gwendolyn Knight, he completed the project in 1941. *Fortune* magazine published about half of the sixty paintings, thrusting Lawrence to the forefront of young New York painters. Shortly after, he married Knight, a native of Barbados, who grew up in St. Louis, and attended Howard University. Lawrence painted the Great Migration as a great American epic that tied African Americans to the larger American epic of "people moving and people getting a better education."[87] "My mother was a domestic worker," he explained, "My father was a cook on the railroad. . . . They were a part of this migration, the migration from the South."[88]

Jacob Lawrence's *The Migration of the Negro* looked at southern blacks gathering their possessions and boarding trains bound north. In the North, they crowded into tenements, attended school, established churches, voted, and, like Lawrence, entered the professions. One panel depicted a domestic worker who might have been Rosa Lee Lawrence. In the North, such migrants confronted white racism and discrimination as well as the ridicule of upper-class blacks. When later asked about his portrayal of an educated, northern black couple, who seemed to symbolize death, Lawrence answered, "Well, of my experience maybe I felt [that way], fortunately we don't have that today, we had the schism of the Southern Negro and the Northern Negro at one time . . . the urban versus the rural." Despite his resentment of black upper-class condescension toward poor southern migrants, Lawrence emphasized the positive. The Great Migration opened the doors for southern blacks. Their participation in World War II and the political power they exercised in the North assured that the gains would not be lost as had happened after World War I. In Harlem and other northern cities, African Americans built lives full of promise, hope, and power. Jacob Lawrence saw this as the meaning of the Great Migration.[89]

Modern dance composer Alvin Ailey shared Lawrence's commitment to a cohesive black community unified by its southern and West African traditions. During World War II, Lulu Ailey had left the Brazos River valley in East Texas for Los Angeles to find work. Having secured a job, Lulu Ailey sent for her only son, Alvin, who arrived in September 1942 on the Texas Pacific Railroad. Ailey's father had abandoned his family three months after Alvin's birth eleven years earlier. At the time of her marriage, Lula was only fifteen. Alvin Ailey never met his father and spoke to him only once on the phone the year that his father died. Lulu Ailey, an intensely religious woman, faithfully attended Sanctified Baptist churches. She insisted that Alvin accompany her to services and oversaw his baptism. The early years in Texas with his mother profoundly marked Ailey. "My feelings about myself have been terrible," he explained, "The whole of where I came from, the Brazos Valley in Texas, picking cotton in my early life, being with my mother and not with my father, living through the 1930s, the lack of a real father, not having enough food sometimes, going around to those churches and Dew Drop Inns, all left an enormous stain and a sense of inferiority that lasted for many years. It felt that no matter what I did, what ballet I made, how beautifully I danced, it was not good enough."[90]

In Los Angeles, Alvin attended George Washington Carver Junior High and later Jefferson High School, both in the South Central neighborhood and both among the best black public schools in the nation. Here, Ailey encountered the fine arts.[91] Only a few blocks away, at the Biltmore Theater in downtown Los Angeles near Azusa Street, Ailey saw Katherine Dunham's African American dance company. Alvin attended every performance of Dunham's three-week engagement. Dunham allowed the attractive and adoring young Ailey to watch her dance from back stage. Enthralled by ballet, modern dance, and the possibility that a black male could dance professionally, Ailey joined the Lester Horton Dance School in Hollywood.[92] Open to nonwhites and male dancers, the Horton Dance Company changed Ailey's life. Trained by Martha Graham, Lester Horton rigorously schooled his students in the principles and techniques of modern dance and ballet. A social radical, Horton embraced the racial diversity of Los Angeles and believed that dance should express a social message. Horton also became Ailey's first lover. In 1953 Horton suddenly died. The company nearly collapsed. Determined to forge ahead, Ailey assumed leadership and accepted an invitation to perform the "Dance of Flowers" at the Erlanger Theater in New York City. Impressed with the work, Harlem dancer Donald McKayle took the young LA dancer under his professional wing. McKayle secured Ailey an assortment of jobs in New York dance companies and introduced him to the city's choreographers and directors. With the support of McKayle and other black dancers, in 1958 Ailey formed the Alvin Ailey American Dance Company. It premiered as a company with Ailey's ballet, *Blues Suite*, performed at the 92nd Street YMHA, a center for New York modern dance.[93]

Blues Suite announced the coming out of the Ailey dance company and the coming of age of black dance. All of the company's dancers were black; its choreographers were black; its director was black; and the ballet was built around African American themes. Set in a southern barrelhouse and accompanied by standard twelve-bar blues songs, *Blues Suite* demonstrated the musical richness of southern black culture, Lulu Ailey's Dew Drop Inns. Affirming the beauty of black people and male sexuality, the dance opened with a railroad whistle, followed by the tolling of church bells—an acknowledgment of the departure from the South, a world left behind. Sensual throughout, *Blues Suite* also hinted at male homosexuality, the source of painful conflict between Alvin and Lulu Ailey, between the rural South and the urban North.[94]

In 1960, again at the 92nd Street Y, Ailey presented *Revelations,* the most popular American ballet ever performed. In *Revelations,* Ailey focused on southern Sanctified religion, the sacred equivalent of his mother's carnal Dew Drop Inns. Addressed to his mother, Ailey organized *Revelations* into three sections— Pilgrim of Sorrow; Take Me to the Waters; and Move, Members Move. In the spectacular ballet, Ailey offered his audience a total theatrical experience, which included exquisite costumes, moving music, beautiful dancing, striking dancers, and a compelling story that traced the African American religious experience from slavery to the flight north. Black spirituals, including "Morning Star," "Precious Lord," "Elijah Rock!," "Wade in the Waters," "Rock My Soul," "Sinner Man," and, his mother's favorite, "I Been Buked," accompanied each of the sixteen dances. *Revelations* opened with the male and female dancers, dressed in yellow and black, standing together in a yellow spotlight. In a cappella offstage, a chorus sang "There Is Trouble All over This World." The elegant dance affirmed the grace, refinement, and beauty of black men and women. "I Been Buked," and "Deliver Daniel" followed, danced in a style unmistakably inspired by Martha Graham.

The visual masterpiece of *Revelation* was "Honor" that began with a parade of female dancers, stylishly strutting across the stage in full-length, flowing white dresses. The lead female dancer trailed behind, carrying an eye-catching, white parasol. The bare-chested, male dancers wore white pants and carried white staffs, festooned with white streamers. Haitian drums played in the background as a choral group sang "Honor unto the Dying Land," an allusion to the South.

Next came "Wade in the Water," a southern baptism, followed by the boisterous "Sinner Man, Where You Gonna Run To?" performed by three male dancers. The beauty of the male dancers and their sexualized presentation in "Sinner Man" alluded to Lulu Ailey's religious reaction to Alvin Ailey's homosexuality. The next dance, "The Day Is Past and Gone," in which a group of female dancers, dressed as church ladies, in bonnets and full-length yellow dresses and holding straw fans, accompanied by males in dress pants and vests, appeared to be his answer. His revelation was the beauty and power of his mother's religion; her revelation was her son's homosexuality. *Revelations* concluded with the rousing "Rocka My Soul." The finale left audiences gasping, smiling, and clapping, spontaneously ratifying the various messages of the ballet. In *Revelations,* Ailey affirmed the beauty and elegance of African American people and their shared, rich, and ancient West African culture. He recounted the African American epic that had formed them into a single people, but he also pointed out that in the passage from slavery in the South to freedom in the North, they had changed. In the South, there was no place for the "Sinner Man to Run To," but in the North that "Day Is Past and Gone." Because of Lulu Ailey's migration to Los Angeles, Alvin Ailey escaped the travails of slavery and southern racism. In the North he became liberated from ignorance, cruelty, poverty, and homophobia.[95]

By the late 1960s, the Ailey dance company was the most successful, independent dance company in the world. Its European performances almost always sold out, and in the 1970s, it also became the most popular dance company in the United States. It stars, Dudley Williams and Judith Jameson, ranked among the nation's premier dancers. The honors climaxed in 1984, when the Alvin Ailey American Dance Company performed at the Metropolitan Opera House at Lincoln Center. Before his death, in 1989, Alvin Ailey had choreographed seventy-nine ballets, permanently established his company at the Clark Center near Lincoln Center, and set up a dance school affiliated with Fordham University to train young black dancers. Ailey's personal Middle Passage from Rogers, Texas, to Los Angeles and his triumph in New York informed his ballets and his efforts on behalf of black dance and dancers. Under the directorship of Judith Jameson, the Alvin Ailey American Dance Company altered the image of African Americans for dance audiences. Like painters William Johnson and Jacob Lawrence, Ailey used his art to unify African Americans and to reach out to European Americans. Because of the support of his mother and Harlem's black community, he succeeded masterfully.

CROSSING OVER

Much like the first Harlem Renaissance, the artists of the second renaissance reached a limited audience—largely other black artists and educated whites and blacks. Most black and white Americans did not know their work. Very likely, most residents of Harlem, at best, had only heard their names. So too, bebop jazz musicians Charlie Parker and Dizzy Gillespie largely played for other jazz musicians and educated blacks and whites. Bebop lacked mass appeal. Not so Harlem's popular music. When the great swing bands of the 1920s and 1930s fell on hard times, Harlem's popular musicians moved to center stage at the Apollo and in other theaters throughout the country. At first, they reached only black audiences, but their music quickly crossed over to white fans. They became national figures, not just black entertainers. At the end of the 1940s, Harlem's Louis Jordan and his Tympany Five ranked among the top rhythm and blues bands in the country, selling tens of millions of records to blacks and whites. Jordan's "jump blues" opened the door that separated black and white popular music and ushered in rock and roll.[96]

Born in Brinkley, Arkansas, in 1908, Louis Jordan first played the tenor sax. He attended Arkansas Baptist College where he learned to read music and play jazz. Like Ma Rainey and Bessie Smith before him, Jordan toured with the Rabbit Foot Minstrels, a group that taught him to play to the audience. In the early 1930s he lived in Philadelphia until he earned his union card in Local 802 to qualify for work in New York clubs. In Harlem, Jordan played at the Elks Rendezvous, and in 1936 he accepted a job with Chick Webb's Savoy house band. Because of Webb's shyness, Jordan introduced the band's numbers and bantered with the audience, joking, dancing, and cutting up as he had done for the Rabbit Foot Minstrels, much as Cab Calloway did at the Cotton Club. Jordan even adopted Calloway-like zoot suits and clowned by wearing oversized white-frame eyeglasses. When Webb died in 1938, Louis Jordan formed the Tympany Five, which consisted of seven musicians—two saxophones, two trumpets, a clarinet, a bass, and a guitar. Jordan explained, "I loved playing jazz with the big band. Loved singing the blues. But I really wanted to be an entertainer—that's me—on my own. I wanted to play for the people, for millions, not just a few hep cats."[97]

An entertainer in the Cab Calloway mold, Jordan played a distinctly black sound that he called "jump blues." Texas bluesman "T. Bone" Walker said, "He plays good blues and he sings them like they were originally sung, too."[98] Jordan's twelve-bar blues structure, with dotted eights and sixteenths, gave to hits such as "The Chick's Too Young to Fry" and "Caldonia (What Makes Your Big Head So

Hard?)" a peppy, cheerful blues sound that made audiences want to dance and forget their troubles. In the 1940s Louis Jordan's recordings regularly reached the top of the race charts and sold well to white audiences. Jordan's flamboyance and the joyous spirit of his band, along with its silly costumes and light-skinned, skimpily clad female singers, appealed to Harlem audiences. His annual two-week Christmas week gig at the Apollo sold out weeks in advance, and his records sold millions. Hollywood film directors often chose the Tympany Five for feature movies. For many, Louis Jordan and his Tympany Five were American popular music during World War II.

As much as any other musician, Louis Jordan led the way for black rhythm and blues to become rock and roll. White rock and roll pioneer Bill Haley called Louis Jordan his musical father. As the record librarian at a small Pennsylvania radio station in the late 1940s, Haley listened to all of the Tympany Five's recordings. Haley recounted, "Why shouldn't a country and western group sing rhythm and blues." The Comets played Jordan's songs until they could duplicate the beat and the eighth and sixteenth notes, melding jump blues with country and western ballads.[99] Chuck Berry also singled out the Tympany Five. "I identify myself with Louis Jordan more than any other artist. . . . If I had to work through eternity [as an artist], it would be Louis Jordan."[100] Louis Jordan's jump blues drew on Harlem's musical diversity—jazz, blues, and show music. His lyrics good-naturedly portrayed life, enabling audiences to laugh and enjoy themselves. Like black religion, rhythm and blues lifted people's spirits and brought joy. Urban and contemporary, live at the Apollo, the jump blues of the Tympany Five affirmed and modified southern black music.

So did James Brown. In 1956, on Amateur Night at the Apollo, fresh from Augusta, Georgia, James Brown left his Harlem audience breathless. They shouted themselves hoarse, danced in the aisles, and demanded encore after encore. Born in Barnwell, South Carolina, about sixty miles west of Charleston, near Bamberg, Brown and other deeply religious southern blacks changed the face of northern cities. Abandoned by his mother, Brown grew up in his aunt's Augusta, Georgia, brothel, which catered to black soldiers stationed nearby. A child of the rapidly changing, postwar South, as a young boy Brown became a singer, modeling himself after visiting black vocalists who performed at the Lenox, the black theater in Augusta. World War II Augusta exposed Brown to a wide assortment of music that included black gospel quartets, touring northern nightclub acts, big band jazz, and Sanctified church music. After the war, Brown formed a gospel quartet called the Famous Flames, which performed in the Savannah River towns up and down the South Carolina–Georgia border. As the lead singer,

Two marines strolling in Harlem (Library of Congress)

Brown's splits, slides, and camel walk made the Flames a local legend, leading to its first recording in 1956, "Please, Please, Please."[101]

No matter where the Flames played or how late, on Sunday morning they faithfully attended church. Brown explained, "These folks were Sanctified—they had the beat. See you get Sanctified and you got holy. Sanctified people got more fire."[102] The recording of "Please, Please, Please" opened the way for Brown's 1956 appearance at the Apollo that made him a major figure on the East Coast black touring circuit. In 1958 he appeared with Fats Domino at County Hall in Charleston, South Carolina, and a year later received a weeklong engagement at the Apollo that enabled him to afford a luxury suite at the Theresa Hotel. By the end of the week, Brown "felt like the Apollo was my natural home."[103] In 1960 the Apollo booked Brown for an almost unprecedented three engagements. He was, by far, the Apollo's most popular performer and black America's hottest singer.

In 1963 Brown recorded his Apollo appearances for his first album, *Live at the Apollo*. Even though white radio stations did not play the album, it became the number two best-selling album of the year. For the first time, more whites purchased his records than did blacks. Brown's successful crossover to a national audience coincided with the increasing popularity of other black rhythm and blues and gospel singers, such as Little Richard, Fats Domino, Ray Charles, the Temptations, the Supremes, and Aretha Franklin. Brown and other black "soul" performers became so popular that white southern cities desegregated their theaters to avoid boycotts by Brown and other black artists, who refused to perform at segregated venues. His most successful songs were "Night Train" (1961), "The Mash Potato" (1962), "Papa's got a Brand New Bag" (1965), and "Licking Stick" (1968). Lyrically and musically repetitious, like Sanctified church music, Brown's songs exhibited a rhythmic intensity and emotional excitement unequaled by any other contemporary music. No one challenged his claim as the "Father of Soul" and the "King of Funk." In his concerts, the audience always "had church." Insistently black, in music and identity, in 1968, amid widespread urban riots, Brown gained national headlines by chanting to his audiences, "Say it Loud, I'm Black and Proud." At the height his popularity, Brown sold his home in Queens and moved back to the "Terri" (territory) in Augusta, where he had grown up. He explained, "My roots, my religion, and my music all come out of the South. Generations of my family, as far back as I can trace them, lived around one little area in South Carolina."[104]

Much more than an entertainer, Brown personified postwar Harlem. Postwar migration tied Harlem ever closer to the South and especially to Low Country Georgia and South Carolina. Unlike earlier migrant waves, postwar southern migrants brought with them not only their traditional southern culture but their newly gained literacy and a familiarity with the world outside the South. In the 1950s, throughout South Carolina and Georgia, black cemeteries proudly displayed the gravestones of thousands of young black males killed in World War II and the Korean War. Deeply religious and traditional in many ways, the brothers, sisters, wives, and children of these fallen soldiers identified with northern black communities as much as with their southern communities. Apollo and Lenox theaters sprouted up across the South. Mindful of Woodrow Wilson's broken promises that followed World War I, after World War II black migrants refused to acquiesce to racial apartheid. Black pride and black rights became as important to their identities as their religion and music. Harlem was their unrivaled Mecca.

The Great Depression shifted Harlem away from its earlier New Negro, middle-class culture toward more southern, working-class values.[105] The rapid rise of Pentecostal and Holiness churches in Harlem after the war and the increasingly southern practices of its old-line Protestant and Catholic congregations reflected the continuing arrival of southern migrants. Harlem's postwar artists addressed southern subjects. The popularity at the Apollo of rhythm and blues and gospel blues bore witness to Harlem's movement away from New Negro gentrification to a more southern and rural Sanctified culture. Even Harlem's formal cultural institutions—the Schomburg Library, the Harlem YMCA and YWCA, the Urban League, the NAACP, the *Amsterdam News*, and its socially prominent churches, fraternities, and sororities—increasingly expressed themselves in the language of southern migrants' Sanctified religion and bluesy music. These Sanctified people not only absorbed Harlem's city ways and political militancy but also carried them back south, sowing seeds of change much as Dizzy Gillespie, the Apollo, Aretha Franklin, Louis Jordan, and James Brown did in popular entertainment. Appropriately, the legendary Harlem Globetrotters basketball team warmed up worldwide audiences with the down-home music of "Sweet Georgia Brown."

By the 1960s, "black and proud" and "Sweet Georgia Brown" had become interrelated parts in a much larger and complex African American epic that included the Carolina-Georgia Low Country, the northern Alabama Hill Country, the Mississippi-Arkansas Delta, and New Orleans and western Louisiana's bayous and cane fields. In the twentieth century, the southern headwaters of Africa America flowed north, not just to Harlem but also to Pittsburgh, Chicago, Los Angeles, and scores of other northern and western cities. Southern slaves remade West African religion and music into Sanctified Christianity and the blues. Similarly, migrants remade their parents' rural southern culture into political activism, popular music, Pentecostalism, fine art, and ballet. Much as West African culture helped define the rural South, so the culture of African American migrants helped define twentieth-century urban America. R. H. Strong, the nineteenth-century American missionary who discovered a complex and dynamic city at Abeokuta, Nigeria, would have recognized Low Country Carolina and Harlem as different but equally legitimate heirs to the ancient cities of West Africa.

MULES AND MEN

•4•

Birmingham

"Hear dat whistle," Siney Bonner, born in slavery, told her WPA interviewer in Birmingham, Alabama, in 1938. Bonner had stopped to chat with a knot of elderly blacks in Norwood, a tattered residential neighborhood of wood-frame shotgun houses, a mile from the blast furnaces at Sloss-Sheffield Steel and Iron. The white interviewer recorded Bonner's conversation in the stylized, black dialect that characterized the WPA slave narratives, "De whistles on dem Big Jacks what pull dese highsteppin' I.C. trains mind me of dem steamboats what used to pull up at the landin' at old Pickensville on de Tombigbee River." She paused in the middle of her "confab" and said, "Course dar wa'nt't no railroads dem days."[1]

Bonner, from Pickensville in Alabama's black belt, migrated to Jones Valley after the Civil War. Before 1870, small black and white farmers had raised cattle and cotton in the remote Appalachian valley. In a generation, the railroad transformed the isolated Jones Valley into the Pittsburgh of the South. Railroads made possible a modern, industrial complex of coal mines, coke ovens, and iron and steel mills that clustered around the newly organized Birmingham. Surrounded by blast furnaces, rolling mills, miles of company houses, and brick churches, with its rigid and precise grid of streets and avenues Birmingham rose out of nowhere. In a valley fifteen miles wide and thirty miles long, by 1938 300,000 black and white workers and a handful of middle-class professionals and managers, merchants and politicians lived and worked.[2]

The Mineral District, so defined by the Alabama industrial commission, included the city of Birmingham and the surrounding Jefferson County. In 1920 Birmingham claimed the largest black population of any southern city and had a larger proportion of black residents (38 percent) than any city outside the South.[3] Birmingham hummed day and night with the sounds of industry. Long and lumbering freight trains rumbled along double-tracks that divided the city in half. Grade crossings, with blinking red lights and warning bells, competed with the sounds of sledgehammers pounding pig iron and the blast of the furnaces that lit up the sky. On the top of Red Mountain, a monumental statue of "Vulcan" overlooked the "Magic City." Middle- and upper-class whites lived out of sight, over the mountains, to the southeast, in bucolically named communities like Mountain Brook and Vestavia Hills.

From 1870 to 1900, thousands of Alabama's poor, rural black sharecroppers, half-croppers, and landless tenant farmers migrated to the new Magic City. Undreamed of wages enticed them to abandon the poverty of Alabama's Black Belt. Unlike the remainder of the Lower South, in Birmingham the region's owners or "Big Mules" offered African Americans hope and economic promise. For them, and for the city's black middle class, Booker T. Washington's "Atlanta Compromise" of accommodation and uplift offered a blueprint for success.

BIRMINGHAM: A HIGH-TONED TOWN

Named after John Jones, an early nineteenth-century settler, Jones Valley before the Civil War was a hunting ground for Cherokee, Creek, and Choctaw.[4] In 1863 Jones Valley claimed a population of only 11,000 that included 2,650 slaves. The four-thousand-acre tract that became Birmingham was "an old rabbit-filled cornfield cleared of stumps and trees."[5] Yet, even before the Civil War, geologists realized that a valley rich in coal, limestone, and iron offered the resources that would trigger Birmingham's birth.[6]

The Warrior Coal Fields, Red Mountain, the Cahaba Fields, and the Black Warrior River defined the region and provided the abundant resources needed to make iron and steel. Alabama's Black Belt, however, offered tens of thousands of underemployed former slaves, and the railroad provided inexpensive and efficient transportation. Well-paid jobs in the valley's mills enticed more than 100,000 rural blacks to the Magic City. In less than a generation, Birmingham became a major rail center in the South, second only to Atlanta.[7]

The black migrants included large numbers of skilled artisans who had worked on the region's plantations as carpenters, masons, blacksmiths, shoemakers, plasterers, gunsmiths, engineers, tailors, bakers, iron puddlers, and boat builders.[8] Not all came from Alabama. Emma Chapman, from Charleston, South Carolina, remembered her parents saying they "expected to find money growing on trees in Alabama."[9] Black women like Chapman took in laundry, and others worked at quilting. "You know, in bees . . . they would all get together and have piece quilts. . . . I didn't never thought I could do something like that but I did," a woman told an interviewer at Sloss Furnace.[10] Wherever they came from and regardless of skills, black workers brought to Birmingham their country ways. Ila Prine, from Mobile explained, "Cose us hab our medicin' sich lak elderbush tea. Hit was red mos' lak whiskey an' us used it for feber."[11]

In 1860, in the skilled trades, blacks in Alabama outnumbered whites by five to one.[12] Early rolling mills in Birmingham, which converted pig iron into wrought-iron bars, required the trained-eye of black puddlers who understood metallurgy and possessed the strength necessary to stir molten iron with a twenty-pound paddle.[13] The 1890s, however, saw the conversion of Birmingham's skilled black artisans into a proletarian working class. By 1900 few skilled black workers remained. African Americans constituted more than 90 percent of the unskilled labor force in Birmingham.[14] Unlike traditional iron making and blacksmithing, after 1900 machines performed much of the skilled work in Birmingham. Large-scale, modern manufacturing and mining required thousands of semiskilled machine operatives and unskilled workers, but only a few skilled workers.[15]

The founders of Birmingham enjoyed the status attributed to them as the "big mules." John T. Miller was Birmingham's biggest mule. After the Civil War, entrepreneur, financer, and landowner Miller convinced the Alabama state legislature to build and then consolidate two regional rail lines. Miller's South and North Railroad and the Alabama and Chattanooga Rail Line intersected at the future site of Birmingham. Miller easily swayed the planter-dominated Alabama legislature. One legislator predicted, "The nigger is going to be made a serf sure as you live."[16] In 1871 Miller, along with several other investors, started to sell parcels of land in the 4,000-acre "Birmingham" tract, named after Britain's largest manufacturing city. Other big mules, Daniel Pratt, his son-in-law Henry De-Bardeleben, and their partner James Sloss, also opened coal mines and blast furnaces in the district. In 1880 DeBardeleben, who co-owned Pratt Coal and Coke, fired his first furnace "Alice," named after his daughter.[17] In the next decade, other southern businessmen built scores of blast furnaces and foundries throughout the district and opened clusters of new coal mines up and down the valley. Alarmed by such dramatic growth, Pittsburgh steel magnate Andrew Carnegie declared Birmingham was "Pittsburgh's most formidable enemy."[18]

Tennessee Coal, Iron, and Railroad Company (TCI) developed into the most important of Birmingham's companies. By 1889 TCI built the region's first open-hearth steel furnace and stimulated the explosive demand for coal. In 1893 the Birmingham district mined 5.5 million tons of coal.[19] Expansion only made the big mules more powerful. Birmingham's new industrialists used their profits to buy more land, build more company housing, and construct monumental stone office buildings and mansions.[20] In 1890 African Americans made up 40 percent of Birmingham's population, and the city's overall population grew from 4,500 in 1880 to 110,000 in 1900.[21]

Such robust growth fed Carnegie's concerns. TCI bought out sixteen local mines and furnace companies. Sloss, whose massive blast furnaces guarded Birmingham's northern boundary, absorbed another dozen. By 1898 Birmingham had become the world's third largest shipping point of iron—much of it sent to Pittsburgh to be processed into steel.[22] DeBardeleben's Pratt Coal and Iron also acquired the mineral rights to more than a half-million acres in the Mineral District. The coal mines that dotted Birmingham's rural hinterland gave rise to dozens of company towns up and down the valley. The company town of Coalburg combined coal resources and rail access. A Sloss-owned coal settlement with a population of one thousand in 1888, Coalberg earned a reputation of being a "first-class railroad town." But Coalberg also housed 150 convicts that the state leased to Sloss to work its mines.[23] In Coalberg, as elsewhere, the demand for unskilled, black labor exceeded the supply. Mill and mine work required massive amounts of brute, human force. Toiling over superheated blast furnaces or digging beneath the ground with pneumatic hammers half the size of a man demanded enormous strength and dexterity. To maintain their demanding production schedules, TCI and Sloss employed thousands who worked in shifts around the clock. To meet the labor shortage the big mules turned to the state legislature and the Alabama prison system.[24]

Rooted in slavery, the convict-lease system allowed mill and mine owners to rent state convicts. Arbitrary, brutal, and violent, convict labor cost mine owner Daniel Pratt nineteen dollars a month for a "full" or "first-class" convict—a grading system borrowed from slavery. A full-hand did the work of a free laborer, who earned fifty dollars a week. In 1874 John T. Miller, the founder of Birmingham, signed a contract with the state for thirty miner-convicts that allowed him to pay "full," "half," or "dead" convicts at different rates. The working conditions in Miller's Newcastle coal mine were so deplorable that locals called it the "Second Black Hole of Calcutta."[25]

By 1894 TCI accounted for 62 percent of Alabama's leased convicts. The state legislature viewed convict labor as beneficial to government and business. It allowed industrialists to pay low wages while it gave county sheriffs a revenue-producing means to sweep up black vagrants and troublemakers.[26] It also assured Alabama of the most abusive and corrupt criminal justice system in the nation. Supervised by white trustees, black convicts faced brutal punishment at every turn. Operators hung recalcitrant convicts on crosses and routinely whipped them. Industrialists, state legislators, prison wardens, and county sheriffs all

Black and white railroad gang, Birmingham, 1920s (Birmingham Public Library Archives, Cat. #1556.21.50)

shared in the largess of the convict-lease system that created a powerful alliance between Alabama public officials and its industrialists.[27]

In 1911 the convict-lease system collapsed, triggered by a catastrophic mine disaster that killed 126 black miners. One miner recalled, "I remembered as if 'twas yesterday when the convict mine over at Banner blew up . . . th'explosion was so awful. . . . There was . . . convicts and eight guards killed in that one."[28] In place of the convict-lease system and to mollify white workers, the city imposed a rigid system of apartheid that legally defined African Americans as second-class citizens and reinforced the urban grid that defined the city by race and class. The Birmingham grid, which divided the city into four quadrants—east, west, north, and south—extended over the Jones Valley that ran northeast to southwest. Outside the city, the Mineral District's black neighborhoods ignored the grid. In small enclaves, just off the tracks and away from company towns, small communities of African American workers lived along dirt streets that wound hither and yon leading nowhere.[29] A woman teacher recalled, "Our little community had unpaved streets, muddy and dusty in turn, filled with litter and debris, where local folks who left 'much to be desired'" in moral standards spent their time making

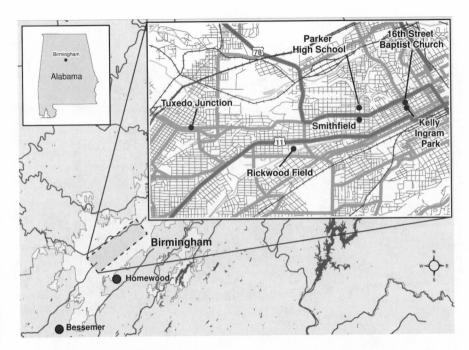

Birmingham Mineral District

"home brew." City planners and politicians separated these disorderly, black neighborhoods from the remainder of district though a series of dead-end and circuitous roads.[30]

Still, as late as 1900 Birmingham lacked formalized rules of segregation. Until the early 1900s, some residential neighborhoods in Birmingham remained racially integrated. Blacks and whites lived along the same streets, some as renters and some in the "quarters," company housing with separate rows for black and white workers.[31] At the same time, in Birmingham, like many southern towns, two parallel and separate downtowns emerged. Black downtown centered on the intersection of Sixteenth Street and Fourth Avenue, anchored by the Sixteenth Street Baptist Church.[32] Designed by Birmingham's only professional black architect, William Rayfield, the Sixteenth Street Baptist congregation built its sanctuary between 1908 and 1911 just as segregation took hold of the city. Sixteenth Street Baptist Church looked like any Baptist Church, that is, any other white Alabama Baptist church. The city's black middle class, a relatively small group of doctors, lawyers, teachers, dentists, Pullman porters, business owners, journalists, and civil servants, made up its congregation. For Birmingham's white elite, the Sixteenth Street Baptist Church represented and spoke for black Birmingham.[33]

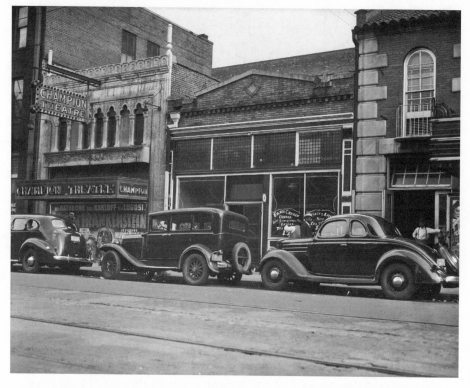

African American downtown, 4th Avenue, Birmingham, 1930s (Birmingham Public Library Archives, Cat. #WBP 4.12)

In the early decades of the twentieth century, Rev. William R. Pettiford presided over Sixteenth Street Baptist Church. Along with editor Oscar Adams of the *Birmingham Recorder* and Arthur George Gaston, an ex-coal miner who served as president of the Booker T. Washington Insurance Company, Rev. Pettiford endorsed Booker T. Washington's program of racial accommodation and uplift. Pettiford also served as the director of black Birmingham's first bank, the Alabama Penny Savings and Loan. Similarly, Oscar Adams used the *Birmingham Reporter* to voice the black elite's concerns, while Gaston built a commercial empire that depended directly on the support of Birmingham's big mules.[34]

Birmingham's black downtown served the entire district. It housed the symbols of the black middle class—Knights of Pythias Hall and the Prince Hall Masonic Lodge, a handful of black barbershops (each, by custom, served either only whites or only blacks), beauty shops, restaurants, and, until 1911, dozens of saloons. In 1911, with the support of the Sixteenth Street Baptist Church, the white Birmingham city council outlawed bars in black neighborhoods. Birmingham's black downtown became the place to go to shop on Saturday mornings and to pray on Sunday mornings with a decidedly middle-class character.

With the passage of the new Alabama Constitution of 1901, African Americans in Birmingham found their lives increasingly confined. In 1880 40 percent of registered voters in Birmingham were black. After the ratification of the 1901 Alabama Constitution, only thirty African Americans retained the franchise.[35] By 1928, of the 85,000 voting-age African Americans in Jefferson County, only 352 were eligible to vote.[36] Starting in 1910, many mining companies, where blacks and whites once worked together and shared union membership, built separate facilities for blacks. Black miners, who accounted for more than half the miners in the district, even received their mail and paychecks at segregated windows.[37] By 1930, in the Magic City, blacks and whites were not allowed to play a game of chance together, sit together on a streetcar, be buried in the same cemetery, eat at the same restaurant, use the same toilet, dwell in the same neighborhood, attend the same schools, or watch a match between black and white boxers.[38] In the 1920s blacks who owned property in white neighborhoods became targets of bombings if they insisted on living in their own dwellings, giving the city the nickname "Bombingham." Lynching and Ku Klux Klan activity also spiked in the 1920s. In July 1920 the *Birmingham Reporter* declared that a wave of racial violence was sweeping the region.[39] In 1924 the Birmingham Klan claimed more than eighteen thousand members, a majority of the white males registered to vote.[40]

The 1907 merger of TCI with U.S. Steel ended the region's industrial independence as well as hastened the end of its experiment with flexible patterns of racial segregation. Engineered by J. P. Morgan, U.S. Steel purchased cash-short TCI for $35 million.[41] Morgan's takeover of TCI created the largest industrial corporation in the United States. In the face of the miners' opposition, U.S. Steel mustered local police, state militia, and black strikebreakers. Lootings, beatings, shootings, and lynching accompanied the 1908 strike.[42] Alabama governor Braxton Comer, following several bursts of violence against strikers and scabs, threatened to arrest all striking miners for vagrancy, making them eligible for the convict-lease system. The union gave in.[43] The specter of the convict-lease system proved too much for the rank and file. In the wake of the strike, union membership evaporated. Accommodation, however, meant no vote and no union membership. The strike did produce an important historical footnote. To maintain morale during the strike, United Mine Workers strikers sang "We'll Overcome." During the strike, the Sea Island spiritual became a union song in Alabama. Forty years later, in the 1950s, "We Shall Overcome" became the marching song of Birmingham's civil rights movement.[44]

ON THE FOURTH OF JULY PEOPLE WOULD BE PLAYING BALL

By 1910 Birmingham had emerged as the center of an archipelago of industrial towns and suburbs. Stretching along rail and streetcar lines that connected downtown Birmingham to Bessemer, ten miles to the southwest, the urban-industrial corridor bristled with activity. The history of the new industrial suburbs paralleled Birmingham's. Local industrialists working as land agents created precisely plotted downtowns that they surrounded with racially defined housing in easy walking distance to the mills, mines, or foundries.[45] Ensley, with its black neighborhood of Tuxedo Park, lay on the western edge of Birmingham. After the town was incorporated by Birmingham in 1910, Ensley's population became increasingly black. Many of the black workers, employed by the gigantic TCI-Ensley steel mill, lived in Martin Quarters in company-owned two-room wood houses, open front to back, called shotgun shacks, a common vernacular house type found all over the South.[46]

Between Ensley and Bessemer, Fairfield, Alabama, took root in 1910. Initially called Corey, Fairfield was renamed after the Connecticut birthplace of U.S. Steel's James Farrell. The new U.S. Steel Fairfield Works provided the town's initial nine thousand acres, which the local land company developed, modeling it after the planned industrial suburbs of Pullman, Illinois, and Gary, Indiana.[47]

In contrast to Ensley and Fairfield, Bessemer sought to become an independent city, not simply a suburb of Birmingham. The creature of Henry DeBardeleben, who named it after the British steel-making process, Bessemer attracted financing from as far away as London and Charleston, South Carolina. Bessemer was carved out of a nine-thousand-acre parcel in 1887, and city planners designed a grid that resembled Birmingham's. Bessemer called itself the "Marvel City." A growing and prosperous downtown sustained two street car lines that ran to Birmingham, a host of limestone buildings, and a handful of modern hotels.[48] Bessemer's population doubled each decade until 1920 when it reached twenty thousand. Located to the immediate west of the city, in front of its sprawling iron works, was Pipe Shop. The adjacent neighborhood, cut off from the rest of the Bessemer grid by dead ends and cul-de-sacs, housed only black workers. In 1909 Joe Brooks recalled life in Pipe Shop: "In Bessemer the streets weren't paved and Bessemer just had horses and buggies . . . and a dirt street. My grandmother just

White Fairfield Industrial baseball team (Birmingham Public Library Archives, Cat. #829.6.108)

did domestic work. We lived in a shot gun house. During that time you could hardly get a house. . . . We didn't have indoor toiletts. The out-house was in the back and there was running water or rather a hydrant on the outside. You had to carry your water inside."[49]

The streets of black Bessemer and its surrounding communities had no outlets. From their homes, black workers could not go directly to downtown Bessemer. They lived apart, conducting their personal lives much as their parents had in rural Alabama. A resident of Pipe Shop explained, "Most of the hog killings took place 'down home' as the people referred reverentially to the hamlets they had lived in before migrating to Bessemer." Pipe Shop's dirt roads only led to the plants and factories nearby. Bessemer's neat Victorian cottages, on the other side of Main Street, were as remote to Pipe Shop's black workers as the estates of Birmingham's white, upper middle class on the west side of Red Mountain. Only on special days, like the Fourth of July, did Bessemer's blacks emerge from confinement. On those days, local African Americans were given access to Bessemer's public park where they celebrated the nation's birthday with moonshine, barbecue, and collard greens.[50]

African American life in the Mineral District developed within the structures of large mills, mines, and company towns. The hardening of racial apartheid, between 1900 and 1930, coincided with the appearance of an elaborate welfare system that gave African American life in Birmingham a distinct cast. The directors of Birmingham's largest coal and iron companies implemented the system.[51] The so-called Birmingham System can be traced to U.S. Steel's acquisition of TCI in 1907 and the 1911 mine disaster that ended the convict-lease system. It emerged slowly, over a number of years, and provided the framework in which a unique blend of African American cultural expression emerged in Birmingham. On ball fields and in churches, at picnics and parades, in schools and lodges, in the Mineral District African Americans built a rich, if rigidly confined, leisure life around baseball, jazz, and gospel music.

In the 1920s Birmingham companies built vast tracts of company housing in the city and its satellite towns. Most consisted of monotonous rows of wood-framed, shotgun shacks, without running water or electricity. TCI constructed twenty racially segregated, company towns in the Mineral District.[52] After World War I, most black industrial workers, twenty thousand in Birmingham alone, lived in these company "quarters." Black workers used company scrip to purchase their food and clothing at company stores, they prayed at company churches, their children attended company schools, and the men played baseball on the company-league teams at the company sponsored annual Labor Day picnic.[53] Within this framework, black workers, much as their ancestors had done in slavery, lived their lives in their own way. They carried their water in buckets drawn from a common hot water tub, barbecued pork on Thursday to eat on Friday, fished and hunted, and ate watermelon that they had grown themselves alongside yams and chickens. The women sewed patchwork quilts for family and neighbors much as their grandmothers had.[54]

Black children attended company schools. Everyone had access to company doctors, many belonged to fraternal and sorority lodges, and their names and accomplishments frequently appeared in company newspapers and magazines. The company scrip, called "clacker," was printed on brown paper with silver ink. Some local merchants accepted the scrip, but Clarence Dean, an employee at Sloss for thirty-five years, remembered bitterly, "They get twenty-five cents out of a dollar. That's how you lost."[55]

The end of the convict-lease system and union militancy was followed by dramatic economic expansion and demographic growth. But industrialists believed that their black workforce lacked sufficient motivation. Plagued by high rates of absenteeism, which saw workers go back to their parents' homes or not show up for work on "stormy" Monday, the industrialists responded.[56] They set up company medical clinics, encouraged church attendance, tightly regulated bars and nightclubs, and encouraged family-oriented activities such as picnics, baseball leagues, and gospel quartets. They borrowed many of their ideas from the Tuskegee Institute's curriculum of vocational training and Christian morality. Indeed, many of the black ministers and teachers hired by the companies as "colored community supervisors" were graduates of Tuskegee, an hour's train-ride from Birmingham. According to research conducted by TCI, the Birmingham System reduced absenteeism, produced more cooperative workers, and discouraged black workers from joining a labor union.[57]

Following the labor unrest early in the century, managers at American Cast Iron Pipe Company (ACIPCO), Sloss, and TCI concluded that, by "lending a Christian hand" to their workers, unions would never again gain a foothold in Birmingham. John Joseph Egan, president of ACIPCO, applied the "Golden Rule" to ensure that "God's Providence was divided fairly among the peoples of the world."[58] Egan offered workers a benign workplace in return for discipline and deference. Benevolent paternalism, colored by white racism, replaced the barbarous convict-lease system. Egan argued that both workers and owners profited from a more prosperous and efficient workplace. He intended to ensure labor peace and create a docile workforce overflowing with gratitude. In 1912 Egan offered company shares to black and white workers who stayed on the job for a prescribed time, provided Christmas Turkeys annually to workers' families, and opened a segregated company bathhouse and community center.[59]

In 1915 ACIPCO set up a night school that taught basic reading skills, "American" habits of thrift and discipline, and the enhancement of the "manual trades." The company also opened an employee savings bank and church.[60] In 1916 ACIPCO built a "negro" school near the plant and in 1920 donated $20,000 to Birmingham to build a white elementary school. *ACIPCO News* devoted three pages, at the back of the monthly magazine, to news about black employees. Proudly, *ACIPCO News* underscored the segregated, if *benign*, nature of industrial life in Birmingham.[61] Starting in 1916, *ACIPCO News* reported on the recreational activities of its employees, particularly its factory teams.

By 1919 ACIPCO, Stockham Pipe and Valve, TCI, Sloss, Republic Steel, and other Birmingham employers fielded scores of black and white baseball teams. In 1928 the *Birmingham Reporter* published schedules for thirty black and white industrial league teams in the Mineral District. Organized in six divisions, teams from Fairfield Steel Works played teams from Lone Star Cement, National Bread Company, and Southern Bell.[62] "Colored baseball" received the same attention as workers' service records, and for good reason. "The object of the baseball game at this institution," wrote Parker Austin, catcher of the ACIPCO Colored Team, "is for the purpose of entertaining the employees of the Company and to develop good sportsmanship."[63]

Black industrial baseball reflected similar values. "We had ball games down in the Quarters. We had enough space to make a ballpark," Richard Gaines recalled. And when they were not playing in the Quarters, black workers watched the company team at Sloss Field, which adjoined the mill in north Birmingham. Segregated company picnics provided occasions for baseball. Birmingham's mills, mines, and foundries sponsored baseball games between employees and between all-star teams from other divisions of the same company. Games were played in honor of "Old Timers" who had just retired, at the conclusion of the annual Labor Day picnic, and just for fun.[64]

In 1916 black industrial baseball began league play. Only three years later, in 1919, black baseball's popularity soared. That year ACIPCO supplied "special" streetcars for blacks to attend the Fourth of July ball game. With five thousand fans expected at Sloss Field, the editors advised readers to get an early start.[65] Labor Day games, which coincided with company picnics across the district, became celebrated events. Marching bands, stands selling hot dogs, goobers, and lemonade, company officials decked out in sashes, the awarding of prizes, and the presence of the local press all ornamented the dozens of simultaneously played baseball games with panache.[66] Employers provided their players, black and white, with first-class uniforms, equipment, and facilities. The black factory leagues featured real-life heroes. A great pitcher or fielder might also work at the furnace or live in the cold-water shotgun house across the street or attend the same Baptist church. Sports heroes and community members were one and the same. Sponsored and equipped by employers, these were black Birmingham's community teams.[67]

In Birmingham, the city's black baseball players played ball for other black players watching in the stands. Their games had all the intimacy and nuances of black life. Players jostled and teased one another. Fans crowded against fences that stood between them and the playing field; talked to players on the bench; shouted at them on the field; made fun of their mistakes, letting them know that their on-field heroism did not make them better than their neighbors. Equality ruled in the early days of Birmingham's black industrial baseball.[68]

In Birmingham, black professional baseball ebbed and flowed between 1905 and 1950. Its source, however, remained the industrial leagues. For much of its history, the great Birmingham Black Barons used the industrial leagues as its farm system. In the 1930s, when the Depression closed down the Negro League and when the Barons momentarily disappeared, the industrial teams continued to maintain and nurture black baseball players. In the 1930s the industrial teams provided employment for aspiring sandlot and semipro players who worked to play. Through the Depression and World War II, the industrial leagues remained intact, moving players from one level to another, teaching skills, and tying together baseball, work, and community. Even during the heyday of black professional baseball, black players who found themselves cut from a professional roster always knew they could find a position on a Birmingham industrial team.[69]

In 1910 Birmingham industrialist Rick Woodward built a modern ball field at the edge of the city that he named Rickwood Field.[70] Directly across the street stood Smithfield, a middle-class African American neighborhood on the city's southern boundary. Smithfield and Rickwood were mirror images of racial segregation. Rickwood Field, an exact copy of Forbes Field (the home of the major league Pittsburgh Pirates) became the home to the white Birmingham Barons. On opening day in 1910, ten thousand wildly cheering fans jammed the park to overflowing. A local band played "Dixie" as the players ran onto the field.[71] Not a black resident from Smithfield, or any other part of Birmingham, sat in the stands of Rickwood that afternoon. The Birmingham Barons, the white minor league team, played exclusively at Rickwood Field from 1910 to 1919. After opening day, the Barons allowed black spectators to watch games from segregated stands in left field. No Negro professional team appeared at Rickwood Field until 1919, when the Birmingham Black Barons played their industrial league rival ACIPCO.[72]

James Arthur Coar founded the Birmingham Coal Barons in 1916. Coar worked for TCI in Ensley where he supervised forty-two men in the transportation division of the company's coal mine. Coar's Coal Black Barons, a team made up of only men in his shop, won the industrial league championship in 1917 and 1918. The team's motto, "High-class, clean baseball," in fact, was Coar's motto. A black Horatio Alger, a disciple of Booker T. Washington, a man who always reported to work on time and handled his team "grandly," Arthur Coar provided the perfect example of middle-class leadership of black working-class sport and culture.

During the 1919 season, the Barons attracted as many as five thousand white "and colored" fans to special games held at Rickwood Field. By the end of July in the first postwar baseball season, the Black Barons took on the South's "other" great professional team, the Atlanta Black Crackers. ACIPCO and the Black Barons competed for coverage in the black press that summer. Each played important games at Rickwood. A Fourth of July contest with ACIPCO pulled in a full house and a twenty-piece band.[73] Later in that summer of 1919, the Black Barons hosted an astounding ten thousand fans to a doubleheader the team split with the Chicago (Negro) Cubs. In a game "of ginger and pep," the Baron's pitcher "Steel Arm Dickey" pitched the club to a win.[74]

In 1920 the Black Barons earned its stripes by playing games against the best teams in the region. Negro League legend C. I. Taylor brought his Indianapolis Clowns to Birmingham for a game in March. Led by the greatest name in Negro League ball, Oscar Charleston, Taylor's team crowded itself into the Dunbar Hotel, black Birmingham's best black hotel.[75] The Barons also hosted the famed Chicago American Giants.[76] Founded by owner-manager Rube Foster, the Chicago Giants were the foremost Negro baseball team in America. Foster played a dominant role in the creation of the first Negro Leagues and was a pioneer in creating unorthodox and daring strategies that characterized Negro baseball.[77]

The transition from an industrial team to a Negro League team took the Barons another three years. From 1920 to 1923, the team played in the "minor" Southern League before joining the Negro National League in 1924. Coar sold the team to Joe Rush, owner of the Rush Hotel, which became a second home to Black Barons' players. Like other Negro League teams, the Black Barons played anyone, anytime, anywhere. Regularly scheduled games were only points of departure for the team. Wherever it traveled, the team played all comers in the region of their scheduled games. It barnstormed from weekend to weekend across the South. Even membership in the Negro National League did not prevent the team from playing challengers whenever they appeared. Improvisation kept the team financially solvent. Negro League baseball offered its players a great deal—fans, fame, and a pocket half-filled with money. But it also included more than 120 games a summer, long trips in old cars, boardinghouses, bad booze, cloying women, and endless card games.[78] The Barons drew well; sometimes as many as twelve thousand fans crammed into Rickwood Field against first-rank teams.

The Chicago American Giants, who "dressed in their private car" and were chauffeured to the ballpark, took the opening-day game in 1925 by a score of 13–6. The Barons lineup included "some of the best Negro ball players in Dixie"; a new manager, Big Smithie; a new pitcher, "Fish" Salmon; and the reliable shortstop "Geechee" Meredith.[79] The Giants' use of chauffeured cabs to transport the team from the hotel to the ballpark revealed much about Negro League baseball. On the one hand, elegant dress, fancy cars, and first-class accommodations brought black players enviable public acclaim. On the other, city law prohibited black players from using Rickwood Field locker rooms. Visiting teams were forced to dress for the game at a segregated black hotel before arriving at the park. They drove to the park in taxis or limousines out of necessity. Their "showboating" one-upped the Birmingham city government's effort to humiliate them.[80]

In 1927 after playing against southern teams from Chattanooga, Memphis, New Orleans, and Nashville, as well as the usual stalwarts from Chicago and Kansas City, the Birmingham Black Barons charged to the forefront of the Negro National League. When hotel owner Joe Rush sold his interest in the team to Oscar Adams, the publisher of the *Birmingham Reporter*, the Barons did not falter. The Barons had recently acquired pitcher Roy Paige, perhaps the greatest pitcher of all time. Roy (for Leroy) Paige played as a Baron for three years, and the team rose to the top of the league on his extraordinary talents. Tall and thin as a whip, the young Paige, who disliked the nickname "Satchel," became a larger than life folk hero.[81] In 1930 Paige left Birmingham for Pittsburgh, where he became the greatest pitcher-showman in the history of Negro League baseball.

Paige's amazing development, like that of the bluesman Robert Johnson, seemed unexplainable. A trickster and a showoff, Paige, to roil the crowd, would call outfielders back to the infield and, then, strike out the side. He told batters what he intended to pitch and still struck them out. And, all the while, he perfected his unhittable fastball. Later, when his fastball lost speed, he developed trick pitches, disguising his pitches by using tobacco juice to make the balls hard to see during the late-afternoon games, and cut the baseballs so they would gyrate unpredictably.[82]

Paige thrived on the intimacy between the crowd and players that characterized black baseball. Fans and players alike knew each other from work or from the community. Even visiting players became friends of fans as they caroused after the game in local black bars and clubs and, at times, even stayed in people's homes. Players and fans "signified" to one another. They teased and toasted and called out insults to everyone's applause and amusement. Every one appreciated verbal agility almost as much as athletic agility. "We jawed at each other," William Greason, a pitcher for the Black Barons, recalled. "And we laughed. We had to laugh to deal with the conditions [of segregation]."[83] On the field, the bending and breaking of rules, the stealing of bases, the taunting of the single umpire, and the razzing of the opposing players were all parts of the game. They were also how black workers had always treated "the Man" or undermined white racism and its arbitrary rules. "We did lots of talking," Greason remembered, "telling the batter what's coming, even though we knew he'd never believe it."[84]

Birmingham embraced the rituals of southern black baseball. The Barons often paraded from downtown to Rickwood in open cars, horns blaring, and on special occasions, were accompanied by a marching band. When the Black Barons opened the season in 1927, Paige's first full year with the team, Birmingham's (white) superintendent of schools instructed his principals to excuse their students from school so they could attend the game.[85] Black baseball became a means by which urban African Americans celebrated and affirmed their community. Baseball, parades, frolics, picnics, medicine shows, and carnivals all broke the routine of work and distracted from the humiliation of segregation. In 1923 the city passed a special exemption to its blue laws and allowed the Barons to play on Sunday. Sabbath baseball, like black baseball during the week, included gambling, booze, and flirting. The moonshine vendor, who wore a long, wool coat even on the steamiest days of summer, prowled the stands with the two dozen pockets sewn into the inside of his coat filled with pints of hootch.[86]

Before and after the game, players gathered in the black downtown not far from Sixteenth Street Baptist Church. In the club and dance hall, located on the upper floors of the Masonic Hall, they hung out and danced to the jazz of Fess Whatley's Industrial High School Band. In retrospect, Bill Greason, who later became a Baptist pastor and played for both the Negro League Barons and the major league St. Louis Browns, recalled, "We had a different sense of team in the Negro Leagues. We played together and hung out together. In the big (white) leagues you had individual stars. With the Barons we had a team."[87]

More than any other social experience in Birmingham, baseball allowed blacks and whites to cross racial boundaries. To get to Rickwood Field, middle-class blacks from Smithfield walked across the street that marked the divide between Birmingham's black and white neighborhoods.[88] Working-class African Americans had to ride the segregated streetcar system to the game. On game day, between ten thousand and twelve thousand black Birmingham residents boarded the streetcars and paid their fares at the front of the car. But because everyone was black and the streetcars were filled to overflowing, they did not all move to the back of the car as city law required. This time, they sat down wherever they wished. Like the story of the African American man who, when he saw the "colored" and "white" signs in the laundromat, smirked as he put his colored clothes in the colored washer and his whites in the white washer, African Americans in Birmingham used every opportunity to laugh at and violate the arbitrary rules of racial segregation.[89]

Birmingham's black middle class found such working-class behavior disturbing. In June 1927 the *Birmingham Reporter* begged the team to sign another pitcher to work in tandem with Paige. The same article also instructed the Barons' manager to pay closer attention to his players' off-field antics. "We want to put

Manager Jones on guard that some of his men are keeping too many late hours," the paper reported. "You cannot keep late hours and give your best each day."[90]

The end of the organized Negro National League in 1930 also crippled the Black Barons. The Great Migration shifted the center of organized Negro baseball north, to Pittsburgh, where the Grays and Crawfords dominated Negro League baseball in the 1930s. In Birmingham, the spotlight of organized black baseball turned back to the industrial leagues. ACIPCO star Lorenzo "Piper" Davis became a local legend, as did Kit Kat Mays, a smooth fielding but light-hitting left fielder from Fairfield, who lived in company quarters and worked in the tin room of the TCI Ensley steel mill. After World War II, Mays's son Willie, born in 1931, joined Kit Kat in the outfield of his father's Gray Sox. With Piper Davis managing, in 1948 seventeen-year-old Willie Mays led the resuscitated Black Barons in the Negro League's last World Series.[91] Possessed of an extraordinary fielding prowess, from his "basket-style" catches, rifle-like throws to home, and breathtaking base running, Mays embodied the panache that characterized the black style of play in Birmingham and the Negro Leagues.[92]

CUTTING MONKEYSHINES AND DANCING ALL NIGHT

Middle-class Smithfield, incorporated into Birmingham in 1910, stood a stone's throw and a world apart from Rickwood. Anchored by Birmingham's emergent middle class, Smithfield lay between the black, industrial suburbs of Ensley to the south and Tuxedo Junction, the streetcar stop where black workers from West Birmingham caught the trolley to outlying mills. Smithfield was the home of Birmingham's sole black secondary school, Industrial High School.[93]

Founded in 1900, the same year Alabama disenfranchised its African American voters, Industrial High embodied the educational and political philosophy of Booker T. Washington. Industrial High also trained an extraordinary group of jazz musicians and directors of southern marching bands. Together, Smithfield, Industrial High, and Tuxedo Junction made Birmingham a major center for southern jazz in the 1920s and 30s. The Birmingham jazz sound, precise, lush, and harmonic, migrated from Industrial High to the dance halls of Tuxedo Junction and, in time, to school bands and church choirs nationally. Thanks to Fess Whatley and Erskine Hawkins, in the decades between the world wars, Birmingham swung.[94]

In 1910 Birmingham annexed the five-hundred-acre plantation of Joseph Smith, as part of the Greater Birmingham Plan. Although before 1920 it was a mixed-race, middle-class community, after World War I Smithfield became increasingly black. By 1928 the area had lost virtually all its white residents but remained a largely middle-class community except for a few working-class black families who lived on Smithfield's back alleys.[95] Smithfield's "alley residents" lived a different and almost invisible life. Sally Davis explained, "So-called middle class parents would look down on the ghetto children—wouldn't want their children to play with them, that sort of thing."[96] For Rev. W. R. Pettiford, architect William Rayfield, editor Oscar Adams, entrepreneur Arthur Coar, and the remainder of Birmingham's "better class of Negroes," Smithfield was a safe enclave, a place where mothers dressed their daughters in frilly dresses for cotillions, and where men slicked back their straightened hair before venturing downtown to visit friends at their fraternity lodges. Smithfield resident Oscar Adams, owner of *Birmingham Reporter* and the Black Barons, also wrote a weekly column for the local white paper entitled, "What Negroes Are Doing in Birmingham."[97]

In 1937 Adams's Smithfield neighbors crowded into his parlor to listen to Joe Louis battle James Braddock for the world heavyweight title. Adams's magnificent console radio provided the draw. Across the street lived Smithfield's richest citizen, Charlie Rowe, whose home sported two poolrooms. Rowe loved to sit on his front porch and read the newspaper. Oscar Adams, at times, had to send his son over to gently instruct Rowe to turn the newspaper right side up.[98] Upperclass blacks in Birmingham belonged to a dozen clubs and fraternal orders, including the Masons, Odd Fellows, the Strollers, and the Coterie. Most attended Sixteenth Street Baptist Church. Like Birmingham's white elite, the Smithfield black elite embraced the black Victorian values of social uplift, racial pride, and self-help.[99]

Among Smithfield's "better class," two educators stood apart—Carrie Tuggle and Arthur Howard Parker. As the first principal of Industrial High School, A. H. Parker directed the school along the lines laid out at Booker T. Washington's Tuskegee Institute. Carrie Tuggle directed the Tuggle Institute, an orphanage that taught middle-class manners and refinement to black foundlings. Arthur Howard Parker and Carrie Tuggle had arrived in Birmingham from different worlds— Parker from a free black family in Springfield, Ohio, and Tuggle from parents who had been born in slavery. Working with Smithfield's clubwomen and black businessmen as well as with Birmingham's white power structure, they built two complementary schools for Birmingham's African American children. The two educators also had a profound influence on black Birmingham's musical culture.

By his own telling, A. H. Parker, born in 1870, came to Alabama as a teacher and a barber. His own father had fled slavery and, thanks to contacts with Ohio abolitionists, opened a barbershop in Springfield. "My father's father was a white man about whom I know nothing," Parker wrote. "My father's mother was the daughter of a Chickasaw Indian."[100] Light-toned, inquisitive, and ambitious, Dr. Parker, as he was known throughout Alabama, had hoped to attend Oberlin College, where his mother had graduated, but he had to withdraw and take up his father's trade. He came to Birmingham in the 1880s, a seventeen-year-old seeking his fortune. Within a few years, he passed his teacher's license examination and taught in Birmingham's black middle school—as one of only ten African Americans teaching in all the Birmingham schools before 1900. Parker reveled in "the prestige that such a position carried among my own people." He wore a "plug hat" and a "Prince Albert Coat," his uniform for the next forty years.[101]

Parker lived in Smithfield in a house designed by local black architect William Rayfield. He joined the Sixteenth Street Baptist Church, and in 1900 he accepted the appointment as principal at the first African American secondary school, Industrial High, in Alabama. His salary was less than half that of a white principal.[102] With the support of the all-white Birmingham Board of Education and Smithfield's black middle class, Industrial High opened its single classroom in 1901. Ten years later, it graduated nineteen seniors and held its commencement at Sixteenth Street Baptist Church. By 1920 Industrial High occupied its permanent site in a new and expanded building in Smithfield, a five-minute walk from Rickwood Field.[103]

From its inception, Industrial High School adhered to the educational philosophy of Booker T. Washington's "Atlanta Compromise." Parker claimed Washington as his "Patron Saint." The curriculum of Industrial High centered on vocational and moral education that Birmingham's big mules and black elites both supported. Situated at the center of black, middle-class Birmingham, the school's working-class students confronted a mixed message. In their classes they learned sewing, cooking, proper dress, printing, the repair of shoes, nursing, and laundry along with "Negro" history and basic mathematics. Such courses were designed to teach students to remain in their place, be productive, and defer to their betters, black and white.[104]

At the same time, at the start of their weekly assemblies, students sang the "Negro National Anthem" to foster racial pride.[105] Parker's school taught Birmingham's working-class children to accept and conform to the local racial and social conventions of an industrial (and segregated) order. In this mission, the liberal arts of philosophy, literature, politics, and history had no place. Birmingham's "better class" of whites and blacks agreed that working-class Negro children should be prepared for lives of dutiful, menial labor. Along with its vocational courses, Industrial High offered classes in Table Manners, Practical Housekeeping, and How to Escort Females.[106]

Most Industrial High faculty members, like Parker, were light skinned. This had a discomforting effect on their dark-skinned, working-class students. Rosa Washington, who attended Industrial High School, remembered, "I felt put down because for years the lighter people put the darker skinned people aside. Parker had more light-skinned teachers."[107] Stone Johnson, who lived near the ACIPCO plant and attended Industrial confirmed Rosa Washington's memory. "Parker did not like me to say it, but there was lots of discrimination. . . . If you weren't high yellow you stayed in the back."[108] The school functioned as a microcosm of black Birmingham. A small and light-skinned middle-class elite taught the industrial working class about proper behavior, self-esteem, and race pride.[109]

The Tuggle Institute for Homeless Boys, founded by Carrie Tuggle in 1903, embraced a similar curriculum. Little is known of Tuggle's early life. After coming to Birmingham in the 1880s, she became a social worker and a Smithfield clubwoman. In 1903 Tuggle opened her orphanage. She worked with black and white middle-class businessmen and clubwomen to raise money for her orphanage. The daughter of a slave and a Mohawk Native American, Tuggle became a major figure in Birmingham's black middle class.[110] As a residential school for unwanted boys, Tuggle Institute taught industrial skills and racial pride. Like Parker, Tuggle also instructed her teachers to teach "responsibility, sobriety, and Christian values." In 1919 William A. Rayfield designed a new building for Tuggle Institute, financed in part by a $2,000 donation from downtown department store owner Louis Pizitz.[111]

A. G. Gaston, black Birmingham's most successful entrepreneur, the owner of insurance, hotel, radio, and funeral businesses, attended Tuggle. So did Industrial High School music teacher and musician John T. (Fess) Whatley and jazz great Erskine Hawkins. The music program of Tuggle Institute and Industrial High popularized jazz in Birmingham among both the working-class graduates and Smithfield's middle-class blacks. In a sense, the two schools provided the "junction" or "crossroads" for black Birmingham, its "Tuxedo Junction," the title of Erskine Hawkins's 1939 jazz hit. A real place, Tuxedo Junction, where working-class blacks caught the streetcar to work, also became in the 1920s and 1930s the center of black Birmingham nightlife.[112]

I'D DINE MY GIRL AND HEAD FOR THE TUX

Jazz had been played in Birmingham for almost forty years when Hawkins penned his signature tune. The city's jazz tradition derived from many sources, which included early twentieth-century all-night dives, like the Rabbit's Foot Saloon,

owned by a white alderman. Early syncopated music featured stringed instruments—fiddles, mandolins, banjos—of the rural and small-town South. In 1901
Ivory "Pop" Williams and Sam Foster introduced New Orleans's horn-style jazz to
the city. An itinerant musician, in the 1890s Williams found work in a local steel
mill and invited his friend and fellow jazz musician Sam Foster to Birmingham. A
multitalented instrumentalist who had played in tent shows and circuses, Williams formed a trio featuring Foster on trumpet that played in black and white
clubs throughout Birmingham for the next thirty years.[113]

Foster introduced Carrie Tuggle to jazz and, in 1905, became the bandmaster
at Tuggle Institute. Known as "High C Foster" because of his ability to play in the
upper register, Foster trained his students to read music and to improvise.[114]
Foster taught John T. Whatley, born in Tuscaloosa, a close boyhood friend of A. G.
Gaston and, later, a teacher of Erskine Hawkins. "High C" also taught his students showmanship. When you play in the upper register, he explained, "Make
them think it's hard for you to do." Foster also taught printing at Tuggle.[115]

John Whatley learned both jazz and printing from Foster. In Birmingham, it
seemed, everyone had an industrial trade. The mills and trains even set the tone
and pace of the city's jazz. J. L. Low, who played saxophone in Birmingham clubs,
described the steel mills that ran around the clock: "Like fire shooting, smoke
belching, giant dragons, the steel mills glowed red."[116] Between 1910 and 1930,
Williams, Foster, and then Whatley played jazz all over town. They played in
North Birmingham, in Ensley at the clubs at the intersection called Tuxedo Junction, at a local amusement park, at frolics, on the Fourth of July and Christmas,
and for the Masons and Elks.[117]

They all taught and gigged. In 1917 Whatley joined the faculty at Industrial
High School where Parker hired him to run the print shop. Fess (for Professor)
Whatley became a one-person jazz school at Industrial, where he turned out
generations of well-trained musicians, an apparent anomaly for such a morally
conscious school. "Whatley bootlegged jazz into the curriculum," explained Dr.
Frank E. "Doc" Adams, the son of Oscar Adams. "He thought it was as important
to play as it was to do math."[118] Principal Parker felt differently. He encouraged
music at Industrial High as long as it was not "ragtime . . . suggestive, and . . .
coarse," a rough description of jazz.[119] Rather, Parker insisted that the school's
children sing the "old Negro songs" at chapel at "least every day."[120]

Quietly, Whatley worked with his young jazz students after hours, or in the
print shop, or on Saturdays. More to Parker's liking, Industrial High also established an enduring tradition of singing in Birmingham. At least monthly, the
entire school turned out for the Community Sing.[121] Sometimes students at "the

Fess Whatley and Industrial High School Band, 1920s (Birmingham Public Library Archives, Cat. #829.1.9)

largest Negro High School in the World" sang "plantation melodies" and at others "lively syncopated songs," accompanied by speeches that commemorated Emancipation Day or Thanksgiving. Industrial High music teachers built a singing tradition that drew in the entire community and taught generations of its students the complexities of four- and eight-part harmony.[122]

Under the direction of choral director Malachi Wilkerson, students at Industrial High sang together all the time. They sang Bach and Rossini as well as "Wade in the Water" and "Lord I Want to Be a Christian." In 1935, on a statewide radio broadcast, the fifteen-hundred-strong student body sang spirituals, such as "Swing Low, Sweet Chariot" and "Standing in the Need of Prayer."[123] As guest artists, popular composer W. C. Handy and William Dawson, composer of the *Negro Folk Symphony* and director of the Tuskegee Choir, performed at Industrial High.[124]

Fess Whatley's jazz classes, however, were Industrial High's most intensively taught courses. Whatley's students included Erskine "The Hawk" Hawkins; Jo Jones, who played drums for Count Basie; Sammy Lowe, a professional saxophone player; and the avant-garde jazz musician Sun-Ra. Whatley formed a preprofessional jazz program at Industrial High School with its own distinct "Birmingham sound." Parker allowed him to direct the school's marching band and ignored the presence of Whatley's "secret" jazz school. Consistent with Industrial High's commitment to uplift and racial pride, Fess taught his students "Whatley's Rules" that advocated love of god, racial uplift, discipline, self-respect, and thrift. Whatley did not allow his students to drink alcohol and insisted that they learn to read music. If a student transgressed, Whatley rapped his knuckles with a stick. Striding around the room, Whatley followed the eyes of his players to make sure that they read from the start of the page. He also enforced "Whatley Time," which required students and band players to arrive early for everything. He sought to form habits that would make his students reliable professional band members.[125]

In 1922 Whatley formed the Jazz Demons, which played across Alabama for the next twenty years. Whatley-trained jazz players could play several instruments, produce complex sounds, knew the stock arrangements of commercial bands, and played all the "scales and proper fingering of notes."[126] By the time Erskine Hawkins arrived at Industrial in the late 1920s, Fess Whatley students were renowned for being able to "read any musical chart or score."[127] Whatley's Rules left little room for improvisation. He wrote out all the solos, and he insisted that his band play exactly what he had written. "They had to learn how to get in and get out."[128] He tolerated the blues and believed that good jazz incorporated the blues. But, for Whatley and his protégé Erskine Hawkins, the sound and the rich sonority of jazz remained primary.[129]

Hawkins's greatness stemmed from his range. He played the saxophone, drums, and trumpet—and baseball. His band-mate, Sammy Lowe, remarked, "We only had two passions, jazz and baseball."[130] Schooled in Whatley's Rules, at Alabama State University Hawkins joined the Alabama State Band.[131] A step removed from the big time, the Alabama State Band functioned for musicians as the industrial baseball league did for ballplayers. Hawkins took over the Alabama State Band and remade it into the Erskine Hawkins Orchestra.[132]

By 1938, with a recording contract and a series of New York gigs, the Erskine Hawkins Orchestra played solid swing jazz. Hawkins perfected the Whatley-Birmingham sound in which he had been trained. His Birmingham jazz combined virtuoso gestures with tight harmony and rhythm. Hawkins's great range on the trumpet led his orchestra in a syncopated, richly harmonic, fully voiced, and precise jazz.[133] His school training taught him how to work with an ensemble. As Lowe remembered, Hawkins would call out the arrangements to fit the

Erskine Hawkins (Birmingham Public Library Archives, Cat. #829.1.52)

tempo, "We always swung, with that rocking beat." And the swing becomes great, Lowe stated, and the jazz extraordinary when "the rhythm is clicking, the sections swinging tightly together, and the soloists are creating ad lib passages right from the heart."[134]

Before going to New York in the late 1930s, Hawkins barnstormed through the

South. He played anywhere and everywhere—dance halls, clubs, joints, lodges, and even beauty pageants and picnics. The personnel of the band, however, remained stable. Sam Lowe (his main arranger) played trumpet; Julian Sash, tenor; Heywood Henry played baritone sax and clarinet; and Avery Parish, the piano. All grew up in Birmingham, and all attended Alabama State or Industrial High. The fourteen-piece band lived, worked, and traveled together in two sec-ondhand Cadillacs. Their favorite gig, however, was at Tuxedo Junction, the name of their most requested song.[135]

At Tuxedo Junction, Twentieth Street and Ensley, the two Birmingham trolley lines crossed. From their company towns to the TCI plant outside of Ensley, black workers jumped off the segregated trams at Tuxedo Junction to change lines. At the crossroads of several roads and trolleys, a two-story building, the Nixon build-ing, attracted commuters and revelers alike. On the ground floor, several taverns took turns sharing the space with a local dentist and a tuxedo rental shop. Up-stairs, the building housed a spacious dance hall. On Friday and Saturday nights, mill workers on their way home from work changed downstairs into their dress clothes and climbed the stairs to hear who was playing. "I'd dine my girl . . . and head for the Tux and dance the night away," one musician remembered.[136] On those nights, "It jumped!"[137]

"Tuxedo Junction" captured the spirit of black Birmingham nightlife in the 1930s. It also epitomized Birmingham's smooth and sophisticated jazz style. "Tuxedo Junction" invited listeners to stamp their feet, to dance.[138] When covered by a white band, "Tuxedo Junction" became one of the most played tunes of World War II. The composition, by Lowe and Hawkins, came about serendipitously. The band had recorded a hit, "Gin Mill Special," and needed a "toe tapper" for the flip side.[139] As Lowe remembered the origins, the tune evolved in 1938–1939 from a riff they played during a warm up and between sets, a soft bluesy chorus that became "Tuxedo Junction." For Lowe, the song conveyed a sense of the real Tuxedo Junction, where "no matter what time it was the trolley cars jammed with workers in blue denims, toting a lunch pail."[140]

"Tuxedo Junction" showcased every aspect of Birmingham swing. It sounded smooth and syncopated, perfect for dancing, and jumping enough to appeal to working-class audiences, who would listen to the song on the juke box in any one of a thousand gin mills and juke joints across the South. Still, it was polished enough to appeal to a New York recording company, RCA. "We made the record-ing in New York," Hawkins told the *Birmingham News* thirty years later, "but our hearts, souls, and spirits were in Birmingham."[141]

"Tuxedo Junction" was the product of the Whatley system of teaching jazz and jazz reading in Birmingham's segregated black schools. Taught in the schools, jazz musicians like Whatley and Hawkins played and wrote a distinctive and lively Saturday night dance music for the black working class of Birmingham. In contrast, "Birmingham Boys," the gospel counterpart to "Tuxedo Junction," came directly out of Birmingham's mills and mines.

BIRMINGHAM HARMONY

Built by black steel workers and coal miners, the Birmingham gospel quartet tradition began in the 1920s. In the 1930s it provided a political voice for black Birmingham workers, who in turn used gospel quartet singing to publicly affirm their collective identity. Derived from 1920s religious and sentimental music, during the Depression Birmingham gospel quartet singing became popular and political. Musically, it formed the foundation for the postwar civil rights movement blending of religion and politics. While black baseball taunted and made fun of "the Man," the gospel quartet challenged the economic and the racial paternalism of the Birmingham System.

The Birmingham Jubilee Singers forged "Birmingham Boys," recorded in 1926, in the mills and mines of the Mineral District. Like jazz, Birmingham gospel quartet music reflected the tight, well-trained harmonic singing taught at Tuggle Institute and Industrial High. It also drew on the spirituals and jubilee singing taught at Fisk University and Tuskegee Institute.[142] Between them, Fisk and Tuskegee trained virtually every music teacher who taught in a black school or directed a black church choir in Alabama, Tennessee, and Mississippi.

The uplifting harmony of the Fisk and Tuskegee spiritual and jubilee singing emotionally bound together the scattered black communities of the lower South. On the surface, it created an image of religiously pious African Americans, at peace with their lot, which southern whites found comforting. In the Mineral District, graduates of Industrial High carried with them to the mining camps, company quarters, and the Sanctified churches of Jones Valley, the refined and inspirational spirituals taught by Malachi Wilkerson and his wife, Julia Wilkerson. Away from middle-class and accommodating Smithfield, these workers drew on black folk music to create a new genre of music, neither genteel nor accommodating, but collectively inspirational.[143]

In small, makeshift, wood-frame sanctuaries, rural blacks in the Mineral District dealt with industrial work in the same way that their ancestors had dealt with slave labor, by summoning the Holy Spirit through prayer, dance, and song. In the company quarters and segregated black neighborhoods of Birmingham, dozens of ministers formed Sanctified Baptist and Pentecostal churches throughout the Mineral District. As an alternative to Sixteenth Street Baptist, these working-class congregations continued the blending of West African spiritualism with Protestant, evangelical Christianity, which had begun in the eighteenth century. The working-class black churches in Birmingham, Bessemer, Fairfield, and other communities in Jones Valley worshiped in storefronts, private homes, vacant lots, or back porches. In 1890 Mount Zion Baptist in Ensley built its church at Tuxedo Junction, just off the intersection at Twentieth and Ensley avenues.[144]

By 1920 the majority of the Mineral District's 115 churches claimed Baptist affiliation. About a dozen, a number that would grow rapidly after World War II, called themselves Pentecostal. Female domestics and male factory and mine workers filled the pews of these Sanctified Baptist and Pentecostal churches. Here workers praised Jesus and ecstatically sang and shouted as they swayed and raised their arms, calling for the Holy Spirit. In the 1920s and 1930s in these working-class churches, a new form of gospel quartet singing originated, distinctive to Birmingham. Gospel quartet singing stressed tight harmony whose lyrics attacked and released. It combined the "pumping bass" taken from foot-pedal-driven, portable Hammond organs, the traditions of shape-note singing, and the precise harmony of Fisk-Tuskegee jubilee singing.[145]

In 1906 John Work, a graduate of Fisk, accepted a teaching position at Tuskegee Institute. The music teachers at Fisk and, after 1906, at Tuskegee stressed discipline, repetition, and practice. They did not require reading music, however. Using the shape-note notation or lining out, music teachers worked with local congregations in a "call and response" mode to introduce the four-part hymn singing. The goal, according to R. C. Foster, Birmingham's first "trainer," was to sing evenly so that you could not "tell who was singing what."[146]

Foster, a deacon at New Zion Baptist Church in Bessemer, came to the district in 1915 from Selma, Alabama. A Tuskegee professor had recommended Foster as the region's first master teacher, or trainer.[147] Such trainers were the musical equivalents of missionaries, and indeed, their goals coincided and reinforced the work of evangelical missionaries. In this case, they were "home missionaries." These grass-roots trainers, in time, formed a corps of "gifted non-academic" teachers who sought to school the musically unschooled in refined and composed jubilee singing. Because most working-class black males and women in the Mineral District did not finish high school, the workplace and the church became the primary homes of gospel quartet singing.[148]

A TCI worker recalled, "We used to be sitting down there in the rail fastening department. I would be working with them, and we'd just go to singing."[149] In the

1920s Gospel quartet groups, some taught and trained by the company, appeared all over the Mineral District. The L & N Singers worked for the Louisville and Nashville Railroad ("4 Trains Daily to Pittsburgh"); the Foster Singers for Woodword's mine and the famous Sterling Jubilee Singers for Bessemer both worked at U.S. Pipe Shop. Quartets performed wherever they could find an audience—in school buildings, churches, lodges, and factories. And like jazz musicians and their cutting contests, they delighted in competing head to head, as audience applause determined the winner. In the 1920s Birmingham's industrial-based groups made Jones Valley the national hotbed of gospel singing.[150]

In the 1930s the movement exploded. During the Depression, the region gave birth to hundreds of gospel quartets, women's and men's groups, amateur and professional. Gospel quartets hewed to the "right way of doing things"—the unadorned and tight harmonic Fisk-Tuskegee style. They also brought to it the blues and jazz played in Tuxedo Junction's dives and dance clubs as well as the exuberant music of Sanctified Christianity. Finally, led by Poterfield Lewis, a local "baser," Birmingham gospel quartets borrowed the pumping organ sound from evangelical choir singing, making the "oompah, oompah," a signature of Birmingham gospel quartet singing for the next fifty years.[151]

The Sterling Jubilee Singers exemplified the Birmingham style. Organized in 1929 in Bessemer and trained by the legendary Charlie Bridges, the Sterling Jubilee singers from U.S. Pipe Shop renamed themselves the CIO Singers in the mid-1930s. They performed at organizing rallies for the Steel Worker's Union, representing themselves as the collective voice of black Birmingham in the Depression.[152]

More than any other quartet, the Birmingham Jubilee Singers mastered the various components of the Birmingham style. Columbia Records sponsored the Jubilee Singers, the first of the Jefferson County Quartets to record, on a national tour accompanied by Ethel Waters. Organized in 1926, when they recorded "Birmingham Boys," the Jubilee Singers featured the shape-note singing, four-part harmony style of unschooled singers. They utilized the blues notes, melisma, falsetto swoops, moans, and syncopation of blues and jazz.[153] Gospel historian Doug Seroff described the Jubilee Singers as a "kind of all-star team" made up of the most talented members of other Birmingham groups.[154]

The Sterling Jubilee Singers' prominence coincided with organizing drives of the American Communist Party and then the Congress of Industrial Organizations (CIO) in the Mineral District. Hosea Hudson, a prominent black communist and labor organizer, was also a gospel quartet singer.[155] Birmingham gospel quartets did not just sing their lyrics, they lived them. Several quartets lived in the quarters at Sloss Mill in North Birmingham. At night, smoke and flame burned yellow and white. There, and in the mines, wearing yellow hard hats, the men sang. And, at "home," in quarters, the women sang, too. The quartets expressed the harsh egalitarianism and forced camaraderie of the Sloss Mill. The four-part (or five- or six-part) harmony, not the solos, expressed the collective feelings of workers and their families in the face of economic hardship and racial oppression. Tom Lacy, who sang in a Birmingham quartet said, "When you are keyed up right nobody's off chord . . . you're all working in a solid chord just like one big voice."[156]

The worker-based gospel quartets ignored the accommodating advice of Smithfield and Red Mountain. The spread of the gospel quartets throughout the Mineral District coincided with the demands of black workers for union representation, federal oversight of working conditions, and the restoration of civil and voting rights. As a quartet, members voted on what songs they sang, where they would sing, when they would sing, and how they would share the money they made. They conducted their musical lives as they wanted Birmingham to conduct its economic and civic lives.[157]

In the cradle of black quartet music, the Blue Jay Singers followed the Jubilee Singers' success in the 1930s by recording its songs, landing a radio show, and touring nationally. Like barnstorming black baseball teams, Birmingham's gospel quartets, such as the Ravizee Singers whose song "He's All and All" remained in the gospel repertoire from 1926 to 1953, bound together southern and northern black communities separated by the Great Migration. Traveling back and forth, from south to north, they flew away to and from black urban communities, like migrating birds. More emotional than the Jubilee Singers, the Blue Jays became a featured quartet in Dallas, Texas, and later with their new name, the Soul Stirrers, they migrated to Chicago where they changed the face of gospel music.[158] The Kings of Harmony traveled the "Gospel Highway" to Cleveland where they helped make the "Forest City" a center of gospel quartet singing. Other quartets traveled to New York, Los Angeles, Atlanta, and New Orleans, making Birmingham Quartet singing, along with Gullah spirituals, Delta Blues, Stride Piano, Texas Blues, and Zydeco, a music of the Great Migration. Claude Jeter, who formed the Four Kings of Harmony in Coalburg, West Virginia, in 1938, had been born in Birmingham in 1914. A coal miner, Jeter, like many others from Alabama, settled in the Upper South before moving all the way to Pittsburgh. When he arrived in Pittsburgh in 1948, he changed the name of the group to the Swan Silvertones. The Swan Silvertones and Jeter brought the gospel quartet sound of the Jones Valley to the steel mills and coal mines of the Monongahela.[159]

The Ravizee Singers (Birmingham Public Library Archives, Cat. #829.1.81)

In April 1916 a train filled to overflowing with black laborers from the Birmingham District pulled into Pittsburgh. Over the next six months, the Pennsylvania Railroad reported that it sold almost five thousand tickets to Birmingham coal miners seeking employment in western Pennsylvania. Birmingham and surrounding Jefferson County became way stations for black labor that left sharecropping for jobs in Birmingham and then caught a train north to Pittsburgh.[160]

In 1916 Alabama claimed a black population of 908,000. From 1917 to 1918, seventy-five thousand, or 8 percent, left the state for the North. The heaviest out-migration came from the agricultural Black Belt counties and Jefferson County and Birmingham. Labor agents, paid by the head by northern steel and coal companies, registered with Birmingham officials and distributed circulars in Birmingham and Bessemer that offered two weeks' pay and transportation. They promised that "all colored ministers can go free" to the promised land where "there are no labor shortages, no strikes, no lockouts; large coal, good wages, and fair treatment."[161]

In February 1917 an agent in Birmingham-Bessemer hired a second train for 191 black workers bound for Pittsburgh. He spent $3,391 for the trip. He "shipped" 4,456 black laborers to Pittsburgh between February and June 1917.[162] Reinforcing the work of migration clubs and echoing the stirring appeals from northern black newspapers, labor agents bragged about daily wages that equaled a week's pay in the South. The allure of a better life found a deep resonance among the black residents of Alabama.

"We are forced to go when one of the things of a grown man wages is only fifty to seventy-five cents per-day for all grades of work," wrote a man from Birmingham to the *Defender* in April 1917. Another sent this message, "I want to come there where I can get work of fairly good wages & educate my children." On April 20 a Birmingham resident wrote that "there is fifteen or twenty familys that wants to come with and we can't phone you here we will be killed they don't want us to leave."[163] Southern white racial attitudes and behaviors, ranging from the imposition of Jim Crow social etiquette to political disenfranchisement, physical violence, and even lynching suddenly found themselves in tension with demand for labor. Fears of reprisals for leaving Alabama echoed through black commu-nities, the labor camps, shotgun houses, and the mill and mine company towns. Still, thousands of blacks boarded the Louisville and Nashville and the Pennsylva-nia Railroads and traveled north to Pittsburgh. In March 1917 a recently arrived migrant wrote home to his Alabama pastor, "I like the money o.k. but I like the South better for my pleasure. This city is too fast for me. . . . It is the largest city I ever saw 45 miles long & equal in breadth & a smoky city . . . some places look like Paradise in this great city." Somewhere, between heaven and hell, Pittsburgh resembled the place they had left.[164]

_⌒_

During the Great Migration, miners and steel workers, laborers and railway work-ers, teachers and ministers, ballplayers, jazz musicians, gospel singers, and quilt-ers all left Birmingham by the thousands. Many, "by the trainload," went to a

Pittsburgh that resembled the Mineral District in so many ways. Workers left Birmingham, Bessemer, Ensley, and Fairfield for work in Pittsburgh's mines and mills because they "wanted a good job." For Charlie Harrell, "There were free trips to Pittsburgh. I grabbed one of them and went."[165] Unfortunately for Harrell, many of the same forces that were reshaping the steel and iron industry in Birmingham were at work in Pittsburgh. In the 1920s, American steel and iron companies introduced new machinery that eliminated many mining and mill jobs. As in Birmingham, Pittsburgh also had more laborers than it had jobs. While Birmingham migrants found work in Pittsburgh, they rarely landed industrial jobs.[166]

No longer labor intensive, by the late 1920s Pittsburgh coal mining and steel milling offered little opportunity for black migrants. Instead, migrants found work in service jobs where they worked as janitors, sanitation workers, bricklayers, carters, jitney-cab drivers, domestics, bartenders, ballplayers, and musicians. More autonomous than blacks in Birmingham, in Pittsburgh working-class and middle-class blacks worked together, less to accommodate the white power structure than to build an independent black community. Along Wiley Avenue in Pittsburgh's Hill District, the Great Migration claimed its social and cultural autonomy. The city's black middle class, its Old Settlers, acculturated southern migrants to urban life. But there, as in Birmingham, Pittsburgh's middle class could not extinguish the flashes of the West African spirit that black rural southerners brought north.

BLUES PIANOS AND TRICKY BASEBALLS

• 5 •

Pittsburgh

In 1849, when John Turfley arrived in Pittsburgh, he joined a small African American community comprising northern-born free blacks and runaway slaves. Many had traveled the Underground Railroad, and most settled along Wylie Avenue, which dominated the largely black "Hill District" that rose up from the river district. Dotted by frame houses and small farms, Wylie Avenue defined what Pittsburghers then called "Little Hayti." Here, the Hill District or simply the Hill fostered a vibrant African American community for the next hundred years.

Wylie Avenue climbed steeply, away from the warehouses, saloons, and shipping agencies that occupied the site of old Fort Pitt at the junction of the Allegheny and Monongahela Rivers. By 1849 downtown Pittsburgh, breathing "smoke and fire," had attracted a working class of Irish and Jewish immigrants. Along with the newly arrived African Americans, they worked as carters, teamsters, and laborers. Pittsburgh's immigrants settled along the nearby slopes of Little Hayti, which was called the "Lower Hill."[1]

The Hill District stood above downtown Pittsburgh and extended to a bluff that overlooked the middle-class community of Oakland to the east. The Hill's main streets, Center Avenue, a block south and below Wylie, and Bedford, several blocks north and above Wylie, rose and fell with the ridges and valleys of the Hill District. From the center of Little Hayti, the city fell away in all directions. Facing downtown, toward the west, the early residents of the Hill could see in a single glance the jumble of wood framed buildings in the downtown and the two rivers, the Monongahela to the south and Allegheny to the north, that carved the region into its distinctive pockets of residence and manufacture.

From their enclave on the Hill, black Old Pittsburghers, the heirs of John

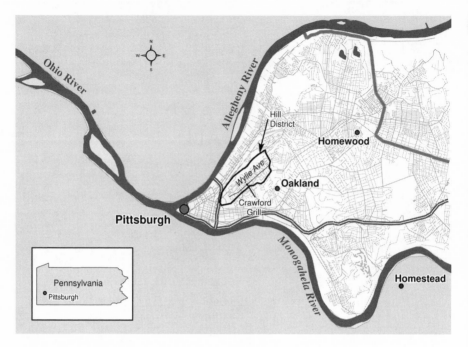

Pittsburgh Mineral District

Turfley, embraced the values of hard work, responsibility, self-help, and racial improvement—values that they would inculcate in the southern black migrants who arrived in Pittsburgh by the thousands between 1916 and 1950. The five male grandchildren of John Turfley, all named Dorsey, became legendary black athletes in pre–World War I Pittsburgh; each played on one of the dozens of amateur, semiprofessional, and industrial teams that flourished in early twentieth-century Pittsburgh.[2]

A small African American, or "colored," middle class dominated the Hill community that John Turfley adopted. Martin Robinson Delaney, identified as the grandson of a "Gullah African," studied medicine and founded an abolitionist paper, the *Mystery*, in 1843. His contemporary, John Vashon, had come west to Pittsburgh in 1829 from Carlisle, Pennsylvania. In Carlisle, Vashon had operated a livery stable and saloon, but in Pittsburgh he opened a downtown barbershop and joined Delaney's antislavery causes. His son, George Bogar Vashon, attended Oberlin College, read law, and, when Pennsylvania denied him admission to the bar, secured admission to the New York State bar. Along with his wife Susan, Vashon taught at a private school for Negro children, the only school available to African Americans until the integration of the city's public education in 1874.[3]

Owen A. Barrett joined Delaney and Vashon, along with Turfley, and formed the black elite of Old Pittsburghers. Barrett owned the drugstore that became a Hill landmark known as Goode's in the 1920s and 1930s. He had officially named his pharmacy after the previous owner, "B. A. Fahnestock's Celebrated Vermifuge."[4]

The small black elite presided over a new generation of African Americans who arrived in Pittsburgh after the Civil War. Often migrating from the Upper South, the new migrants settled in the Third and Fifth wards of the Hill, establishing an African American residential pattern that survived until the Depression. Many blacks, from Virginia and especially from Richmond and the Shenandoah Valley, settled in several other neighborhoods—Homewood-Brushton, Homestead, and the Northside. Before 1920, African Americans composed less than 50 percent of the population in any single district in the city.[5] Living side by side with Italian, Irish, and Jewish immigrants and later Poles, Czechs, and Hungarians, Pittsburgh's late nineteenth-century black residents lived in integrated neighborhoods, sharing much of their public lives with whites.

In the first southern, black migration to Pittsburgh, the city's African American population grew from about 2,000 in 1870 to more than 20,000 in 1900. The overall population of Pittsburgh grew at the same rate, from 50,000 to 450,000. Fueled by unprecedented growth in iron, steel, coal, and railroad building, the discovery of oil in Western Pennsylvania, and the emergence of banking, in a single generation Pittsburgh became a modern industrial colossus.

By 1900 Pittsburgh supplied almost half the nation's open hearth steel and coke. Carnegie Steel, alone, employed more than twenty-five thousand workers. The city served as home to Gulf Oil, owned by the Mellon family, the electrical empire of George Westinghouse, Pittsburgh Plate Glass, and pickle magnate H. J. Heinz. By 1906 Pittsburgh rivaled Chicago as a commercial center and became the sixth largest, and the dirtiest, city in the nation.[6] At the turn of the century, when an average industrial white worker earned five dollars a week, Andrew Carnegie earned approximately twenty-five million untaxed dollars. Only 1 percent of Pittsburgh's black population gained middle-class status. The city, which Lincoln Steffens described as bathed in "volcanic light upon the cloud of mist and smoke," before World War I drew a wave of blacks to work in its lowest-paid jobs, where they lived along winding streets, steep hills, and canyons.[7]

In 1902 Robert L. Vann, a twenty-two-year-old North Carolinian arrived in Pittsburgh by train. Vann had worked as a teamster in North Carolina, then as a waiter at a resort hotel in Boston, and attended Virginia Union University. These experiences taught him the virtues of self-improvement, hard work, and racial uplift that Booker T. Washington espoused. Nothing, however, prepared Vann for

Street parade on the Hill, 1940s (Charles "Teenie" Harris, American, 1908–1998; black and white Agfa safety film; 4 × 5 in.; Carnegie Museum of Art, Pittsburgh, Heinz Family Fund; copyright © 2004 Carnegie Museum of Art, Charles "Teenie" Harris Archive; photograph © 2007 Carnegie Museum of Art, Pittsburgh)

the "booming steel industry that filled the hillsides . . . with fiery coke ovens, multi-ton Bessemer converters and huge open-hearth furnaces which glowed day and night."[8]

Vann's light complexion, dark flowing hair, and college degree gave him access to the social world of Pittsburgh's African American Old Pittsburghers. Old Pittsburghers, many from Virginia and Maryland and often light-skinned and educated, formed a self-conscious society of private cotillions, garden parties, summer hayrides, and exclusive musical and literary clubs. They spent much of their time together at resorts, and some of the males indulged in the racy sporting life of the Lower Hill. At Frank Sutton's Hotel on Sixth and Wylie, Old Pittsburghers gambled alongside white crapshooters and card players, rubbed elbows with famed boxing champion Jack Johnson who held court at the hotel, and dined with the famous black minstrel-actor Bert Williams.[9]

In 1901 Old Pittsburghers founded the all-male Loendi Club, named after an African lake. "Bedecked with rich carpets, fine tapestries, and beautiful pictures," the Loendi Club provided the city's middle-class African Americans the trappings of Victorian refinement and elegance. The Loendi Club had purchased a building on the Upper Hill, near the intersection of Wylie and Fullerton for $10,000.[10] In 1894 Old Pittsburgher women had earlier established the Aurora Reading Club as a center for charity work.[11] In Homestead, the local black elite, led by Anna Posey, the wife of entrepreneur Cumberland Posey, formed a Social and Literary Club. Vann used his Old Pittsburgher connections to gain admission to the Western University of Pennsylvania Law School. He also worked as a Pennsylvania Railroad dining-car waiter and, in 1908, secured a clerk's job with the city.[12]

As one of only five black lawyers in Pittsburgh in 1910, Vann contributed poems to a fledgling newsletter for Pittsburgh's black community. Started by Edwin Harleson and other employees at the Heinz Company, the *Courier*, named after the *News and Courier* in Harleson's hometown of Charleston, South Carolina, published its first four-page edition in 1910.[13] That same year Vann recruited investors for the paper and, along with "Captain" Cumberland Willis Posey, became an officer of the *Courier* and its voice. He served as editor, treasurer, and legal counsel for the paper for the next thirty years. Posey, one of the most prosperous and powerful African Americans in the Pittsburgh region was already a dominant figure in Homestead. Born in Cumberland, Maryland, in 1858, Posey moved to Homestead in 1892 from Ohio where he had worked as a river pilot. There, he bought several coal barges and founded a shipbuilding company.[14]

The Poseys lived in a gracious, wood-frame house on 13th Street in Homestead that looked down on the library that Andrew Carnegie built for the community. Posey served on the Homestead school board, speculated on real estate, directed a local bank, participated in the town's African American upper-class cultural activities, and owned the largest black business in the Pittsburgh district, the Diamond Coke and Coal Company. He built his coke and coal company with the money and credit he had earned with his barge and ship company. Posey's fortune gave him access to the Old Pittsburgh Loendi Club. His son, Cumberland Willis Posey Jr., born in 1891, attended Holy Ghost (Duquesne) University and Penn State. "Cum" Posey became a legendary basketball star, and in 1911 he joined a local baseball team called the Murdock Grays.[15]

The Grays had begun at the turn of the twentieth century as a team composed of black and a few white millworkers. The team became all black by 1910. "Cum" Posey, along with his brother Seward and the famed Dorsey brothers, had played both football and basketball on two all-black teams, the Monticellos and the Collins Tigers, before he joined the Grays.[16] In 1916 the twenty-five year-old Posey took over as the Gray's booking agent and then became team manager of the renamed Homestead Grays. He did not pay his players salaries until the early 1920s when the Grays earned the reputation as one of the best black semiprofessional teams in the country. Between 1911 and 1925, the Posey-men, as the *Homestead Daily Messenger* called them, were an extension of Old Pittsburgh with Posey as the most successful sports entrepreneur in the region.[17]

Homestead was a microcosm of Pittsburgh's African American community. Born of industrial expansion, the steel town, an extension of Carnegie's Homestead Works at the river's edge, reached up the steep hillside that overlooked the mill. In 1879 the village of Homestead boasted a population of 302. By 1900 the Homestead Works employed more than twelve thousand workers. The *Pittsburgh Survey* labeled Homestead a "town of saloons."[18] Divided by class and race, Homestead had two main streets, Eighth, where European-born workers could drink at fifty taverns within walking distance of the Homestead Works, and Sixth, which served as the town's Wylie Avenue.

Along Sixth, the commercial center of "the Ward," black workers availed themselves of a string of saloons and brothels, pawnshops and pool halls.[19] Black workers had arrived in Homestead in the 1890s as strikebreakers. After the strike they accepted jobs as nonunion workers in skilled positions at the works. Skilled workers, like Posey, lived up along the wooded hillside, at "Hilltop." Their lofty perch distinguished them from the majority of Homestead's African Americans, who worked as domestics and manual laborers and lived down in "the Ward."

The black families who lived on the Hilltop attended Clark Memorial AME church, founded in the early 1890s. They used the church to welcome newcomers into Homestead and, in the 1920s, U.S. Steel donated money for a new Clark Memorial Church. The church supported a range of social and educational activities that instructed the congregation with appropriate behavior. Alongside its Sunday school, the church sponsored classes in responsible finances and cautioned its parishioners to beware of the gamblers, loan sharks, and whores that "infested" the streets of the Ward.[20]

In 1906 in the Ward, Homestead's black working class founded a church in a blacksmith shop but moved it to a storefront on Sixth Street, where it became the Second Baptist Church.[21] Its first pastor, J. D. Horton, worked in the mill, and the church offered black working-class migrants southern religion in contrast to the upper-class Victorian ways of Clark Memorial.[22] Many southern-born workers believed that Clark Memorial discriminated against dark-skinned worshipers. They chose, instead, Second Baptist and storefront Pentecostal churches.[23]

In the first decade of the twentieth century only a few working-class African Americans in Homestead rose through the ranks of the Homestead Works. In 1907, 17 percent of the blacks who worked in the Homestead steel mill held skilled positions. Observers attributed this statistical success to the belief of the foremen of the "shape up" crews that English-speaking workers were easier to manage.[24] Many black migrants to the Pittsburgh district "leapfrogged" from the countryside to urban industrial centers where white unions had excluded them. Many Pittsburgh migrants who came from Birmingham had previously worked extensively on farms with draft animals or on southern railroad crews.

The short-lived period of modest success enhanced the influence of Old Pittsburghers. The values of hard work, racial uplift, and decorum, endorsed by the *Courier*, middle-class churches, and the private men's and women's clubs, seemed to have benefited the men and women who migrated to Pittsburgh between 1880 and 1910. Old Pittsburghers took it as their mission to instruct the majority of African Americans who labored in the mills and the mines, worked as porters and teamsters, as puddlers and carpenters, and as barbers, beauticians, janitors, cooks, laundresses, and servants.

The cultural dominance of Old Pittsburghers expressed itself in the sacred and secular music of black Pittsburgh. The WPA *History of the Negro in Pittsburgh* portrayed the years between 1890 and 1910 as the "golden age" of church music in the city. A community, which had begun with two black Methodist churches on the Hill in 1850, had grown to more than twenty churches in 1920, the majority Baptist.[25] AME Choir masters provided formal musical training to their congregations. A reporter described the St. James AME Church service, "The members are all naturally musical, but almost all studied music and are rapid sight readers."[26] Many who sang in the church choirs also formed secular quartets, quintets, and sextets that performed European art music. Groups like the Black Swan, the Ladies Four in Hand, and the Lindsay Quartet gave concerts throughout the region. The Lindsay Quartet, named after Colonel Lindsay of Carnegie Steel, who donated instruments and uniforms, first performed in honor of Charles Schwab, the president of U.S. Steel.[27] When famed singer Marian Anderson came to Pittsburgh in 1920, her recital of European art songs won standing ovations.[28]

Divided by geography and scattered among immigrant working-class communities, Pittsburgh's twenty-five thousand African Americans lived in several inter-related communities. Pioneers like the Turfley-Dorsey clan, professionals like Posey and Vann, and a handful of skilled iron and steel workers lived on the heights of the Hill and Homestead, above the mass of black working men and women who lived below them. The tenfold increase in African Americans in the city from 1900 to 1910 derived from the migration of workers from the South—iron puddlers from Richmond, skilled steel workers and miners from Birmingham, independent business owners, barbers, railway porters, teamsters, plasterers, masons, and carpenters, as well as service workers who catered to wealthy whites as janitors, waiters, maids, and later elevator operators and shipping clerks.[29] In these years, U.S. Steel employed only 507 blacks out of a total of 25,000 steel workers.[30]

Many in the service class lived on the Lower Hill within walking distance of the heart of the city. The Hill housed several clusters of African Americans before World War I. Along Fullerton, Wylie, Clark, and Center avenues, blacks lived interspersed with foreign-born whites.[31] Few of Pittsburgh's African Americans who arrived before the Great Migration hailed from the Lower South. Most came from the upper tier of southern states—North Carolina, Virginia, Maryland, West Virginia, Kentucky, and Tennessee. They endured the humiliations of white Pittsburgh when waiters salted their coffee in downtown restaurants, nickelodeon parlors charged them double the price they charged whites, hotels insisted that they use the freight elevator, and white-dominated unions refused them membership.[32] Undaunted, southern migrants followed the advice of the black elite. They worked hard and minded their manners. Many blacks in Pittsburgh sought to expand their access to public schools and parks and to improve "the race" in the places allotted to them. Instructed by the Old Pittsburgh elite, African Americans formed churches and neighborhood centers, ball teams and music schools, choral and fraternal groups, men's and women's reading and social groups, and bands and orchestras that promoted racial pride and social uplift. On the eve of World War I, black Pittsburgh was a precocious and exemplary new Negro community.

GET YOUR LETTER FROM HOME

"Things became awful," recalled "Big Jim" Dorsey, "loud and wrong Negroes came bounding into Pittsburgh. They had switchblades, loud tempers, and very quickly the white population began restricting Negro privileges in the city by closing doors that had always been open to us."[33] Between 1910 and 1920, the black population of Pittsburgh jumped from 26,000 to 38,000. Most of the increase occurred during World War I. The region's satellite cities of Braddock, Rankin, and Homestead more than doubled their African American population. By 1930, 55,000 blacks called Pittsburgh home, giving the city the sixth-largest black population in the nation. In 1930, 78,000 African Americans lived in the Western Pennsylvania District.[34] Statistics do not account for the ebbs and flows of the black migration to Pittsburgh. The census data underestimated the number of blacks who traveled north. Of the 25,000 blacks who lived in Pittsburgh in 1910, as many as half had moved away, back to the coal fields of West Virginia or to the farms of Georgia and Alabama. Altogether, 25,000 new black migrants arrived in Pittsburgh from 1916 to 1919.[35]

Pittsburgh's black population rose from 37,500 in 1920 to 62,200 in 1940. In these two decades, the city's African American population grew more rapidly than the city's overall increase. Two spurts of unemployment in the 1920s were followed by the decade-long Great Depression, when only 50 percent of Pittsburgh's black male population found employment. By 1930 the city had become home to a large, impoverished, and unskilled black working class, many of whom were migrants from Birmingham.

A study of black migrants to Pittsburgh, completed in 1917 and based on a sample of five hundred questionnaires, showed a cross section of the Great Migration from Alabama to Pittsburgh. Compiled by Abraham Epstein and entitled *The Negro Migrant in Pittsburgh*, the study documented that migrants from Alabama outnumbered all the other migrants from the next three largest states of origin—Georgia, North Carolina, and Florida.[36] A young woman interviewed by the Urban League, Jonnie F, had moved from Montgomery, Alabama, to Birmingham, where she worked as a domestic before migrating to Pittsburgh. She told her interviewer that she could lift a "hundred pound ... just like my brother."[37] The vast majority of Alabamians came as young and single men, many hoping to return south. Yet many found in their new city a kind of "Birmingham of the North," where patterns of geography, residence, and employment were familiar. A significant proportion of Pittsburgh's new migrants had worked in skilled and semiskilled jobs in Birmingham's mills and mines. In Pittsburgh, employers reclassified them as "common laborers" just as had happened in Birmingham.[38]

At the Carnegie, Westinghouse, and Jones and Laughlin mills, black workers initially found jobs. Their numbers increased from 25 in 1916 to 900 in 1918 at Westinghouse and from 1,500 to 4,000 at Carnegie and Jones and Laughlin over the same two years. Pittsburgh's mills and factories classified between 90 and 100 percent of their black workers as unskilled and paid them accordingly.[39] The initial burst of southern migrants overwhelmed Pittsburgh. Employers and social services alike crowded new workers into boardinghouses on the Hill where they shared beds on "double shifts." Employers leased warehouses and filled them with double bunk beds, industrial army barracks for the transient young men who slept in shifts two or three to a bed. The Urban League, whose staff helped find work for 1,094 migrants in 1917, reported that one steel mill connected several boxcars along its rail siding, cut slit windows for ventilation, and added a makeshift stairway to create an "instant dormitory."[40] In the mining camps in satellite cities of Braddock, Duquesne, and McKeesport black workers lived in company bunkhouses comparable to those in Ensley, Fairfield, and Bessemer. In Homestead, new arrivals found rooms as lodgers in the Ward. On the Hill in 1920, a third of the residences listed one or more male lodgers living in rooms.[41]

The expansion of black Pittsburgh's workforce led to the bitter and unsuccessful steel strike of 1919. Union leaders turned their backs on black workers. When the 25,000 area steel workers struck, only two dozen African Americans joined. Owners kept the mills operating by importing black strikebreakers.[42] A black man from Alabama recalled, "All we knew we was getting a job. . . I wanted to work. I didn't know what the strike was all about."[43] The Pyrrhic victory for the steel mills ushered in a decade-long period of rapid growth followed by contraction. Recessions in 1921 and again in 1923 resulted in mass layoffs for black steel workers. Of the 17,222 blacks employed in seven major industries in 1923, only 7,636 retained their jobs a year later.[44] The pattern repeated itself in the coal mines, where African Americans found themselves reclassified into unskilled jobs, assigned by the union to jobs that whites refused, and then brought into the mines by the owners during a strike in mid-decade as scabs.[45]

By mid-decade, African American migrants to Pittsburgh constituted a massive, mostly unskilled, urban working class. Their daily lives suffered from the spikes in unemployment, racial hostility, and discrimination. When employment slackened in the mills and mines, many African Americans remained in the city shifting from industrial to domestic and service work as teamsters and sanitation workers and in construction. On the Hill, especially the Third Ward of the Lower Hill, new patterns of racial demography emerged. As early as 1910, black residents on the Hill, composed 21 percent of the population. Twenty years later, the Hill was 45 percent black. By the late 1920s, two of the census tracts in the Lower Hill had become more than 80 percent black. Older white residents moved away from the Lower Hill in the 1920s as did well-to-do African Americans, who relocated either to the Fifth Ward, to Sugar Top on the eastern heights, to Beltzhoover on the Northside, or to Homewood-Brushton. Homewood-Brushton, just beyond East Liberty, where middle-class African Americans maintained the "genteel tradition," saw its black population climb from 310 in 1910 to more than 4,000 in 1930.[46]

The Hill's shops and clubs, meeting halls and taverns, pool halls and groceries, churches and parks attracted African Americans from across Pittsburgh. Wylie Avenue, which ran down the spine of the Hill, became the commercial and entertainment gathering point for all black Pittsburghers. This occurred even as the proportion of black-owned small businesses declined with the departure of middle- and upper-class blacks to Homewood.[47] On the eve of the Depression, the Hill had become a poor, black, urban neighborhood. Social workers labeled its housing as "slums" and described it as "over-crowded" and "unfit."

> Narrow streets are lined with tawdry houses, dingy red, their scarred doorways and tottering porches often reached by crumbling wooden steps. . . . The Hill is a district of small businesses trying to prosper—dingy pool rooms, the yellow-fronted Big 4 Barbershop or the Garish green Cold Turkey Barbershop; red-fronted variety stores; smudgy ill-smelling restaurants—Tom's Lunch, Mother's Lunch, Southern Bar-B-Q, Lucky Chop Suey, Rosas Beauty Salon, or the Paradise Shoe Shine.[48]

Yet, to some, the Hill remained Pittsburgh's Harlem, a neighborhood that "spoke the language of jazz." It catered to southern immigrants with dream books, folk remedies, policy rackets, and voodoo fixes that existed side by side with the Loendi Club and the Wylie Avenue Literary Society. On the Hill, where rent parties and wine rooms flourished upstairs and a dozen bars jumped all Saturday night downstairs, vendors strolled the streets each evening selling their wares, whether pies, coal, ice, or watermelons that they hawked as "Red to the Rind! Red to the Rind! Get Your Letter from Home!"[49]

By 1930 the Hill was still home to twenty-five thousand African Americans, but the jobs promised by the steel and coal industries had disappeared. During the Depression, unemployment reduced many to subsistence and made return to the South impossible. The hostility that migrants faced spoke with two distinct voices—white racism and black classism. White racism kept southern African Americans out of unions, neighborhoods, hospitals, swimming pools, hotels, restaurants, and restricted them in movie theaters, ballparks, playgrounds, and music halls. Old Pittsburghers' class prejudice, at once benign and patronizing, looked down at them as "boll weevil" Negroes, with "cotton in their hair." Old Pittsburghers wanted the migrants to lower their voices, work hard, and improve the race.

GET YOUR MONEY IN THE FOURTH INNING

In the early 1920s Jim Dorsey worked with other Old Pittsburghers and social workers to refine the behavior of southern migrants. The city government, the Urban League, the YMCA, and the Westinghouse and Edgar Thompson mills hired Old Pittsburghers as "Negro welfare workers" to settle the migrants.[50]

These light-skinned, college-educated men and women helped migrants find jobs, obtain an education, and locate decent housing. The Urban League hired Grace Loundes, a social worker, to oversee a "morals court" to deal with immigrant problems—prostitution, abuse, and abandonment.[51] The Urban League praised Loundes as "a beautiful woman from South Carolina who had found her way into the 400—the crème de la crème of Pittsburgh Negro society." Loundes replaced her "Geechee" dialect with "cultural standard English" and moved from Schenley Heights, at the far eastern edge of the Hill, to work at the Morals Court.

Robert Earl Johnson, who worked at the mile-long Edgar Thomson–U.S. Steel mill in Braddock, was born in Virginia and graduated from Morgan State University in Maryland. A nationally famed distance runner and an Olympian in 1920 and 1924, Johnson had worked as a mathematics tutor at the YMCA between 1916 and 1919.[52] Johnson belonged to the Loendi Club and Omega Psi Phi, worshiped at an AME church, and voted as a registered Republican. In national track meets, he wore Edgar Thompson's colors and coached the mill's black track squad as well as its industrial baseball team.[53] In 1922 Johnson took his ball team into a semipro Negro baseball league that featured a rival team from Westinghouse. Johnson entered his team in the Greater Pittsburgh League, recruited good college players from schools like Wilberforce, and sent his best to the Homestead Grays. The *Courier* called Johnson "the Edgar Thompson Marvel" and lauded his Olympic bronze medal as the "biggest surprise of the 1924 Olympics."[54] Johnson's prominence tied him closely with Posey and Dorsey and gave the Grays access to his best players.[55]

Five years earlier, in October 1917, Westinghouse opened courses in its technical night school to "colored men." While the company featured black-faced comedians at its plant banquet in 1921, Westinghouse inaugurated a "colored" employees association, WEMCO.[56] In 1922 WEMCO's black baseball team featured Harold Tinker, a shortstop from Birmingham, Alabama. Pittsburgh's black industrial baseball league was only a small part of organized black baseball in Pittsburgh, which was dominated by Cumberland Posey's Homestead Grays.[57]

Posey, a close friend of both Dorsey and Johnson, booked games against white industrial teams in the early years of the decade. For a time, he also played left field and batted leadoff for the Grays.[58] In the 1920s there was money to be made, and Posey converted the Grays from a local semipro team into a national power. As Posey told one of his pitchers, "Get your money in the fourth inning. Don't throw another ball."[59]

Other regional teams competed with the Grays. The best of the black industrial teams no longer relied on local talent to fill their rosters. At a time when African

Spectators at baseball game, Forbes Field (ca. 1945–1950; Charles "Teenie" Harris, American, 1908–1998; black and white Ansco safety film; 4 × 5 in.; Carnegie Museum of Art, Pittsburgh, Heinz Family Fund; copyright © 2004 Carnegie Museum of Art, Charles "Teenie" Harris Archive; photograph © 2007 Carnegie Museum of Art, Pittsburgh)

American employment in the steel mills and other heavy industry plummeted, black ball players found themselves in demand. Some, like Frank Moody, who played for the Carnegie–Illinois Steel team in the U.S. Steel League, were hired just to play ball. "They didn't like to do it openly," he recalled.[60] The industrial teams recruited others for the summer months only and assigned them easy jobs so they could play ball games in the late afternoon. Harold Tinker and his friend Charlie Hughes went from Westinghouse to the professional Crawfords. They "just took us. Took us with them," he recalled.[61]

Between 1925 and 1930, Posey built the Grays into the best Negro team in the country. He announced his intention do so in the middle of the 1925 season when he signed the legendary pitcher "Smokey Joe" Williams. Between forty-three and fifty years old at the time, the Louisiana-born Williams had pitched Negro baseball for a quarter century. Tall, part American Indian, and canny, Williams threw a

Baseball game, scoring at Greenlee Field (ca. 1935; Charles "Teenie" Harris, American, 1908–1998; black and white Agfa safety film; 4 × 5 in.; Carnegie Museum of Art, Pittsburgh, Heinz Family Fund; copyright © 2004 Carnegie Museum of Art, Charles "Teenie" Harris Archive; photograph © 2007 Carnegie Museum of Art, Pittsburgh)

fastball that "seemed to be coming off a mountain top."[62] Williams joined a Grays' pitching staff that included two Negro League players already on salary, a player from the New York Lincoln Giants and spitball specialist Sam "Lefty" Streeter from the Birmingham Black Barons.[63]

In 1926 the team won more than one hundred games. This spurred Posey to add a group of Negro League all-star players to the Grays. He signed future Hall of Famers "Cool Papa" Bell, Judy Johnson, Willie Foster, and Martin Dihigo. When the Grays also signed Oscar Charleston, it became one of the best teams of the era—black or white. Charleston, a tough, no-nonsense man, had played ball with Buffalo Soldiers of the Twenty-fourth Infantry in Manila. His teammates said that he was so strong he could open the seams of a baseball with his bare hands. He sometimes played all nine positions in a single game and was so athletic that he could charge a ball hit to center field, complete a flip, and still catch the ball.[64] Charleston's showboating style, perfected under the tutelage of his mentor, Negro

League founder Rube Foster, hid a more intense psychological strategy—to show up and intimidate the other team. Even as an elder statesman of Negro baseball, Charleston "played in the southern style" with verve and panache.[65]

With his array of stellar players, Posey scheduled more and more games against teams in the established Negro Leagues. The Grays joined the Negro American League in 1928, but when the Depression killed off organized black baseball, Posey returned the Grays to independent status. He saved the team by restoring a policy of playing all challengers. He could not accomplish this without an infusion of cash, and like so many Negro League owners, Posey turned to a local gambler for support. Rufus "Sonnyman" Johnson was the numbers "banker" in Homestead.[66] Johnson owned the Sky Rocket nightclub and operated the jukebox rental business for the entire Pittsburgh area. Johnson's silent partnership saved the Grays and allowed Posey to recruit the best players available. Thanks to Johnson, in 1930 the Grays owned two spanking-new Buicks and drove to games in style.[67]

IN THE JOINTS, CRAWFORD'S ROOTERS

Johnson's presence coincided with the rise of the Pittsburgh Crawfords, a team that challenged the Grays for dominance in the Negro League. Like the Grays, the upstart Crawfords traced its origins to a time when Pittsburgh's racial boundaries were vague.[68] Even so, by the early 1920s, the Hill's expanding black population needed a larger center. The building of a second recreational facility on the Hill, the Crawford Bathhouse, at the intersection of Crawford and Wylie Avenues, raised the issue of racial separation. The Crawford Bathhouse functioned as both a recreational facility and a settlement house. It offered adult classes and a kindergarten in addition to a swimming pool. City park supervisors asked Jim Dorsey to take charge of the new facility. The *Courier* reported that Dorsey was also instructed to "hire a Third Ward black politician as janitor.[69] The following summer, one of Pittsburgh's two African American papers, the *American*, reported a new sign posted on the Crawford Bathhouse wall—"This House is open for bathing purposes to the Negro citizens of Pittsburgh."[70] The *American* accused the city of "shunting Negroes off" to Washington Park even as it barred blacks from other swimming pools in the city.[71] At the same time, the YMCA of Pittsburgh, under pressure from Pittsburgh's other black newspaper, the *Courier*, successfully pressed for a separate all-black Y on Center Avenue. By 1923 the Hill supported two new institutions—the Center Avenue Y and the Crawford Bathhouse. The Old Pittsburgh elite hoped these facilities would ease migrants' adjustment to urban life and separate them from whites. The combination of city patronage and black middle-class support built the two institutions that defined and segregated the Hill for the next generation.[72]

In 1926 the Crawford Bathhouse organized a ragtag neighborhood sandlot baseball team called the Crawford Recreation Team, the Crawford Bathhouse Team, or the Crawford Colored Giants. Most often they were simply called the Crawfords.[73] It took years before the Pittsburgh Crawfords, a team of black, migrant, and working-class Pittsburgh, challenged the powerful Homestead Grays for local and then national dominance. Crawford games at Ammon Field, on Bedford Avenue at the top of the Hill, began at three or six o'clock. When a crowd gathered, the bleachers filled to overflowing. On a June day in 1930, in front of a crowd estimated at more than five thousand, a young Crawfords' catcher named Josh Gibson smacked four hits.[74]

As a local semipro team before 1930, the Crawfords survived from week to week passing the hat among its fans. As the darlings of the Hill, the Crawfords clamored for a confrontation with the Grays. "Hell, you had more games played on the corner," recalled Clarence Clark, "You had your Grays rooters and in the joints Crawford rooters."[75] Then, during the 1930 off-season, the Crawfords changed hands. Bar owner, politico, and boxing aficionado Gus "Big Red" Greenlee said, "I'll write a check." He became the owner.[76] Within two years, Greenlee built the Crawfords into the best in Negro League baseball.

Greenlee, a college graduate and veteran of World War I, possessed the credentials necessary for membership in the Old Pittsburgh elite, except he was a southern migrant. He came to the city by hopping a freight in 1916. He worked in the mills and fought in France before he returned to Pittsburgh 1920. During the 1920s, Greenlee bought several restaurants and clubs, moved his residence to the affluent Homewood neighborhood, and assumed control of the numbers racket on the north side. A cigar in his jaws and standing six foot three inches, the imposing Greenlee made the Crawford Grill, at Wylie Avenue and Townsend, into his headquarters.[77]

Greenlee's Crawford Grill served as a fashionable gathering place for Pittsburgh's black elite. When the Grill featured a known jazz band, patrons dressed to the nines, dining in front of murals of the Caribbean. Duke Ellington, Louis Armstrong, and Joe Louis all played or held court at the Crawford Grill. During game day, the Crawford ball players dressed for their Ammon field home games downstairs. They stashed their street clothes near the cash registers and counting tables. Occasionally, Greenlee hired his players to stand outside the club as lookouts, affecting nonchalance.[78]

Crawford Grill, the best jazz spot on the Hill (ca. 1950; Charles "Teenie" Harris, American, 1908–1998; black and white Kodak safety film; 4 × 5 in.; Carnegie Museum of Art, Pittsburgh, Heinz Family Fund; copyright © 2004 Carnegie Museum of Art, Charles "Teenie" Harris Archive; photograph © 2007 Carnegie Museum of Art, Pittsburgh)

In only two years, Greenlee moved the Crawfords into the first rank of black baseball teams. Wealthy during the Depression, Greenlee spent his money without apparent regard to outcome. By 1932 he had added Oscar Charleston, Judy Johnson, "Cool Papa" Bell, Jimmy Crutchfield, Ted "Double Duty" Radcliff, and Josh Gibson to the Crawford roster. Most came from the Grays, including Gibson, who played for the Crawfords in 1931. Greenlee's crowning achievement came with the acquisition of future Hall of Fame pitcher and showman Satchel Paige, whom he acquired from the Birmingham Black Barons in 1931. All told, the Crawfords signed three other Black Barons to the team, giving them a distinctly Birmingham flavor.

In 1932 Greenlee shelled out an estimated $100,000 to build his own ballpark, Greenlee Field, a few blocks up Bedford Avenue from Ammon Field. He added lights the next year and also organized the Negro League's annual East-West all-star game in Chicago. One observer remarked that he built his own field because Greenlee "wouldn't use a white man's field if he didn't have to." At the segregated Forbes Field, the National League Pirates did not allow the Grays to change in the clubhouse. Instead, they dressed at the nearby Center Avenue Y.[79]

Over the next five years, the Crawfords dominated black baseball. Then, as suddenly as the team had risen, the Crawfords collapsed. Greenlee's fortune, dependent on police protection, vanished in the wake of citywide political re-form.[80] Without the numbers, Greenlee could not support his team. In 1938 Greenlee demolished his ballpark. Most of the Crawford star players, including Gibson and Paige, resigned with the Grays. In 1939 Greenlee gave up his position as president of the Negro National League that he had helped form in 1933.[81] The Grays returned to their previous glory, winning pennants regularly until the integration of baseball in 1947.

The development of black baseball in Pittsburgh did not overcome the inher-ent class tension between the city's black elite and its migrant working class. By playing at Oakland's Forbes Field, the Grays accommodated itself to an outdated sense of coexistence with white Pittsburgh. Accepting the limitations of segre-gated seating and exclusion from the clubhouse, the Grays and Posey gratefully accepted what white elites granted them. Black Pittsburghers who attended Gray's games in Oakland often found as many whites in the stands as blacks. The game felt more like a major-league contest, as if the Pirates were playing. The fans dressed and behaved with appropriate New Negro decorum. They took picnic baskets and the men wore ties. "We dressed for games at Forbes like we were going to church."[82]

In contrast, playing on the Hill, announcing their games with handbills posted on telephone poles, filling Greenlee Field's 7,200 seats to overflowing, and en-couraging local fans to sip beer, the Crawfords played in a down-home atmo-sphere of a southern barbeque.[83] Fans heckled opposing teams and referees from their seats and engaged players who lived down the street from them in conversa-tion. "Players and the crowd were always mingling," recalled Robert Lavelle, a longtime resident of the Hill, "even during the game."[84] With an opposing runner on second, a fan rose in the stands and with a megaphone commanded, "You take one step off the base and I blow your head off." He had a shotgun in his other hand. Greenlee cupped his hands and called out from behind the Crawfords' dugout to his player, "Just stay on the bag."[85]

At Greenlee Field, fans bet on the games openly. Unlike white baseball, traumatized by the Black Sox scandal of 1919, Negro baseball had "nothing to fix." When the Crawfords played at home, fans bet a quarter on almost anything—the next pitch or where the ball might be hit. And they did it loudly. "Like if I got .50 on the Monarchs, the guy in the next seat or the row behind says 'he wants a piece of that.'" But when the Crawfords played the Black Barons from Birmingham, where many migrants had come from, the stakes rose. Against the Grays, "These games were big betting."[86] When the Grays came to Greenlee Field, "the place be rambin' packed," explained the Crawfords' batboy Elijah Miller in 2004.[87]

Greenlee Park was, in the words of one Hill resident, a "Negro" ballpark. If the Grays were the establishment team, the Crawfords belonged to the migrants.[88] The ballpark echoed to jive and banter.[89] As Harold Tinker remembered, "When we walked out on that field it was like going to another world. I looked up at those stands in center field, what a thrill."[90] During the two teams' four-way double-headers, Crawfords against the Kansas City Monarchs and the Grays against the Baltimore Elite Giants, the stands shook, and the entire Hill pulsed with excitement.[91]

TRICKY BASEBALL, OR YOU'LL GET NOTHIN' TODAY

The great black stars of the Crawfords—"Cool Papa" Bell, Josh Gibson, Satchel Paige, and Oscar Charleston—lived double lives. As black men who resided in the neighborhood, on the Hill, they mingled, shopped, shot pool, and leaned their elbows against the bar alongside anyone else. As ball players, on and off the field, their lives seemed larger than life. Their heroic stature magnified the Hill during the Depression, transforming a neighborhood of ordinary people, of shared distress and poverty, into a place of extraordinary energy and excitement. Few moments in American life equaled the excitement at the Crawford Grill when Greenlee threw a party for Satchel Paige in 1934. The revelers, who included Broadway dancer Bill "Bojangles" Robinson, dined like royalty.[92]

Spectators at Crawford games remembered "Cool Papa" Bell as being "some kind of fast"—so fast that "it looked like his feet weren't even touching the ground," that "he could steal second base standing up" or "could out-run a rabbit." In the neighborhood, Bell dressed like a businessman, exhibited impeccable manners, and treated everyone with polite respect.[93] Paige perfected his baseball and showman skills in Pittsburgh, first with the Crawfords and, after 1937, with the Grays. Paige's grin and bravado catapulted him into the hearts and wallets of fans across black America. He became wealthy and beloved in an era of widespread poverty and misery. Possessed of unbounded confidence, Paige named his pitches—"bee ball," "long Tom," "trouble," and "the barber." He worked to create his legend.[94] On the road, however, he lived a quiet and solitary life, disappearing for an afternoon and returning to his hotel room with a hamper filled with fish that he had caught. Then, to the dismay of his roommates, he fried them up in his room over a hot plate.[95]

Josh Gibson, whom major-league owner Bill Veeck called the "best hitter I ever saw," hit home runs so hard "they went off like nickel rockets."[96] Harold Tinker, his teammate on the Crawfords, called Gibson "the most tremendous hitter I've ever come across." Robert Lavelle, who lived on the Hill most of his life, remembered Gibson as the most phenomenal hitter of his time. Like Jackie Robinson a decade later, Gibson became the hero to local blacks on the Hill. But he also lived among them, on Bedford Street, not far from Greenlee field. Gibson, according to one story, hit a ball so high that the umpire called him out when the ball came down the next day in Washington, D.C. Yet Gibson never made it to the major leagues. John Watkins remembered walking up Bedford in 1946 where he saw his friend Levi Williams carrying a wreath to put on the porch of Gibson's house. Having heard that Jackie Robinson had just signed with the Major League Brooklyn Dodgers, the greatest catcher to ever play baseball died "of a broken heart."[97]

Gibson, Paige, Charleston, and Bell left mythic legacies and lived public lives as black folk heroes. For African Americans, prowess and guile often saved the day, manipulated the Man, pleased the crowd, or tickled the funny bone. Cool Papa Bell explained, "We put emphasis on what I call tricky baseball. We tried to play with our heads more than our muscles."[98]

Negro League life on the road, barnstorming from town to town, speeding away from danger, "had a southern feeling."[99] Players amused themselves during all-night rides by singing gospel songs or telling tall tales.[100] They spoke the language of the South and loved southern food. Paige asserted, "You take all those . . . southern boys . . . first thing you know they all go haywire, living on top of the world, walking . . . with their jackets that say Pittsburgh Crawfords. The older fellows, we had neckties on when we went to dinner."[101] The Crawfords included five players from the Birmingham Black Barons, and the majority of Pittsburgh's professional black baseball players—James Bell from Starkville, Mississippi; Leroy Paige from Mobile, Alabama; Jimmy Crutchfield from Ardmore,

Missouri; and Josh Gibson from Buena Vista, Georgia—came from the South. They grew up in sharecropping families and moved north during the Great Migration.

"Tricky baseball" was a southern style of black baseball codified by Rube Foster. Black baseball players relied on innate talent, discipline, and improvisation. The August 7, 1930, game between the Homestead Grays and the Kansas City Monarchs epitomized the southern style of Negro League ball. A classic pitchers' duel between the Grays' Smokey Joe Williams and the Monarchs' Chet Brewer, the game showcased tricky baseball at its best. Known as the "Battle of the Butchered Balls," it lasted twelve innings.[102] At age fifty, Williams confronted the young Brewer. Playing at night, the teams met under the portable lights that the Monarchs carried with them on barnstorming tours. The dim lighting enhanced the mythic quality of the game and played tricks on the hitters' vision. Brewer surrendered four hits and struck out nineteen, including ten in a row between the seventh and tenth innings. Still, he lost the game, 1–0. Williams allowed only a single hit over twelve innings and struck out twenty-five batters. Brewer "twirled" a masterful emery ball. Smokey Joe Williams dropped to side arm in the shadowy evening. Williams also covered the ball with dark tobacco juice which made it almost impossible to see.[103] The pitchers' stamina, the number of strikeouts, and the length of the game made it one of the Negro Leagues greatest games.

Tricky baseball, however, happened every game. Sam Streeter, who played for the Birmingham Black Barons, the Grays, and the Crawfords, was known as the "Spitter King."[104] Pitchers worked with catchers and infielders to apply Vaseline, hair tonic, or saliva to the ball, or they "cut" the ball, scuffing the leather with sharpened fingernails, emery boars, and bottle caps. They varied their deliveries—sidearm, submarine, hesitation—as part of a repertoire to fool the batter.[105] Tricky baseball, in truth, southern baseball, combined Rube Foster's practice of unorthodox strategy—bunt and run, double steal, using the center fielder as the pickoff man at second, the hidden-ball trick—with a time-honored version of "getting over."

A term borrowed from sharecroppers' efforts to undermine white authority, getting over meant getting away with something by pulling the wool over the Man's eyes. The Negro Leagues adopted centuries-old traditions of black rebellion and resistance and carried them north. Because there were no reserve clauses in Negro League baseball, players were not legally bound to an owner. Whenever they wished, like a southern sharecropper, they could "skip off" to play for another team. Players came and went with the money.

Tricky baseball sought the edge wherever a player could find one. The single umpire, an amateur with authority, stood behind the mound in the Negro Leagues and often had his back turned away from a base runner speeding around second. Bell, his feet churning, frequently reached third on a hit by cutting across the infield in front of second base. Black baseball players cut and doctored pitches, caught fly balls with basket catches, performed flips, and generally showed off even as they played hard-nosed ball. They brought these attitudes into baseball, drawn from southern blacks efforts "beat the system" of Jim Crow segregation that rewarded individuals for their toughness, resilience, and carefully masked contempt for authority.

In 1948, while still pitching in the Negro Leagues, Leroy Paige received a late-season call up to the Cleveland Indians in its drive for the pennant. In his late forties, Paige could no longer display all the skills he had mastered in the Negro Leagues. His "Long Tom" fastball was gone but not his guile. Paige threw overhand, sidearm, and underhand, wiggled his glove at the top of his delivery to distract the batter, and unleashed his famed "hesitation pitch," a change-up with a hitch in his motion. "I don't stop," he said to a reporter, "I stop my stride quick but my arm is still moving." He paused, "Sure it's a trick pitch."[106]

Southern African American migrants viewed black baseball as an expression of their culture. They spoke with vivid language and images to describe their heroes—"so fast," "so far," and "so strong." In contrast, Old Pittsburghers accepted as holy scripture the *Courier*'s middle-class slogan, "Enough hard work could make a man successful," or the masthead of the *Courier,* which read, "Work, Integrity, Tact, Temperance, Prudence, Courage, Faith." Old Pittsburgh ideals taught the value of middle-class diligence, propriety, and prosperity. The *Courier* and Vann monopolized the published record of black Pittsburgh. On the Hill, however, migrants from Alabama, Georgia, and Mississippi spoke their own language that showed as little respect for the "Queen's English" as it did for the Man. Buck Leonard, the Grays' answer to Josh Gibson in the 1930s, yelled to Leroy Paige that Paige had doctored the ball. As the crowd roared in response, Leonard asked for a new batch of baseballs. Paige replied, "You can throw them all out, 'cause you'll get nothing today." As usual, Paige won, this time on speed, not trickery.

Playing tricky baseball, like talking black, was a choice, not a necessity. It affirmed who you were and whom you disrespected. It did not mean that you could not play or speak like a white man. Rather, unlike Old Pittsburghers, migrants played for other black people. It meant they were proud to be black and had no desire to become white.[107]

THE HOUSE, THE CLUB, AND THE PIANO

August Wilson, the author of nine plays set on the Hill, was born in Pittsburgh in 1945. His father, a German American baker named Frederic August Kittle, and his African American mother, Daisy Wilson, lived together until 1950. When Kittle left, Daisy Wilson moved her family to a small two-room apartment on Bedford Avenue, across the street from the Crawfords' Ammon Field. When his mother died in 1965, the twenty-year-old August added Wilson to his name in her honor. Largely self-taught, he wrote scraps of poetry and prose on the paper napkins at Eddie's Spaghetti House where he worked.[108] From Eddie's chrome lunch counter, diners could see the Crawford Grill directly across Wylie Avenue. When Wilson began to write his Pittsburgh plays, Wylie Avenue and the Hill had already deteriorated. Wilson's plays brought the Hill back to life as they charted its history from the start of the migration to the present.

Two of August Wilson's Pittsburgh plays, *Fences* (1985) and *The Piano Lesson* (1987), addressed the interplay of baseball and music in black Pittsburgh. Wilson set *Fences*, a story of regret and missed opportunity, in the 1950s. He placed *The Piano Lesson*, a story of survival and cultural awakening, in the 1930s. Each play explored the complex legacy of African American life on the Hill. In *Fences,* Wilson's bitter Troy Maxon revealed the ambivalence of Josh Gibson's generation of Negro League stars—talented and overlooked. These proud men, passed over and forgotten when Major League Baseball became integrated in the late 1940s, became sporting vagabonds, playing for dimes dropping into the passed hat. The disappearance of the Negro Leagues, the death of black baseball in Pittsburgh, stripped the community of one of its cultural cornerstones.

In Wilson's *Piano Lesson*, the family's piano, long the symbol of middle-class African Americans' refined culture, also bore the images of West African spirituality. Poor southern migrants saw the piano as only a pretentious commodity. Wilson uses the piano to create a flash point between the competing needs of Boy Willy and his sister Berniece. Willy, just out of prison in the South, wanted to sell the piano to buy back the land his family had sharecropped in Mississippi. His sister Berniece, living in Pittsburgh, holds onto the piano with all her will. It symbolizes her urban world. It commands attention in the parlor of her home and is the symbol of her family's history and its middle-class aspirations.

Wilson "discovered" his own West African heritage in *The Piano Lesson*. In the last scene of the play, the family gathers and experiences a ghostly presence that commands Berniece, Wilson's symbol of pride and culture, play the family piano. Handed down through many generations of African Americans, the piano is

Pittsburgh piano jazz: Earl Hines, Erroll Garner, Billy Eckstein, Maxine Sullivan, and Mary Lou Williams (ca. 1948; Charles "Teenie" Harris, American, 1908–1998; black and white Ansco safety film; 4 × 5 in.; Carnegie Museum of Art, Pittsburgh, Heinz Family Fund; copyright © 2004 Carnegie Museum of Art, Charles "Teenie" Harris Archive; photograph © 2007 Carnegie Museum of Art, Pittsburgh)

covered with strange, West African symbols. Wilson's stage directions announced, "She crosses to the piano. She begins to play. The song is found piece by piece." Wilson described the song Berniece played: "With each repetition it gains in strength. It is intended as an exorcism and a dressing for battle. *A rustle of wind blowing across two continents.*"[109]

To black Pittsburgh, the piano jazz music played on the Hill blew from two directions. Pittsburgh jazz embodied the aspirations of its middle class and the musical heritage of its working people. Urban and sophisticated, Pittsburgh jazz emerged from the public schools where music instructor, Carl McVicker, shaped its development. Dozens of important jazz players identified with Pittsburgh jazz, including Stanley Turentine, Billy Eckstein, and George Benson. After World War I, Pittsburgh jazz musicians, literally, received piano lessons at Westinghouse High School, the cradle of Pittsburgh jazz. Nurtured by the public school system and by the private music academies that shared the musical tastes of Old Pittsburghers, Pittsburgh jazz was also sustained by the local black musicians' union, known as "the Club." Local 471 offered a counterpoint on the Hill to the academic training provided at Westinghouse High School, known locally as "the House." Together, the Club and the House created Pittsburgh's distinctive piano jazz.[110]

The public school system cradled this tradition of elegant swing jazz. Since 1874 the Pittsburgh school board had sought to disperse African American children throughout its school system to prevent the formation of all-black schools. All of its largest high schools, Schenley, Peabody, and Westinghouse, served mixed racial populations. Located along the seams of Pittsburgh's ethnic neighborhoods, each high school contained a sizable minority of African American students. Not until 1937, however, did the school board hire black teachers. The education of black Pittsburgh fell to the hands of white teachers. While denied jobs in the school system, Old Pittsburghers supported the school board's educational agenda of discipline, hard work, deference to authority, and cultural refinement.[111]

Among the city's high schools, George Westinghouse High School was the grandest. Named for the inventor of the air-break, whose plant employed thirty-five thousand electrical workers in the city, Westinghouse High dominated the city's musical education. Westinghouse generously endowed the school with the stipulation that it educate working-class children with the values of American success. He also asked that it be named George Westinghouse High School. Founded in 1923, Westinghouse High School was part of the company's effort of welfare capitalism. With a student population of sixteen hundred and an auditorium with the company logo displayed conspicuously on its walls, the school's spacious and elegant neoclassical building marked the boundary between Homewood-Brushton and Point Breeze. In the 1930s and 1940s, Westinghouse High School's African American enrollments stood at about 20 percent.[112] It provided integrated courses, sports, dramatic presentations, and music.[113] From the start, Westinghouse became the premiere high school for Pittsburgh African Americans, the pride of Homewood and, under the tutelage of Carl McVicker, the guardian of Pittsburgh jazz.

McVicker taught a refined, technically proficient jazz at Westinghouse. His students were taught according to the tastes of Old Pittsburghers and their middle-class preference for the piano. Tall and gangly, a white graduate of Carnegie Tech, McVicker began teaching in 1927. Assigned to teach instrumental music, McVicker, also the director of the Westinghouse High School swing band, proclaimed, "I wanted any kid in my program who was serious."[114] McVicker also belonged to the floating faculty of the private Pittsburgh Music Institute (PMI) that many black music students from Homewood attended. Gentle and unassuming, McVicker drilled his students in the basics of music education. He insisted that his students read music. He prepared several generations of Westinghouse students for professional musical careers, schooling them in the European classics, in formal composition and harmony as well as in jazz.

Adolph Doug Cook, a lifelong Pittsburgh jazz musician, learned flute, piano, and vibes at Westinghouse with "Mac." McVicker also taught Cook at PMI in nearby Oakland. "They went by the rules. But part of it was that you have to know the rules to break them," he explained.[115] McVicker taught classical music and theory, encouraged his students to take private lessons, and fostered a competitive ethos in his jazz band. McVicker allowed student musicians to challenge their classmates for the ranked seats in the band, which also taught them how to confront others.[116] In the mid-1930s, Billy Strayhorn and his white classmate, clarinetist Jerome Eisner, studied with McVicker. Both working-class kids, Eisner and Strayhorn received the best of McVicker's generosity. He secured them gigs at the local streetcar barns, in central Homewood, and at the neighborhood's unofficial supper clubs that opened on Sunday evenings.[117]

Despite the apparent racial tranquillity of Pittsburgh's public schools, African Americans remained aware of the boundaries and limitations imposed on them. "We became over-achievers," said Nelson Harrison, a black horn-player. "Competition was . . . a coping mechanism" they deployed to tell the "racist teachers and principal that they could not stop us." In the 1930s, when a black girl seemed poised to become Westinghouse's first African American valedictorian, the principal demanded that McVicker "lower that nigger's grade." McVicker complied and changed an A to a B. Many blacks in Homewood never forgave him.[118]

McVicker's musical influence was reinforced by a variety of institutions and personalities. The local studios of PMI and the classes of Mary Caldwell Dawson, founder of the Negro Opera Company in Homewood, offered young musicians private instruction. The Dawson School "trained singers and skilled readers" for Pittsburgh's black musical community.[119] A neighborhood music shop, Volkwein's, offered young black musicians a welcoming place to gather, jam, and try out secondhand instruments. Together, Westinghouse, McVicker, the Dawson School, PMI, private tutors, and Volkwein's supported a classically influenced, well-trained, technically skilled, and refined music for Homewood's black musicians. In contrast to the increasingly working-class character of the Hill, Homewood offered a distinctly middle-class culture. Billy Strayhorn lived along Tioga Street Rear, an unpaved alley a block from stately Homewood Avenue, but most of his classmates lived on Monticello Avenue, qualifying them as among the "better class" of African Americans.[120] Rich or poor, Pittsburgh jazz became a music of middle-class taste and aspirations, forged in the schools in and around Homewood.

Many Pittsburgh jazz musicians learned to play in the genteel Homewood school of music. When they graduated and turned professional, they earned their "chops" in the working-class clubs of the Hill. In the back rooms of after-hours clubs, the second floor of Greenlee's Crawford Grille, and the headquarters of the black musicians union, Local 471, the Hill confronted Homewood-trained musicians with the working-class world of a majority of the city's African Americans.[121] In the 1930s and 1940s, Wylie Avenue joints such as the Flamingo, Collins Inn, the Humming Bird, and the Leader House jumped with "jive." Up and down Wylie, where a "jew-baby" played for drinks with a "lambs tongue" and blew "their tops" with a "reefer" before they "bust your conk," jazz played all night long. The black workers flocked to the Hill to listen and dance to jazz. For every middle-class family that displayed a piano in the front parlor, the Hill offered a bar, saloon, taproom, and club.[122]

"The Club" of Local 471 occupied a building at 1231 Wylie Avenue on the Lower Hill. Three stories high, the Club had a piano bar on the entry level that featured a white baby grand available to anyone who wanted to play. Upstairs, the Club maintained a bandstand surrounded with tables and chairs for dining and a small kitchen. On the third floor, it provided a larger space for big band rehearsals that could use the entire floor. The union held its weekly meetings on the third floor. To many, the Club never closed, always hopping, day and night, with music, drink, and talk.

"It was one of the great experiences of my life," said Joe Kennedy Jr., who played with the Ahmad Jamal Trio, "The all-night jam sessions at 1213 Wylie Avenue were just marvelous."[123] Pittsburgh's black musicians, visiting jazz artists both black and white, and kids earning their stripes all showed up at the Club to play. It was a place to show off in cutting contests and a place to pass along lore. "We had a blackboard, and we had jam sessions, and they put the changes to all the numbers. And each week we had to learn the changes to a different number . . . different guys wrote them down."[124] Joining the Local meant jobs. Union scale meant better-paying jobs from "these jive promoters and agents."[125] As a teenager, Fritz Jones joined the union even before he graduated from school. Later Jones changed his name to Ahmad Jamal, who as a teacher wrote his chord changes on the Club's blackboard. "I was lucky to be a part of that great family," remembered Charles Austin, "We had a death benefit you know, we'd pitch in money, we looked out for each other, we cared about each other."[126]

DO YOU HEAR THE PITTSBURGH CATS PLAY?

The "raggedy" piano in August Wilson's play and the old upright piano in Billy Strayhorn's home played jazz both on the Hill and in Homewood. David Hajdu, Strayhorn's biographer, wrote, "The thoroughly furnished parlor was arranged around a piano, a symbol of cultured gentility rare on Tioga Street Rear."[127] Five piano players, Earl "Fatha" Hines, Erroll Garner, Mary Lou Williams, Billy Strayhorn, and Ahmad Jamal, contributed to Pittsburgh jazz piano. The five Pittsburgh jazz pianists developed a style and defined an age. Hines, Williams, and Strayhorn belonged to the era of Old Pittsburghers, whose southern families arrived before the Great Migration. Garner and Jamal belonged to the Great Migration. Only Hines, who attended Schenley High School, did not study music at Westinghouse and had no musical connection to Carl McVicker.

Each of the Pittsburgh Five enjoyed long careers in Chicago and New York, and three garnered fame from other musicians with whom they played: Hines with Armstrong, Williams with Andy Kirk, and Strayhorn with Ellington. Garner, the only one who did not read music—so perfect was his pitch and ear—played with everyone, and Jamal worked in trios and quartets that enabled him to work in relative isolation from the larger jazz community. But, they all claimed Pittsburgh as a musical home.

When the twenty-year-old Earl Hines hit the road in the mid-1920s, he combined his mother's church music with the classical training of his German music teacher. Three years later, in Chicago, Hines teamed with Louis Armstrong, adapting his jazz to Armstrong's "hot" style. Rhythmically powerful, Hines's technique abandoned the stride piano tradition and produced a more inventive, improvisational, and virtuoso approach. Adding offbeat accents, stretching the melody, and embracing arpeggios, Hines offered a new piano style, at once rhythmically innovative and melodically linear. Known as "Fatha," Hines drove his music, pushing it down the road, clearing out whatever lay in its path.

Like a magician, Hines revealed and then immediately took back his tunes. Setting the melody, or the rhythm, with one hand, he undermined it with the other. He then returned to where he had begun. A simple tune like "Moonlight in Vermont" became a rich exploration of rhythmic variations. He laid out linearly on the piano the West African polyrhythms of his mother's church. Hines's trumpet style of right-hand playing enabled him to stay with Armstrong, who, without warning, changed directions on a dime. The unexpected, the unanticipated, became Hines's trademark. Superficially a player of ordinary tunes, easily confused with supper club jazz, Hines was a musicians' musician. He tried out, explored, elaborated, and taught new techniques that he embedded in the familiar. Hines invented Pittsburgh piano jazz.[128]

Hines swung. And he adopted the rhythm of hot jazz.[129] Abandoning the oompah-pah-like two-two beat, Hines played a swinging four-four beat with incredible dexterity and speed. His "killer-dillers" drove dancers wild and said "try me if you can." Swing became the vehicle for the array of black "Kings" and "Dukes" and "Counts" that followed. No mistake that Hines's nickname, "Fatha" from father, anointed him as the founder. In the late 1920s and early 1930s, when white or "sweet" jazz bands sought commercial success, they left the "hot" jazz of Hines and Armstrong behind.[130]

If Hines was the father of Pittsburgh's jazz piano, Mary Lou Williams was its midwife. Five years younger than Hines, Williams practiced with him as a child. Later she secured Erroll Garner's first gigs and gave Ahmad Jamal his first recording session. Like Hines, the southern-born Williams came from a musical family, lived in an integrated neighborhood, and developed an innovative left hand. Unlike Hines, Williams learned to play by ear; only later, at Westinghouse, did she learn to read music. A child prodigy, Williams played with male and adult jazz musicians in Pittsburgh before the age of ten. In her teens, she went on the road, where she studied harmony, composition, and arranging.[131]

Born with a caul over her eyes, a West African symbol of second sight that she believed gave her art a special vision, Williams was graced with charm and talent.[132] She took the jazz she learned on the street—the blues and boogie-woogie—and integrated them into piano jazz. Jazz, she wrote, did not come from books but from "poor black people." As a child, she scuffled for quarters on the Hill, played on demand for the Mellon family, and barnstormed with a minstrel show outfit. One of her teachers told her, "Play the left-hand louder than the right. It's where the beat and the feeling is."[133] At nineteen, she joined Andy Kirk, the leader of a Kansas City swing band. Williams toured with Kirk for more than a decade and became the band's arranger. Williams constantly expanded her range, pounding her left hand, breaking the stride with what she called "walking tens," and stomping the blues.[134] Perfect pitch allowed her to play anything she heard, and her musical intelligence allowed her to carry a tune on the piano with her left hand while she scribbled arrangements with her right.

Williams's eclectic approach resulted in a series of styles that constantly changed, but she never abandoned the foundation of her music. Even as she adapted swing with the Kirk band, playing blues-laced jazz that stretched out linearly, she always came back to the blues and boogie-woogie. "Night Life," a tune she wrote at the age of seventeen, sounded like a spiritual, joyous and powerful, as well as the blues. It moved back and forth between the two. Three years later, her "Clean Pickin'" (1930) swung, even as she retained a stomping rhythm with her left hand. The notes from her right hand flew, fluid and dexterous, a contrast to the hard-hitting "trumpet" style of Hines.[135] By 1940, after a decade with Kirk, Williams's style blended swing, blues, and boogie. No longer content to move back and forth from one to the other, she brought them together, which gave her swing a distinctive hop and drive. Still, as a woman, Williams remained obscured, hidden behind the men with whom she worked.

Billy Strayhorn relied less on Mary Lou Williams than on blind luck for his entrée into piano jazz. Like Williams's musical introduction, Strayhorn's early musicianship was breathtaking. The child of southern working-class migrants, he played spirituals when he returned to the family home in North Carolina. Cultivated by McVicker at Westinghouse as a classical pianist, Strayhorn played Grieg and Liszt at school recitals and wandered into Volkwein's for private lessons. A prodigy, Strayhorn had demonstrated piano mastery even before his legs were long enough to allow his feet to touch the floor. At Westinghouse, he studied theory and harmony with Jane Alexander, who had also taught Williams. A disciplinarian, Alexander often left Strayhorn in charge of the class.[136]

Strayhorn's closest friend, a Jewish clarinetist named Jerome Eisner, introduced him to the jazz world of nearby East Liberty. Strayhorn did not play or even listen to jazz before 1937. In 1938 he and Eisner formed a small combo that dabbled in swing standards like "Body and Soul."[137] Strayhorn earned his chops by playing against all comers. His ability to play a classical repertoire and adapt it to jazz was Strayhorn's special gift. And it fit perfectly into Duke Ellington's lush synthesis of jazz and blues. Like Williams's work, Strayhorn's arranging, together with his ear, allowed him to play what he heard and translate it to a jazz band. His first important composition, "Lush Life," exhibited his musical gift. Urban and sophisticated, with Cole Porter lyrics, "Lush Life"'s poetry complemented the harmonic, yet bluesy, piano accompaniment.

> I used to visit all the very gay places,
> Those come what may places
> Where one relaxes on the axis
> Of the wheel of life
> To get the feel of life
> From jazz and cocktails.[138]

In late 1938 Billy Strayhorn met George Greenlee, the nephew of Gus. On the third floor of the Crawford, high above the counting rooms and the piano bar, Gus

Greenlee introduced Strayhorn to Duke Ellington, who had come to Pittsburgh for a weeklong downtown engagement. Ellington invited Strayhorn to play for him. The next day, in the Duke's dressing room, Strayhorn played "Sophisticated Lady" twice—once the Ellington version and then "as I would play it." Ellington called for his baritone sax player, Harry Carney, and asked Strayhorn to play the tune again: "Listen to this kid play." Strayhorn, the composer of the Ellington Orchestra's theme, "Take the 'A' Train," joined Ellington as his arranger and second pianist, moved to New York, and never looked back.[139]

Mary Lou Williams's relationship with Erroll Garner, eleven years her junior, began at the same time as the Ellington-Strayhorn friendship. Garner, also a child prodigy, member of a musical family, and a product of Westinghouse High School, met Williams in 1938. At Westinghouse, Garner was considered a musical genius. When Kirk's band played in Pittsburgh, Williams found "such a little guy playing so much." As she attempted to teach him to read music, Erroll resisted. Williams confessed that he "was born with more than most musicians could accomplish in a life-time."[140]

Garner's resistance to reading affected his career. The local musicians' union required passage of a sight-reading test. The union refused to issue him a card, and Garner had to earn his living outside Pittsburgh.[141] Still, Garner always returned to Pittsburgh, to the Hill. He became one of the first black jazz players to perform in downtown Pittsburgh, at clubs like Mercur's Music Bar. Like Strayhorn, Garner crossed boundaries and passed through the barrier of segregation in Pittsburgh. Strayhorn's friends, Alice and Jerome Eisner, arranged for Garner's gig at Mercur's by confronting the codes of race prejudice that resulted in phrases like, "We don't serve no niggers here" or "Tell Jasper [Garner] he can't play here."[142]

The left-handed Garner, all five feet two of him, sustained the Pittsburgh tradition of powerful piano jazz. Even in his idiosyncratic style, Garner displayed a combination of neoclassical harmony, left-handed rhythmic use of locked chords, and the swing produced by his right hand that he played slightly behind his left. His signature ballad, "Misty," began as a straightforward tune. Garner played the song slowly to accent the theme and variation format. Sounding as if Debussy or Satie had composed it, Garner's "Misty" seeped out into the evening night, cool and stately, elegant and lush. The kid from Pittsburgh, who played every instrument in McVicker's band, including the tuba, but who chose not to read music, played a unique style that embodied the best of Pittsburgh jazz.[143]

Ahmad Jamal, born in 1930 as Fritz Jones, also exemplified the best of Pittsburgh jazz. Combining the taste and techniques of his predecessors, Jamal navigated the postwar jazz world which saw bebop challenge the dominance of swing.

A student of McVicker's and the Dawson school, Jones loved music first, then jazz. In 1950 Jones changed his name and converted to Islam. As a jazz musician, Jamal ignored the intensity of bebop, and like Miles Davis, played the spaces, the silences, the still moments that drew the listener into the tune.[144]

Like so many of Pittsburgh's other great jazz players, Jamal's musical talent became obvious at a young age. Pete Henderson, who played with Jamal and went to Westinghouse with him, remembered:

> Yeah, Fritzy took theory. So, he said, "Man come on let's go in Volkwein's with me" to get this book. We went in there and Fritz looked like a little kid . . . and the guy says, you know how whiteys were, "What do you want with a book like that?" . . . I said did you ever hear him play. And he went over and started playing the piano. From everywhere, upstairs, out on the street, the store was packed. I said "didn't I tell you." He was flabbergasted, man. It was the same attitude when I went to get the trumpet. They said, "Niggers don't know nothing, man." But Fritzy lit the place up."[145]

In 1946 Fritz sat in with the house band at the union local. Stan Getz, in town with Woody Herman's Second Herd, arrived, and as local jazz musicians showed off Jones's extraordinary piano talent, Getz picked up his horn and announced, "I can play with this kid." As several Pittsburgh musicians recalled, Getz asked Jones to play a song in C, and they sped into the number. At each chorus, Jones modulated the harmonic structure and shifted the runs of the chord progressions, making the tune "brighter and brighter." Ten minutes later Getz stood up, packed up his horn, and announced "I quit."[146] For Jones's Westinghouse school pal, Nelson Harrison, the night and the confrontation at the Club demonstrated the relationship between competition and racial resistance. The still-segregated black musicians' union in Pittsburgh welcomed all jazz players.[147] And to onlookers, the contest between Jones and Getz seemed like a Joe Louis victory. Even the white Pittsburgh musicians, who witnessed the match, understood the racial significance of Jones's triumph over a white star jazz performer.[148]

Jones, who learned to play the piano at age three, began lessons at seven and played Liszt at eleven. He dreamed of a professional classical career and aspired to attend Juilliard. Instead, to "earn a living," he joined the musicians' union and played anywhere he could. His working-class parents, one a steel worker, the other a domestic, could not afford Juilliard. "Economic circumstances" led him down the road to jazz. He understood that Pittsburgh was a great piano jazz city. "I don't earn a living playing Liszt or Bartok," he told a French interviewer, "I earn a living playing Jamal." He added, "You might say that we are the Bachs, Bartoks and Mozarts of our time, that is, we are the improvisers."[149]

Fritz Jones (Ahmad Jamal) at "the Club" (ca. 1947; Charles "Teenie" Harris, American, 1908–1998; black and white Agfa safety film; 4 × 5 in.; Carnegie Museum of Art, Pittsburgh, Heinz Family Fund; copyright © 2004 Carnegie Museum of Art, Charles "Teenie" Harris Archive; photograph © 2007 Carnegie Museum of Art, Pittsburgh)

In 1951, at twenty years old, Ahmad Jamal formed his first trio, the Three Strings—piano, bass, and guitar. Later he expanded to the Four Strings and added the drums. Together, the trio and quartet became Jamal's musical voice. In the 1950s he moved to Chicago, with a stop in New York, where Miles Davis first heard him. "Listen to the way Jamal uses space," Davis said in an interview for the *Jazz Review*. "He lets it go so that you can feel the rhythm section . . . it's not crowded."[150]

Erroll Garner played an even more critical role in the evolution of Jamal's style. Jamal described Garner "as a decisive source of inspiration." Garner's rich sonority, the sophistication of his music, impressed Jamal from an early age.[151] Like Williams and Strayhorn, the blues remained central to Jamal's music. "The blues are very important," he told his French interviewer, "they allowed me to make a living for years, but, [really] there is only the blues in music."[152]

The blues, the use of the flatted fifth, the blue note, derived from West African modal music that underlay the piano jazz music of Pittsburgh.[153] In Jamal's hands the blues became integrated into an urban jazz expression, a blending of the "trumpet" style of Hines, the boogie-woogie of Williams, the lush sensibility of Strayhorn, and the harmonics of Garner. In his earliest recorded tunes like "The Surrey with the Fringe on Top" (1951) and "Ahmad's Blues" (1952), Jamal drew on these influences and added the common denominator of swing.[154] Propelled by the tension between right and left hands, the melody and harmony often leading the rhythm, Jamal's music took flight. No longer dance music, Jamal's swing became a chamber alternative to the intensely emotional cascade of bebop.

Jamal recorded his most famous tune, "Poinciana," twice in the mid-1950s, first with his standard trio in 1953 and then again with a drummer in 1955. The contrasts in rhythm and the added dimension of Latin-influenced syncopation demonstrated the ways in which he elaborated his musical ideas. More exotic the second time around, the tune became an exploration of new rhythms superimposed on a blues-based melody. Subtle, rich, and full of Garner's sonority, the tune led Jamal to the height of success. "Poinciana" became his trademark piece, a number forever associated with his name. But, like much of his work in the 1950s, Jamal's recording owed its fame equally to the tradition of Pittsburgh piano jazz.

Born in Homewood, nurtured at Westinghouse High School, the Pittsburgh jazz piano style found sustenance on the Hill. The urban piano jazz that emerged from Pittsburgh's black community between 1920 and 1950 reflected the amalgam of the blues, classical tastes and training, the tradition of an innovative left-hand, the tension between competition and community, the spirit of inventiveness, and the rhythm of swing. The piano jazz tradition echoed the social and cultural circumstances of African Americans in twentieth century Pittsburgh.

The forge, mine, and factory shaped African American life in the "other" steel city of Birmingham. In Pittsburgh, the presence of a pre-Migration middle class proved an equally powerful force, as symbolically central to Pittsburgh's African American culture as Wilson's piano was to Boy Willie and Berniece. Newly arrived migrants found in Pittsburgh a black upper class all too ready to instruct them in the art of survival. At a time of economic distress, which saw working-class blacks banished from the factory floor, Old Pittsburghers taught them the social skills necessary to find jobs in the city's newly emerging service economy as domestics and as entertainers. Pittsburgh's New Negroes schooled the new working class. But, as in Birmingham, no matter how dramatically migrants changed to adapt to their new urban worlds, they also maintained their ties to a rural African American heritage rooted in West Africa as evident in the blues piano of Mary Lou Williams and the tricky baseball of Leroy Paige.

WALKIN' EGYPT

• **6** •

Mississippi Delta

TWO MIGRATIONS

During the twentieth century, African Americans left Mississippi in two waves. The first Great Migration coincided with the First World War. In this phase, African Americans left from most of the regions in the state except the Delta. Many first went to Memphis and then to Chicago. Then, during and after the Second World War, most Mississippi migrants to Chicago came from the Delta. By 1945 the entire South Side of Chicago had become a southern black community contained within a largely white city—a black metropolis.[1] Like other African American migrants, Mississippians brought with them their West African–derived southern culture, a rich mixture of Delta blues and Sanctified Christianity.

The first Great Migration in Mississippi had two currents. One ran north in search of jobs in the labor-starved factories, and a second ran westward from the Black Belt into the Delta's rich cotton land. While tens of thousands of black Mississippians moved north, tripling the black population of Chicago from 44,000 to 120,000, thousands more moved to the Delta. The two phases of the Great Migration were set in motion by a world war that coincided with agricultural depressions that affected different parts of the state at different times.[2]

Mississippi contained three agricultural regions. The orchards and truck farms of the Piney Woods in the southeast and the alluvial swamps and forests of the Yazoo-Mississippi Delta in the northwest were divided by the Mississippi Hill Country, an area that extended through the middle of the state from the Tennessee border southward. While the cotton-rich Delta remained impervious to the boll weevil until the 1930s, after 1910 the boll weevil devastated the Hill counties of central Mississippi. "The boll weevil makes cotton culture for the time

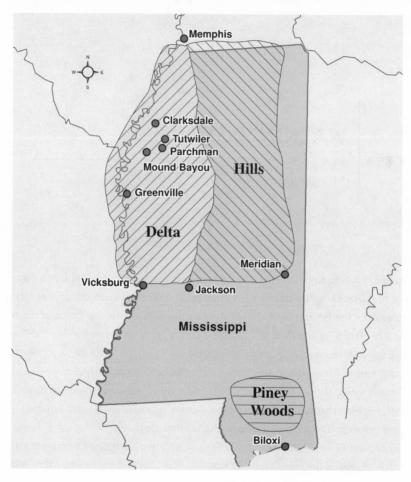

Mississippi Delta

being out of the question in the Mississippi 'Hills,' " intoned the U.S. Department of Labor study entitled *Negro Migration, 1916–1917*.[3]

After slavery, African Americans had scattered themselves unevenly through-out the state. Relatively few blacks lived in the Piney Woods while an ever-increas-ing number of blacks, most sharecroppers or share renters, dominated the Delta. In regions with few African Americans—in the Coastal Meadows and the Piney Woods—more than 50 percent of black farmers owned their own land and, until 1903, had prospered.[4] Between 1910 and 1920, when the five central counties of the Delta increased their African American population by forty-five thousand, most came from Hills.[5] Other Hill Country blacks moved to the state's largest cities—Jackson, Mobile, and Hattiesburg—while others left the state altogether, moving either west to Texas or north, first to Memphis and St. Louis and then to Detroit and Chicago. Chicago received "heavy migrations of sawmill Negroes from around Laurel and Hattiesburg and other smaller towns. Of 109 Mississippi Negroes who applied for employment from a labor agent in Chicago, 20 came from Hattiesburg, 2 from Laurel, 6 from Gulfport.[6] During the second decade of the twentieth century, the southern half of the state contributed much more significantly to "the exodus than the poorer and more isolated regions of the north and east."[7] African American migrants searched for better jobs, better schools, and safety. They moved as individuals and in groups. Sometimes whole communities and church congregations left as one. Despite warnings and pleas from Mississippi whites and blacks to stay, thousands accepted the offer of northern labor agents and bid Mississippi farewell.[8]

African American migrants left Mississippi in the wake of the agricultural depression that triggered an unprecedented surge of racial violence. Disenfranchised by the new Mississippi constitution of 1890, terrorized by the Klan and Hill County white-cappers, and subject to convict labor, peonage, and lynching, thousands of black Mississippians voted with their feet.[9] Prized for their labor and feared because of their numbers, during and after World War I African Americans faced random beatings, terror, and death for alleged violations of the elaborate, humiliating, and confusing codes of Jim Crow. When they crossed the Ohio River, one group of migrants burst into song:

I done come out de land of Egypt
Ain't dat good news.[10]

WALKIN' EGYPT

"I was borned in Frankin, Loos'iana," James Cornelius, a Confederate veteran, told interviewers in the 1930s. "My mammy come from Virginny," Dora Franks of Aberdeen recalled. "My daddy was my young Marster. His name was Marster George Brewer." Henri Necaise of Nicholson, at age 105, told an interviewer, "I was born in Harrison County (near the Gulf) 19 miles from Pass Christian, 'long de ridge road from de swamp near Wolf River. . . . Us was all French. My father was a white man, Anatole Necaise." Susan Snow of Meridian came from Wilcox County, Alabama, and Isaac Stier of Natchez remembered, "My mammy was

Ellen Stier an' my pappy was Jordon Stier. He was brought to dis country by a slave dealer from Nashville, Tennessee. Dey traveled all de way through de Injun Country on foot."

James Lucas was born on October 11, 1833, on the plantation of Confederate president Jefferson Davis "in a cotton fiel in cotton pickin' time, an' de wimmins fixed my mammyup so she didn' hardly lose no time atall. My mammy sho' was healthy. Her name was Silvey an' her mammy come over to dis country in a big ship. Somebody give her de name o' Betty, but twant her right name. Folks couldn' understan' a word she say. *It was some sort o' gibberish dey called gullah-talk, an' it soun' dat funny.*"[11]

Many slaves brought with them to Mississippi aspects of Gullah culture that James Lucas identified as "African." Their language, customs, songs, medicine, and religion bore the Low Country's distinctive mark. Others, whose ancestors had entered the United States though New Orleans, exhibited features of Haiti. Conjuring and herbalism, call-and-response work songs, and sanctified spirituals, the ring shout, and Gullah tales blended together to form a rich West African–influenced African American culture. During slavery, Mississippi blacks worshiped and sang in the brush arbors in the woods near their cabins, out of sight of white owners, slave patrols, and overseers. Slave religion in Mississippi remained underground, largely invisible to whites, a consequence of the 1831 state law that prohibited any "slave, free negro, or mulatto," from preaching the Gospel.[12] The prohibition forced slaves to mask their private lives, insulating their religion from the planters' Anglo-Protestantism.

Anna Baker, of Aberdeen, expressed her sense of her West African spirit. "I was buried in de water lak de Savior. I's a real Baptis'. De Hold Sperrit sho' come into my heart." She continued, "I b'lieves in de Sperrit. I b'leieves all o'us when us dies is sperrits. Us jus' hovers 'roun' in de sky a-ridin' on de clouds." Baptism, the immersion of body and soul in the river, remained a central sacrament in Mississippi slave religion. Like the Yoruba initiation ceremonies, Afro-Baptists in Mississippi practiced their rituals. According to Yoruba belief, the *orisha* Oshun, possessor of great wealth and beauty, took her subjects with her to the "bottom of the river" where "she reigns in glory." Afro-Baptists in their baptismal rites symbolically transported the believer from the mortal realm to the immortal, anticipating their passing into the spiritual realm at death. "I jined de New Zion Baptist Church here in Magnolia an' was Baptized in de Tanghipoa River one Sunday evenin'. I was so happy dat I shouted, me an' my wife bofe," James Cornelius told his interviewer. His shouts of joy echoed the culture to which he remained intensely connected. Similarly, Jim Allen prayed and sang with a preacher who "would say, 'Pull down de line and let de spirit be a witness, workin' fer faith in de future from on high.' "[13]

Mississippi slaves improvised brush arbor churches that harkened back to Low Country Gullah practice. "Us Niggers didn' have no secret meetin's. All us had was church meetin's in arbours out in de woods. De preachers 'ud exhortus dat us was de chillun o' Israel in de widernedd an' de Lawd done sont us to take dis lan' o' milk an' honey." And we can feel it in the text as Charlie Davenport takes in a breath to add, "But how us gwine a-take lan' what's already been took?" Davenport expressed a sense of ironic contradiction, the gap between his own experience and white perception of it, when it came to conjuring. "Plenty folks b'leived in charms, but I didn' take no stock in such truck. But I don't lak for de moon to shine on me when I'm a sleepin'."

Like the Gullah, Mississippi slaves turned their mirrors to the wall when someone was "funeralized," hunted in the woods for "Samson snake" roots to "doctor 'em wid," and called on spells to set and then fix a conjure. "If we heerd a little old shiverin' own (owl) we'd th'ro salt in de fire an' th'ow a broom 'cross de do' fer folks say dat 'twas a sign of bad luck, an'a charm had to worked fas' to keep sumpin' terrible from happenin'." These West African customs—charms used to destroy or restore the social equilibrium of the community—possessed the "power to make things right."[14] In the WPA narratives, ex-slaves described a spiritualism that offered a clear alternative to the Protestant and Catholic practices of their masters.[15] Susan Snow of Meridian told her interviewer, "I was a devil 'till I got 'legion. . . . I had a vision. I tol' it to a white lady an' she say, 'Susie, dat's 'ligion a-callin' you. . . . I didn't join de church 'till 1891, after I had a second vision. . . . I done put my badness b'hin' me."

Slave religious practice also adapted features of frontier revivalist Christianity to shelter West African spirit possession. "We had preachin' and singin'. Old Daddy Young sho' could make 'em shout and roll. Us have to hol' some of 'em dey'd get so happy." Practiced in secret and at night, the slaves' African-Baptism ("dey took me to de river an' it took two of 'em to put me under. When I come up I tol' 'em, 'turn me loose, I b'lieve I can walk right on top o' de water') expressed joy, awe, and a sense of the extraordinary. Snow explained, "De meetin's last from early in the mawnin' 'till late at night. When dark come, de men folks would hang up a wash pot, botton up'ards, *in de little brush church-house we had,* so's it would catch de noise an de oberseer wouldn't hear us singin' and shoutin' . . . you should'a seen some of de niggers get 'ligion. De best was was to cary 'em to de cemetery an' let 'em stand ober a grave. Dey would start singin' and shoutin' 'bout seein' fire an' brimstone: den day would sing some mo' an' look plum sanctified."[16] The African

American sing and shout was an expression of the traditional West African rituals of dance, song, and rhythm that constituted the ring shout. "At de wake we clapped our han's and kept time wid our feet – *Walkin' Egypt*, dey calls it."[17]

The song and shout of "Walking Egypt" expressed a yearning for a leader, for a Moses to carry slaves to freedom. "There are millions of my people on the plantations of the south," Harriet Tubman reportedly said, "I must go down, like Moses into Egypt, to lead them out."[18] "Walking Egypt" took the form of the ring shout, the shuffling, counterclockwise dance movement performed in the brush arbors or hush harbors of the field and revival meeting, where "[we] kept time with our feet" and "chant and hum all night." Following the Civil War, the first white observers described the ring shout. They reported that "the benches are pushed back to the wall, and old and young, men and women . . . all stand up in the middle of the floor, and when the 'spirichil' is struck up, begin first walking and by-and-by shuffling round, one after the other in a ring. The foot is hardly taken off the floor, and the progression is mainly due to a jerking, hitching motion, which agitated the entire shouter, and soon brings out streams of perspiration."[19]

In 1933 folklorist Lydia Parrish attended an African American folk festival in Broadfield, Georgia, where she witnessed a "tall Negro" lead sixty "sawyers" in a "shout." Noting that Negroes "hide their Africanisms" from whites, Parrish described the ring shout in terms that echoed back to "Walking Egypt." Following the leader's raised arms, which he crossed as a "sign of the judgment," the shouters moved first slowly then rapidly, "as if in a trance." Parish thought it evident from the "peculiar heart-clutching quality" in their rhythm that they "were possessed." As song followed song, those who looked on were moved to weeping, but "the Negroes appeared unaware of their surroundings."[20] During slavery, African Mississippians forged an Afro-Baptism that harbored the old within the practice of the new. Filled with the Holy Spirit, employing the language of Christianity and the emotional intensity of West African religion, they preserved their ancient heritage.[21]

During the Great Migration, African Americans expressed the idea of heading "home" in their aspiration for a better life on the "other side." In their spirituals, slaves had associated freedom with death but also imagined a biblical return home from the wilderness of slavery, "betwixt and between"—between bondage in Egypt and the freedom of the Promised Land. Susan Snow merged the political with the spiritual. She combined a vision of inner freedom with a yearning for liberation. The songs held people together, bound them as one against their bondage, taking them home—to freedom, to the "other side," to a better place, to a spiritualized Africa.

Going to church, Mound Bayou, Mississippi, 1939 (Library of Congress)

Home expressed the transcendent in African American slave culture. Transcendence could be reached during the shout, in ecstatic expression, in receiving the spirit, but also in its poetry. The slave song

> Did yo' ever
> Stan' on de mountain
> Wash yo' hans
> In a cloud?

resonated in the memory of Berry Smith of Forest, Mississippi. Estimated to be 116 years old in 1937, Berry remembered, "I was twelve years old when the stars fell. They fell late at night an' dey lighted up de whole earth. All de chaps was a-runnin' 'roun' for 'em, but none of us ever kotched one."[22]

Expressed in the present tense, "when the stars begin to fall," also told of Nat Turner's rebellion, finding in that rebellion a figure of the Judgment Day, intertwining the incantation of *mournin'* as an expression of grief, sorrow, and the approach of the new day.

> Oh what a mournin' (sister),
> Oh what a mournin' (brudder),
> Oh what a mournin' [dat day sister]
> When de stars begin to fall.[23]

For Mississippi African Americans, the spiritual always infused the material. There was no separation of the sacred and the secular. Life and death, baptism and burial, heeling by roots and herbs, conjuring and praying, mourning and morning, inner spiritual freedom and political liberty were always intertwined.

The 1938 Federal Writers Project *Mississippi: The WPA Guide to the Magnolia State* devoted three pages to "Negro life." In a state where African Americans made up a majority of the population, Mississippi's *WPA Guide* proved maddeningly patronizing yet remarkably perceptive. The writers identified religion at the heart of Negro culture and described it as "sensuous," "emotional," and "weirdly African." The *WPA Guide* described Rev. Cindy Marshall, minister of a Sanctified church in the Delta county of Leflore, who led her congregation to "moan, groan, and inject other psychological stimuli." Her followers "called her good Shepherd. Reverend Marshall always closed her services with a dance during which she would sit in a corner and sing. 'It ain't no sin t'dance so long as you don't cross yo feet.'" In Marshall's church, the "singing is done in earnest . . . until its weird harmony and spiritual uplift forces hands to clap rhythmically with the steady cadence of the drum."[24] In 1938 the ring shout remained central to Mississippi African American religious practice. Rev. Marshall's words—"it ain't no sin t'dance"—echoed nineteenth-century Gullah slave preachers who had explained, "Hit ain't railly dancin' lest de feets is crossed," and "dancin' ain't sinful iffen de foots ain't crossed."[25]

Following emancipation, Mississippi's African Americans practiced their religion openly. The patterns and rituals of Afro-Baptism provided cultural continuity in a world of flux. Afro-Baptism retained important West African components. Emotional fervor and the ecstatic nature of worship, intense preaching styles, and the call and response between preacher and congregation derived from the West African ring shout and the brush arbor of slavery. When Afro-Mississippians worshiped, they did so largely as Baptists. In the last decade of the nineteenth century, Holiness churches attracted congregations that closely resembled Sanctified Baptist churches. Sanctified churches appealed to increasingly poor and disenfranchised Mississippi African Americans. Rejecting some white forms of worship, Sanctified Baptist, Holiness, and Pentecostal churches sustained the rituals derived from the ring shout and the brush arbor.

FIRST TRAIN TO MEMPHIS

Tucked into the southeast corner of Tennessee, by 1900 Memphis had become the largest city on the Mississippi north of New Orleans. In 1900 its population had reached 100,000. African Americans constituted half the city's population, squeezed into the Greasy Plank, a tenement district of small streets, alleys, and mud flats that ran from Church's Park, just off Beale Street, to the Mississippi River at the south end of town. Nearby Beale Street served as the center of black life that included dozens of saloons, joints, theaters, and movie houses, mostly owned by Italians like Vigello Maffei, the owner of Pee-Wee's Salon, or the Barasso Brothers who in 1909, founded the Theater Owners Booking Agency (TOBA) and controlled black theater and entertainment throughout the South. Mayor, or Boss, E. H. Crump left unpoliced Memphis's Beale Street. Memphis earned a reputation as a wide-open city. Crump's Memphis teemed with characters like the desperado Two-Gun Charlie, who prowled Beale with pearl-handled revolvers.[26]

Black migrants to Memphis found work in local sawmills and rail yards and as dockworkers along the river. They earned a dollar a day, crowded into Church's Park at night, played on Beale on Saturday nights, and prayed in their churches on Sundays. By 1920 Rev. Charles Mason worked at the center of African American religious life in Memphis. Founder and bishop of the Church of God in Christ (COGIC), Mason presided at the Mason Temple, the Church of God's "upper room" where celebrants "tarried with the Holy Ghost."[27] In 1895 Mason had founded the Church of God in Christ in Lexington, Mississippi. Born in Memphis, trained as a Missionary Baptist minister, in 1907 Mason participated in the Azusa Street Pentecostal Revival in Los Angeles. Led by a black Houston minister, William Joseph Seymour, the Azusa Street Revival lasted from 1906 through 1908. Seymour preached the Holiness doctrine of Sanctification, and the necessity of receiving the Holy Spirit as a sign of holiness. The Azusa Street Revival had invited white as well as black believers. Seymour insisted on glossolalia, the trancelike practice of "speaking in tongues," as essential proof of salvation. Mason, too, accepted speaking in tongues and aligned his COGIC church with Seymour's Pentecostalism.[28]

Under Mason, COGIC churches attracted poor, working-class African Americans who had recently arrived in cities. Here, they found a spiritualized, energized form of Christianity that many urban African American Methodist and Baptist churches had abandoned as pagan and country. When Baptist churches in Mississippi eliminated the shout and the holy dance, many African Americans turned instead to the Holiness and Pentecostal churches.[29] Mason brought the "shout" music of the Azusa Street Revival to the urban South. Sung in an intense call-and-response style, the shout incorporated polyrhythms and hand and foot stomping of the ring shout. COGIC music used instruments—guitar, bass, and percussion—and its singers adopted the ornamentation of glides, note bending, and falsetto of the blues.[30]

Mason sponsored annual conventions of the Church of God in Christ in Memphis. He dubbed the convention the "big congregation" and, during the 1920s, attracted more than five thousand believers to its annual three-week revivals in November. The conventions made Memphis into a center of COGIC music and gave "shouting" singers like Arizona Dranes and Bessie Johnson a national audience. The COGIC style emphasized a rough, almost ferocious emotional delivery. Bessie Johnson sang with and against her choir, sawing her husky growl over the rhythms of its response.[31] COGIC singer Arizona Dranes, who lost her sight in the influenza epidemic of 1919, and Elder Curry, a disciple of Mason's, recorded the song "Memphis Flu."

> Nineteen hundred and twenty-nine
> Men and women, you were dyin' (Glory) . . .
> Death was creepin' through the air
> [What they got, for their sins] you were saved
> God's almighty hand.[32]

By 1930 Memphis had almost as many black Mississippians living in the city (35,000) as Chicago (38,000). Confined to a segregated and impoverished district, their music and religion helped them adjust to urban life. For many, Memphis served as a stepping-stone from the Delta to Chicago.[33]

THE DELTA

Before the Civil War, most of Mississippi was settled farming country, except for the Delta. As late as 1860, most of the Mississippi Delta, a plain of fertile land that extended along the Mississippi River from Vicksburg to Memphis and east to bluffs of the Yazoo River, remained a wilderness. Rich, flat lands shaped the region. For the next sixty years the Delta maintained a fragile balance between extraordinary natural wealth and far-reaching poverty, bound together by cotton. By 1867, only the Delta's river counties were settled. Most of the region remained a lush jungle-like plain of "great forest trees and a growth of ever-green cane and bamboo, through which no rider could pass." Steamy and humid in the summer, chill and damp in the winter, the Delta flooded each spring during the "rainy season" as wild panthers and bears roamed freely among the cypress, ash, cottonwood, oak, maple, hickory, pecan, and tupelos—whose ancient trunks stood as wide as six feet at their base.[34] To southern white writers the Delta seemed an exotic, wild place.

The Delta that I first knew was a land of unleveed small rivers, bayous, lakes, slough pools, ponds and swamps; pools where water lilies grew, ponds where crawdads pushed masterpieces of carved masonry into high towers . . . and swamps where Cypress grew to unbelievable heights; their bodies straight as arrows and their roots so widely spread it looked as though the trees themselves were set in a framework of roots. Frequently these roots curled around each other and pushed themselves into carved humps. We called them "cypress knees."[35]

After the Civil War, the Delta, the last American frontier east of the Mississippi, was one of the few places in the South that offered economic opportunity. Land could be bought for five dollars an acre in the river counties to the west. Blacks found work in the sawmills and turpentine camps in the swamps. A number of African Americans secured small farms or rented land to farm. In the last three decades of the nineteenth century, the Delta offered opportunity to blacks and whites.[36] The railroad and the Mississippi River levees remade the Delta from wilderness to plantation empire. African American labor built the levees, cleared the land, laid the tracks, planted and harvested the cotton, and prepared it for shipment. As Alfred Stone, a Greenville planter, acknowledged,

> The railroad rights of way through its [the Delta's] forests have been cut out by the Negro, and every mile of track laid by his hands. These forest lands have been converted by him into fertile fields, and their subsequent cultivation has called for his constant service. The levees upon which the Delta depends for protection from floods have been erected mainly by the Negro, and the daily labor in field and town, in planting and building, in operating gins and compresses and oil mills, in moving trains, in handling the great staple of the country . . . is but the Negro's daily toil.[37]

The river's annual floods gave the Delta the uncommon wealth in its soil. The river seemed timeless, enduring, and unconquerable while the railroads kept the Delta's time and drew it into the modern world. A half-dozen times each day, trains with picturesque names—the grand City of New Orleans, the Peavine, and Yellow Dog—marked the hours. While the main line of the Illinois Central divided the Delta from the remainder of the state, its feeder tracks ran through a hundred towns and villages. The railroad proved an unwitting, but not unwilling, handmaiden to Jim Crow. Its tracks divided each town into white and black, and the segregated seating of its passenger trains pioneered racial segregation of public accommodations. In 1890 the new Mississippi constitution excluded blacks from citizenship and reinforced the power of white landowners.[38] Bluesman

Mississippi John Hurt of Avalon sang about African American railroad workers, the "Gandy Dancers," who laid the railroad track. Hart reworked the John Henry legend into "Spike Driver Blues": "This old hammer killed John Henry, can't kill me, can't kill me," he sang in 1928.[39]

By 1892 the Illinois Central operated more than eight hundred miles of track in the Delta. The Y & MV provided service to New Orleans and Memphis and earned a local nickname, the Yellow Dog. Further south in the Delta, the Yellow Dog line crossed the Southern Railroad, marking the crossroads of blues folklore where "the southern cross the dog."[40] The penetration of the Yellow Dog into the interior of the Delta spurred cotton cultivation, ginning, and oil pressing, along with lumber, sawmill, and turpentine production. At the same time, along the Mississippi the vast federal levee construction projects dotted the river's banks with levee camps. By 1890 25 percent of all African Americans in Mississippi resided in the Delta. By 1900 seven of the state's ten blackest counties were Delta counties.[41]

The unceasing demand for labor made it possible for some African Americans to acquire a foothold in the Delta. In the 1870s and 1880s, as renters, leasers, and even owners, African Americans became farmers. Lumber mills also spawned small communities where African Americans could draw up favorable contracts allowing them to rent land against their cash-crop receipts. In the Delta's interior, renters predominated until 1890.[42] Over the next thirty years, black landowners and renters declined dramatically, a consequence of falling cotton prices and declining land values. By 1920 landless black sharecroppers worked two-thirds of the Delta's farms.[43]

Vast plantations dominated the Delta's Mississippi River and northern counties. Centered in Scott, Mississippi, and owned by a British consortium of cotton mills, Delta and Pine Land Company commanded an operation of thirty-seven thousand acres—more than double the acreage owned by *all* black farmers in the Delta. These enormous cotton plantations consisted of hundreds of self-contained sharecropping communities. The scattered settlements housed sharecroppers in wood-frame, unpainted shotgun houses, two-rooms deep whose doors opened directly onto vast stretches of cotton fields. At the season's start, landowners provided sharecroppers seed, fertilizer, the use of a mule, and the house to see black families through the year. They called it "the furnish."[44]

With credit and goods available at the plantation store, sharecroppers had little need to leave the fields. Makeshift schools and churches, cotton gins, and juke joints completed the plantation community. At the harvest came "the settle." Overseers figured prices for cotton grown and picked against the debts in the

Nugent Plantation, Mississippi Delta, 1939 (Library of Congress)

plantation store. The cropper family paid its share, between one-third and one-half, before it received a cash settlement. In good years, a family might earn a dollar a day. In bad ones, it fell into debt. The furnish and the settle bounded the lives of black sharecroppers in the Delta.

At first, to attract labor, Delta plantation owners enforced a relatively liberal system of race relations. They represented themselves as guardians of their laborers against the resentments of poor whites. "That was the way it worked," remembered Joe Rice Dockery, explaining how he bailed "his" Negroes out of the local jail. "And you had a decided interest in seeing that that person was let free to come home to be with his large family so he could go to work the next morning."[45] The Republican Party sponsored "fusion" political tickets in the 1880s that allowed some Negro representation on local election tickets. Before 1890, Mississippi's African Americans struggled with mixed success to hold office—sheriff, state house representative, county official—thanks to their participation as "fusion" candidates in the state's Republican Party.[46] The constitution of 1890, however, ended this practice. In the Delta, African Americans found themselves wholly dependent on the goodwill of large planters. Only in Mound Bayou, an independent African American town, could Delta blacks control their lives. Three years earlier, the sole African American delegate at the 1890 state convention, Isaiah T. Montgomery, had helped found Mound Bayou, the "Jewel of the Delta."

JEWEL OF THE DELTA

In most ways Mound Bayou varied little from the rest of the Delta. The consolidation of the Illinois Central Railroad in the 1880s opened the Delta's interior, some 4.5 million acres, to development. African American agents, working for the railroad's land interests, contacted Isaiah Montgomery, an ex-slave of Jefferson Davis and the owner of the Davis's plantation following the Civil War. The railroad agents enticed Montgomery to invest in the novel idea of an all-black agricultural community in Bolivar County, a dozen miles east of the Mississippi, midway between Memphis and Vicksburg. In 1887 Montgomery visited the site and purchased a tract of 840 acres for $6,000. He resold part of his holdings to his cousins, Benjamin Green and Joshua Montgomery. Together, the men surveyed and platted the land into forty-acre parcels, with space for a town. By the spring of 1888, the town of Mound Bayou boasted forty residents who lived in log cabins, a lively sawmill camp, and a number of forty-acre cotton farms outside the town.[47]

At first, Mound Bayou prospered. In 1909 Mound Bayou claimed thirteen stores, a train depot, a sawmill, three cotton gins, a newspaper, drugstores, boardinghouses, a hotel, several eateries, barbershops, livery stables, and a bank. The Bank of Mound Bayou, founded by Charles Banks of Clarksdale, a graduate of Rust College, opened its doors in 1903. Isaiah Montgomery, his daughter Mary Booze, and Banks became fixtures in Mound Bayou's Republican Party. Between 1895 and 1909, Montgomery and Banks promoted Mound Bayou with good success. Using their standing in the Republican Party and the National Negro Business League, they enticed President Theodore Roosevelt to visit Mound Bayou, where he made a campaign whistle-stop in 1907.

This visit coincided with the high point of the town's economic history. In 1913–1914, recession hit Mound Bayou and undermined the ability of local farmers to make their mortgage payments. By 1911 a majority of Mound Bayou cotton farmers had been forced to sign second mortgages on their farms. They faced the prospect of falling into tenancy and sharecropping. Slumping land values made it difficult for indebted farmers to stay afloat. For wealthy blacks, like Mary Booze, inexpensive land and surplus labor seemed godsends. She purchased large tracts of farm acreage at low prices and acquired all the sharecroppers she needed.[48]

Desperate, Mound Bayou town leaders sought outside help. The town's population almost doubled between 1907 and 1912, reaching nine thousand. A thousand others lived and worked in the town. All depended on the success of the cotton crop. In November 1912, to celebrate its twenty-fifth anniversary, Booker T. Washington spoke on the virtues of black entrepreneurship at the opening of the nearly finished cottonseed oil mill that many hoped would restore the town's economy.[49]

When Washington sounded the opening steam whistle, the gin was neither complete nor fully financed. Short of funds, Montgomery looked for outside investors. In 1914 he traveled to Chicago to visit Provident and Olivet Baptist churches. Next, he approached Chicago philanthropist Julius Rosenwald of Sears-Roebuck for a loan. Despite his efforts, the mill never came into full operation. The Bank of Mound Bayou failed in 1914, and when Booker T. Washington died in 1915, the town lost its most important promoter. After 1915 Mound Bayou's economic base rapidly eroded, marking the decline of African American fortunes in the Delta. Only Mary Booze, who embraced the sharecropping plantation system, thrived.

Despite such failures, Mound Bayou remained a symbol of African American pride and independence in segregated Mississippi. But it was an empty symbol. The self-help ethic of Booker T. Washington and the community's accommodation to segregation failed to bring prosperity. Its spiritual life, however, thrived. In 1888, a handful of Mound Bayou Afro-Baptists posed for a group photograph. Framed by a six-foot-long logging saw and an axe, the men in Sunday best and work clothes, sported Stetsons. The women wore bonnets and calico. Montgomery brought many of them, including his cousins Joshua Montgomery and Benjamin Green, from the Davis Bend plantation that he and his father, Benjamin T. Montgomery, had owned and operated until the estate fell bankrupt in 1885.[50]

In 1872, at Davis Bend, Benjamin Green and 114 other African American plantation workers attended a revival in a "grove of trees." Afterward, they were baptized in the river. The previous day, 130 had been reborn—for a total of 244 persons on a plantation of 300. A Freedman's Bureau agent described the revival as "the most emotional and demonstrative kind":

> Women go into a frenzy of excitement and roll on the floor for two or three hours together, screaming and crying "Lord take me," "Jesus save me," 'till utterly exhausted they fall asleep or experience something which they call "coming through" when they jump up in ecstasy of joy shouting "Glory, glory, glory, hallelujah" at the top of their voices . . . men walk around the house on their knees shouting. . . . And then they sing . . . all joining at the top of their voices, swaying their bodies to the time of the music, and clapping their hands in the most frantic manner.[51]

In 1887 the founders of the Delta town of Mound Bayou also gathered to form a new church. "Records show that these 'believers in Christ' erected a 'Brush Arbor' which served as a meeting ground" for the small frontier community. The original founding families of Mound Bayou worshiped at their brush arbor until they built their first church, Green Grove Baptist, on the same spot. In 1905 First Baptist replaced Green Grove with a redbrick building, its cornerstone initialed by the local chapter of the Knights of Tabor, which has remained for more than a century as the Baptist center of Mound Bayou. The weekly bulletin of First Baptist commemorates to this day the brush arbor origins of the church.[52]

Self-government enabled Mound Bayou to escape the formal humiliations of segregation. Mound Bayou suffered no curfew and its children attended their own public school. With one exception, Mound Bayou had neither "White Only" nor "Colored Entry" signs. Only the railroad station, which state law mandated, maintained separate waiting rooms. The stationmaster commandeered the smallest room in the depot and dutifully affixed a "White Only" sign. During the height of racial violence in Mississippi, Mound Bayou's African Americans lived in safety, under their own control.[53] "Imagine. It was safe here," remembered Preston Holmes. "We could vote, have our own sheriff, post-master, and school teachers, telephone exchange. And let me tell you it wasn't like that, not at all, within miles of here. Still isn't."[54]

In this all-black sanctuary, its people remained faithful to their Afro-Baptist beliefs. Despite the loss of the mill to white creditors, the closing of the gins, and two fires in 1926 and 1941, African Americans in Mound Bayou sustained their religion. Several churches practiced full-baptism using the "sand pit," a quarried pond just north of town, for the ritual. Baptisms in Mound Bayou often occurred in an August revival, at lay-by time, following the second chopping and before the harvest. During the revival celebrants walked from the mourner's bench at the front of the church to the outside baptism, white robes flowing, to be received into the church.[55]

In a similar fashion, Mound Bayou's Sons and Daughters of the Knights of Tabor explicitly affirmed its West African heritage. With roots in nineteenth-century myths of black rebellion, the Knights of Tabor became a burial society in the twentieth century and built its headquarters in Mound Bayou. The Knights of Tabor played a key civic role in Mound Bayou. The Taborians gave Mound Bayou a strong, religiously influenced, secret fraternal organization during its most difficult times. The Taborians' fraternal symbol was engraved on the cornerstone of First Baptist. A local teacher, Perry Smith, persuaded the Knights of Tabor to build the Delta's first African American hospital. Taborian Hospital, completed in 1942, allowed black patients, "for the first time, to walk through the front door of a medical facility, rather than through the side-entrance marked 'colored.' "[56]

The town's Founder's Day, with Taborians in regular attendance, began with a singing of "Lift Every Voice and Sing," James Weldon Johnson's "Negro National Anthem." It also included religious invocation, prayer, and Alfred Brumley's hymn "I'll Fly Away." Already a staple in the black Baptist repertoire, "I'll Fly Away" claimed an unusual origin.[57] Brumley, a white gospel quartet singer and farmer from the Ozarks, composed "I'll Fly Away" in 1931 while picking cotton. Brumley remembered an old work song, "The Prisoner's Song," and adapted its freedom "to fly out of that cotton field."[58] Brumley sold thousands of recordings of his first published song. For African American sharecroppers, still laboring in the fields of the Delta, the song offered a way out. " 'Some glad morning,' " recalled Rev. Willie Morganfield, a Baptist pastor and cousin to blues singer Muddy Waters, "gave us hope."[59] Brumley remembered a line from an old ballad, "Like a bird from prison bars have flown," which fit the Afro-Baptist belief of the reunification of the spirit at death.[60]

> Some glad morning when this life is o'er
> I'll fly a-way
> To a home on God's celestial shore,
> I'll fly a-way.
>
> I'll fly a-way, oh glory,
> I'll fly a-way.
> I'll fly a-way, in the morning
> When I die, hallelujah, by and by
> I'll fly a-way.[61]

African American religion survived in the Delta. The shout—and the continuum of dance, drum, and song, where "fast" spirituals made for pushing back the benches—remained in the small churches tucked away on country crossroads and on the edge of remote Delta plantations. In towns like Mound Bayou, where class and politics often eroded the communal spirit of the brush arbor, townsfolk and farmers, and then political bigwigs and ordinary shopkeepers, kept their social distance. As the gap between town and country, wealth and poverty, grew in Mound Bayou, so did the distance between churches. By 1930 half a dozen churches—Baptist, Holiness, Catholic, and AME—had established congregations in the town and in the surrounding farmland. While the First Baptist Church remained central to Mound Bayou's religious life, its own ritual practices became less demonstrative, less emotional, leaving the spirit of the shout behind, except during late summer revival. Out in the country tenants and renters continued to pray and worship as their ancestors had.[62]

HOW LONG BEFORE I CAN CHANGE MY CLOTHES

Only fifteen miles fron Mound Bayou, Parchman, Mississippi, became home to the state's notorious penitentiary. Parchman Farm's best-known inmate, Booker T. Washington White, was the blues singer "Bukka" White. In 1930 White cut several spirituals, including "The Promise True and Grand" in his first recording session. The twenty-one year-old White had lived in the Delta for several years, staying with a sharecropping uncle, playing and singing in local barrelhouses. In 1937 White was sentenced to life imprisonment at the state prison, Parchman Farm, for shooting a man. He would later write,

> I won't forget me the day you had me in Parchman jail,
>   Wid no one even comin' to go my bail.
> How long before I can change my clothes.
> How long before I can change my clothes.

Three years later, the governor of Mississippi, Paul Johnson, released White to record for Okeh records.[63]

Parchman Farm was part of the prison reform movement implemented by Governor James Kimble Vardaman, "The White Chief." Elected governor of Mississippi in 1903 on the slogan of "A Vote for Vardaman Is a Vote for White Supremacy," Vardaman galvanized class resentment of the Hills and directed it equally against blacks and Delta planters. Vardaman's administration began construction on Parchman in 1904 and opened it as a profit-making institution a year later. The Mississippi State Penitentiary at Parchman replaced the convict-lease system in operation since 1868 that had allowed the state to lease its mostly African American prisoners to plantation owners. As in the Birmingham Mineral District, owners provided convicts with food, clothes, and shelter in exchange for labor. Planters also received a subsidy from the state for prisoner "maintenance." Vardaman did not object to the brutality of the convict-lease system but only to the unfair advantage it granted to wealthy planters in the Delta.[64]

A racist demagogue, who wore a white linen suit, a black brimmed hat, and flowing long hair, Vardaman was born in the Hills. He made his reputation as a white supremacist as a newspaper editor in Greenwood, in the interior of the Delta. Here, Vardaman cultivated his Hills resentment of Delta planters. Vardaman also opposed funding for Negro schools. Vardaman's governorship coincided with an upsurge in antiblack violence that included public spectacles of official executions and vigilante lynching. Delta planters condemned the lynching epidemic. A Delta newspaper called them "Negro Barbeques." The Percys of

Parchman Farm, First Building, 1903 (Peter Rutkoff)

Greenville, the Dockerys near Cleveland, and later writer David Cohn all considered lynching brutal, distasteful, and low class. Much of their opposition, however, was due to their paternalist attitudes that considered "their" Negroes loyal
and childlike rather than the bestial sex-fiends of Vardaman's imagination.[65] Only
Hodding Carter, editor of the *Greenville Democrat,* challenged the Delta's prevailing upper-class genteel racism.[66]

Bukka White's commuted sentence typified racial justice in Mississippi. Local
sheriffs and courts imposed capital punishment and life sentences on blacks who
committed serious crimes against whites, especially crimes that involved sex
between black males and white females. In contrast, Mississippi courts rarely
punished blacks severely for crimes of violence against other blacks. Many whites
believed that by nature blacks behaved as brutes and criminals.[67] Or as Joe Rice
Dockery put it, "I've always said in the Negro race, as far as I'm concerned, there
never was any premeditated crime."[68]

According to prison lore, the Parchman sergeant, "Long-Chain" Charlie, appeared in county lockups and drove convicted felons, like White, by wagon to
Parchman Farm. The prison's main entrance stood off State Highway 49 about
fifteen miles of dirt road shortcuts from Mound Bayou and forty miles south of

Clarksdale. The Mississippi penitentiary at Parchman spread out over twenty thousand acres, making it one of the largest plantations in the Delta. It occupied forty-six square miles.[69] Parchman looked like any other large Delta plantation, indistinguishable from Senator James Eastland's plantation next door. The land lay flat and stretched out to meet the sky. Its cotton fields were broken by rows of small wood houses in which the guards lived. The state penal administration chose Parchman's wardens for their ability to produce a profit. Parchman's inmates worked for the state under conditions "worse than slavery," remarkably close to those of surrounding sharecroppers. In its best years, Parchman earned a million dollars for the state, and in 1933 it qualified for a federal farm subsidy of $75,000 for laying aside cotton acreage.[70]

Long-Chain Charlie, an incarnation of a number of Mister Charlies who wielded arbitrary authority in the Delta, wore a revolver and a long leather strap hanging from his belt. The sergeant roughly shoved prisoners, like Bukka White, before a long wood counter, where they received their uniforms—green, horizontally striped, loose fitting pants and shirts, called "ring arounds." Women at Parchman, fifty out of a population of two thousand in the mid-1930s, wore vertical striped formless dresses, or "up and downs." Ninety percent of the ring arounds at Parchman were African American, strictly segregated from white prisoners. Mister Charlie told the new inmates: "Mine y' own bus'ness, eyes down and lips zipped."[71]

About a fifth of Parchman's prisoners served as trustees, or shooters, armed with 30–30 rifles and dressed in "up and downs."[72] But all prisoners worked. "We worked from before you could see until you couldn't see."[73] Parchman farm earned a fierce reputation for being as brutal and hard a place as existed in twentieth-century America. Trustees who killed escapees were rewarded with sentence commutation. No one escaped. The prison graveyard was filled with the headstones of inmates whose remains no one claimed.

Under the guise of prison reform, Parchman inaugurated a practice of conjugal visitations in the 1920s. Officials believed that the regular, though not frequent, presence of women would improve the work. On the fifth Sundays of months with more than four sabbaths, the midnight train from Jackson arrived at Parchman station on the Yellow Dog line carrying "Big Leg Rosies with big legged drawers." The Midnight Special might even bring a cherished gift, a Rosie with a pardon in her hand for the ring arounds who awaited her arrival. "Heah come yo' woman, a pardon in 'er han' / Gonna say to da boss, Ah wants mah man."[74]

The Parchman execution on December 7, 1934, of Roy, a convict known as a "hard sinner" and a "bad Negro," created the legend of "Stagolee." A man who refused all who came forward to save him, Roy relished his last supper of "cigars and chicken and dumplings" with no remorse.[75]

When de devil wife see Stack comin'
She got up in a quirl, —
"Here come dat bad nigger
an' he's jus' from the under worl."[76]

The linking of his heroism with his "under worl" origins also linked him to West Africa. Behind his mask of the devil lay the trickster Elegba, who survived like the Hodoo doctor, in a "mean world alone."

African Americans at Parchman clung to their culture. They brought the work songs and field hollers into the prison from the scores of Delta turpentine, sawmill, levee, and railroad camps. They adapted them to Parchman where conditions were cruel, harsh, and limiting. Incarceration at Parchman meant hard labor from dawn to dusk. The Parchman work song, the "Midnight Special," Stagolee, hodoo doctors, and overcoming affirmed their African American identities. Misery and cruelty at Parchman mirrored and magnified the conditions of the Delta. The saying that the Delta was "Mississippi's Mississippi" paralleled the equally revealing saying that Parchman was "the Delta's Delta."

HIGH WATER EVERYWHERE

Parchman embodied the racial brutality of the Delta. Unbridled viciousness did not end at the prison's gates. It permeated Delta life. No event more clearly showed the oppressive and violent life of African Americans in the Delta than the great Mississippi flood of 1927.

Go look at the weather
I believe its goin' to be a flood
I believe my baby's gone quit me
Because I can feel it in my blood.[77]

The passion of feeling "it in my blood" saturated the events of the Great Flood. Of incredible, biblical proportions, the Mississippi River unleashed a wall of water a hundred feet high and three-quarters of a mile across into the Delta from the "crevasse" at Greenville in April 1927. It left death and destruction everywhere. In ten days, the flood covered a million acres under ten feet of water, left 185,000 people homeless, drowned hundreds, and exposed the myth of white planter paternalism.[78]

In Memphis, the Pentecostal voice of Elder Lonnie McIntorsh, a black man with brilliant blue eyes, told his flock about the flood—an event so devastating that it must be God's punishment for sin. McIntorsh's intensity, his "shouting" style, turned a historical event into a biblical tragedy.

It was in nineteen and twenty-seven
It was an awful time to know.
Through many storms and thunderin',
God let the water flow.

Well it poured through the land
And it killed poor beasts and man
For the people had got so wicked,
They wouldn't hear God's command.[79]

The Great Flood accelerated the transition between the so-called classic blues of the 1920s, the polished vaudeville blues of Ma Rainey, Bessie Smith, and Memphis Minnie, and the rough country sound of the Delta Blues of the 1930s. The Great Flood did its greatest damage to the Delta, but it affected the nation—from the headwaters of the rivers and tributaries of the Mississippi system in the Rockies and Appalachians to the great delta in New Orleans. The flood made a hero and president out of Herbert Hoover and made New Deal programs like the Tennessee Valley Authority inevitable features of American life. It also provided fresh material for Delta bluesmen.[80]

In the late 1920s, Howard C. Speir, a Jackson, Mississippi, furniture store owner and talent scout for several record companies, "discovered" Charlie Patton and persuaded him to record "High Water Everywhere," a ballad about the 1927 flood. In it Patton expressed the futility of escape.

Lord, the whole round country, Lord, river has overflowed
Lord, the whole round country, man, is overflowed
You know I can't stay here, I'll go where it's high boy
I'd go to the hilly country, but, they got me barred.[81]

Patton recorded "High Water Everywhere" two and a half years after the flood. Very likely, Patton used an improvised studio at Joe Rice Dockery's plantation near Cleveland, Mississippi. He told it from a black point of view, "I'd go to the hilly country, but, they got me barred." When blacks tried to leave the flooded Delta, they confronted violence from the white-capping counties in the Hills and from Greenville in the Delta. The planter-dominated Greenville Levee Commission organized miles of tent camps along the earthen embankments along the Mississippi River. Directed by white captains or overseers, blacks from the levee camps dug and hauled earth and rock to shore up the levee. With all of Greenville County under water, thirteen thousand African Americans, children, women, and men, lived and worked on the levees. The Mississippi state National Guard was under orders not to leave.[82]

William Alexander Percy, son of Republican senator Leroy Percy, Vardaman's political chief rival, headed relief efforts in Greenville. Percy, a poet, considered himself a friend of the local black population. As levee commissioner, Percy ordered, "No able bodied Negro is entitled to be fed unless he is tagged as a laborer."[83] In early June 1927, when the Levee Commission, the Red Cross, and the federal relief program required all Negroes to work on the levees, they also forbade anyone from departing, and banned all northern labor agents from the camps.[84] As General Curtis T. Green, National Guard general, explained to NAACP head Walter White, the policy aimed to keep the men on the levees until each planter had enough money to "claim his niggers." When a white police officer shot and killed a black male who tried to run off, Greenville faced crisis. Shortly after the shooting, Percy addressed Greenville's African Americans gathered at a Baptist church. For months, Percy told his audience, he had worked tirelessly for them and "during this time you did nothing for yourselves or us. . . . I am not the murderer . . . the murderer is you. Down on your knees, murderers, and beg your God not to punish you as you deserve."[85]

During the flood, an estimated fifty thousand Delta residents fell ill with pellagra, and a year after the levee break twelve thousand local residents still depended on Red Cross relief for food and shelter. The Great Flood was an economic calamity for the Delta, but for African Americans it was a cataclysmic disaster, as Patton had commemorated.

So high the water was risin' our men sinkin' down
Man the water was risin' at places all around,
boy they's all around.
It was fifty men and children come to sink and drown.[86]

The 1927 flood marked a parting of the way for Delta blacks. Percy's response laid bare the racism of the planter elite. Never before had Afro-Baptist spirituals and Delta blues seemed so manifestly true. The flood became the historical "crossroads" for Delta African Americans. Now, like other black Mississippians, they turned northward to Chicago. But not until 1940, when northern factories stepped up production in preparation for World War II, did the migration north from the

Delta turn into a human flood of even greater significance than the 1927 Mississippi flood.

In the first quarter of the twentieth century, "Son" House, Robert Johnson, and Charlie Patton formulated the guitar-based Delta blues. Each recorded only a handful of records, but those recordings served as the foundation of post–World War II American popular music. Patton and House preached for parts of their lives and shared a rough-edged, vocal style that expressed the suffering and resignation of other African Americans in the Delta. Johnson's evocation of Devils, Hell Hounds, and Bad Men spoke to the reckless and self-destructive side of Delta life that centered on illicit sex, heavy drinking, and violence. The blues functioned as a musical "crossroads" that could lead to the church and to the juke joint. The moaning, the call-and-response lyrics, the percussive tones, and the powerful rhythm shaped African American music, sacred and profane, wherever Delta bluesmen played their guitars.[87]

During the 1930s Delta bluesmen played across the Delta. Refusing to become sharecroppers, they could make three dollars a night at a fish fry or a house party. They adopted an itinerant life, thumbing rides on the backs of pickup trucks and jumping slow trains like the Pea Vine and the Yellow Dog. The bluesmen enjoyed a good life during the Depression when they offered everyone else relief from their daily misery. When they could afford it, they dressed in flashy outfits. When they could not, they dressed indifferently, indistinguishable from their audience. "Young, poor and mobile, they traveled from the countryside to the towns and cities and back again."[88]

Their blues stories dealt with movement, especially the railroad on which poor Delta African Americans depended ("How long, how long, babe / Has that evenin' train been gone"),[89] or the automobile ("I said flash your lights, mama / your horn won't even blow"),[90] or sex ("Hitch up my pony saddl' up my black mare / I'm gonna find a rider, oh baby in this world somewhere").[91]

In the blues, "the devil was in the turn-around," explained Paul Oscher, who played harp for Muddy Waters. In the turnaround, the music between the verse and the chorus, bluesmen stamped their identity on a song. The turnaround brought a tune back to its beginning. It completed the circle, making the blues a ring.[92] In the turnaround, the bluesman added his signature to a song that he had borrowed from other bluesmen. In railroad parlance, the turnaround was the roundhouse where crews turned the engine around, a crossroads that tied one place to another. Son House, Robert Johnson, and Charlie Patton formed an inner circle of Delta bluesmen. They crisscrossed the Delta for a decade, in fast cars, on slow trains. They preached and they sang.

Eddie James House Jr., "Son," came from Lyon, a small town near Clarksdale. House worked and drifted throughout the South and began to play guitar only in the late 1920s. When House took up the bottleneck guitar, he thought that he had left his religious upbringing behind. But, like many Delta blues players, Son House's music drew on the church and spirituals. In "John the Revelator," House left no doubt about the spiritual sources of his music. Son House played with great tonal resonance in "My Black Moma" and "Preaching the Blues." His bottle-neck style created a spare and sharp vibration, a West African inspired "whirring" that snaked in and around the words as his song "John the Revelator," illustrates.

> Tell me who's that writin',
> John the Revelator
> Tell me who's that writin',
> John the Revelator
> Who's that writin',
> John the Revelator,
> wrote the book of the seven seals.

Following a two-year stint at Parchman for killing another man, House played around Lyons, a short ride from Clarksdale. House's songs relied heavily on religious feelings and imagery, even as they seemed to criticize it.

> Oh, I went in my room, bowed down to pray
> Oh, I went in my room, bowed down to pray
> Till the blues come along, and they blowed my spirit away.[93]

The song attested to House's struggle with the church—"I'm gonna be a Baptist preacher, and I sure won't have to work." House explained, "I'm preaching on this side and the blues on that side. I says, well I'll just put them together and name it 'Preaching the Blues.' "[94]

House sang "Preaching the Blues" as an emotionally intense, highly pitched and strained spiritual with hints of work-song exhales. He accompanied the song with his trademark bottleneck style and simple turnaround followed by three upward picks. In contrast, Robert Johnson's version, "Up Jumped the Devil," recorded in 1936, moved like an express train. Johnson's open-tuned, bottleneck guitar resembled House's, but Johnson's pace and technique left House's older style behind.

Beer and juke joint, Clarksdale, Mississippi, 1939 (Library of Congress)

The blu-u-ses
    Is a low-down shakin' chil
    (spoken, "Yes, preach' em now")
Mmmmmm mmmmmm
    Is a low-down shakin' chill
You ain't never had 'em, I
    hope you never will.[95]

Johnson emerged as the great innovator of the blues sometime in 1933, shortly after his legendary crossroads encounter with the Devil. The transformation, in fact, allowed Johnson to adapt a raucous boogie-woogie blues piano style to the guitar thanks to a new open-tuning stringing. With this new tuning technique, Johnson learned to play intricate, piano-based accompaniments on the blues guitar. Johnson's 1936 recording sessions opened the way for more energetic and complex music that culminated in his "Sweet Home Chicago" that derived from more than twenty-three earlier versions.[96]

Oh, baby, don't you want to go, oh
Baby don't you want to go,

Back to the land of California
To my sweet home Chicago.

Charlie Patton, the son of a Sanctified minister, never traveled to Chicago but lived most of his life on the Dockery Plantation in the central Delta. Four hundred sharecropping families worked the plantation of eighteen thousand acres. Patton and Son House crossed paths at Dockery and again in the late 1920s in Clarksdale. Patton lived for a while in Marigold, a small town two miles south of Mound Bayou. Patton never parted ways with his religious upbringing. Like House, he insinuated his religious beliefs into the blues.[97] Patton recast a traditional spiritual into "You're Gonna Need Somebody When You Die," recorded in 1929. He retained the spiritual's pattern and added a short sermon in the middle of the song. Later, Robert Johnson turned Patton's song into a railroad song and retitled it "Last Fair Deal Gone Down." Johnson preserved the religious melody and structure but stated it in secular terms.

It's the last fair deal goin' down
It's the last fair deal goin' down
It's the last fair deal goin' down, Good Lord.
On that Gulfport Island Road.

The country blues of the Mississippi Delta combined the percussive pulse of the guitar with rough and unpolished vocal styles that blended West African sacred and secular themes. In the 1930s, Clarksdale, in Coahoma County, attracted bluesmen from across the Delta where they laid the foundation for even more dramatic musical changes.

THE SEABIRD BLUES

Clarksdale's boosters called their town the "golden buckle on the cotton belt." More millionaires per capita lived in Clarksdale than any other place in America. The Clarksdale Chamber of Commerce called Clarksdale "The Wonder City of the Delta." It included "19 churches divided among the following denominations: Baptist, Methodists, 1st Presbyterian . . . *and in addition there are ten negro churches.*"[98] The 1941 Fisk University music recording project, led by black ethnomusicologists John Work and Lewis Jones and accompanied by Alan Lomax, identified eight black churches and more than one hundred ministers.[99]

While blacks remained disenfranchised in Clarksdale, they composed 72 percent of the population of Coahoma County and more than 80 percent of Clarksdale's twelve thousand inhabitants. Typical of the Delta, race and class determined the neighborhoods of Clarksdale. Poor and middle-class whites lived close to one other, near the "Brickyard," a small Negro middle-class neighborhood. Upper-middle-class whites lived on the other side of town, across the Sunflower River and over a bridge to the downtown with its banks, post office, and library. Working-class blacks and day laborers lived in the Roundyard, a neighborhood just off the Negro Business District separated from white downtown by the railroad tracks. The black middle class of the Brickyard often disapproved of the Roundyard's ways.[100]

Clarkdale's whites shopped in the city's fifty-one food stores, twenty-two restaurants, eight furniture and appliance stores, five lumberyards, eleven automobile dealers, and nine drugstores. While these businesses opened their doors to blacks, they insisted blacks use separate "colored" entrances. Often they kept separate ledgers for their "colored" customers, identified by the initials COL beside their names, and preferred to serve black customers on Saturday afternoons and evenings, when whites stayed home. Whites owned all the businesses in the white downtown and often sent trucks out to the plantations to bring patrons into town on Saturdays, especially during the harvest.[101]

The Negro Business District clustered near the corner of Fourth and Issaquena streets. Most businesses were owned by blacks, Jews, Chinese, and Italian families. Clarksdale's small immigrant population, "about twenty-five or thirty families of Jewish storekeepers . . . a few Greeks . . . a few Syrian families . . . and a few Chinamen engaged in laundries . . . and some dope on the side," lived in between, often unwelcome by both black and white.[102] The district included Clarksdale's only black hotel, the Savoy theater, a single furniture store, three gas stations, a host of jukes, cafés, and beer parlors, barbershops, beauty parlors, groceries, and a funeral parlor. The two largest black churches stood directly across the street from the Dipsie Doodle, a favorite hangout for plantation workers in the 1930s where on Saturday nights they danced, ate tamales, drank beer, and listened to the blues on the juke's Seabird, as the bright new Seeburg jukebox was called.[103]

In the late 1930s, many plantations hired day laborers from Clarksdale. Early in the mornings, plantation trucks appeared at Fourth and Issaquena streets, where farm owners picked up laborers. When the need arose, plantations chartered Greyhound buses. By late summer 1941, labor agents appeared in Clarksdale from Missouri and Arkansas. Even before Pearl Harbor, the international demand for cotton had raised prices and wages in the Delta. In a single week, in July 1941, prices and demand doubled. "Not since 1926 had the wages reached such a level. Everybody was in the fields. People who had been working for meager wages in the town quit their jobs." Labor became so scarce in Clarksdale that "white women were driving through the Negro residential district seeking someone who would work for them."[104]

The labor shortage led Delta plantation owners to shift from mules to tractors. McKinley Morganfield, known locally as Muddy Waters, secured a job as a tractor driver at Stovall Plantation and supplemented his income by operating a juke joint in his home. He also played in Clarksdale on a regular basis. Clarksdale's juke joints exposed Waters to the host of itinerant blues musicians who passed through. "When I heard Son House I should have broke my bottleneck."[105] Waters could have said the same about Charlie Patton and Robert Johnson. When the Fisk team, including Lomax, recorded Waters in 1941, they found a mature Delta blues player who sounded as if he had been playing with these legends for all his life.

"That's a song I made up. . . . I was just walking the road and I heard a church song," Muddy Waters told Lomax in August 1941. The Fisk group found Muddy at Stovall Plantation where he had lived since the age of three with his grandmother. Stovall farmed 3,500 acres of cotton and employed ninety sharecropping families. Waters's household farmed about 40 acres. Starting at the age of nine, Muddy (that "little muddy baby") spent much of his time picking and chopping cotton. He received almost no formal schooling. Coahoma County had no high schools for blacks and only a few poorly funded and staffed elementary schools. Stovall black children received their education at home and in church.[106]

Stovall was a self-contained world. Unpainted cabins, mostly shotgun, see-through wood structures, occasionally three-room affairs, lined up along the main dirt road of the plantation. Back doors opened right out into the fields. Many, lined with newspaper and heated by wood-burning stoves, contained neither electricity nor plumbing. Sharecroppers dressed in the two sets of work clothes and shoes that Stovall provided as part of the furnish.[107] The gin and work shed dominated life on Stovall. A large wood structure, the work shed housed tools and mules and, after 1940, tractors.[108] On Stovall, a small church, Oak Ridge Baptist, completed the plantation community. Oak Ridge Baptist gave Stovall's African Americans a place to "jubliate." At Oak Ridge Baptist, they shouted during the hot and humid August revivals that coincided with lay-by time. They sang "Get Right with You Jesus" when penitents walked to the mourners bench to join the church.[109] The Oak Ridge congregation also performed a shuffle known as "Rocking Daniel," which they danced without crossing their feet.[110] Stovall's owner, Howard Stovall, liked a good tune and often hired local musicians to play

Jitterbugging, Clarksdale, Mississippi, 1939 (Library of Congress)

at family parties. As a young man, McKinley Morganfield played and heard the music at Stovall on all plantation occasions. To sing the blues, he said, you "had to go to church to get this particular thing in your soul."[111]

McKinley's uncle hoped that his own son Willie and his nephew McKinley would become ministers. In a sense, they did. Willie Morganfield became a Baptist preacher and famous gospel singer in Birmingham, Alabama, then in Cleveland, Ohio, and finally, back in Clarksdale. His cousin McKinley never joined the church, but his music never left it. In 1936 Willie's family left Stovall for Clarksdale where Rev. Louis Mathews Morganfield had been called to pastor. In Clarksdale, Muddy Waters had steeped himself in the rich blues music of the Delta. In 1941 and again in 1942 the Fisk Project directors recorded Muddy Waters. Of the five songs he played, two, "You Got to Take Sick and Die One of These Days," and "Why Don't You Live So God Can Use You," derived directly from church hymns. "You Got to Take Sick" was based on two sung sermons recorded in Chicago in 1929 and 1934. Waters drew on the recordings for his version. Muddy Waters's "You Got to Take Sick" combined his slide guitar whine with a chuch-a-chuch train rhythm. Waters explained that change, even death, was inevitable.[112]

You got to take sick and die one of these days,

You got to take sick and die one of these days,

All the medicine you can buy and all the doctors you can hire,

You got to take sick and die one of these days.

I BE'S TROUBLED

When Muddy Waters left for Chicago in 1943, he took with him the rich historical legacy of the Delta blues. Drawn from spirituals and work songs, bluesmen played in the jukes on Saturday nights and in their churches on Sundays. Their music shouted and shimmied, told tall tales and true stories. They conjured with black cat bones and mojo, wore red flannel and bore children at home, and mastered the verbal give-and-take known as "signifying." As he wrote in "I Be's Troubled," [I'm] gonna pack my suitcase / and make my getaway."[113]

Waters played "I Be's Troubled" on the steel-string slide guitar with an open tuning that combined the rhythmic and instrumental elements of Delta blues style with the lyric and sentiment of Baptist spirituals. The slide guitar style allowed Waters to shape and search for notes and sounds. Steel-string bottleneck playing incorporated the Muslim-influenced wavering, or melismatic effect, that combined with an open or drone string that gave some West African–derived music a single tonal center. West African musicians had often played single-string bows, sometimes resonating against the body or into the earth to achieve the same melismatic, droning effect that African American musicians incorporated into the one-stringed family of diddly-bows or nineteenth-century multiple-stringed banjoes.[114] "I Be's Troubled" bore the stamp of the Delta's West African and American heritage.

The lyric of the song brought together several other African American traditions. "I Be's Troubled" combined the obvious theme of loss and sorrow, in this case of a lost love, and evoked the familiar spiritual idea of troubles ("Nobody Knows The Trouble I've Had") with movement ("Trabelin' On"). Songs about spiritual and physical weariness, about being troubled and wanting to travel beyond the present, nurtured the blues. Even the syntax of the title, "I Be's Troubled," revealed Waters's cultural roots. Many West African languages and African American Gullah did not distinguished between past and present in some verb usage. In the rice lands slaves used "be," to describe habitual actions, past or present, plus the action verb—"you orter *be* carry money with you." "I Be's Troubled" could mean "I was troubled for some time," not embodying the grammati-

Belgrade Plantation commissary, Clarksdale, Mississippi, 1936 (Library of Congress)

cal error of using "be" for "am."[115] "I Be's Troubled" expressed the enduring quality of suffering. And, in the Delta, the only cure for suffering was to leave.

In the Delta, the annual settle between owner and cropper offered an opportunity for cheating through manipulation of simple arithmetic figures and the charging of unscrupulously high interest rates on the furnish. Often the only response available to the sharecropper was "skipping off" or "getting over." In "I Be's Troubled," Waters urged his listeners to "get-over" the troubles of heartache and exploitation and to "skip off." In 1941 this meant Chicago.

In Chicago, Muddy Waters recorded "I Be's Troubled" for Aristocrat Records under the title "I Can't Be Satisfied." It reflected Waters's altered perspective from the South to the North, of someone who had "skipped off."

> Well, I'm goin' away to leave
> Won't be back for more
> Goin' back down south, child
> Don't you want to go.

Beer hall, Mound Bayou, Mississippi, 1939 (Library of Congress)

Woman I'm troubled, I be all worried in mind
Well baby I just can't be satisfied.

The song also revised its Gullah-derived syntax. Originally written as "I Be's Satisfied," the verb "to be" an expression of past, present, and future, when Waters recorded it in Chicago, he altered the title to "I Can't Be Satisfied," placing it clearly in the present.

By the time the Coahoma project team arrived in the Delta, Robert Johnson had already died, murdered, residents said, in 1937 or 1938. In 1940 thirty-eight thousand black Mississippians already lived in their "sweet home Chicago," more than had resided in all Mississippi cities and towns in 1910.[116] Indeed, by 1930 more Mississippi-born African Americans lived in Chicago than in any city in Mississippi.[117] The Second World War accelerated this staggering movement of people. It also radically altered the Delta. By 1945 the mechanization of cotton farming made sharecropping economically impractical even as the demand for workers in the North offered a way out of the Delta's economic and racial oppression. Tens of thousands of African Americans from the Delta made their way to Detroit, Cleveland, St. Louis, and especially to Chicago.

From Clarksdale, Greenville, Greenwood, Indianola, Batesville, and Vicksburg, more than 100,000 African Americans from the Mississippi Delta carried their

Delta music and religion with them north. In Chicago, they remade South Forty-seventh Street and its "Bucket of Blood" into communities that resembled the black section of Clarksdale and other Delta towns. Chicago poet Gwendolyn Brooks peopled her South Side Chicago "Street in Bronzeville" with Delta characters—the bluesman, Stagolee, the Baptist preacher, juke ladies, and Parchman felons. They, and tens of thousands of other African Americans, chose to "Fly Away" to "Sweet Chicago," where once again they could "Walk Egypt" and "Rock Daniel."[118]

BRONZEVILLE'S PINKSTER KINGS

•7•

South Side Chicago

African Americans have lived and worked in Chicago since its founding. At the time of the American Revolution, Jean Baptiste Point du Sable, a "French-speaking black man" who built a log cabin on the mouth of the Chicago River may have been the city's first settler.[1] By 1910 forty-four thousand African Americans lived in Chicago, the nation's second largest city. Most resided along Chicago's Black Belt, a strip of dilapidated wood-frame houses south of downtown, bound on three sides by railroad tracks. The African American South Side extended south from the Loop along State Street to 31st Street. The city's pre-Migration Black Belt straddled State Street for its entire thirty blocks. Most African Americans in the Black Belt sent their children to the area's virtually all-black schools, attended local black churches, and shopped in white-owned businesses that served the community. On the eve of World War I and the Great Migration, African Americans constituted only 2 percent of Chicago's population. They included, however, a self-consciously important group of middle-class "Old Settler" families who had lived in Chicago since the Civil War.[2]

On May 15, 1917, Robert Abbott, editor of Chicago's leading African American newspaper, the *Chicago Defender,* in many ways the voice of Old Settler opinion, launched a "Great Northern Drive." The *Defender* urged southern African Americans to leave the plantations, poverty, and racism of the South behind to seek freedom and opportunity in Chicago. The *Defender's* Old Testament rhetoric— "The Flight out of Egypt," and "Bound for the Promised Land"—coincided with Abbott's program of economic and political independence for what he called "the race." By 1920 the African American population of Chicago had more than doubled to 109,000. Sheer numbers pushed the boundaries of black Chicago east toward Cottage Grove Avenue, west toward Wentworth, and south toward 55th Street. While some African Americans in Chicago lived in smaller enclaves on the

West Side, the vast majority of those who came to the city in the Great Migration crowded into the South Side Black Belt.

African Americans left the South for the promise of independence and a decent way of life. They willingly abandoned a racially hostile society in the South and entered the maelstrom of America's most dynamic city. They came from the sawmill and turpentine camps of the rural South, from the devastated cotton fields of Alabama, Mississippi, and Georgia, and from the cities of Memphis, Jackson, Mobile, Birmingham, and Montgomery. They poured into Chicago by train and found their way to the rooming houses and boardinghouses in the South Side Black Belt. Aided at first by African American self-help organizations like the Urban League and the Phyllis Wheatley Association, the migrants responded to the *Defender*'s call to search for better jobs, better education, and better lives. African Americans poured into the city even in the face of Chicago realtors' and politicians' determination to confine them to substandard and overpriced slum housing, which created conditions that set off Chicago's race riot in midsummer 1919.[3]

By 1930 Chicago's African American population had doubled again to 233,000. Then, despite the devastating effects of the Depression, Chicago's black population continued to climb. In 1940 it reached 277,000, more than 8 percent of the city's people. By 1960 Chicago's black population trebled again to 812,000, the vast majority of whom lived on the congested South Side. In this vast black metropolis, African Americans lived apart in their own self-defined world that resembled the Mississippi Delta as much as Chicago.

On the South Side, African Americans found themselves geographically confined, economically and politically limited, socially excluded, and racially feared. Their growing numbers fed white racial hostility that led to conflicts over housing, neighborhoods, and jobs. Newly arrived blacks pushed out against white resistance to their expansion. African Americans paid between 10 and 25 percent more than whites did for equivalent housing. For half a century, the *Defender*'s "promised land" resembled a combat zone. In 1918 a banner bearing the words "They Shall Not Pass," stretched across Grand Boulevard at 43rd Street. The banner, hung by the white Hyde Park–Kenmore Property Owners Association, expressed the vitriol of white resistance to African American expansion. Even so, on the South Side, within its narrow strip of residences and businesses, African Americans built an autonomous, largely self-governing, urban community that included blues joints and jazz clubs, gospel choirs, Sanctified churches, festivals, mayoral elections, dance clubs, gambling, prostitution, speakeasies, and sports.

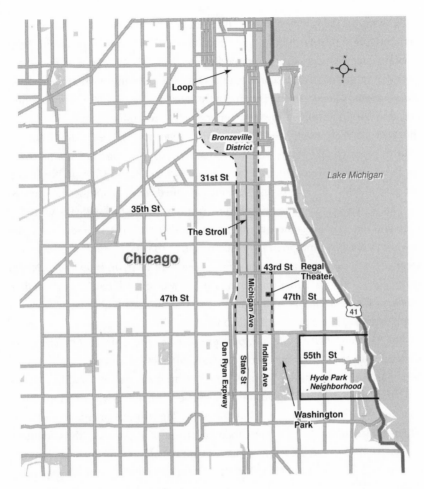

South Side Chicago

I CAN FRANKLY SAY THERE WAS NO DISCRIMINATION

As migrants arrived in Chicago, Old Settlers viewed them as threats to their hard won middle-class status and to the city's racial peace. As in Pittsburgh, after the initial shock Old Settlers took the migrants under their wing and helped them find jobs and housing. Then, they realized that the migrants' large numbers meant votes for the local Republican Party machine and power for themselves. Different in class, place of origin, and social behavior, light-skinned Old Settlers accepted darker-skinned migrants as an ambiguous gift.[4]

Newcomers did not always view Old Settlers as their betters. By force of numbers, migrants introduced the South Side and Chicago to their southern, West
African–inspired ways. Chicago's middle-class, black elite treated the first wave of
southern migrants as unwelcome guests. Old Settlers, many of whom came from
New Orleans, Canada, or the Upper South states of Missouri, Kentucky, Tennessee, and Virginia, judged the newcomers backward and ignorant. "There is a
different class of people who come into Chicago during the exodus from the
South," reported Old Settler Joan Snowden in 1938. "Chicago was not prepared
for these people. They criticized these people who came to Chicago [for] living
promiscuously."[5] Snowden, age seventy, explained that her mother had hosted
the Old Settler's Club in their home in 1905 and belonged to the Phyllis Wheatley
Club and the Urban League and that her friends were "very cultured."[6] Gertrude
Davis was born in Chicago in 1873. She served as the Old Settler's president and
recalled, "My mother was born in upper New York of Irish, Indian, and Negro
parentage . . . but my father was not mixed. He was just colored." Like Snowden,
Davis recalled her life in Chicago before the Migration with nostalgia: "I can say
frankly that I knew of no discrimination."[7]

Bell Harper Graves Fountain, past president of the Chicago Association of
Colored Women's clubs, member of the Old Settler's Club since 1874, also served
as a charter member of the Young Women's Christian Association. She and her
husband ran an undertaking business. While he was reading William Lloyd Garrison, an interviewer questioned Fountain about "discrimination and prejudices."
When told that the WPA project focused on the Old Settlers, Mrs. Fountain
replied, "Oh, you're at the wrong house as I am not old." Of mixed Irish, English,
Negro, and Indian parentage, Mrs. Fountain attended Quinn Chapel AME
Church, and had supported the creation of Provident Hospital, "the first colored
hospital in Chicago." Fountain praised the new migrants. "Before they came we
didn't live or own any of those mansions on South Parkway . . . the only thing that
caused quite a bit of trouble was that the white man exploited our people." She
added, "When I went to school there was no discrimination. There were so few
Negroes."[8]

The society pages of the *Defender* reflected such Old Settler attitudes. Robert
Abbott, editor of the *Defender*, embodied the Old Settler ambivalences toward new
migrants. A black-skinned southerner, Abbott came from St. Simons Island in
the Georgia Sea Islands, the son of a slave, who traced his lineage to the West
African Igbo. Abbott grew up surrounded by Gullah culture and language. Yet, he
banned the word "black" from the *Defender*'s style sheet. Raised on the outskirts
of Savannah by his mother and his German-speaking stepfather, Rev. John Steng-

stacke, Abbott also bridled at the term "Geechee," the Georgia equivalent of Gullah. Yet, at the end of his life, he turned to the Gullah folk traditions of root doctoring and conjuring that he had earlier described as ignorant superstitions.[9]

Abbott's feelings about race were reflected in the *Defender*. Educated at Hampton Institute, Abbott arrived in Chicago in 1893 to sing at the World's Fair. For a decade, he worked as a printer. When an Old Settler church rejected his application to join its choir, Abbott attributed the snub to his dark skin. In 1905 he founded the *Defender* as a "race" paper, which admonished African Americans to stand as one and overcome the class biases manifest in Du Boisian elitism and Washingtonian complacency. "American race prejudice must be destroyed," he published on the *Defender's* masthead. By the 1920s the *Defender* was the nation's largest black newspaper and had made Abbott into a millionaire.[10]

Chicago's Old Settler readers of the *Defender* were often light skinned, frequently college educated, refined, and self-consciously cultured. They included Pullman Porters, postal workers, a handful of professionals, and servants of the rich. They attended Quinn Chapel AME, Olivet, and Pilgrim Baptist churches, worked for the Urban League and the Phyllis Wheatley Association, attended the all-black Wendell Phillips High School, founded the city's black Provident Hospital, served on the Chicago police force, formed the all-black Eighth Regiment of the Chicago National Guard, and voted Republican. Highly visible, they represented only a small fraction of Chicago's African Americans. *The Wonderbook,* published in the 1920s by the Intercollegiate Club, an Old Settler social organization, identified only 963 professionals and 243 public officials out of 27,317 African Americans employed in 1910.[11]

In contrast, in 1910, 16,389 Chicago African Americans worked in "domestic and personal service."[12] A decade later, the percentages were even more skewed. New jobs in the slaughterhouses and the steel mills boosted black industrial employment dramatically. African Americans represented 20 percent of Chicago's blast furnace workers and 32 percent of stockyard laborers. In 1920, 63 percent of African Americans in Chicago worked in unskilled labor, another 32 percent in clerical and semiskilled jobs, and fewer than 5 percent were professionals or business owners.[13] During the 1920s, the percentage of African Americans in unskilled labor increased, with new opportunities in garbage collection, laundry, coal, and lumber replacing the loss of jobs in the slaughterhouses and packinghouses. Most employed African American women worked as domestics. In 1930 only "one fifth of the Negroes were above the rank of semi-skilled workers."[14] While the number of African American professionals in Chicago doubled between 1920 and 1930, their proportion of the black population decreased. In a community of a quarter of a million people, in 1930 only 308 African Americans held "regular" teaching positions in the Chicago public schools.[15]

In the 1920s Old Settlers worked diligently to refine southern migrants. "Don't use Vile Language in Public Places" "Don't loaf or talk loud in Public," instructed the *Defender*. The Urban League urged that new arrivals "refrain from wearing dust caps, bungalow aprons, house clothing, and bedroom shoes out of doors."[16] Whites told the southern migrants where they could not live and what they could not do. Old Settlers taught them how to behave so that middle-class whites would accept them as poor cousins. Fresh from the South, migrants entertained no illusions about white prejudice, and they had no intention of behaving like middle-class whites. They had come to Chicago for economic opportunity and personal freedom, not to repudiate their West African heritage.

THE STROLL: WHERE THE CHARITY CHILDREN PLAY

In the 1920s Old Settler "instructions" for sobriety, respectability, hard work, and ambition became the watchwords of Wendell Phillips High School. "Gradually colored since 1916," in 1928 the school moved from the old Black Belt, below 30th Street, to a new building on 39th. Phillips employed sixteen African American faculty members out of a total of forty-seven teachers. Phillips graduates included journalist David Kellum, who wrote for the *Defender*, several dentists and teachers, and a handful of "colored" athletes who played at Big Ten universities in the 1920s. Members of Wendell Phillips's Intercollegiate Club upheld the Old Settler values of economic and racial uplift, implicitly tailoring them to the new working classes in Chicago's South Side.

"Develop Your Economic Possibilities" the authors of the *Negro in Chicago* wrote. They touted the progress of such black-owned businesses as Powell's Garage and Filling Station, the Binga State Bank, the Overton Hygienic Company, and "manufacturers of pork sausage . . . ice cream . . . and candy."[17] The Black Belt expanded to include an entertainment district, centered on 35th and State, known as "The Stroll."[18] The push down the corridor between State and South Parkway opened new and sometimes palatial housing for Chicago's black middle and upper middle classes. Striking greystone townhouses stood along either side of the tree-lined South Parkway, where only a decade earlier wealthy whites had taken their ritual Sunday carriage promenades to the racetrack just below Washington Park. In a process of "musical houses," new migrants inherited the less desirable housing and storefronts that the black middle class abandoned.

The 35th and State crossroads anchored the new African American community. The massive buildings of the Wabash Avenue YMCA on 37th Street, the Eighth Regiment Armory at 35th and South Giles, the Binga State Bank at 36th and State, the Liberty Life Building on the corner of 35th and South Parkway, and the Chicago Defender Building on Indiana between 34th and 35th defined the new South Side. In 1929 entrepreneur Tony Overton located his newspaper, the *Chicago Bee*, and his cosmetics business, the Overton Hygienic Company, on 36th and State, in effect, marking the expanded boundary of the South Side.[19] At the end of the decade, the South Side's commercial district shifted southward to 47th Street, the site of the popular Regal Theater and Savoy Ballroom "for Negroes." For the next two decades, the Savoy-Regal complex dominated the entertainment of the South Side. On the eve of the Depression, black Chicago maintained two downtowns—one for commerce and culture at 35th and the other for pleasure near 47th.[20]

Chicago Old Settler poet Gwendolyn Brooks rooted her work in the South Side Black Belt. Her poem, "A Song in the Front Yard," yearned for the Stroll—and feared it:

I want to go down in the back yard now
And maybe down the alley,
To where the charity children play.
I want a good time today.[21]

Robert Abbott published Brooks's schoolgirl poems in the *Defender*. The mature, Pulitzer Prize–winning Brooks published her collection, *Street in Bronzeville*, in the late 1940s. While Brooks lived in the front yard and wondered about the alley, Abbott feared its discovery. Together, they voiced the anxieties that preyed on Old Settlers.

Painter Archibald Motley Jr. harbored no such reservations. He painted the Stroll and its migrants in their full and vibrant glory. The race riot of 1919 taught Motley that his relatively privileged life in the mostly white neighborhood of Englewood would not protect him from racial violence and hatred. Light-skinned, the son of a schoolteacher from New Orleans and a Pullman porter, Motley attended the art school at the Art Institute of Chicago. When the race riot broke out, he lived with his family, the sole African American family, in Englewood. White neighbors had asked the Motleys to sign a covenant on their deed that restricted sale of their house to whites. Despite assurances that they would not be excluded, Archibald Motley senior refused when he realized, "I couldn't even leave my property to my own children."[22] During the riot, the senior Motley barricaded his family behind the doors of the house they had lived in since 1907.

Standing watch with a loaded gun, his white neighbors protected the family from marauding Irish gangs.[23]

By 1927 thirty-six year old Archie Motley was recognized as one of Chicago's preeminent painters. He exhibited his paintings throughout the state and in 1928 received the prestigious Harmon Foundation Award, a Guggenheim Fellowship, and a one-person show in New York. At the start of his career, Motley painted portraits, but in the late 1920s he started to paint the South Side. The Old Settler Intercollegiate Club reproduced Motley's staid but well-painted portraits of Old Settler life. In *Grandmother*, painted in 1924, Motley portrayed his grandmother's world that included Emily Motley's Bible and Roman Catholic crucifix.[24] Motley painted his grandmother as part of a set of portraits that depicted the full range of class and color on the South Side. From young to old, dark to light, domestic servant to socialite, Motley offered a parade of people drawn from the Stroll. "I was trying to fill . . . the whole gamut," he told an interviewer later, "the race as a whole, not only, you know, being terribly black, but those that were very light and those that were in between . . . they're not all the same color, they're not all black, they're not as they used to say years ago, high yellow, they're not all brown."[25]

Like Gwendolyn Brooks, Motley lived along the front of the street but, unlike Brooks, he went downtown, to have "some wonderful fun." Motley first recognized his social isolation in grade school, "I used to go everyday to that poolroom to make sketches of them [migrants]," he remembered. "I made it a habit to go to the places they gathered . . . churches, movie houses, dance halls, skating rinks, sporting houses . . . gambling houses."[26] Motley searched for "them" along the Stroll.

The Black Belt's expansion after the First World War moved the red-light district with it south to 35th. There, the new jazz clubs, the "black-and-tan" cabarets of the twenties—the Elite Café No. 2, the DeLuxe, Dreamland, Plantation, and Apex—introduced jazz to all comers at all times of day and night. During the day, visiting Elks and Baptists walked up State Street while "women . . . wearing head rags of gaudy hues" watched from second-story windows. At night, the Stroll moved to the rhythm of its clubs and joints, to the swirl of streetwalkers' and shop girls' green and red dresses, and under the gaze of men in straw hats and bowlers. In and out of the "black and tans," the dance halls, and the cabarets, crowds ambled. Motley painted the neon lights playing on their faces and sidewalks, illuminating the variety of skin tones that he found fascinating.[27]

During the 1920s, the influx of New Orleans–based jazz musicians, like King Oliver and Louis Armstrong, introduced Chicago to a new music. New Orleans jazz blended piano ragtime with "gut bucket" blues groans, shouts, and whoops.

Popularized by radio, phonograph recording, and the South Side's array of clubs, cabarets, and rent parties, in the 1920s jazz became the music of the Black Belt. Oliver and his Dixie Syncopators pioneered jazz at the Plantation Café. His protégé, cornet player Louis Armstrong, reworked the New Orleans Dixieland style of Oliver into a hot, new urban jazz that swung. Armstrong's pulsating music, his improvisational genius, and show-stopping personality popularized jazz and introduced Americans outside the South to the rhythms, tones, and complexities of West African–inspired southern music. By the mid-twenties, music lovers proclaimed Armstrong the "King of the Stroll" and the 1920s "the Jazz Age."[28]

The New Orleans origins of Motley and Armstrong reflected the complexity of Chicago's South Side. In the 1920s many of Chicago's migrants had come from southern cities—New Orleans, Memphis, Atlanta, Mobile, Savannah, and Charleston. The Stroll resembled New Orleans's French Quarter more than the Cotton Belt. Bending rules about racial mixing, welcoming whites to its notorious "black and tans," and offering music, dance, liquor, and sex from dusk until dawn, the Stroll transported the freedom of New Orleans, Beale Street, and other southern cities to Chicago. While some Old Settlers found the Stroll licentious, new migrants, especially rural migrants, found it overwhelming. The Stroll offered a place in between: between Old Settlers and migrants, between blacks and whites, between Victorian respectability and modern disdain, between the rural South and the urban North, between the Jazz Age and the Great Depression.

Motley returned again and again to the Stroll. His paintings documented its changes. In the 1920s he pictured the new migrants, hands stuffed in their pockets and sheen in their hair, and their hopeful smiles filled his paintings. In the 1930s Motley shifted his gaze to 47th Street, inside its clubs and pool halls, to the joints where the new migrants hung out drinking whiskey, smoking cigars, and playing cards. In *The Plotters* (1934), *The Boys in the Back Room* (1934), and particularly *The Liar* (1936), Motley presented working men and women as confined and restrained. In *The Liar,* Motley contrasted a naive, adoring migrant with a cynical, winking citified man. The painting pointed out the hardened skeptics who knew better than to believe in their dreams. Motley set *Tongues (Holy Rollers)* (1929) in the rural South, but it easily could have taken place in one of the dozens of Holiness and Sanctified churches in the South Side. "Jesus Saves" proclaimed the legend on the wall. The congregation and preacher swayed and belted out their songs to the hand-clapping and foot-stomping music of a guitar and tambourine, a world apart from Armstrong's Stroll and Brooks's and Motley's Old Settlers.[29]

"The Liar," by Archibald Motley Jr. (Valerie Gerrard Browne)

A RHYTHM WE HELD ONTO FROM SLAVERY TIMES

In the 1920s most African Americans in Chicago belonged to a Baptist congregation. The preference of southern rural migrants for the shouting tradition led to
the growth of black Holiness and Pentecostal churches such as the Church of God
in Christ (COGIC). Most rural southern migrants belonged to either a Sanctified
Baptist church or a storefront Holiness or Pentecostal church.[30]

Motley's depiction of the "fronts," the small storefront churches that dotted
the South Side, attested to the persistence of traditional religious practices. Old
Settler churches, Methodist (AME) and Baptist, conducted formal and subdued
services, accompanied by European hymn singing. Migrants found such services
spiritually lacking, without warmth and feeling. New migrants either turned to
more southern churches or forced Old Settler churches to adopt southern ways.

Crowd outside of fashionable African American church after Easter Sunday service, Black Belt, Chicago (Library of Congress)

Olivet Baptist, founded in 1850 as Chicago's oldest African American Baptist church and the mother church to twelve other congregations, grew from six hundred parishioners in 1902 to four thousand in 1915 to eight thousand in 1918. Two of its pastors, Elijah John Fisher and his successor Lacey Kirk Williams, changed Olivet from a "sin and salvation" church into an agent of social welfare. Under the leadership of Fisher and Williams, Olivet provided its members housing, jobs, and health assistance programs, an African American version of Hull House. Fisher's daughter, Matte Fisher, one of Chicago's first African American social workers, interviewed migrants to determine how best to serve them. Williams sent congregants to the 12th Street railroad station to greet and assist newly arrived migrants. Southerners swelled Olivet's ranks even as it moved southward with other Old Settlers. In 1927 Olivet relocated from 27th and Dearborn to 31st and South Parkway. Olivet took over the former white First Baptist Church. By the end of the decade, Olivet had become the largest African American church in the United States.[31]

In contrast, Pilgrim Baptist Church opened at the beginning of the Migration. In 1915 several families met in the home of a West Side family. The church moved from living room to living room in the neighborhood, leading to the name "Pilgrim," until it rented a South Side storefont on Wentworth at South 49th. In 1918

Pilgrim Baptist moved again to 37th and Indiana and again, in 1922, to an Adler and Sullivan–designed, former synagogue on 33rd and Indiana. In the early 1930s, Pilgrim joined Olivet as one of the great African American churches on Chicago's South Side. Several other churches emulated their success. Liberty Baptist, founded in 1918 at the home of a Bertie Boone, swelled from 120 congregants in 1925 to 3,500 in 1938.[32]

The Reverend Thomas Emerson Brown, a steel worker from Mississippi, chose another path. Brown arrived in Chicago in 1915 and, soon after, launched his ministry from an apartment on 37th and LaSalle above an abandoned saloon. Five families in the South Side working-class enclave, known as the "Bucket of Blood," urged Brown to form a new church, which they named Progressive Baptist Church. Progressive chose not to move south, away from its LaSalle-Federal-Wentworth neighborhood. Rather, Brown built Progressive's massive congregation on its working-class, Mississippi migrant base.[33]

By 1927, out of the roughly three hundred African American churches in Chicago, fifty-five of the largest boasted a total membership of sixty-six thousand, whereas some of the smaller churches had as few as two dozen members. These small churches met wherever they could secure space in family sitting rooms, funeral parlors, and storefronts. At first seen as remnants of older and passing southern rural life, by the 1950s most South Siders were affiliated with either a Sanctified Baptist, Holiness, or Pentecostal church.

Olivet and Pilgrim joined Abbott's campaign to uplift "the race" and to ease migrants' transition to the city. Their pastors and deacons still saw no need to provide an old-time, Sanctified service that many southerners longed for. The shift of many successful African American Baptist and Methodist churches from "demonstrative to deliberative" churches and from "simplicity to stateliness" left migrants cut off from their southern traditions.[34] A number of independent nondenominational, Holiness, and Pentecostal churches offered the spiritualized worship services many southern migrants craved. These new churches grew at the expense of the established Baptist and African American Methodist churches. In 1928 the combined thirty-five AME, AME Zion, and Christian Methodist Episcopal congregations represented 12 percent of Chicago's African American churches. A decade later, the percentage had dropped to 9 percent. At the same time, the percentage of Holiness and Pentecostal churches grew from 19 to 23 percent. Many were small congregations located north of 47th Street.[35]

New arrivals, greeted by social service representatives from churches like Olivet, attended church with their mainline hosts but often searched for a more familiar, southern alternative. One member of a migrant church said of her

St. Peter's Rock Baptist Church, Chicago (Library of Congress)

service, "I like [it] better . . . because the service was more like the service they had at home." She liked the minister, too. "I like his preaching better than I do the preachers that were educated in the North. The sound is so different."[36]

Not all the new churches that began as South Side storefronts in the 1920s traced their origins to southern dissatisfaction with northern styles. In September 1923 more than a hundred parishioners of St. Mary's AME Church at 53rd and Federal gathered in an apartment at Williamson's Funeral Parlor. Mrs. Marjorie Stewart Joyner, a wealthy Old Settler clubwoman and an executive in Madame C. J. Walker's cosmetic empire, had invited the new congregation to declare its independence from the AME bishop. The new nondenominational congregation, "established to commemorate the untiring work of women in the first Negro church in Chicago," limped along on a shoestring budget for a decade.[37] Then, in 1931, on the verge of bankruptcy, having collected barely $3,000 from its entire congregation for the year, Cosmopolitan Community Church found a new pastor.

Forty-year-old Mary Green Evans had worked as an itinerant evangelist and AME organizational fundraiser in Indiana. She joined Cosmopolitan Community Church following her own difficulties with the male-domination of the district in Indianapolis. By the end of the decade, Cosmopolitan had grown eightfold. Evans established a tithing tradition where more than one-third of the congregation, in the midst of the Depression, gave a tenth of their income, refurbished the building on 52nd and South Wabash, and claimed an income of more than $20,000.[38] A woman of renowned rhetorical and organizational ability, Mary Evans extended her church into the community. The church built two playgrounds, a community house, and a home for the elderly. Later it provided locations for Boy and Girl Scout Troops and launched a neighborhood nursery school. Like the old-line churches Olivet and Pilgrim Baptist, Cosmopolitan Community Church extended an Old Settler–style embrace to the newly arrived.

From the beginning of the Great Migration, both lay and clerical African American women, like Marjorie Stewart Joyner and Mary Green Evans, played critical roles in the leadership of Chicago's first female church. By the mid-1930s, Evans organized the members of her congregation into twelve fundraising committees, one for each member's birth-month. Later, she added two more, each of which regularly outperformed the others. Committee 13 belonged solely to the pastor, Dr. Evans, as she called herself, and Committee 14 to the stalwart Marjorie Stewart Joyner. At Cosmopolitan Community Church, African American women presided and raised the roof both spiritually and materially.

Elder Lucy Smith, pastor of All Nations Pentecostal Church, had migrated to Chicago from Georgia in 1910. Born in 1875 as Lucy Madden, Elder Smith had worked for most of her life as a sharecropper, moving to Atlanta for a few years before migrating north. Lucy Smith joined Olivet Baptist but stayed only a short time. She affiliated briefly with Ebenezer Baptist, before joining a Pentecostal congregation in 1914, Stone Church at 37th and Indiana. Stone Church, just south of the pre-Migration Black Belt, had a white congregation. There, in the wake of the Azusa Street Pentecostal Revival, Smith received her call and was baptized by the Holy Ghost.[39] In 1916 she established her own church, whose mission was based on the signs of Pentecost and her gifts of "divine healing."[40]

For the next decade, Lucy Smith wandered the South Side leading a small band of worshipers, the All Nations Pentecostal Church. All Nations set up its tents wherever Smith could find a vacant lot. In 1926 she built a permanent home at 3716 South Langley. In the 1920s, the city had designated a narrow strip of the Black Belt, just south of the Stroll, for slum clearance. Impoverished residents turned to churches like Progressive Baptist and All Nations for support. Calling herself the "preacher to the disinherited," Elder Smith organized a social as well as spiritual uplift program that provided food and clothing to the needy in her congregation. By the mid-1930s, Smith was Chicago's premier radio preacher.

She attracted food donations to her church from a wide spectrum of listeners who responded to her healing powers.[41]

Offerings at Smith's services provided the money to build a new church on Oakwood Boulevard.[42] Smith developed a particularly close relationship with Mary Evans following a "miraculous healing" in 1941.[43] The spirit of West African religion united the two women, who thrived in a religious community traditionally dominated by males. Elder Smith's conversion to Pentecostalism led the Church of All Nations to embrace Sanctified singing in its service. Combining syncopation derived from ragtime with the traditional chorded structure of Protestant hymns, the "gospel" beat of pioneering Sanctified singers like Arizona Dranes harked back to the piercing cries of the shout. Dranes, like a dozen other blind Sanctified voices in the 1920s, performed in churches, in tents, and on the streets. The power of her voice and "its piercing quality . . . cut through the clapping and stamping of church services."[44] Emotional and spirited, Sanctified singing reflected the shouting of the small Pentecostal and Holiness churches that the new migrants longed for. Singer Mahalia Jackson remembered, "These people had no choir and no organ. They used the drum, the cymbal, the tambourine, and the steel triangle. Everybody . . . clapped and stomped their feet and sang with their whole bodies. They had a beat, a powerful beat, a rhythm we held on to from slavery days."[45]

Elder Smith's All Nations Church held the beat. Its parishioners shouted the "holy dance" and embraced the energy of the praise house.[46] Smith's own granddaughter Lucy played the piano at the age of four. She studied with the gospel pioneer Roberta Martin, who married Lucy's father.[47] At age sixteen "Little Lucy" Smith was All Nations' organist and singer. During the 1930s, Little Lucy became a local star with a voice that made her "the sweetest singer in the world."[48] Smith belonged to a generation of Chicago gospel singers and performers who transformed African American sacred music by bringing it back home. In Chicago, Smith's teacher, Roberta Martin, the powerful Mahalia Jackson, and pianist-composer Thomas A. Dorsey created a new gospel music for African Americans. By bringing the blues into church music, they restored the elements, the flavor, and the style of the black folk spiritual tradition that no amount of politeness or "stateliness" could ever extinguish.[49] The blues inflection of Chicago gospel sounded, in the words of Mahalia Jackson, "like a letter from home," the music "colored people left behind." It provided them with a compass to navigate the northern present.[50] In Chicago, the blues revived the spirit of religious music. Charles Mason, founding bishop of the Pentecostal Church of God in Christ (COGIC) proclaimed, "Why should the devil have all the good music."[51]

PRECIOUS LORD, TAKE MY HAND

Thomas A. Dorsey codified Chicago gospel blues. Dorsey brought together several elements of African American music to create a new sacred music. To the traditions of gospel hymns and anthems, Sanctified singing, and folk and concert spirituals, he added the blues, with its pentatonic scales, bent notes, and improvisational embellishment. Willie Webb, a contemporary gospel musician, said, "Dorsey wrote down what was 'out there.' He was not the first to use blues elements, but he was the first to write it down."[52] At a time when the South Side had fallen into the depths of the Depression, Dorsey offered musical consolation. His compositions shared the swing of Chicago jazz, of Louis Armstrong's syncopated "West End Blues," and they also spoke to the black urban experience of Depression-era Chicago. As one writer recorded of black Chicago during the 1930s, "This is the heart of the Black Belt. Signs read 'We Repairs: radios, stoves, electric irons, sewing machines.' Windows broken, stuffed with rags or covered with cardboard. A four story tenement advertises 'five rooms for fifteen dollars.' Nearby, cafes, taverns, groceries and a barber. The grocery store displays a sign 'we accept relief orders.' "[53]

Dorsey drew on musical ideas that had surfaced in the 1920s. In 1921 the publication by the National Baptist Convention of *Gospel Pearls* gave African American Baptists a rich body of music that many old-line Chicago churches regarded as "low-down, low-class."[54] *Gospel Pearls* embraced a wide range of songs that included the music of Sanctified churches and traditional hymns, from "ecstatic" Holiness shouts to "Stand by Me."[55] When Thomas A. Dorsey introduced Ebenezer and then Pilgrim Baptist churches to his bluesy gospel songs, *Gospel Pearls* had prepared the way. In the 1920s church musicales showed off trained choirs and European repertoires. Many of the southern migrants, who had initially swelled these churches to overflowing, had left to start new churches. Those who stayed expressed a desire for more lively religion and music. The ministerial and lay leaders of Olivet, Pilgrim, and Ebenezer sought to balance the needs of "shouters" and "nonshouters." In the early 1930s, newly created gospel choirs were relegated to basements, while church chorale groups and their orchestras practiced in the sanctuary. An old-line choir director remarked, "The Negro people liked Gospel 'cause it goes back to Africa."[56]

When Georgia-born Thomas A. Dorsey came to Chicago he was known as "Barrel House Tom," an accomplished honky-tonk piano player. Dorsey's migrant experience and his roots in the southern church left their imprint on his music. The son of a minister, "Barrel House Tom" became "Georgia Tom" in the mid-

1920s when he cut a pioneering "hokum" record, "Tight Like That." The success of the 1928 novelty record earned extra money for Dorsey, who had worked nights in Gary steel mills while he both studied composition and accompanied Ma Rainey, the legendary blues singer.[57] In the 1920s Rainey, Bessie Smith, and Clara Smith brought blues out of the black vaudeville circuit and into the mainstream of popular music. "Race" records brought these "Queens of the Blues" to a wide, national audience.[58] Dorsey took Rainey into religious music. "She possessed her listeners; they swayed, they rocked, they moaned and groaned, as they felt the blues with her."[59] In Rainey's music Dorsey found the southern elements of Pentecostal music, the call and response, ecstatic expression ("raising the roof"), hand clapping, and foot stomping. He recalled, "I always had rhythm in my bones. I like the solid beat. I like the moaning and groaning tone. You know how they rock and shout in church. I like it."[60]

Between 1928 and 1932, Dorsey restored the blues to Baptist music. The blues added the shouts, embellishments, flattened thirds, and "blue" notes that old-line churches had repressed.[61] When the pastors of Ebenezer and Pilgrim recognized the attachment of their migrant congregations to the old music, they allowed Dorsey's moaning style back into the sanctuary. In 1932 Pilgrim Baptist Church appointed Dorsey as its gospel chorus director. Dorsey's first important gospel blues, "Take My Hand, Precious Lord," established him as Chicago's preeminent gospel music composer. Written in the wake of the deaths of his wife and newborn son in August 1932, "Precious Lord" marked Dorsey's abandonment of the blues for the gospel blues. "Georgia Tom" had died.

> Precious Lord take my hand,
> Lead me on, let me stand
> I am tired, I am weak, I am worn.
> Through the storm, through the night
> Lead me on to the light,
> Take my hand Precious Lord, lead me home.

"Precious Lord" belonged to Chicago's impoverished black community. The song reached back to the spiritual traditions of the praise house and the brush arbor. But, by Dorsey's placement of a single "haunting" blue note on the word "hand," it also vibrated with the blues.[62]

Dorsey did not work in isolation. Mahalia Jackson and Roberta Martin also helped formulate Chicago's gospel music in the 1930s. Jackson's style came directly from Sanctified singing and shouting—"a full throated tone, delivered with a holy beat and a body rhythm to accent that beat."[63] In 1930 the nineteen-year-old

"Hallie," who had come from New Orleans, accepted Dorsey's invitation to "demonstrate" his music. Dorsey wrote and published songs that Jackson sang on the "Gospel Highway," the national network of churches, conventions, and radio programs that Dorsey directed from Chicago. Jackson and Dorsey worked together for the next twenty years. Recording and financial success, however, eluded Jackson. To supplement her income, she enrolled in a local beauty school and opened "Mahalia's Beauty Salon" where she worked until 1948, when her recording of "Move on up a Little Higher" brought her national attention and the title "Gospel Queen." "Move on up a Little Higher" became Jackson's "going to heaven workouts," a house wrecker that brought audiences to their feet, clapping and shouting. Jackson's driving rhythm and beat moved singer and audience to a "frenzy of intensity almost demanding a release of holler and shout."[64] At the funeral following Martin Luther King Jr.'s assassination in 1968, Jackson sang "Take My Hand, Precious Lord" at the COGIC Mason Temple in Memphis.

Roberta Martin came to Chicago with her family in 1917. She had grown up in Helena, Arkansas, across the Mississippi from Clarksdale. Graduating from Wendell Phillips High School, Martin worked with Dorsey at Ebenezer Baptist Church and formed her own "quartet" of five young men, drawn from Ebenezer and Pilgrim. The Roberta Martin Singers sang a refined gospel sound, first as an all male group and then, in the early 1940s, with two female voices. Working without a bass, Martin blended soprano, tenor, and baritone voices to create a refined, more harmonic gospel style in contrast to Mahalia Jackson's powerful shout. Martin's devices of "few tones, small intervals, and resolutions around a principal tone" that relied on the pentatonic scale derived from West African music.[65] Together, Dorsey, Jackson, and Martin offered a range of gospel music that drew on Sanctified shouts and mainline hymns. They altered gospel music, making it urban without losing touch with its rural roots.

BUD BILLIKEN AND BRONZEVILLE'S PINKSTER KINGS

The South Side's southern and West African sprit was not confined to the church and the dance hall. In the 1930s Chicago's African American migrants inaugurated two intertwined public rituals, Bud Billiken Day and the election of the mayor of Bronzeville. Bud Billiken Day began in 1930 as a midsummer frolic, a diversion from the routines of workaday Chicago. Within a decade, it became Chicago's African American New Year, Decoration Day, Fourth of July, and Mardi Gras all rolled into one. "It was the greatest parade Chicago has seen since

Charles Lindberg," bragged the *Chicago Defender*, sponsor of the first Bud Billiken Day in mid-August 1930.[66]

A year after the stock market crashed, Robert Abbott used the festival to prop up his struggling *Defender* newspaper. Organized as a sales gimmick, for seventy-five years Bud Billiken Day became the South Side's great community occasion. As the Bud Billiken Day Parade grew larger, longer, and grander, its ranks filled with thousands of recently arrived migrants, whose parents and grandparents had marched in southern Decoration and Emancipation Day celebrations. In 1934 Bud Billiken Day merged with a second *Defender*-sponsored event, the election of the mayor of Bronzeville. Together, they gave the South Side a modern-day West African–inspired Pinkster Day festival that linked the South Side to northern African American communities in the eighteenth and nineteenth centuries.

Abbott and the *Defender* initiated the two events, but almost immediately Bronzeville claimed them as its own. The Bud Billiken Day Parade and the mayor of Bronzeville election became the cultural property of the South Side. In the 1930s, during Bud Billiken Day, Chicago African Americans dressed up in their Sunday best in defiance of the hardships of the Depression, much as their slave ancestors had done on Christmas and Watch Night. When they chose their honorary mayor of Bronzeville, they declared their political independence from white Chicago.[67]

Sharply at ten o'clock on Saturday morning, August 16, 1930, Major N. Clark Smith, former bandmaster at Tuskegee Institute and current music director of Wendell Phillips High School, launched the inaugural parade. Smith proudly led the procession of floats and cars, flanked by a flotilla of screaming motorcycles, down the boulevard. They marched, "high stepping" in a cakewalk down the length of South Parkway. The parade passed the elegant greystones and former synagogues that had become part of the South Side, ending at the northern end of Washington Park. Between 51st and 55th streets, the holiday throng played baseball, gobbled down gallons of free ice cream, and cheered the hundred bathing beauty contestants in a soaking, mid-August rain. In the teeth of the Depression, Bud Billiken Day participants "put on the ritz." Young girls posed for the bathing beauty contest held at the duck pond in the northern corner of Washington Park. Dorothy Mae Duke, reported the *Defender*, won first prize, "a 35$ blue automobile equipped with a windshield, rubber tires, a horn, and 1930 license plates," courtesy of the L. Fish Furniture Company.[68]

The first Bud Billiken Day Parade marched to the southern boundary of black Chicago. The route, from 35th Street south to 55th Street, along Grand Boulevard and South Parkway and into the northern and western quadrant of Washington Park, publicly marked out the current boundary of the African American South Side.[69] In 1930 African Americans lived only along the north and northwest sides of Washington Park.

The idea of the parade can be traced back to 1923, the year that novelist Willard Motley invented the cartoon character of Bud Billiken for the *Defender*.[70] When Motley left Chicago in 1929, the *Defender* parlayed the character into a successful national promotion gimmick.[71] Using Billiken as the newspaper's mascot, Abbott organized dozens of Bud Billiken Clubs for children who pledged to read the *Defender*.[72]

The "Rules of the Bud Billiken Club" emphasized middle-class respectability and race pride.[73] Billiken urged young black readers to honor their parents, their nation, and their church.[74] In 1930 *Defender* staff writer David Kellum assumed the Billiken persona, a role he maintained well into the 1940s. Despite Abbott's intention to boost circulation and to instruct migrants on appropriate behavior, Bud Billiken Day took on a life of its own as it changed from a kids' promotion to a summertime jubilee, becoming an urban African American celebration. In 1933, the parade's fourth year, Abbott rode in an open white Rolls Royce and reviewed the entire parade that included Crown Prince Allaoumi of Nigeria "and his witch doctor, Abdou of Kano, the most powerful member of the Yoruba tribe." The West Africans, decked in gold, "as an emblem of power," came from the Century of Progress exhibit of "Darkest Africa" at the 1933 World's Fair. The "witch doctor," according to the *Defender*, played a "queer but beautiful music, flanked with tom-toms and royal drums of the ancient province."[75]

"If there ain't 45,000 people out there today, there ain't a hound dog in Georgia," wrote a *Defender* columnist. Another exclaimed, "It saved the Race." Twelve bright red trucks, donated by the Great Atlantic and Pacific Tea Company, carried children from deep within the congested South Side to the open space of Washington Park. The paper burst with pride at the sight of African American police officers. "Eight of them in line—eight straight-shouldered young men of the Race, who resplendent in the uniforms of red coats, blue trousers, Sam Brown belts and white cork hats announced to the world that they were a part of the arm of the law."[76]

At the height of the Depression, Chicago's African Americans consumed thousands of Amos 'n' Andy candy bars, donated by the two Chicago-based radio stars, untold gallons of ice-cream, and danced to the "rhythm rocking melodies" of Duke Ellington and his Cotton Club Orchestra. Ellington graciously shared the bandstand with Earl Hines and several other local groups; the Duke reigned as

Duke Ellington at Bud Billiken Day, 1933 (Chicago Public Library, Vivian G. Harsh Research Collection of Afro-American History and Literature)

true African American royalty. Nominated by the *Defender,* Ellington drew crowds of black working-class migrants, like the young Nathaniel Coles, who found himself entranced by Barney Bigard's clarinet on "Mood Indigo."[77] Coles and other Chicago blacks played and picnicked in Washington Park, unmindful of the poverty and white hostility that surrounded them.

The parade, as the *Defender* reporter observed, sent thousands of participants "swinging down South Parkway with banners and flags flyin', the bands and drum corps playin' and all the Billiken's yellin' and singin'. . . . There was old Bud himself, . . . his whistle danglin' around his neck, standin' on the running board of a big tourin' car leadin' the marchers."[78]

Bud Kellum led a squadron of "fifteen motorcycles, their sirens wide open," down South Parkway and boasted "plus fours, sport shoes, and eye glasses." Not to be outdone, the famed drum major Hannibal Scurlock cakewalked in classic African American style. "Just look at that drum major," the *Defender* exclaimed as Scurlock tossed "that big diamond-studded baton! Up it goes, to the top of the houses, and he keeps walkin' as though it wasn't there—and suddenly he sticks out his hand, careless like, grabs it and twirls it around his neck, while he struts proud as a peacock." A decade later, Cub Scout Bill Lowry, the son of a Washington Park postal worker, attended his first Bud Billiken Day Parade. Lowry never forgot the drum major, "In his high hat, high stepping, up and down the parade line," Lowry paused, "strutting just like the drum major at the Tuskegee-Wilberforce Game at Soldier Field."[79]

Merchants on the South Side, white and black, outdid each other in their generosity and advertising. They donated almost anything as long as it had their name on it. Their white crepe-papered floats glided slowly before a cheering and swaying throng, lined six deep along the parade route. For a day, Bud Billiken offered a moment of heaven on earth. Red delivery trucks, strutting drum majors, wailing sirens, white floats, and uniformed police and soldiers, bedecked in blue and gold, joined visiting African dignitaries. Kellum in an outrageously elegant white coat and tails as Bud Billiken, Abbott in his white Rolls, and thousands of children all marched together down the grandest street on the South Side and into their park. Picnics and baseball, the staples of southern African American Fourth of July celebrations and August revivals, marked the festivities in Washington Park.

Southern migrants had long celebrated mid-August as lay-by time, a moment of tranquillity between the second chopping, or weeding, and the laborious cotton harvest of the fall. At lay-by time, plantation churches brought the newly converted into the fold. Afterward, they marched, singing, to the river in white robes to be baptized.[80] By the mid-1930s, several South Side Baptist churches had abandoned Lake Michigan as a site for summer baptism. Instead, led by Progressive Baptist's Rev. T. E. Brown, migrants used the duck pond and the lagoons in Washington Park. Clad in white, standing along the banks, the congregants gathered and, one by one, received the sacred water ritual of rebirth, much as they would have in Mound Bayou or Ghana. In Washington Park on Sundays during the 1930s, African American baptism remade a civic space into a sacred space.

Sixty-five years earlier, in Charleston, South Carolina, African Americans also transformed a white public space in a black space. In March 1865 four thousand black Charlestonians assembled at the Citadel, the symbol of the Confederacy, and walked the length of the city. Two "colored marshals" led the parade, "sitting high above the crowd on horseback with red, white and blue rosettes and blue sashes." Fifty butchers, colored fire units, a brass band, blacksmiths, and the "car of liberty"—a float with a moving diorama depicting the "death of slavery"—also marched.[81] African American marching bands "literally danced down the street," disrupting the martial ritual of parade "with music and dance performance that

Baptism in Washington Park Lagoon (*Chicago Daily Tribune*, August 8, 1938)

allow for circular movement reminiscent of the ring shout."[82] The drum major, with his torso tilted back, his baton held high, and his face looking over his shoulder, assumed a Kongo pose of West African balance and pride.[83]

In Charleston, African Americans transformed the Gullah "Watch Night" into a New Year's Day parade that celebrated the Emancipation Proclamation. Other African Americans in Missouri, Tennessee, and Mississippi celebrated Emancipation Day in August. As occurred during Juneteenth in Texas, on these summer days African Americans "learned they were free."[84] During these celebrations, the whole community turned out, occupied normally forbidden territory, crossed boundaries, and for a brief moment took over the town.[85] In Chicago, on Bud Billiken Day, African Americans recast these celebrations. The invitation to African dignitaries, the parade's splendid uniforms, its high-stepping and dashing drum majors, its smartly attired officials, braided dignitaries in open cars, West African–inspired music, and the dance of its majorettes sashaying side to side as they marched down South Parkway to the rhythmic encouragement of thousands of onlookers all attested to their West African heritage.[86]

On their arrival in North America, West African Americans had organized other public festivals, most notably the Pinkster Day celebrations in eighteenth-century New York.[87] West African processional customs included wearing beautiful clothing, gold rings, and bracelets. In parades, princes dressed in ostrich plumes walked with "children swishing elephant tails, umbrella carriers, drum-

mers, minstrels, linguists, gun-bearers, and executioners."[88] Pinkster Day, celebrated in New York State until the 1840s, like Bud Billiken Day, Americanized
West African traditions. At Pinkster Day, slaves elected their own "King Charlie"
to rule over their holiday. Observers reported on the regal charm and bearing of
the Pinkster kings.[89]

Nineteenth-century African Americans in New York had dressed distinctively,
parading in silk scarves and gold earrings, a complex cultural expression of pride
and derision.[90] The Bud Billiken Day Parade, protected by its own uniformed
militia, accompanied by its police, the Scouts, and veterans, authorized South
Side residents to walk straight down South Parkway and then claim Washington
Park as their own. Bud Billiken Day drew more than 150,000 participants. On the
second Saturday of August, South Side African Americans marched with pride.
In Washington Park, they danced, played ball, picnicked, and listened to the best
jazz in the land.

CHICAGO'S FIRST BLACK MAYOR

After 1933, in the spirit of Pinkster holidays, the Bud Billiken Parade became the
focus of an intense electoral contest. In 1933 James Gentry, newspaper reporter
and theater critic for the Chicago Bee, a short-lived rival to the Defender, devised a
local election in which South Side blacks voted for their own mayor.[91] No record
exists of the "election" of Chicago's first black mayor, but it was likely no more than
a wooden ballot box placed on the counter at the Palm Tavern on 47th Street. The
next year, however, the ever-opportunistic Abbott hired Gentry and took over
sponsorship of the election. On October 27, 1934, the Defender announced in bold
headlines: "JAMES KNIGHT, BRONZEVILLE MAYOR, PICKS 'CABINET' NOV. 1."

Knight owned the Palm Tavern, the site of the Bronzeville mayoral election box,
an elegant and popular 47th street hangout, that featured a neon-light palm tree on
its rear wall and real potted palms at the end of each leather-cushioned booth.[92]
Customers happily cast their mayoral ballots for the bar's genial proprietor, the
first elected Pinkster king, the "mayor of Bronzeville." Gentry and Abbott coined
the name "Bronzeville," which included the welter of black Chicago neighborhoods,
the South Side, the near South Side, Grand Boulevard, Douglass, and Washington
Park. Bronzeville, Darktown, or Black Bottom ran "from 18th to 68th streets,
Wentworth to Cottage Grove." Altogether, Palm Tavern patrons cast 127,000 ballots
(there were no limits on how many times an individual could vote).[93]

Bronzeville's new mayor, reputedly the local policy king of Chicago, presided
over his inaugural ball at Bacon's Casino, a middle-class nightclub on 48th Street

that hosted about a hundred guests, including Republican Alderman William Dawson, several lawyers, and at least two police captains. Rumor had it that the mayor of Chicago, Ed "Big Red" Kelly, would arrive "at midnight."[94] Knight held his title for only six months before the *Defender* announced the next campaign. In June 1935 the paper explained that nominations were open for mayor, now described as the "official spokesman for the 300,000 or more citizens residing in Bronzeville."[95] By the end of June, the citizens of Bronzeville had nominated thirty-seven candidates. The *Defender* declared that the top four would be chosen for a runoff. As the "Bronzeville Editor" observed, "You'll find deputy sheriffs, sign-painters, bondsmen, nightclub proprietors, dentists, doctors, lawyers, coroners, undertakers, matchmakers, taxi cab magnates, colonels and insurance men listed."[96] The *Defender* held a considerable stake in the race. The paper supported the "Mayor of Bronzeville Campaign" to boost its depression-weary subscribers. Voters obtained ballots by clipping coupons from the paper, even though the *Defender* covered its own race as any other news event. "Candidates Rush to Get on Bronzeville Band Wagon," read one headline in late June followed by "Bronzeville Candidates in Final Mayoralty Drive."[97]

By the time of the runoff election, the paper's plans for the August Bud Billiken Day parade and picnic were well underway. The paper scheduled the runoff election for the first week of September and announced the results at a grand soirée at the Savoy. "The Million Dollar Savoy Ballroom at 47th and South Parkway" had also hosted the *Defender*'s Thirtieth Anniversary program that crowned Irma McCoy as "Miss Chicago Defender." "Four thousand carefree" and well-turned-out Bronzeville voters danced at the "Coronation Ball" to the Earl "Fatha" Hines Orchestra. "I'll show up Paul Whiteman, Ray Nobel and all the rest," bragged the Pittsburgh-born Hines. Dubbed "King of the Ivories," Hines declared, "You haven't heard a thing 'till you get a load of my cats swinging away."[98] Late in the evening, the crowd, which "spent the night in carefree frolic," learned that undertaker W. T. Brown had been elected the second mayor of Bronzeville. As Valda, the "best 'shake' dancer" in town strutted her stuff, Mayor Edward J. Kelly "wired a long-telegram of regret" that he could not attend.[99] Brown won the election by twenty-one thousand votes. James "Gentle Jimmy" Gentry, "The Maker of Mayors," presided over the coronation ceremonies.

For the remainder of the decade the overlapping civic rituals of Bud Billiken Day and the mayor of Bronzeville election continued with great fanfare. The 1937 parade secured a permit for all of Washington Park, transforming the entire space into Chicago's first and largest all-black public park. Bill Lowry remembered, "We used to joke as kids during the war, that if Hitler wanted to win the war he'd have to knock out all the blacks in Chicago. All he'd have to do is drop a bomb on Washington Park during Bud Billiken Day."[100] The expanded Bud Billiken Day reflected the continued migration from the South, which pushed African Americans further down the narrow racial corridor between Wentworth and Cottage Grove. White Chicagoans refused to allow Bronzeville to expand East or West, but by the late 1930s, black Chicago extended south, past Washington Park. In 1938, by nominating boxer Joe Louis as mayor, the voters of Bronzeville expressed their determination to fight for expanded civil rights. The adoration of Louis, who in 1938 knocked out German heavyweight champion Max Schmelling, prompted the Brown Bomber's nomination. Declining graciously, Louis agreed to ride in the Bud Billiken Day Parade in an open car reserved for dignitaries, a place of honor that he occupied for years to come. Louis, who let his fists speak for all of African America, announced his participation in the Billiken Day parade the same week that the *Defender* reported the lynching of a black man in Rolling Green, Mississippi, and the attack on a Chicago "Race youth" by white "hoodlums," who had run down and beat a black sixteen-year-old on the corner of 24th and South Parkway.[101]

The 1938 *Defender* raised the stakes again by promising the winner a "beautiful brand new automobile." In 1939 the paper offered a free trip to the New York World's Fair, escorted by the female winner of the "Win a Trip to the Fair Contest." Starting in 1939, the mayor of Bronzeville election sponsored its own beauty pageant. The *Defender* ran the mayoralty and beauty elections side by side. The finalists for each contest, Chicago's Pinkster royalty, rode atop an oversized float in the Bud Billiken Day parade.

In the 1930s male candidates for mayor were identified first by occupation and then by social class. In contrast, African American women were identified solely by social class. Of the thirty women who put their names forward in 1939, half came from Old Settler social clubs like "Les Petites Amies," "La Creole," and "Matronettes," whose light-skinned membership dominated the *Defender*'s social page. Most attended a socially prominent church, such as Olivet, Pilgrim, and Hope Presbyterian. Only a few—clerks, beauticians, and "unaffiliated"—came from modest backgrounds.[102] Successful, self-made, southern-born men matched themselves with refined heirs of the city's old-line, Old Settler sepia elite.

In 1940, a political turning point in Bronzeville, most of Chicago's black political leaders, after eight years of courtship, finally, shifted over to the Democratic Party. Consequently, for the first time, the mayor of Bronzeville election took on serious social and racial issues. Former mayor Robert Miller attacked housing conditions in Bronzeville. "I am opposed to kitchenettes and I believe they should be abolished," he declared in his "platform." A week later, Clinton Brown criticized the Chicago municipal government, the mayor's office, and the police department for failing to protect the residents of Bronzeville from "banditry and vandalism." Brown denounced police brutality and called for more black teachers in the public schools, especially at Bronzeville's new Du Sable High School with its nearly all-white faculty. Neither challenger, however, defeated the sitting mayor, Joseph Hughes of Woodlawn. Hughes, a native of Louisiana and a successful tavern owner in Bronzeville, easily defeated his rivals. A child of the Great Migration, by 1940 Hughes had become Bronzeville's king.

No longer just a popularity contest, in the 1940s, the mayor of Bronzeville election had become a serious event. Candidates openly campaigned for votes in the primary season before Bud Billiken Day. Neighborhood and citizen committees organized for their favorite candidate. The race for mayor was now a serious black civic ritual. Elected by southern migrants, the mayor of Bronzeville served where the people lacked power. "It wasn't the real thing," reflected community leader, realtor, and author Dempsey Travis, "but until we got Harold [Washington] it was our only thing."[103] Represented by a symbolic government in Bronzeville, but no longer victims of the brutal violence of the South, Bronzeville voters remained second-class citizens in Chicago.[104] Politically, in the 1930s many black South Side voters maintained their loyalty to the Republican Party, the party of Lincoln. In 1935, to the astonishment of many, William Dawson, the longtime Republican alderman of Bronzeville's second ward, endorsed Democrat "Big Ed" Kelly for city mayor. Dawson, a member of Bronzeville's Progressive Baptist Church, carried 80 percent of Chicago's black vote into the Democratic Party. Kelly's Democratic machine accepted Dawson as his African American emissary to Bronzeville and extended to the district political patronage.[105]

Despite the veneer of Chicago's actual patterns of black voting and representation, Bud Billiken Day and the election of the mayor of Bronzeville rested on a shared sense of apartness that Chicago African Americans experienced daily. The election of the mayor of Bronzeville declared their independence as well as underlined their exclusion from power in Chicago. But each election, as the number of votes cast grew, demonstrated the South Side's latent power. At the end of the Second World War, heralding the arrival of another 250,000 African Americans, Chicago blacks were beginning to flex their political muscles. Far more than the facade of the urban machine, Bud Billiken Day and the mayor of Bronzeville election had prepared them for democratic politics. In the 1950s and 1960, South Side voters redefined Chicago politics by mobilizing its masses with symbols of their West African kinship.

GOOD GOD, ALMIGHTY, THIS MUST BE HEAVEN

The Second Great Migration accelerated the formation of a black working class in Chicago with its own culture. The appearance of a distinctly urban blues in Chicago marked the shift of dominance in the South Side from Old Settlers to migrants. Delta blues and gospel blues both appealed to the new migrants, many of whom joined Sanctified Baptist or Pentecostal-Holiness churches. Riding the tide of postwar prosperity, Chicago blues and gospel music radiated from South Side joints and churches that lined 47th Street. The promise of good-paying northern jobs combined with the mechanization of cotton in the Delta, had swelled Bronzeville's black population. Blues singer Ko-Ko Taylor remembered, "I'd been making fifty cent a day. Chop cotton a whole week and you don't get but three dollars . . . came here and got five dollars a day. That was big money."[106]

For Taylor and other African Americans from the Delta, Chicago offered unlimited promise. "I came to Chicago on a Greyhound bus," she recalled, "and when that bus got almost there we saw all of these lights and everything lit up [along 63rd Street]. There was so many bright lights and things and I said, 'Good God, Almighty, this must be heaven.'" Prentiss Brown from Greenville, Mississippi, saw Chicago in a different light: "The first time I saw Chicago . . . coming from Vicksburg, which was a very small city . . . I saw a huge raggedy city . . . The backs of the buildings is what I can picture, I can never forget, with all the wooden stairs, and the raggedy buildings . . . In Vicksburg we had homes. But here (in Chicago) I can remember walking into some of the 'flats' as they called it. And they had just kitchenettes, all over the place."[107]

African Americans from the Mississippi Delta made up nearly one-half of the migration to Chicago between 1940 and 1950. They remade Bronzeville into their own neighborhood. Prentiss Brown from Greenville considered 47th Street as his new home away from home. "Let me tell you, there was no place like 47th Street in the '50s and the '40s, anyone who wanted to go to anyplace we'd go on 47th Street, because all your clubs, and everything, that's where it was, and your eateries and everything was on 47th Street. I lived on 48th and Calumet and I was on 47th Street every day."[108] Anchored by the South Center department store–office building and the Regal Theater, 47th Street became the crossroads of black Chicago. On a given weekend, the Palm Tavern might feature Josephine Baker, back from Paris, and the Regal might headline Duke Ellington.

In the 1940s, the largest and most successful black business remained "policy," the back-door lottery sold like penny life insurance—hence the name, based on the "numbers" of the daily stock closings. The Jones Brothers who owned the

"Rabbits for Sale," by Wayne Miller (used with artist's permission)

local Ben Franklin store and Jim Knight at the Palm Tavern, as the South Side policy kings, ran vast networks of numbers runners who worked every South Side neighborhood. Bill Lowry recalled, "Every artist at the time would come through the Regal, and I was a runner . . . backstage and as these people would come in, Duke Ellington and George Kirby and Ella and Billie Holiday. I was the guy that would run and get their sandwiches, their cigarettes, their booze or whatever it is they wanted."[109]

Most of Bronzeville's legitimate businesses, as in the Delta, were owned and operated by whites, often Jewish. Capital poor and inexperienced in business, black businesses, such as Woodson's shoe store, languished. Unable to maintain an extensive inventory of styles and sizes, Woodson's displayed row upon row of shoeboxes, most empty, stacked neatly on floor-to-ceiling shelves.[110]

By the late 1940s, the growing population pushed the South Side's boundaries southward well beyond Bronzeville. Whites responded violently. Battles, reminiscent of the post–World War I era, raged in neighborhoods like Woodlawn. At the Airport Homes, west of the South Side, in 1940, white protest forced the city government and the Chicago housing authority to adopt a slum clearance program that included construction of one thousand low-rise Ida B. Wells apartments at 37th and South Park.[111] The powerful South Side politician, William Dawson, supported the Ida Wells projects, which provided Dawson an enormous pool of patronage jobs, including one for the legendary "Two-Gun Pete."

South Side resident Prentiss Brown remembered Two-Gun Pete. "He was a police officer there. He was noted for keeping his district corners and things straight. He would come by and if you was on the corner he would tell you when I go around the block I don't want you here when I get back." Mary Wiley, who like Brown came to Chicago from Greenville, Mississippi, added, "He was black and he was put there on 47th Street and he was put there to keep the niggers together —that's why he was there—by the white man, the establishment. And he did his job well, just like they told him. And the chances are that he was from the deep South . . . and he learned how to do that from the white man . . . who was probably Irish or something. . . . So he learned his job well."[112]

In 1945 Dr. James Scott, the two-term mayor of Bronzeville, suddenly withdrew his name from the mayor of Bronzeville ballot and threw his support to rival R. H. Harris. Harris had arrived in Chicago just before the war. Originally from Texas, Harris sang lead in the famous gospel group, the Soul Stirrers, and operated the Five Soul Stirrers Cleaners on 47th Street.

The Soul Stirrers achieved local fame with its version of Thomas Dorsey's "Precious Lord" and its regular Sunday appearances on the black radio station WIND. Harris's ability to move his listeners, to make them shout, came from his Sanctified "old time religion," which the Soul Stirrers embodied.[113] Harris's election signaled the shift in power on the South Side from prewar Old Settler culture to Harris's Sanctified religious culture. Together the postwar flood of Delta migrants, the construction of massive public housing in the South Side, and the displacement of Old Settler leaders by charismatic migrants, like Harris, brought to a close the first phase of the Great Migration to Chicago and ushered in the second phase.

As the "Baddest Man on the Gospel Highway," R. H. Harris knew how to "leave a church in shambles."[114] In Texas, R.H. had joined the Soul Stirrers in 1937, when the group had already abandoned the Fisk Jubilee style of singing. Jubilee quartets had originated in 1905 when male quartets split off from the mixed choirs that sang concertized spirituals designed to "elevate the standards of the [Baptist] denomination."[115] The Birmingham quartet tradition, starting with the Foster singers in 1915, featured a more Sanctified style. The Sanctified gospel quartet emphasized call-and-response shouting, swaying body movements that evoked the ring shout, and spontaneous praises like "Thank you, Jesus" and "That's right."

Harris and the Soul Stirrers added a "swing lead" and a "walk around."[116] A second lead expanded the quartet to five, with a second baritone who walked the stage and sang the verses while the quartet sang the chorus. Harris, "overcome by the spirit," moved back and forth to a fever pitch and often jumped off the stage without "missing a beat."[117] The ecstatic energy depended, according to gospel lore, on a "Sister Flute," an imagined member of the audience who "falls out" when she catches the spirit. "When you get Sister Flute you get the house."[118] Like a Pentecostal-Holiness preacher, Harris and the Soul Stirrers brought their audiences to a state of spiritual ecstasy. "That man could just move a church," recalled an early admirer. Folk music collector Alan Lomax exclaimed, they possessed "the most incredible polyrhythmic stuff you've ever heard."[119]

Thanks to the Soul Stirrers ten-year run on WIND, Harris's group became the South Side's preeminent gospel quartet. An extensive touring schedule took the group to every state in the union and brought national prominence. In the late 1940s, Harris grew weary of the "moral snares, most of them female," that awaited him on the road. When Harris announced his retirement, at a concert at Du Sable High in September 1950, the overflow crowd of two thousand felt "as if a bomb had dropped."[120] The Soul Stirrers' admirers found ample consolation in the group's new lead singer, Sam Cooke, the son of a Sanctified minister from Clarksdale, Mississippi. Cooke electrified the gospel quartet tradition, making it urban and even more bluesy.

Polyrhythmic and sexual, driving and spirited, the Soul Stirrers urban gospel quartet style drew heavily on Delta blues. Cooke's yodeling, or whooping, that jumped octaves, tied his music directly to rural southern field hollers that derived from the Congo-Angola region of Central West Africa.[121] In 1903 Harvard musicologist Charles Peabody first identified the survivals of West African music in the Brickyard district of Clarksdale where Cooke had grown up.[122] In the Brickyard, in the holiness church of Sam's father, the Reverend Cooke, the music "brought in the spirit" with cymbals, tambourines, and drums. An observer recalled that the church "looked like a juke joint on a . . . hot Saturday night."[123]

Cooke took his family to Chicago in 1932 and established a Holiness congregation on 32nd and Cottage Grove, one of the poorest neighborhoods on the South

Side. In 1942 Rev. Cooke baptized his twelve-year-old son, Sam, and urged him to join the Soul Stirrers–inspired gospel group, the Highway QCs.[124] From there, Cooke moved to the Soul Stirrers, and before long he replaced R. H. Harris as the lead singer. Cooke sang with a "sweet," floating voice that contrasted with the gritty, shouting style of the group's tenor Paul Foster.[125] By 1953 the Soul Stirrers had become Cooke's group and Harris a historical footnote. In the Soul Stirrers' 1954 record "He'll Make a Way," Cooke whooped, sang in falsetto, and crooned while the quartet backed him up. The song started out as a gospel number but shifted to a smooth and syncopated version of the pop hit, "Sea of Love." Cooke's voice pulled the song forward. His embellishment and moaning infused the song with a sexuality that became his hallmark. His youthful good looks and "light lyrical tenor" brought in the women.[126]

Cooke had the same effect on the gospel quartet that fellow Clarksdale native Muddy Waters had on the Delta blues. Both men borrowed from their Delta predecessors, both were master musicians, both worked their audiences, and each borrowed from the other. Cooke sang in church on Sunday mornings and to religious groups. Waters sang in blues bars and joints on Saturday nights. Bill Branch, the son of Mississippi migrants, commented, "I could see that many of the people we went to church with were also going to parties in the various bars . . . These are all church going people, I just did not ever realize (growing up) that people did these things, and they never missed a beat."[127]

I CAN'T BE SATISFIED

Cooke's first gospel group, the Highway QCs, had met in a storefront on South State Street just around the corner from the neighborhood jazz joint, the Macomba Lounge, owned by Phil and Leonard Chess. When in Chicago, Billy Eckstein, Ella Fitzgerald, Lester Young, and occasionally Count Basie dropped by after hours to perform at the Macomba. The Chess brothers also ran a blues bar, the 708 Liquor Store, on the corner of Langley and 47th Street known locally as "708." The Chess brothers were Czech Jewish immigrants who arrived in the South Side in the 1920s and remained after their neighborhood "turned" black. In 1948, the brothers brought out a record label, Aristocrat, which sold in 180 South Side mom and pop grocery stores and beauty shops.[128]

When the Chess brothers first heard Muddy Waters in 1948, they did not think his country blues fit the South Side's taste for jazz, or the currently popular jump-blues of Louis Jordan. Waters had no trouble, however, finding work in the dozens of blues joints on the fringes of the South and West sides. He sang at rent parties, on street corners, and along Maxwell Street. During the day, he drove a truck, which paid more in a day than he had earned for a week driving a tractor at Stovall.[129] Still, the Chess brothers took a chance and recorded Waters's Stovall number "I Be's Troubled." Performed on an acoustic guitar with an electric pickup, "to cut through the noise" of South Side bars, Muddy Waters's now renamed "I Can't Be Satisfied" brought the Delta blues to Chicago.[130] For a man who once wanted to become "a heck of a preacher, a heck of a ball player, or a heck of a musician," music had won out.[131]

Waters played in and out of the Bronzeville blues clubs north of 47th Street. These storefront clubs operated like the nearby storefront churches, places where working blacks from Mississippi hung out to hear their music—"You could go to Herb's on Sunday afternoon, you knew you were gonna see someone from Green-ville," said one cabbie.[132] In the words of Clarkesdale bluesman Earl Hooker, north of 47th Street was "where the blues people lived."[133] In 1950 Waters cut his first hit for Chess, "Louisiana Blues." It evoked the Deep South's conjure doctors and mojo charms, red flannel bags filled with oil and pierced by a needle that intertwined with South Side migrants' Sanctified faith.[134] "Louisiana Blues" drew on rural blues with its repetition of traditional blues lines, like "I'm going down Louisiana, baby, behind the sun." Waters's use of an electric pickup on his acoustic guitar in his first Chess recording changed the rural Delta blues into a new, peppy and loud, urban blues. With "Louisiana Blues," Waters had found his persona, the hoodoo-voodoo man.

> I'm goin' down in Louisiana get me a mojo hand,
> I'm goin' down in Louisiana get me a mojo hand,
> I wanna show all you good looking women just how to treat your man.[135]

In 1951 Waters assembled a blues band—second guitar, drums, bass, and harp —for "Long Distance Call," a song that climbed to near the top of the new "rhythm and blues" chart that replaced the old "race" category.[136] Backed by his electrified band, in "Long Distance Call" Waters sang a migration story that told of urban loneliness and sexual betrayal. Waters's singer-teller waited for the phone to ring ("You say you love me, baby, why don't you call me on the phone sometime"), imploring a lover back home ("I'll give you a brand-new Cadillac and show you just how good a man can be"). When the call finally came, he heard a voice on the other end telling him, "Muddy Waters, there's another mule kicking in your stall." In the middle, Waters stopped the song to step out of his bluesman/bad-man persona and reappeared as the Reverend Morganfield. Waters-Morganfield chanted, "I was standing by my door one day, and my woman say, she say, she say . . ."

"Dancing at the 45th Street Bar That Catered to the Slaughterhouse Workers," by Wayne Miller (used with artist's permission)

In the mid-1950s Muddy Waters released his signature song, "Hoochie-Coochie Man," written by Willie Dixon. Dixon's use of black cat bones, John the Conqueror root, and mojo tied his song to Louisiana slaves and the West African legend of lucky sevens, "On the seventh hour, of the seventh day."[137] According to blues historian Robert Palmer, West African–inspired voodoo-hoodoo rituals and beliefs helped sell Waters's records to a rapidly growing working-class migrant audience. Waters explained, "Black people really believed in this hoodoo."[138] Bill Branch, from Mississippi, remembered:

There were just some things you didn't do. You never ever leave your hair any place . . . if some of your hair would come out in a comb, the only way to dispose of it is burn it, because if you throw it in running water, the person would lose their mind. . . . I find myself very, very cautious at the barber shop. . . . I always watch and wonder what they do with it. [And] Never let a pregnant woman do your hair, because when my mother was pregnant she cut my father's hair and it never grew back.[139]

Willie Dixon, Waters's "Hoochie-Coochie Man," came to Chicago in 1935 from Vicksburg. "The blues call on God as much as a spiritual song do," Dixon wrote. He explained that his religious parents taught him that the "home" in "Swing Low Sweet Chariot" was in Africa.[140] As a teenager, Dixon, a poet, wrote his own versions of the West African–inspired "Signifying Monkey" poems and toasts, peddled them on the street, and brought them with him to Chicago. He recalled his favorite toast:

The elephant looked at it from the corner of his eye
Sayin' you better find someone to fight your size
So the lion jumped up and made a funny pass
And the elephant knocked him on his hairy ass.[141]

Dixon's success with Waters led to his job as Chess Records artist and repertoire (A&R) man. Between 1954 and 1965, he oversaw the golden age of Chicago blues, when Chess produced hits by a pantheon of blues musicians, the vast majority from the Delta, including Chester Burnett (Howlin' Wolf) from Ruleville. Howlin' Wolf had met Charlie Patton at Dockery Plantation, played with Son House, and learned the harmonica from Rice Miller. The Wolf adopted his new name after the war when, living in West Memphis, he hosted a radio program and needed a "handle."[142] He did not move to Chicago until 1952, when, at age forty-two, he recorded his first record with Chess and Dixon.

Like Howlin' Wolf, B. B. King had been born in the Delta and was raised in a minister's household. After the war, King lived in Memphis with his cousin Bukka White. On Memphis radio, King hosted the "Sepia Swing Club" and called himself Blues Boy King.[143] Blues singer Ko-Ko Taylor came from a sharecropper family outside of Memphis, where she too learned to sing in church. "My daddy said everybody in his house had to go to church on Sunday. And we did . . . that's how I got to learn about singing . . . 'cause my love for singing started with the Gospel in the church." She remembered listening to B. B. King on the radio. "He was on 15 minutes a day and we all made sure to catch him . . . and James Cotton and Junior Wells."[144] Taylor arrived in Chicago in 1953. She found work as a laundress and sang in basement clubs on the South Side where Dixon heard her. Full of sexual bravado, Taylor recounted, "There were some really great singers, you know, back in their day . . . like Bessie Smith. I always respected Bessie."[145] But, like B. B. King, Ko-Ko Taylor sounded like a church singer, the growl in her voice heavy and rough. "You know, girl, the way you sing, it moves," Dixon told her when he signed her to a Chess contract.[146]

Dixon did not want her to become another Billie Holiday. Instead, he wanted Taylor to highlight her bold sexuality. Her great hit, "Wang-Dang-Doodle," derived from an old lesbian-hokum number, "Bull Daggers Ball." In his rewrite, "Wang-Dang Doodle," Dixon cleaned up the original, removing such characters as "Fast Fuckin' Fannie." Instead, Taylor sang about Double Crossing Ed, Abyssinia Ned, Piston Pete, Washboard Sam, Shakin' Boxcar Joe, and Jennie May, with "snuff juice everywhere."[147] Dixon and Taylor brought Bronzeville to life, peopled with larger-than-life characters familiar to the South Side's southern migrants.

WHERE THE BLUES PEOPLE LIVE

Black Chicago awakened in the first week of September 1955 to the shocking images of Emmett Till published by *Jet Magazine*. The photographs of the fourteen-year-old Till, his mutilated body visible in an open casket, were impossibly obscene.[148] The brutal murder of Emmett Till, in the heart of the Mississippi Delta, brought national attention back to Mound Bayou. Till's Chicago mother, Cloyte Murdock of *Ebony Magazine*, and Michigan congressman Charles Digs, while attending the trial in Money, stayed at the home of Mound Bayou civil rights leader Dr. T. R. M. Howard, a physician in Mound Bayou's Knight's of Tabor Hospital. Till's death horrified the nation, but even more so did the acquittal of his two murderers despite incontrovertible evidence. Till's murder made clear just how far Chicago's Mississippi migrants had traveled.

It also reminded them of how much farther they had to go, even in Chicago. From 1950 to 1965, Chicago mayor Richard Daley, the Chicago Housing Authority, and key South Side Democratic politicians endorsed a new public housing policy that, overnight, transformed the South Side from a poor black community into an urban disaster.[149] In the 1950s Chicago's African American population grew by an astonishing 320,000, from 492,000 to 812,000, 24 percent of the city's people. The migrants pressed against the largely white neighborhoods of Morgan Park and Englewood. Determined to limit the expansion of blacks into adjacent neighborhoods, Chicago chose to expand the South Side upward. It built a cordon of massive concrete public housing projects on the South Side's western boundary, a seven-mile-long, half-mile-wide wall of high-rise warehouses for poor African Americans that reinforced the impenetrable concrete created by the Dan Ryan Expressway.

The leader of Bronzeville's Second Ward and its congressional representative, William Dawson, worked with William Daley, Democratic politician from the neighboring, Irish Catholic Bridgeport. For twenty years, Dawson had played Chicago's game of patronage and loyalty with remarkable success, earning him the title of the "Booker T. Washington of Chicago politics." He parlayed his influence into federal employment—mostly post office jobs—for his most loyal constituents.[150] In the early 1950s Dawson and Daley worked hand in hand to make their wards key to Democratic control of Chicago city government. In the 1955 mayoral election, Dawson's support secured enough South Side votes to give Daley a plurality of 100,000 votes.[151]

Determined to run Chicago by himself, Daley undercut Dawson's power in the Second Ward by curtailing patronage. Initially, Dawson had opposed slum clearance and urban renewal projects. In 1950, taking advantage of the Federal Housing Act of 1949, city planning and zoning commissions had selected several Bronzeville tracts with substandard housing for demolition. African Americans lived in the kitchenette apartments carved out of this warren of wood-frame, asbestos-shingled houses.[152] By 1956 the Chicago Housing Authority constructed fifteen thousand units of public housing in Bronzeville. In 1962 the city expanded this core by laying out the twenty-eight identical, sixteen-story buildings of the Robert Taylor "Homes" that anchored Bronzeville's public projects south along State Street, from 34th to 55th streets. Directly west of the new public housing projects, the city targeted an additional band of tenements along LaSalle, Wentworth, and Federal avenues that included, at 4423 Wentworth, "Rosie's Beauty Shop and Manicuring." The Federal-Wentworth area had served for more than fifty years as a boundary between black Bronzeville and white Bridgeport, between Dawson and Daley.

The City of Chicago, cooperating with state and federal agencies, tore down mile after mile of black working-class "slums." In their place they constructed a gaping, below-grade swath to accommodate an urban interstate and light rail system. The Dan Ryan Expressway created a virtually impenetrable barrier between Bronzeville and Bridgeport—a twelve-lane chasm of isolation and protection. At the very moment when Chicago's middle-class African Americans could finally afford to move to more suburban subdivisions in South Chicago, Bronzeville had been rendered even poorer and more isolated. Unlike New York and Pittsburgh, where similar programs of urban renewal simply carved up old working-class and black neighborhoods, the Bronzeville public projects reinforced segregated life, keeping the neighborhood geographically intact while insuring its social disintegration. In the meantime, South Side middle-class blacks left for homes in the southern suburbs. By 1960 little was left of prewar Bronzeville except its newly constructed projects that housed Chicago's desperately poor. Controlled by drug dealers, prostitutes, and gangs, Bronzeville public housing became the preparatory schools of the Illinois prison system.

Located at 3705 LaSalle, in the most desolate section of Bronzeville, Progressive Baptist Church fought back. As a Mississippi-immigrant and working-class church, Progressive Baptist had become Chicago's largest African American church. In the early 1950s, its congregation numbered six thousand active members.[153] The pastor of Progressive Baptist, Thomas Emerson (T. E.) Brown, made his church into a social welfare agency. "Many of his flock worked in the stockyards and railroad yards. Others have jobs as servants or in factories that dominate in the highly industrialized area," explained a local reporter. "We served as a social agency as well as a house of worship," said Rev. Dr. Brown. "So many who come North, they get lost and they get lonely."[154]

Brown's success depended on his fiscal organization. In the 1920s Brown abolished the Baptist practice of tithing at Progressive and replaced it with a system of small, regular, and organized donations.[155] He also organized a series of internal clubs of forty parishioners each. The club leader, usually a middle-aged woman, at weekly meetings distributed dime cards to each member.[156] One dime at a time, one card at a time, one group at a time, Progressive Baptist prospered. As soon as a club reached forty members, Brown organized another. Such clubs as Old Veterans, Monthly Rose, Get Busy, and Keep a Glow provided a core of energetic fundraisers. In the early 1960s the *Defender* reported that Progressive's "free will" policy raised an estimated $10,000 a month.[157] Brown worked tirelessly behind the scenes for his parishioners. Phone calls downtown secured city jobs, and soft-spoken words to banks obtained loans.[158]

In March 1955 Brown broke ground for a new sanctuary that would seat four thousand worshipers at 3700 LaSalle, directly across from its old building. Even though the neighborhood had been targeted for slum clearance, the city approved the permits for the LaSalle site in August 1955.[159] A year later, in the middle of construction, Chicago's Public Works Department condemned the church property, offering to pay Progressive $230,000 restitution. Engineering studies, officials argued, required the demolition of LaSalle Street. Both Progressive sites were to be buried by Dan Ryan Expressway. For the next four years, Brown and his congregation fought to save the church. Brown rejected all city entreaties to relocate away from his constituents.[160]

On April 1, 1961, once again, Brown broke ground for a new Progressive Baptist Church. This time his negotiations with the city yielded a windfall. The city agreed to purchase a new site for the church, provide a half-million dollars to cover the cost of relocation, and another half-million in compensation.[161] A few months later, contractors laid one hundred yards of concrete track, set hydraulic jacks under the partially built church, hoisted it onto rollers, and moved it onto a new foundation at 3658 South Wentworth. Progressive Baptist, a million dollars richer, sat on the Bridgeport side of the yet-to-be built Dan Ryan Expressway. Daley and Brown clearly practiced good Chicago politics. In addition, the church received a site large enough for substantial parking and for the construction of a building to house the elderly.

_ᴄ͟ᴐ_

Demography, politics, and residential segregation undermined the integrity of Bronzeville. For those who equated Bronzeville with the Great Migration, the movement of rural southern blacks out of the Delta and other Deep South regions seemed to reveal a futile struggle in the face of discrimination and poverty. But as federal census takers made clear, by 1960 only a fraction of migrants and their children lived in city projects. Most had moved on to other neighborhoods, purchased homes, and conscientiously sent their children to school and church. They conducted their lives as citizens of Chicago, not a beleaguered racial minority. When Emmett Till died in Money, Mississippi, his Chicago mother, her Chicago church, and much of the South Side insisted that his murderers be punished. They acted as a community and asserted their voice as they had learned to do in their music, their religion, in the annual Bud Billiken Day Parade, and in the mayor of Bronzeville election.

In music stores, nightclubs, and playing fields throughout Chicago, in the city's Sanctified and Pentecostal churches, in its schoolrooms and business offices, migrants from the Mississippi Delta and other places in the South, left their mark on the Windy City. The Robert Taylor projects made clear how much more was needed to be done. But few in 1919 could have imagined that in 1983 Chicago voters would elect Harold Washington, a "native son" of Bronzeville, as mayor of Chicago or that in the 1970s most elected officials and police officers in the Mississippi Delta would be black. The Great Migration did not just change Chicago and Mississippi; it changed America.[162]

DIXIE SPECIAL

• 8 •

Houston

Eli Whitney's invention of the cotton gin in 1792 set off the western march of slavery. Following Mexican independence from Spain in 1820, settlers from the slave South streamed into Texas, lured by the region's rich black soil. These first Anglo-Texans brought with them thousands of African Americans. Most passed through New Orleans, the booming port of the Mississippi Valley and the primary slave market for the domestic slave trade. In the decades before the Civil War, slave owners in Virginia, Maryland, North Carolina, and coastal South Carolina and Georgia had shipped their surplus slaves to New Orleans where slave dealers auctioned them off to Gulf State cotton and sugar planters. In the slave pens bordering the French Quarter, slaves from the Upper South and Gullah slaves from the Carolina Low Country joined French Creole slaves from southern Louisiana for western passage to the expanding rice and cotton fields of East Texas.[1]

On the eve of the Civil War, nearly 182,000 slaves lived in Texas, most around Galveston and Houston. According to the accounts of former Texas slaves, recorded in the Works Progress Administration slave narratives, only a few Texas slaves came directly from Africa. Most had arrived from the Chesapeake and Carolinas by way of Louisiana, where their parents and grandparents had undergone creolization in the older slave regions.[2] Long before their arrival in Texas, almost all had become African Americans, although they came from a variety of African American communities.[3] Texas slaves constituted the most culturally diverse black population in North America. On the basis of 1860 census samplings, roughly two-fifths of black Texans came from the upper South—Virginia, Maryland, Kentucky, Tennessee, and Arkansas. Another two-fifths hailed from the Gullah regions of the Carolina and Georgia Low Country and the Cotton Belt across Georgia, Florida, Alabama, Mississippi, and northern Louisiana. The remainder came from the French Creole population of New Orleans and southern Louisiana. In 1860 slaves constituted about 30 percent of the Texas population. Census takers counted only a thousand slaves in Houston out of a total Harris County slave population of five thousand. Still, slaves constituted half of the population of surrounding Harris County. Houston's one thousand slaves represented the largest concentration of urban slaves west of New Orleans. According to the census, only eight were free; if accurate, this was the fewest number of free blacks in any antebellum American city.[4]

Living in a frontier region, with few cities and almost no free blacks, Afro-Texans left few records of slave life. Two things stand out in the two hundred or so Texas slave narratives recorded by the WPA. In most ways, East Texas slavery resembled the slavery in the remainder of the slave South. Slave owners bought and sold slaves as they saw fit and often separated husbands from wives and children from parents. Masters punished slaves at their discretion, often brutally, and slave owners provided slaves only meager housing, food, and clothing. Slaves who ventured off their plantations at night, frequently, found themselves whipped and beaten by vigilante slave patrols or, in the case of women, sexually molested. Masters discouraged slave literacy and sought to control their slaves' religious life. Almost all Texas slaves lived on farms or plantations that grew cotton, rice, sugar, livestock, or foodstuffs. Others, largely males, worked in lumber camps or as dockworkers, or they herded cattle. Many, such as Will Adams from San Jacinto County, were born in Texas. Of mixed Creek and West African ancestry, Adams professed belief in West African and Native American spirits and root medicine. He also described slave entertainment: "On Saturday and Sunday nights they'd dance and sing all night long. They didn't dance like today, they dance the round dance and jig and pigeon wing, and some would jump up and see how many times he could kick his feet before they hit the ground. They had an old fiddle and some of them would take two bones in each hand and rattle them."[5]

Adams's description of slave dances underlined a feature of Texas slavery. Even though slave owners enjoyed nearly unlimited legal power over their human chattel, former Texas slaves remembered rich private lives that took place away from the supervision of their masters. Slaves married individuals of their choice, celebrated their unions by "jumping the broom," and named their children after relatives or West African days of the week. Parents passed infants over the bodies of newly deceased relatives so their spirits would look after the infants. Adams remembered worshiping at night "in the hollow" around an upside down sugar barrel that he believed absorbed the noise—a "hush arbor." During the Civil War, he recalled that his congregation "prayed for the North to win." As Madison Bruin remembered, "My mother wore the Yankee flag under her dress like a petticoat when the Confederates came raiding. Other times she wore it on top of the dress."[6]

Wash Wilson recounted, "The black folks' quarters were log cabins with stick and dirt chimneys. They had their own garden round each cabin and some chickens, but there weren't any cows like in Louisiana. Here there were lots of possums in the bottoms and we went coon and possum hunting. I liked cornbread and greens, cooked with hog jowls or strip bacon.... I got married in a suit of doeskin jeans.... I married Cornelia Horde and she wore a pretty blue gingham.... We had five children, Calvin and Early and Mary and Fred and Frank."[7] A devout Christian, Wilson explained, "The Masters before and after freedom didn't like the religious meetings, so we naturally slipped off at night, down at the bottoms or somewhere. Sometimes we sang and prayed all night.... When the niggers go around singing 'Steal Away to Jesus' that means there's going to be a religious meeting that night." The church meetings included boisterous dance and song. Wilson affirmed the Gullah belief: "Dancing ain't sinful ... if the feet ain't crossed. We dance in the arbor meetings but we sure didn't have our feet crossed."[8]

Wilson also expressed belief in West African–derived ideas of spirits and haunts. "The best watch dog you can get for the hoodoo is a frizzly chicken ... cause it scratches up every trick laid down against its owners.... A frizzly chicken comes out of the shell backward and that's why he's the devil's own."[9] Throughout the Texas slave narratives, former slaves described themselves as devout Christians but also expressed belief in conjurers and ancestral spirits. Charley Mitchell declared that in the cemetery "dead folks come out by twos at night and go in the church and hold a service." Also at night, the congregation would sneak down to the bayou to baptize new church members.[10] Richard Caruthers described a prayer meeting in the hollow where "Some got so joyous they started to holler loud and we had to stop up their mouth. I saw niggers get so full of the Lord and so happy they dropped unconscious."[11] Ellen Payne admitted that she still shouts at meetings: "I don't have nothing to do with it. It hits me just like a streak of lightning, and there's no holding it."[12] Florence Ruffins explained the connection between her parents' spiritualism and her own Sanctified Christianity. Ruffins's parents saw ghosts, but she did not. Instead, according to Ruffin, she felt the Holy Spirit. In church, she "learned to say spirit instead of ghost. Now the church says the preacher can bring the ghost, but they call it the spirit.... It's the spiritualism of the church." For Ruffin, "the Lord" will banish ghosts. Former Texas slaves testified to an Africanized or Sanctified Christianity that included

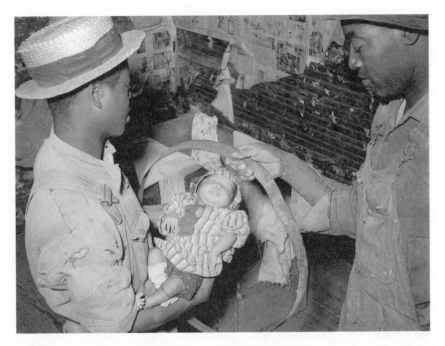

A sick baby being passed through "hoops for stretches" in Texas, 1930s (WPA, Library of Congress)

full-immersion baptism, spirit possession, sacred dance and shouting, call-and-response services, and speaking in tongues. Many traced the belief in conjuring, haunts, and ghosts to South Carolina Gullah ways. Lorenz Ezell recounted that "when he told other blacks that he was from South Carolina, they said, 'Oh, he's bound to make a heap.' I could be a conjurer doctor and make plenty of money."[13]

Texas formed the western border of Dixie. Most white Texans came from the slave South. From the start, Texas embraced a multiracial population that included Afro-Texans, Anglo-Texans, Mexican Texans, and Native Americans. Most of its southern residents followed southern folkways, many derived from West Africa, and a plantation code of honor. Except for Native Americans, virtually everyone adhered to some form of Christianity, either Catholic, Protestant, or Sanctified. In 1860, when Texas seceded from the Union, it was as much a western as a southern state. Texans exhibited the traits of inhabitants of other arid and semiarid, sparsely populated regions of North America. The plantation system extended less than a hundred miles inland from the Gulf Coast. By the Civil War, white settlement had reached westward to San Antonio, and as many Texans relied on ranching for a living as on plantation slavery. In 1860 only one in four whites in Texas owned slaves, but nearly everyone owned a horse and a gun, even the slaves.[14]

Many former slaves expressed strong identities as Texans. James Cape, whose parents were West Africans, proudly pointed out that he had served in the Confederacy as a horse tender and later as a cowboy.[15] Martin Jackson called himself a "black Texan." His name combined his dual African-Texan identity. "We had to register as someone so we could be citizens. Well . . . I made up my mind. I'd find a different one (than my master's). One of my grandfathers in Africa was called Joaceo, and so I decided to be Jackson."[16] Born in Louisiana, Amos Lincoln claimed an African grandfather, soldiered, worked as a cowboy, tracked Indians and wolves, drove cattle, and endured the dry weather.[17] Tom Mills, though born in Alabama, gave an extended account of a black Texas cowboy. When he was still a young boy, Mills's family moved to Texas near Corpus Christi. At age twenty-two, he married Ada Costa. "She had on a white dress dragging the ground in the back what you used to call trains. I had on one of those frock-tail coats, black broadcloth suit. . . . We danced all night. . . . I was a damn fool, wanted to dance all the time. I inherited that from my mother. . . . When I got to working for myself, it was cow work. I did horseback work for fifty years. Many a year passed that I never missed a day in the saddle."[18]

As a frontier region, Texas offered African Americans opportunities that did not exist in the remainder of the South. Discontented slaves could either run away to live with an Indian group or cross the border into Mexico, which did not recognize slavery. Men learned to ride horses, track animals, herd cattle and sheep, and handle a gun. Mounted on a horse, dressed in buckskins, wearing a Stetson or sombrero, and sporting a carbine and a revolver, a black Texan did not look nor act as a slave. He could shoot a rifle, ride a horse, wrangle a bull, go where he wished, drink in a saloon, swagger down the street, speak with a drawl, and carry a chip on his shoulder. From the origin of the Lone Star State, black in Texas did not mean what it meant in Alabama or Georgia. It meant inequality and servility, but it also meant the courage and freedom of a warrior. When southern slaves set foot in Texas, they also became westerners.

The state song, "The Yellow Rose of Texas," illustrates black Texans' twofold identity as southerners and westerners. According to legend, Emily West, a mulatto, became a Texas spy in the army of Santa Ana when the Mexican general captured her in a skirmish before the battle of San Jacinto. By her account, West seduced Santa Ana on the eve of the battle, which enabled the Texas army, led by Sam Houston, to capture the Mexican commander while he lay in the arms of

West. Emily West's black lover wrote "The Yellow Rose of Texas" to honor his love. In the 1930s, white Texans de-racialized the song when they made it the state's anthem. Its original words make the racial identity of Emily West clear:

> There's a yellow rose in Texas
> That I am going to see
> No other darky knows her
> No one, only me
> She cried so when I left her
> It like to broke my heart
> And if I ever find her
> We nevermore will part.
>
> She's the sweetest rose of color
> This darky ever knew
> Her eyes are bright as diamonds
> They sparkle like the dew
> You may talk about dearest May
> And sing of Rosa Lee
> But the yellow rose of Texas
> Beats the belles of Tennessee.[19]

JUNETEENTH

On May 27, 1865, Confederate commander Kirby Smith ordered all Texas troops to rally in Houston. Only a handful showed. In despair, on June 2, Smith surrendered the last remaining Confederate army to the Union commander at Galveston. On June 19 Union general Gordon Granger read General Order Three to an assembly of whites and blacks in Galveston: "The people of Texas are informed that all slaves are free. This involves an absolute equality between personal rights and rights of property between former masters and slaves." Smith's surrender and Granger's proclamation freed nearly a quarter million slaves in Texas. For the next 150 years, black Texans celebrated their freedom on "Juneteenth," the anniversary of Granger's general order. By 1870 the black population of Texas had increased nearly 40 percent over the preceding decade from 182,921 to 253,475. In the next decade, it jumped another 55 percent and another 25 percent in each of the next two decades. In 1900, more than 620,000 African Americans called Texas home, more than in any other western state. At the start of the twentieth century, Texas offered black Americans their best hope for economic and personal security. In the four decades following emancipation, the Lone Star, not the North Star, beckoned black southerners, especially to Houston.

Houston's black population increased at the same rate as the state's overall black population from 3,691 in 1870 to about 15,000 in 1900. The same forces that drew black southerners to Texas and Houston attracted even more white southerners. From 1870 to 1900, Houston's white population increased more than 500 percent from 5,691 in 1870 to 30,000 in 1900. In 1870 two out of five Houstonians were African Americans. In 1900 less than one in three Houstonians were black. In 1870 blacks constituted about 30 percent of the Texas population. In 1900 the proportion had dropped to about 20 percent. As in Texas generally, each decade saw the number of blacks in Houston increase dramatically even while their proportion of the population declined. For blacks in Texas, freedom never approached the "absolute equality" of General Order Three. The tapping of the Spindle Top oil field in 1902 and the opening of the Houston ship-channel in 1914 brought dramatic changes to Houston, but not black equality. Better off than other black southerners, black Texans celebrated Juneteenth out of hope for equality, not its achievement.

Every June 19, black Texans, especially those in Galveston and Houston, gathered to celebrate their freedom. Ritually, they publicly read the preamble to the Declaration of Independence that declared all men were created equal, Lincoln's Gettysburg Address that called for "a new birth of freedom," the Emancipation Proclamation, and General Order Three, which prohibited the use of race as a disqualification for voting. Following the readings and speeches, the assembled celebrants, dressed in their best clothes, paraded to a picnic ground where they set off fireworks, ate barbecue, and danced.[20]

At first, the Union army, supported by the national Republican Party, protected former slaves and helped them adjust to freedom. White Texas voters, however, remained loyal to their prewar Democratic Party. In 1866 a newly ratified Texas Constitution barred blacks from voting, office holding, and jury service, and limited their legal testimony. The all-white, Democratic Texas legislature reinstated much of the state's pre–Civil War slave code. The legislature segregated public transportation and education, approved a whites-only homestead law, enacted an apprenticeship law that allowed employers to control black children until they reached the age of twenty-one or married, approved a contract labor statute that bound whole families, and ratified a vagrancy law that tied black prisoners to long-term labor contracts on rice and cotton plantations. In response to such actions, in 1866 northern voters gave Republicans overwhelming majorities in the federal Congress, which disqualified most Confederates from office holding and voting. Backed by a Republican-dominated federal government and protected by Union soldiers, on July 4, 1867, 20 whites and 150 blacks formed the Texas Republican Party.[21]

In 1870 Republicans gained a majority in both houses of the Texas legislature and won the governorship. The new state legislature included 14 blacks and 106 whites. The Republican-controlled legislature repealed most of the race-based statutes enacted in 1866 and established a system of black public schools in Texas cities. From the start, Texas racially segregated public education—white teachers taught white students in all-white schools and black teachers taught black students in all-black schools. Moreover, despite the presence of Union soldiers, in the rural areas of Texas secret white organizations, such as the Ku Klux Klan, intimidated Republican voters and officeholders. In the 1870s the all-white Democratic Party returned to power. Except for isolated, all-black communities such as Houston's Fourth Ward, Texas became an uncontested, white-man's country.[22]

So complete was the white Democratic Party's victory in Texas that the state legislature never bothered to disenfranchise black voters. As long as blacks voted Republican and the Republican Party remained impotent, Texas whites cared little if blacks cast meaningless votes. Backed by the state government and an increasingly indifferent federal government, local white Democrats, even in areas that boasted black majorities, county by county, city by city, by means fair and foul, drove Republicans from power and imposed on Texas unchallenged white rule. Indeed, the only visible sign of Confederate defeat and Union triumph was the formal ending of chattel slavery, the continued celebration of Juneteenth by Texas blacks, and the presence of federal troops along the Texas Indian frontier and Mexican border.[23]

Texans supported the policing of Native Americans by the U.S. Army. White Texans, however, deeply resented the black soldiers of the Twenty-fifth Corps. A remnant of the 180,000 black soldiers who had served during the Civil War, black soldiers of the Twenty-fifth Corps patrolled the Indian and Mexican frontiers.[24] Nearly two-thirds of the Union soldiers who occupied Texas following Kirby Smith's surrender came from the black Twenty-fifth Corps. For former Confederates, these black Union soldiers made defeat all the more galling. When black soldiers ventured into Texas towns, they often faced white harassment and in some instances violence. In response to the murder of two black Union soldiers by the deputy marshal of Jefferson, Texas, the Union commander, General Philip Sheridan, refused to prosecute the killer. Sheridan explained his inaction: "The trial of a white man for the murder of a freedman in Texas would be a farce."[25] In 1869 Sheridan ordered black federal troops in Texas to serve only west of the

100th Meridian, the boundary between the white settlements of East Texas and the Indian lands of West Texas.

After 1865, the War Department reorganized the Twenty-fifth Corps into the Ninth and Tenth Cavalry and the Twenty-fourth and Twenty-fifth Infantry, placing the black regiments under the command of white officers. The four regiments, like other western soldiers, policed reservations, served in frontier stockades, escorted westward-bound wagon trains, chased down hostile Indian bands, patrolled the Mexican border, and enforced the United States' control of the Trans-Mississippi West. Black soldiers received numerous citations for bravery in combat, occasionally indulged in acts of cruelty and unprovoked violence, and at other times acted as courageous arbitrators between helpless Native Americans and violent whites. Unlike white soldiers, they became targets of white hostility and violence, sometimes even from fellow white soldiers and commanders. Unlike many other western commanders, when John Pershing assumed command of the Tenth Cavalry, he staunchly defended his black "buffalo soldiers," so called by Native Americans because of the soldiers' coarse, dark hair that they thought resembled a buffalo. Pershing found his black cavalry reliable and brave. Because of his identification with the Tenth Cavalry, Pershing acquired the nickname "Nigger Jack." When given command of the American army in Europe during World War I, his fellow officers changed his nickname to the less offensive "Black Jack" Pershing.[26]

African Americans accounted for about 5 percent of federal soldiers in the West. African Americans also made up about 5 percent of the region's cattle herders. In Texas, freedmen worked on ranches throughout the state and accompanied the cattle drives that originated in South Texas and worked their way to the rail yards of Kansas. A few successful black cowboys acquired ranches and joined thousands of other freedmen who lived in rural Texas, most as farm laborers but some as landed ranchers. The largest black landowner in Texas, Daniel Webster, owned a ten-thousand-acre ranch in Mitchell County. Most, however, worked as ranch hands or ran small, fifty- to a hundred-acre ranches scattered across the state.[27] In 1900 Texas was the only western state in which a majority of its African Americans lived in rural areas. Even so, black Texans drifted westward and cityward in response to rural white violence and urban opportunities. By 1900, one in three black Texans lived in a city, nearly 15,000 of those in Houston.

With emancipation, many former slaves had sought sanctuary in Houston. In the heart of the East Texas Black Belt, Houston beckoned freedmen from throughout East Texas and especially plantation workers from the Brazo River Bottoms. On a fifty-acre tract called Freedmen's Town, in Houston's Fourth Ward, black migrants formed Houston's first black community. The settlers of Freedmen's Town built simple shotgun houses that contained two to three rooms. Freedmen clustered together in the Fourth Ward much as they had in their plantation quarters, but now they controlled their private lives. Many worked as laborers or domestics while others opened vegetable stands, butcher and blacksmith shops, and a string of taverns along San Felipe Road where it entered Houston (now West Dallas). On Juneteenth, July Fourth, and Watch Night, the residents of Freedmen's Town paraded and picnicked in celebration of black emancipation and racial solidarity.[28]

In 1870 Fourth Ward church leaders, supported by northern missionary societies, opened the Gregory Institute to train young blacks for the skilled trades. In 1870 one in twenty-five black families in the Fourth Ward owned its own home. Almost all of Houston's black-owned businesses were situated in the Fourth Ward, most serving other blacks. Freedmen's Town claimed most of Houston's black churches, including Houston's first black church, Trinity African Methodist Episcopal Church, Houston's first Baptist congregation, Antioch Baptist Church, and the lodge houses of the city's black Prince Hall Masons, Knights of Pythias, and Odd Fellows.[29]

African Americans in Freedmen's Town laid out Founders' Cemetery that overlooked Buffalo Bayou. In 1867 Elias Dibble formed the Trinity Methodist Church in Freedmen's Town followed in 1872 by Jack Yates's establishment of the Antioch Baptist Church. Both churches housed Freedmen Bureau schools. When the Houston city government barred blacks from city parks in 1871, the residents of Freedmen's Town moved their Juneteenth celebration to a ten-acre lot in the Third Ward at the intersection of Dowling and Elgin, on the city's northeast side. On June 19, 1873, Houston's African American community celebrated its first Juneteenth in Emancipation Park. Maintained and owned by black Houstonians, on June 19 and July 4, Emancipation Park became the center of black Houston. A parade from Freedmen's Town to Emancipation Park marked the three-day-long festivities that, by 1900, included barbecue, free lemonade, carnival rides, races, and a variety of contests. Each June 19 Houston's black leaders ceremonially read the Juneteenth Proclamation, on July 4 they read the Declaration of Independence, and on January 1 the Emancipation Proclamation.[30] In time, the park commission developed Emancipation Park into a year-round facility with recreational fields, playground equipment, outhouses, a racetrack, two outdoor dance floors, and a beer tavern. In Emancipation Park, Houston African Americans never doubted the importance of emancipation or its unfulfilled promises.[31]

BLACK BAPTISTS ON BUFFALO BAYOU

Houston lay along the banks of Buffalo Bayou, a tidal river that maintained a six-foot depth for the thirty miles it meandered between Houston and Galveston. With Galveston, Houston served as the Gulf port of the East Texas cotton and rice belts and the administrative center of Harris County. Not until 1900 did the population of Houston surpass that of Galveston, and not until 1920 did it exceed San Antonio and Dallas. The opening of the Spindle Top oil field in 1902 transformed Houston into the center of the world's petroleum industry, setting off the extraordinary growth that Houston enjoyed throughout the twentieth century. In 1914 the Army Corp of Engineers completed the Houston Ship Channel to Galveston that straightened Buffalo Bayou and deepened the channel to twenty-five feet. Taking advantage of Houston's saltwater access, the Southern Pacific, Central Missouri, and other national railroads built rail lines to the city. In 1930 Houston ranked as the eighth-largest port in the nation and the nation's largest cotton and petroleum port. Before World War II, no other city in the South enjoyed such sustained growth.[32]

Houston's prosperity offered African Americans a unique, southern opportunity. Unlike most other southern cities, each year the Houston economy created thousands of new jobs, most unskilled and semiskilled. African Americans in rural Texas and neighboring Louisiana, condemned to sharecropping or tenant farming, poured into the "Bayou City." Black migrants found inexpensive housing in the Fourth Ward southwest of downtown, the newer Fifth Ward east of downtown near the rail yards and the ship channel, and the Third Ward near Emancipation Park. Almost no free blacks had lived in Houston during slavery, so, the city's first black leaders were almost all former slaves, mostly rural laborers from cotton, rice, and sugar plantations. Outnumbering whites by two to one in the plantation regions and forced to live apart from whites in the slave quarters, Texas and Louisiana slaves lived in their own world, largely invisible to whites.[33]

Emancipation, momentarily, broke through the walls that separated white and black Texans. Black children attended Freedmen Bureau and later missionary society schools where they learned the same subjects and skills that white children learned in Texas public schools. In a few instances, blacks and whites worshiped together, especially Methodists. Under the auspices of the Republican Party and the protection of the Union army, black and white Republicans supported common candidates for public office. In 1870 black Republicans looked forward to a racially nondiscriminatory society. Those hopes ended in 1873 when

A Masonic lodge on Dawley Avenue in Houston's Third Ward (Will Scott)

the all-white Texas Democratic Party reversed the efforts of the Republican Party to integrate former slaves into Texas life.

After 1876, Louisiana followed virtually the same course as Texas. By 1900, African Americans in both states had lost most of their rights as citizens and lived apart in all-black worlds.[34] Slavery had poorly prepared Texas and Louisiana African Americans for freedom. A largely illiterate and rural people, freedmen struggled in post–Civil War Houston. They found themselves excluded from skilled trades and the trained professions, and they lacked the entrepreneurial skills and capital to succeed in business. After 1870, white hostility forced African Americans to turn inward and reaffirm the culture and social ties that had served them during slavery. In post-Reconstruction Texas and Louisiana, African Americans clung to the remnants of their slave culture and developed a strong sense of racial community. In churches and lodges, they formalized many of the West African–influenced customs of slavery. In East Texas and South Louisiana, these old ways found new homes in the newly organized Sanctified Baptist churches of the region. Nowhere was this more so than in Houston and surrounding Harris County.

In 1866 I. S. Campbell formed Antioch Baptist Church, Houston's first black Baptist congregation. At first, it met in a brush arbor on the southern bank of Buffalo Bayou, convenient for full-immersion baptisms. In 1868 the church moved to a temporary building in Freedmen's Town on the corner of Rusk and Bagby streets. A year later, Jack Yates, a former slave, became the pastor of Antioch Baptist Church. In 1879 Yates moved his congregation to a permanent building on nearby Robin Street. Earlier, in 1867, Rev. Elias Dibble had formed Houston's first black Methodist church, Trinity Methodist, also in Freedmen's Town. Until World War I, almost all African Americans in Houston belonged to either a Baptist or a Methodist church. Most, however, worshiped as Baptists. At times in Houston, black and Baptist seemed interchangeable terms. In 1910 Houston's *Red Book,* a directory of the city's black community, estimated that 80 percent of the city's African Americans attended a Baptist church. Firmly rooted in slavery, Texas Baptists affirmed a form of Africanized Christianity similar to other Sanctified southern churches, also rooted in slavery.[35]

Afro-Baptism embodied creolized, West African beliefs. Upper- and middle-class Christians, black and white, viewed Afro-Baptism as a crude, magic-ridden, and emotional religion restricted to the poor and ignorant. They believed it would disappear when African Americans became educated and acculturated to Anglo-American life. Racial segregation, however, fortified West African–based slave ways. Under the rubric of the Knights of Pythias, the Odd Fellows, and the Prince Hall Masonic Order, black males in Houston preserved many the ceremonies and initiation rituals of West African–inspired secret slave societies. These all-male secret societies served as the guardians of black Houston. Secret lodges provided food and shelter to the poor, buried the dead, conducted annual parades, formed the boards of deacons in the city's black Baptist churches, and supervised Juneteenth and Fourth of July celebrations in Emancipation Park. In Houston, the cornerstones of many black churches bore the Masonic seal.[36]

Because of its invisibility and the oral character of its liturgy, few records exist of early Texas Afro-Baptism. The WPA slave narratives offer insight into the religious beliefs and practices of Texas slaves just before emancipation but do not address post-emancipation religious practice. In the 1940s the Julius Rosenwald Fund commissioned Henry Faulk to record a few Central Texas, black Baptist church services.[37] In the 1980s, drawing on these sources and his personal observations as church-organist for the St. John Progressive Baptist Church in Austin, ethnomusicologist Walter F. Pitts Jr. analyzed and described the Texas Afro-Baptist liturgy. As a guest-organist over a five-year period in the 1980s, Pitts participated in, observed, and recorded the services of more than a dozen different Texas black Baptist churches. Together, these three sources offer a rare glimpse into the sacred rituals of Afro-Baptism.[38]

Afro-Baptists in central Texas divided their services into two discrete parts—

the devotion and the service, each initiated by the congregation's senior deacons. To prepare the congregation for the service, in a cappella a senior deacon lined out a traditional hymn, often taken from nineteenth-century Protestant hymnals. The deacon chanted the song at a dirgelike pace and tone, leading the congregation line by line in a call-and-response exchange. After the opening chant, he or another senior deacon, in the stylized language of the King James Bible, offered a ritualized prayer in the same somber tone. Following the prayer, a second deacon lined out a second old hymn followed by another stylized prayer also in the seventeenth-century language of the King James Bible. One by one, worshipers entered the plain-style sanctuary, took their seats in the straight-backed wooden pews, and joined the service. Deacons stationed at the doors barred anyone from leaving and cautioned children to cease talking and to assume a reverent attitude. The opening devotion lasted a half hour or more. Throughout, the predominantly female congregation, dressed in white, maintained a subdued manner and duti- fully followed the lead of the male deacons. An outside observer could easily have mistaken this prelude to Sunday worship as a funeral service.[39]

The preparatory devotion ended when a deacon signaled the choir. The choir responded in song, accompanied by the piano. On hearing the minister's foot- steps, the deacons opened the altar door and admitted him, followed by the assistant ministers. On the minister's appearance, the robed choir broke out into a joyous, upbeat hymn such as "Oh Happy Day," now, accompanied by the piano, an organ, a drum set, and an electric guitar. At the end of the hymn, the minister read a verse of scripture that provided the theme for his chanted prayer accompanied by the pianist, which brought on an emotional crescendo punctuated by shouts from worshipers of "Blessed Jesus," "Yes, Preacher," and "Thank You Jesus." Wor- shipers waved their straightened arms above their heads with open palms to the ceiling, some spoke in tongues and others fainted. The minister ended the prayer by slowing the cadence to restore calm, accompanied only by the piano.

Following the prayer, an assistant minister announced upcoming events and church news to the composed congregation. The deacons then collected the offer- ing after which the choral director led the choir in a powerful, body-swaying hymn that featured solos of the best voices and musicians in the church. Visitors, un- familiar with Sanctified services, found themselves moved by the power and quality of the music and often, to their own surprise, leaped to their feet, clapped their hands, and swayed rhythmically with the choir. When the choir finally ended its singing of verse upon verse of jubilant song, the congregation understood themselves to be in the presence of the Holy Spirit, in an ecstatic and holy space radically at odds with the outside world.[40]

Facing an aroused congregation, the minister took over. He started slowly, in a series of rhythmically chanted lines. He spoke in a vernacular "black English," free of the formalism and archaic words of the King James Bible and the queen's middle-class English. Like the congregation and choir, the minister left the older, archaic world and language of the devotion and entered the spiritualized realm of the here and now using the language of the here and now. With each line, his sermon intensified and the congregation's responses became louder as it appealed to the Holy Spirit. Some worshipers stood, some swayed, others smiled rapturously, a few spoke in tongues, while others fainted. All felt the presence of the Holy Spirit, who lifted their burdens. The sermon and the congregation's ecstasy lasted from a half-hour to several hours depending on the Holy Spirit. Neither the minister nor the deacons nor the congregation could predict or control the Sanctified service. It took on a life of its own. The congregation, through ritualized prayer and sacred song, had invited the Holy Spirit and prepared for its visit. But the worshipers had no control over its actions. Afro-Baptists revered and faithfully worshiped Jehovah and Jesus, but only the Holy Spirit provided them the spiritual joy and strength to endure the tribulations of the outside, profane world.

The preliminary devotion paralleled the initiation rites of many West African religions and secret societies. During the devotion, congregants left the unsanctified world of daily existence and prepared themselves for the sanctified world of the spiritual world's joy, praise, and love. When the sacred phase of the service began, sealed off from the outside world by the deacons, the worshipers opened their hearts to the Holy Spirit, who bridged the living and the dead, the present and the future, a world free from the traumas of life, slavery, apartheid, and racial prejudice. In the presence of the Holy Spirit, they found unqualified love. All were equally worthy. All were equally qualified for Jesus's redemption. During the sacred service, they passed from their profane lives and ecstatically experienced their passage into the realm of God. Marked by their full-immersion baptism, they "crossed the River Jordan" in their "Old Ship of Zion" and "stole away to Jesus" as they "flew away" to "Glory Land."[41]

The orally transmitted liturgy of black Baptism drew on the shared ideas of various West African religions and fused them with southern Protestantism. Like the black Masons, who on the surface looked like white Masons and who adopted the public symbols of the white Masonic Order, behind a veil of secrecy African Americans preserved and affirmed the West African ways of their ancestors. Afro-Baptism enabled African Americans the means to sustain hope in the face of unimaginable adversity.[42] The rituals of the Prince Hall Masons, in a similar fashion, symbolically reenacted West African initiation rituals when their members moved their hands counterclockwise on the shoulders of the person in front of them. On Juneteenth, the Fourth of July, and New Years Day, black Houstonians in public, but invisible to whites, affirmed their spiritual ties to West Africa.

HOLY SPEECH AT AZUSA STREET

In 1869 when Jack Yates assumed the pulpit of Antioch Baptist Church, he viewed Afro-Baptism as the linchpin of a powerful black community that had freed itself from slavery. Within three years, however, whites drove blacks out of public life in Houston and Texas. White Texans made it clear that, while slavery had ended, white supremacy had not. Antioch Baptist Church, no longer a force of citywide power, became a spiritual sanctuary for Houston's beleaguered black community. Bolstered by their Sanctified Christianity, neither Yates nor other Houston African Americans were willing to return to the brush arbors of slavery. Emancipation had given them the freedom to move about, to control their personal lives, to own property, to legally constitute families, and in Freedmen's Town to build a semi-autonomous black community with its own schools, stores, lodges, taverns, playing fields, cemeteries, leaders, churches, and West African ways.

For three decades following emancipation, slavery cast its dark shadow over the memories of black Houston. Until 1900, most black Houstonians had either experienced slavery personally or learned about it from their parents. In 1890 most remained illiterate, only about 15 percent owned their own homes, 85 percent of the women worked as domestics, and about the same percentage of men labored in unskilled jobs. Four out of five attended Afro-Baptist churches, but virtually no one voted. African American formal education followed Booker T. Washington's Tuskegee model of vocational and agricultural training to become the "hewers of wood and bearers of water" for the South's whites. Blacks lived throughout the city, but concentrated in the Fourth Ward and conducted their lives largely apart from white Houston. They remained a rural, at best small-town, southern people whose circumstances had changed little since emancipation. They had little reason to imagine any significant change in the future. They had exchanged their brush arbors for Baptist churches, slavery for menial wage labor, and their slave quarters for Freedmen's Town. Otherwise, they lived much as their parents had lived.

In 1890 Houston remained a small, southern city. In the 1890s Houston, like the remainder of the South, began to change but not always for the better for its African American residents. Between 1890 and 1900, the percentage of blacks in the city dropped 5 percent. The arrival of large numbers of white migrants explained part of the relative decline, but the departure of hundreds of African Americans to Los Angeles contributed to the loss. With the extension of the Southern Pacific Railroad to Los Angeles, blacks from Texas and other areas of the South gained passage to the far West. Los Angeles and Houston emerged as the most important centers of African American life in the West. The first indication of the intimate tie between Los Angeles and black Texans occurred during the 1906–8 Azusa Street Pentecostal Revival.[43]

Unlike southern Afro-Baptism, the Azusa Street Pentecostals in Los Angeles openly challenged racial segregation. Most converts to Pentecostalism had earlier belonged to a Holiness church. The Holiness movement derived from Methodism. The founder of Methodism, John Wesley, had preached a doctrine of "perfectionism," which asserted that true Christian saints underwent a second, powerful, and life-changing conversion, called "sanctification," much as Saint Paul experienced on the road to Damascus. After their sanctification, saints led perfect Christian lives, free of sin, confident of their salvation. Throughout the nineteenth century, Holiness factions periodically surfaced in Methodist congregations throughout the country but most frequently in Missouri, Arkansas, southern Indiana, western Pennsylvania, and Ohio. In 1904 in Wales, a Holiness revival reported a new phenomenon. Several persons touched by the Holy Spirit spoke in tongues, an incomprehensible speech that accompanied the possession of the individual by the Holy Spirit. Pentecostals believed that true saints underwent a third and even more powerful event, possession by the Holy Spirit, as manifested by "speaking in tongues" much as the disciples of Jesus had on the day of Pentecost, following his crucifixion and resurrection. Other Holiness revivals occasionally reported an individual who spoke in tongues, but these were isolated, apparently, random occurrences.

Then, in 1906, an itinerant, black Houston evangelist, William Seymour, while in Los Angeles, conducted a two-year-long revival during which hundreds of individuals "spoke in tongues." Dozens reported that Seymour healed them of sickness and crippling injuries. Seymour's Azusa Street Revival led directly to the Pentecostal movement and the formation of several new Pentecostal-Holiness churches. While Pentecostalism originated in Los Angeles, it enjoyed its greatest success among poor blacks and whites in Texas, Oklahoma, Arkansas, and Missouri.[44] Drawing heavily on features of black, Sanctified Baptist churches, Pentecostal ministers appealed to the poor, especially urban and African American poor. In the 1940s Pentecostal churches challenged the Baptists for denominational supremacy among Houston blacks. An urban religion, Pentecostalism merged the orthodox Christian notion of God with the puritanical holiness of

Methodism and the spirit-possession and ecstasy of Afro-Baptism. Seymour had first found the Holy Spirit in Houston.

William Seymour was born in 1870 in Centreville, Louisiana. He grew up in the Reconstruction South, the child of former slaves in Ku Klux Klan–plagued northern Louisiana. Seymour never accepted white supremacy or black subordination. As a child, he turned to the Bible for guidance, and in his family church he absorbed the Afro-Baptist synthesis of West African and Protestant religion. These included God's mandate of freedom and racial equality, the primacy of the Holy Spirit, ecstatic visions and trances, ritual music, dance, faith healing, and the imminent coming of the Second Advent of Christ, who would usher in a Holy Commonwealth on earth. In 1895, refusing to accept racial oppression by Louisiana whites, at age twenty-five, Seymour moved to Indianapolis where he joined a predominantly white Episcopal congregation. A "seeker," in 1900 Seymour moved to Cincinnati to participate in an interracial Holiness group called the Evening Light Saints. Seymour joined the Evening Light Saints at the time when he also contracted small pox that left him blind in the left eye. In 1903 he moved to Houston, where he sought out Charles Fox Parham, a white Holiness minister who spoke in tongues or "glossolalia," a sign to Seymour of the approaching Advent. Parham appreciated Seymour's interest but refused to admit a black man to his all-white Houston Bible School. Instead, he allowed Seymour to listen outside the classroom through an open window and to sit at the rear of his church during evening services. A woman, who had worshiped with Seymour in Houston, moved to Los Angles. In her Los Angeles home, she formed a black Holiness congregation, which invited Seymour to become its leader. In 1906 Seymour arrived at the Southern Pacific Railroad terminal in Los Angeles, a short walk to his new church on Sante Fe Street in the city's warehouse district.[45]

To Seymour's surprise, the Sante Fe Holiness congregation did not agree with his notion of speaking in tongues and dismissed him. Undiscouraged, he met in the homes of a handful of followers. On invitation, Seymour also visited the sick bed of Irish Lee. Seymour prayed for Lee to receive the Holy Ghost, whereupon Lee spoke in tongues and recovered. At the evening service that night, having heard Lee's testimony, others in the black congregation spoke in tongues. The congregation concluded that the advent of the second Pentecost had begun. As the meetings gained in size, the congregation rented an abandoned Methodist church at 312 Azusa Street, between Little Tokyo and the black South Central neighborhood. At Azusa Street, Seymour, much as his parents in their Louisiana brush arbor church, placed the pulpit on the same level as the congregation and formed a holy circle of pews around the pulpit.[46] According to the church's first publication, the Pentecostal movement drew "all together in one body of love, one church, one body of Christ."[47]

The Azusa Street services attracted widespread public attention because of their multiracial composition and eccentric conduct. Never before had Los Angeles witnessed a black minister lead a congregation that included as many whites as blacks as well as large numbers of Asian and Hispanic Americans. Without regard to race or gender, the Azusa Revival attracted the city's poor and downtrodden, including a large number of black, female domestic workers. In the presence of the Holy Spirit, all joined to form a single body with a single religious impulse —to receive the Holy Spirit on the advent of the Second Coming of the Kingdom of God. In a state of ecstasy and possessed by the Holy Spirit, worshipers spoke in tongues, sang, danced, and fell into trances. One participant recounted, "Suddenly, people rose to their feet. Everywhere hands shot toward heaven. Mine went up, and I hadn't tried to raise them. So did the hands of small children and even those of babies in the arms of black mothers. Big, strong men began to cry out loud, then women. I felt like crying too. I didn't know. I just felt, 'Thank you, God, for letting me be here with You.'"[48]

To outside observers, the congregation had lost all sense and decorum. Men and women, blacks and whites fell into each other's arms, sharing the joy of redemption. In the throes of spiritual ecstasy, worshipers ignored racial and gender conventions. In the presence of the Holy Ghost, all became equal. No longer outcasts or objects of contempt, the poor of Los Angeles saw themselves as God's chosen saints, the vanguard of the Second Coming. Material wealth, racial bigotry, and gender inequality all became parts of the profane and rapidly disappearing world of human sinfulness. At Azusa Street, worshipers found a purer, more Godly world that brought unbounded joy.[49]

The revival lasted another two years. Seymour's congregation purchased the Azusa Street building. Subscriptions to its newspaper, the *Apostolic Faith,* exceeded fifty thousand. By 1909, Azusa Street missionaries had established churches throughout the United States but were most successful in the South and in northern cities with large contingents of southern migrants. Seymour's Houston mentor, Charles Parham, formed the whites-only Assembly of God Church that excluded women from its ministry. A black Baptist-Holiness minister from Mississippi, C. H. Mason, attended the Azusa Street revival and, on his return from Los Angeles, founded the Church of God in Christ. Centered in Memphis, COGIC became the nation's largest and most influential Pentecostal church. Unlike the Assembly of God, COGIC remained racially inclusive. Most COGIC members had grown up in rural Sanctified, black Baptist churches. Indeed, for many, Pentecostalism became a reformed, urban-version of rural Afro-Baptism.[50]

Much of Seymour's Pentecostalism derived from his parents' slave religion. Hand clapping, foot stomping, arm waving, shouting, rhythmic song and music, magical healing, spirit possession, and speaking in tongues all characterized Afro-Christianity. Having grown up in the highly spiritual Afro-Baptism of Louisiana, Seymour sought out a similar experience in a racially inclusive church. In the Episcopal Church he found racial inclusiveness, and in the Holiness Church he found puritanical morality and millennial expectations, but neither exhibited the spiritualism of Afro-Baptism. Fellow southerner Charles Parham's speaking in tongues linked Seymour's acquired Holiness beliefs with his inherited African spirituality. Parham, like so many other white Southerners influenced by Afro-Christianity, could not transcend his racism. At Azusa Street, free of southern racism, Seymour and other members of his southern, multiracial, expatriate community formed a new religion that embodied the racial diversity of Los Angles, the theology of the Holiness movement, and the spirituality of Afro-Baptism. For the descendants of West African slaves, the Christian Trinity replaced the multitude of African gods; the Holy Ghost replaced spirit possession; faith healing replaced root medicine, hoodoo spells, and incantations; and racial and gender equality replaced notions of male superiority and racial exclusiveness.[51]

Much like Afro-Baptism, Pentecostal services followed rituals rooted in West African secret societies. Most Pentecostal services, especially in the South, began with a devotion led by a church elder, followed by the procession of the minister and choir. The choir offered a rousing hymn that followed an elder's chanted opening prayer. Then a deacon made the announcements after which the minister appeared and began his chanted sermon, punctuated by the organ, drums, or other instruments, all directed toward members' possession by the Holy Spirit as evidenced by speaking in tongues, trances, joyful shouting, singing, dancing, and full-immersion baptism. In most Pentecostal services, women with ritual responsibilities wore white. Frequently, churches used a standard organ, a piano, a set of snare drums as well as a Hammond organ that could play the complex rhythms and tones of African American sacred music. Pentecostal services ended with a benediction followed by the minister's and congregants' embrace of one another.[52]

Several things in Pentecostalism pointed toward West Africa—holy dance and shouting, the chants of affirmation, white liturgical clothing, the formal welcoming of guests, and unrehearsed ecstatic behavior. Pentecostal churches encouraged spontaneous shouts and dancing that derived from the emotional preparation in West African initiation rites. Such ritualized affirmations from worshipers such as "Yes Jesus," "Praise Jesus," "Thank You Jesus," "Amen Preacher," expressed the participatory communalism of Pentecostal congregations where everyone was either a spiritual sister or brother. The white liturgical dress of attendants, especially of women, derived from the Yoruba identification of white with purity, while full immersion baptism harked back to Yoruba river deities. The formal welcoming and identification of guests, which included the visitor's home, pastor, and church, reached out to fellow members of the African diaspora. Most importantly, spirit possession and ecstatic trances marked the presence of the Holy Ghost, the sanctification of the service. No Pentecostal or other Sanctified congregation has "had church" unless the service included a spiritual awakening that removed worshipers from their profane worlds and drew them into the sacred world.[53]

After the Azusa Street Revival, rural black migrants to Houston gravitated to the newly formed Church of God in Christ and other Pentecostal churches. Such churches openly recruited the rural poor. Instead of discouraging religious enthusiasm as inappropriate and socially embarrassing, Pentecostal congregations described such behavior as manifestations of holiness. Illiteracy, countrified dress and speech, poverty, and openly expressed spirituality became badges of honor, passports into an urban, exile community that included other uprooted African Americans. In Houston's Sanctified churches, rural blacks found a home that welcomed rather than judged them. Sanctified churches assisted rural newcomers to locate housing, introduced them to potential mates, found them employment, and encouraged such middle-class values as cleanliness, hard work, temperance, sexual chastity, literacy, and disbelief in magic and "pagan superstitions." Pentecostal and other Sanctified churches accepted rural refugees for what they were, helped with their immediate needs, and reformed their behavior in ways that equipped migrants for urban life.

MUTINY ON THE BAYOU

Rural blacks flocked to Houston because it offered opportunities and freedoms unavailable elsewhere in the South. By World War I, Houston had built elementary schools in every ward, including the predominantly black Fourth Ward. In 1910 Houston boasted the highest black literacy rate in the South, the highest rate of homeownership, and the highest rate of church membership.[54] Before World War I, black life in Houston centered in Freedmen's Town. The fifty-block community included Booker T. Washington High School, Gregory Elementary School, a black

Carnegie Library, and the four-story Pilgrim Professional Building. Freedmen's Town also included the powerful Antioch Methodist Church, Good Hope Mission-ary Baptist Church, Shiloh Missionary Baptist Church, Bethel Baptist Church, and Pilgrim Congregational Church, as well as the Union Hospital. In 1910, 90 per-cent of Houston's black-owned businesses were located in the Fourth Ward. They included groceries, cafés, boardinghouses, hotels, restaurants, funeral homes, honky-tonks, bars, and brothels. Most residents lived in either shotgun houses or two-story frame houses with porches and fenced-in vegetable gardens in the back. Owners frequently added on rooms to accommodate their expanding households and even moved their houses from one lot to another, leading to the quip that Freedmen's Town was a community of an ever "growing and moving people."[55]

Because of Houston's large number of black voters in Freemen's Town, the Republican Party survived into the 1930s. Moreover, in the wake of the Spindle Top oil boom, Houston and its surrounding communities added thousands of new jobs each year, many for blacks. Black dockworkers claimed half of the union jobs in the ports of Houston and Galveston. The railroads that served the ship channel and the East Texas oil field also employed large numbers of African American males as construction workers, maintenance, and Pullman car porters. Most telling, Houston and surrounding Harris County recorded only two public lynchings in the fifty-year span from the end of Reconstruction until 1930, one of the best records in Texas.[56]

Such good news, however, occurred in the context of a rigidly enforced system of racial apartheid that brooked no opposition. Until the 1950s, Houston main-tained segregated school systems, limited the employment opportunities for black and Hispanic laborers, and racially segregated access to restaurants, hotels, public transportation, public parks, and housing. In all things racial, Houston accepted and enforced the southern system of white superiority and black ser-vility. On its public buildings, the Stars and Bars of the Confederacy flew just below the Lone Star flag. Any challenge to the city's racial apartheid brought immediate and, often, brutal punishment. But unlike other ex-Confederate states, the U.S. Army maintained a visible presence in Texas.[57] White Texans, however, refused to respect the army's black soldiers as agents of public authority. In 1870 an all-white jury acquitted a white man who murdered a black soldier. In 1878 at Fort Concho a mob tore the stripes from a black sergeant's uniform, and in 1881 a San Angelo jury acquitted a white shepherd for gunning down an unarmed black trooper. Other incidents occurred during the mobilization and demobilization for the Spanish-American War. Texas and federal authorities stationed black units away from white settlements and cautioned soldiers to stay away from white bars

Inscription on an African American gravestone. Life in Houston was often like crossing a troubled water. Olive Wood Cemetery, Houston (Will Scott)

and saloons. At times, however, military needs required stationing black units near towns.[58]

In 1906, concerned with border security along the Rio Grande, the War Department ordered several units of the Twenty-fifth Infantry to Brownsville, Texas. White Brownsville authorities aggravated the usual white-black tensions. Local bars and restaurants refused to serve black soldiers, and a federal customs agent pistol-whipped a black private when he failed to step off the sidewalk for a white woman. A week later, a federal border guard threw a black soldier off a bridge into the Rio Grande when the soldier tried to return to Brownsville from a visit to Matamoros, the cross-border Mexican town. Shortly after the bridge incident, a white woman accused a black infantryman of assault. The post commander ordered all black soldiers to remain at the fort, but on August 13 a dozen soldiers left the military base and fired into several buildings along the river. The shots killed a Mexican bartender and wounded a deputy sheriff and the editor of the Spanish-language newspaper. Texas authorities arrested eleven of the black soldiers and asked the War Department to remove all members of the Twenty-fifth Infantry from Texas. Acknowledging white provocation, the War Department confirmed that black soldiers had attacked Brownsville civilians. Unable to determine the guilty parties, the War Department transferred the entire Twenty-fifth Infantry to Oklahoma. President Theodore Roosevelt, who had commanded the Twenty-fifth during the Spanish American War, backed the summary court-martial that led to the dishonorable discharge of 167 men from the Twenty-fifth for banding "together to shelter their own criminals."[59]

Despite such treatment, African Americans in Texas remained loyal to the federal government. In preparation for European combat in 1917, the army ordered nearly seven hundred soldiers and officers of the Twenty-fourth Infantry's Third Battalion to Fort Logan, outside Houston. At the same time, the War Department launched a nationwide campaign to root out prostitution near all army and navy bases. The department pressured local authorities to close down red-light districts and tightly regulate bars and dance halls. The wartime closings included New Orleans's famed Storyville and Houston's Reservation.

In the Fourth Ward, the Reservation housed about five hundred prostitutes, black and white, who worked within easy walking distance of downtown Houston and in the city's nighttime entertainment district along San Felipe Avenue. On the Reservation, Houston males could visit prostitutes at a bordello of their racial choice. The closing of the Reservation coincided with the arrival of the Twenty-fourth Infantry. The new regulation forced Houston prostitutes to ply their trade on the streets, in full public view. On leave, the soldiers of the Twenty-fourth could no longer discreetly visit the black bordellos and nightspots on the Reservation. Instead, they prowled the city for prostitutes. The nighttime presence of several hundred black soldiers, roaming the streets of downtown Houston in search of alcohol, entertainment, gambling, and sex unnerved Houston whites. Not since Reconstruction had racial tensions in Houston been so high.[60]

In August the Houston police launched a campaign of intimidation and violence against black soldiers. The first incident occurred on August 18 when two policemen beat and arrested two black soldiers. On the same day, Houston police beat two more soldiers, who protested being called "niggers." The next day a deputy sheriff pistol-whipped a soldier for sitting in the "whites only" seats along the sidewalk. On August 23 two Houston police officers, Rufus Daniels and Lee Sparks, beat and arrested a black soldier for protesting the arrest of a black housewife. Believing the police had killed the soldier, members of the Twenty-fourth gathered to revenge the alleged killing. White officers tried to quell the mob, but when a soldier yelled, "To hell with France, get to work right here," Sergeant Vida Henry led about one hundred men, most from Company I, into Houston. They found Sparks and Daniels in the San Felipe District where they killed Daniels and three other police. Next, Sergeant Henry ordered the soldiers to attack the police station. Most refused and returned to camp. The remainder went into hiding in Freedmen's Town. By morning, the police and military had restored order. The police killed Vida Henry and three other black soldiers; the rioters killed ten white civilians, five white police officers, and one Mexican American.[61]

Stunned, the army tried 118 soldiers for mutiny in three separate trials. On November 30 a military court sentenced 13 soldiers to death. In the early morning of December 11, the army privately executed the 13 condemned men before they could appeal their sentences. Altogether, the army executed 29 soldiers, imprisoned 53 for life, and acquitted 7. The army sentenced the other 16 to prison for two to fifteen years.[62] Not since the Nat Turner slave insurrection, in 1832, had an American court ordered the execution of so many African Americans. Even the Virginia slave court allowed Nat Turner to appeal his conviction to the governor of Virginia, and it publicly announced his execution and publicly hung him. Shortly after the trials, Congress prohibited the participation in combat of the Ninth and Tenth Cavalry and the Twenty-fourth and Twenty-fifth Infantry, in effect demoting them from soldiers to military lackeys. Together, with the East St. Louis race riot, which had occurred a month earlier, the Houston Mutiny in August 1917 marked the beginning of a quarter century of deteriorating race relations in Houston and the remainder of the nation. No one along Buffalo Bayou, however, would ever forget the Buffalo Soldiers' last stand.

CREOLE CROSSROAD

The rising tide of white racism ushered in by World War I coincided with Houston's shift from a regional port and local agricultural center to a national industrial and transportation center. The arrival of new rail lines in the 1920s drew a wave of Louisiana black Creoles to the city. The Southern Pacific Railroad's construction of a large rail yard near the Houston-Galveston Ship Channel attracted an influx of Francophone, black Creoles from southern Louisiana. In the Fifth Ward, these Creoles formed a community of French-speaking black Catholics. "Frenchtown," on the south side of the Southern Pacific tracks, became the first stop on the western migration of black Louisiana Creoles to Los Angeles, Oakland, and San Francisco.

Frenchtown comprised about twenty city blocks of swampy land that bordered the Englewood Yards of the Southern Pacific Railroad. The Southern Pacific Railroad not only employed black Creoles but provided them direct and inexpensive transportation back to the French-speaking parishes of southern Louisiana. Many of Frenchtown's five hundred or so families even built their homes out of worn-out Southern Pacific boxcars. Others built Louisiana double-pen houses with a porch on the front and a kitchen in the back, while still others built traditional shotgun houses. No matter the style, Frenchtown houses, like the sharecroppers' houses in southern Louisiana, included a front porch.[63] In a letter home, a Creole boasted about his nine-to-five job for two dollars a day, "Dear Couzan, this is heav'n over here, we only work half a day."[64] The rail yards provided the back fence for Our Mother of Mercy Catholic Church and School that fronted on Sumpter Street. Two blocks south, an assortment of Creole groceries, gumbo restaurants, barber and tailor shops, the Creole Knights Temple, and juke joints formed the business section of Frenchtown on Deschaumes and its cross streets. A few blocks west of Frenchtown, on Lyons Street, Stanley Drugs advertised Voudon root medicine and talismans. Creole families in Frenchtown behaved much as they had in rural Louisiana. They planted vegetable gardens in their back yards, caught crayfish in swampy ponds, raised chickens that roamed the streets and alleys, and took turns hosting neighborhood *boucheries,* during which they ceremonially butchered a hog and distributed its meat, feet, tail, head, blood, and entrails to family and friends.[65] The western outpost for southern Louisiana black Creoles, Frenchtown gave them a familiar passageway into urban America.[66]

During slavery, black Creoles had worked the sugar plantations of southern Louisiana.[67] More than any other mainland, North American colony, Louisiana was a racially mixed society, much like other Caribbean colonies. In its largest city,

New Orleans, *gens de couleur libres* or free mulattoes at times outnumbered black slaves. In New Orleans and the Creole parishes of southern Louisiana, racial mixing was the norm.[68] In the eighteenth century Louisiana became a self-sustaining slave community. After 1730, most Louisiana slaves were Creoles, that is, born in North America, not West Africa. As had happened in Low Country Carolina, "creolization" transformed Louisiana slaves from a wide variety of West African ethnic groups into a culturally unified, African American, French-speaking people. In Louisiana after 1760, individuals born in West Africa made up less than a third of the region's slaves. Unlike Haiti, Jamaica, Cuba, Santo Dominguez, Barbados, and Brazil, early on Louisiana became an African American melting pot, not a conglomeration of recently arrived, ethnically distinct West and Central African peoples.[69] Isolated in Louisiana, Mandi, Bambara, Fanti, Gambian, and Senegalese along with Guinea, Yoruba, Igbo, Kongo, and Mali slaves contrived a Francophone pidgin made up of West African, Native American, and French languages. These African French Creoles preserved modified forms of West and Central African architecture, cuisine, religion, and music.[70]

The Louisiana climate and physical environment resembled West Africa, especially its heat, humidity, and tropical diseases. Like West Africans, Louisiana slaves cultivated and ate rice, okra, hot peppers, yams, peanuts, red beans, black-eyed peas, fish, pork, chicken, and shell fish. Louisiana slaves dressed in light-weight, loose-fitting, brightly colored clothing. Women wore head cloths and carried burdens on their heads. Slaves built compact houses with porches that took advantage of natural breezes and shade, and in their festivities men and women danced nude the "bamboua," the "chica," and the "ombligada"—the latter, a navel-to-navel dance, accompanied by African drums, rattles, foot stomping, clapping, and string instruments. Outside observers frequently noted the African elements in the Catholicism of black Creoles.[71]

Even more than in the Protestant Carolina Low Country, in Catholic Louisiana, black Creoles retained West and Central African religious practices. Unlike Protestantism, Catholicism embraced a rich array of icons and relics, many tied to the Virgin Mary and the cults of saints. In Louisiana, African gods assumed the names of Catholic saints; the rituals of West African river gods became Christian baptism; magical amulets translated into sacred Catholic relics; and African spiritual intermediaries resembled Jesus, who received supplicants' prayers on behalf of deceased ancestors.[72] Before the French Revolution, Francophone creolization obscured the West African sources of Creole Christianity; nonetheless, it permeated all aspects of Louisiana life, whether you were a black slave, a *gens de couleur libres,* or a white planter. After 1791, however, no one could overlook the West African

A New Orleans version of a shotgun house (Will Scott)

presence in Louisiana. In that year, Toussaint L'Ouverture led a slave revolt that culminated in the formation of the Haitian Republic on western end of the island of Saint Dominguez. Fearing the spread of further slave revolts, frightened Saint Dominguez slaveholders fled to Louisiana with their slaves. Saint Dominguez slaves adhered to Voudon, a highly Africanized form of Christianity.[73]

Few religions have been more misunderstood and misrepresented than Voudon. Since its appearance in Louisiana, Catholic and Protestant Christians have described Voudon as a form of black magic based on primitive African superstitions that promoted sexual promiscuity, violent revenge, and magical healing. Voudon (or Voodoo) was quite different, although it derived from West African sources, embraced magic, and offered its adherents protection from mortal enemies and malevolent spirits. Recently, religious scholar Elizabeth McAlister witnessed a Voudon baptism that conformed to nineteenth- and earlier twentieth-century accounts. According to McAlister, the *oungan* or priest prayed, offered food, and sang to Dambala, the serpent deity, on behalf of a one-year-old baby. The baptism took place on the Saturday night nearest St. Patrick's Day, named for the

Catholic saint associated with snakes in Ireland and whom Voudon associated with the Dambala. The ritual combined aspects of Dahomey, Yoruba, Kongo, and Catholic religious practice.[74]

Voudon, like Christianity, affirmed a single creator God, whom Voudon priests called Gran Met or Great Master. In West African religion and Voudon, the creator God remained aloof from human affairs. Only the intervention of lesser gods or spirits could arouse his interest and help. Lesser gods included Elegba (trickster), Dambala (serpent), Ogou (iron), and scores of others. Voudon priests appealed to such lesser gods or spirits for divine intervention on behalf of congregants through offerings, prayers, songs, and dance. The priest summoned these lesser gods to a spiritually prepared Voudon sanctuary to aid the living. Once appeased, the spirits passed back into the spiritual world where they intervened with the Gran Met on behalf of the believer. The Voudon priest, whom McAlister observed, baptized the infant "in the name of the Father, the Son, and the Holy Spirit."[75]

Also like Christianity, Voudon portrayed reality as radically divided between spiritual and physical realms, between the dead (immortal) and the living (mortal). Water separated the physical world of sensory experience from the divine realm of spiritual consciousness. To join the spiritual world, supplicants underwent rigorous initiation rites that culminated in full-immersion baptism—the passage from the physical to the spiritual. When possessed by a spirit, supplicants fell into trances, lost control of their bodies, and babbled incomprehensibly. They became ecstatic and sometimes experienced magical healing. At death, the spirit left the body and passed across the water into the spiritual realm. To ensure the peaceful passage of the departed, family and friends offered prayers, songs, food, and drink to the spirit of the departed to guarantee its goodwill and help. In Voudon, the living were intimately tied to the dead. In southern Louisiana, as in much of the Anglo-South, the living never forgot the dead; most did not even believe the dead were gone. Passing meant transformation, not death.[76]

The parallels between Voudon and Catholicism were striking. Both posited two radically different worlds, both gave priority to the unseen, spiritual realm, in both the living invoked rituals on behalf of the dead, both embraced a panoply of godlike intermediaries, both affirmed a single creator God who oversaw all reality, and both religions utilized magical rites and baptism. Voudon appealed especially to newly arrived Caribbean and African slaves. It had much less impact on French-speaking, Catholic gens de couleur libres and whites. But in the slave pens and quarters of New Orleans and in the sugar and rice lands of southern Louisiana, West African religious ideas survived in the Catholicism of black Creoles.[77]

Louisiana migrants also brought to Frenchtown their West African–influenced dance music called "lala."[78] After World War II, in Houston a rural, Francophone, and accordion-based lala music evolved into zydeco, a rhythm and blues music that sounded like nothing else outside Louisiana, Mali, and Madagascar. The exact origins of lala are obscure. But like other African American music, it derived from slave field hollers, black church spirituals, and European dance music. In the decades following emancipation, black, southern Louisiana farm workers, mostly sharecroppers, hosted impromptu dance parties to raise money, similar to Harlem rent parties. Early in the week, the women in a family spread the word that they planned to hold a house party on the upcoming Saturday. "On weekends, after working six days a week in them days, sunup to sundown on Saturday nights they'd go to this country house and have a dance," explained Roy Carrier.[79] The host arranged for a lala band, which included an accordion, a rub board, and sometimes a drum and guitar, to play for twenty-five cents per admission. The sponsors offered gumbo for another fifteen cents. On Saturday afternoon before the dance, the men in the family removed all the furniture from the two main rooms in the sharecropper shack and lined the walls with benches. Twenty to thirty dancers packed the two fifteen-by-twenty-foot rooms while others rested outside. Occasionally, the floors collapsed. In that case, the host took the dance outside, and the next week, everyone pitched in to rebuild the broken floors. In the black Creole communities of southern Louisiana, only the Catholic Church surpassed lala dances in importance.[80]

Lala borrowed heavily from late nineteenth- and early twentieth-century European dance music, especially the waltz and the two-step. Like ragtime, except for its syncopation and the use of the rub board, few hearing lala would have considered it African American. Its most prominent features were its French Cajun lyrics, the distinct, rattlesnake-like sound of the rub board, and the one-note button accordion. Invented in 1820 in Austria, the accordion was adopted by black New Orleans musicians who found that the peppy and inexpensive accordion sound could be heard over loud dancing.[81] Accordion players had no difficulty playing the waltz and the two-step, but because the keyboard buttons played notes only on the diatonic scale, black musicians found it difficult to play non-diatonic "blue notes." For white Cajuns, whose music conformed to the diatonic scale, accordion-based lala suited their musical taste, which led many black lala accordion players to play for white Cajun audiences. These included Amédé Ardoin, considered by many the first zydeco accordionist.[82]

A small, disagreeable black man, Ardoin conformed to the "bad man" image that bluesmen, most famously, Robert Johnson, often cultivated. While playing,

Ardoin openly flirted with women and, reputedly, slept with many of them. More controversial, some were white women. Before World War II, despite a long, interrelated history and culture, white Cajuns in southern Louisiana enforced a rigid system of racial apartheid on their black Creole neighbors and kin.[83] When a black accordionist like Ardoin played at a white Cajun house, his host required him to stay on the porch and play through an open window. Some racially conscious hosts even insisted that the black accordionist wear white gloves so that white dancers would not have to dance to music played by black hands. Early in his career, Ardoin, like Robert Johnson, played his instrument indifferently. Then, according to his testimony, at twelve o'clock one midnight, he stood at a crossroads with a black cat where a tall black figure took his soul and cat. The next night, and every night thereafter, Ardoin played like the devil. Apparently, at the crossroads, Elegba had given Amédé Ardoin the gift of music.[84] In 1934 Ardoin traveled to Texas and then to New York City to record his lala, black Creole accordion waltz and two-step music. His white Cajun friend, Dennis McGee, accompanied him on the fiddle.[85] In 1941 Ardoin died in a state mental home.[86]

When black Creoles arrived in Frenchtown following World War I, they remained loyal to their Francophone, lala dance music. Lala music was rural, French, and only marginally West African. It owed more to an Austrian instrument maker and the European waltz than it did to West African musicians. In Houston, country-born Frenchtown Creoles confronted other African Americans, who neither understood French nor liked to dance the "Amédé Two Step." The World War II influx of poor, southern farm workers included black sharecroppers who preferred the blues to Ardoin's French dance music. Even so, few could resist the energy and freshness of the Red Hot Louisiana Band from Opelousas that featured Clifton Chenier on accordion, Cleveland Chenier on rub board, and Paul "Little Buck" Senegal on guitar. Together, they remade rural Louisiana lala into big city, Houston zydeco.[87]

World War II set in motion fundamental change in eastern Texas and southern Louisiana. Federal conscription forced thousands of young men to leave their rural communities and confront a much more complex, urban world. The war touched even those who avoided the draft. Shipyards, petroleum drilling and refining, and other military-related industries offered good-paying jobs to blacks and whites, women and men. The region bounded by Galveston, Beaumont, and Houston boomed. Trapped by sharecropping and the Depression, southern Louisiana Creoles found the East Texas golden triangle irresistible. Frenchtown became their home away from home. Most wartime Creole migrants were young males who arrived without their families and parents. Employed and single, in their off-hours they flocked to the newly opened black clubs in Frenchtown and in the non-Creole areas of the Fifth and Third wards to hear Lightin' Hopkins, T-Bone Walker, Blind Lemon Jefferson, and other East Texas bluesmen. No longer confined to chaperoned house parties and Catholic church-dances, young Creole males reached out. Southern Louisiana remained their homeland, but Houston had become their home, a modern, African American crossroads. After World War II, blues-based zydeco made its appearance in the El Dorado Ballroom, Irene's Café, the Silver Slipper, and other Creole clubs.[88]

World War II brought Cleveland Chenier to East Texas. The son of a black sharecropper and a lala accordionist, Chenier took a job in the oil fields near Port Arthur. At night and on weekends, he gigged at barbecues, house dances, picnics, and Creole honky-tonks. Soon, his brother Clifton joined him, and the brothers formed the Red Hot Louisiana Band. Clifton Chenier found himself drawn to the blues and rhythm and blues, especially the music of Lightin' Hopkins, T-Bone Walker, and Muddy Waters. Audiences preferred his new bluesy style to the old lala dance numbers that his father had played in Opelousas. Chenier used the new piano accordion rather than his father's single-note, button accordion because it allowed him to play blues notes. The addition of Buck Senegal's electric guitar, a drum set, Cleveland Chenier's rub board playing, and an increasing use of English lyrics separated Chenier's Red Hot Louisiana Band from other French lala bands. The new music embraced bluesy elements drawn from field shouts and Francophone spirituals. The washboard derived directly from the ring shouts of Louisiana slaves, while Buck Senegal's blues guitar reached back to Senegal.

The European button accordion, together with the white Cajun preference for waltz music, had suppressed much of this West African heritage. But in postwar Houston's black wards, Lightnin' Hopkins and other Houston blues and rhythm and blues musicians gave lala a fresh breath of African American sound. In 1949 Hopkins recorded a French-flavored, rhythm and blues song entitled "Zolo Go." In it he used an organ to imitate the accordion. For Hopkins, "Zolo Go" was a word play on "zottico," a term that young Houston Creoles used to refer to an accordion dance. In 1955 Marie Lee Phelps, in a *Houston Post* article, referred to Creole music as "zottico," the first published use of the term, which Chenier altered to "zydeco."[89]

In 1955 Chenier recorded in Creole "Ay-Tete Fee" (Hey, Little Girl) for Special Records. The song established zydeco and created a demand for the Red Hot Louisiana Band in East Texas.[90] A second breakthrough came for Chenier and zydeco in 1964 when Lightnin' Hopkins introduced Los Angeles record producer

Chris Strachwitz to Chenier in a Frenchtown club. "When we got to the little beer joint, what I heard quickly brought on a rush," recounted Strachwitz. Chenier's recordings on Strachwitz's Arhoolie Records brought Chenier and zydeco international attention.[91]

Zydeco enabled Frenchtown Creoles to bridge Houston's racial divide. In 1958 Clarence Gallien, who had moved from Opelousas to Frenchtown, asked the priest at St. Francis of Assisi Catholic Church to sponsor a zydeco dance as a church fundraiser. The priest approved. The first dance did well enough that Gallien invited Chenier and the Red Hot Louisiana Band to play the following Saturday. When it sold out, the church realized that zydeco dances raised much more money than Saturday night bingo. Other Houston Catholic churches quickly followed. The competition led the diocese to organize a zydeco circuit that gave each church its own Saturday night turn. In 1960 the idea spread to the black Creole communities in Los Angeles and Oakland. The Catholic zydeco circuit in Texas and California not only introduced large numbers of white Catholics to zydeco; it led Hispanic musicians to form their own zydeco bands. While a purist might object to a Hispanic zydeco band that used the accordion and rub board to play Hispanic sounds and rhythms, from a historical perspective it represented the continued creolization of lala. Such creolization affirmed the dynamic, eclectic, and improvisational character of West African music, which puritans find distasteful.[92]

TEXAS BLUES

The depression of the 1930s hit black Houston especially hard. Many of the hard-won gains of the 1920s evaporated in the 1930s. African Americans received some city and state relief and others gained employment on the federal government's WPA and Public Works Administration (PWA) projects, although at lower wages than whites who did the same work. American entry into World War II in December 1941 opened up new opportunities for blacks. The war economy drew thousands of young, rural workers to Houston.[93] In 1940 86,000 African Americans lived in Houston; in 1950, Houston's black population had swelled to 125,000, a nearly 50 percent increase. Public facilities, schools, and housing failed to keep up with demand. The war also marked a shift of Houston's black population out of the old Fourth Ward in central Houston to the Third Ward and the Fifth Ward.[94]

Crowded into tenements, these new, young black Houstonians changed the Third Ward that adjoined Emancipation Park. The northern two-thirds of the

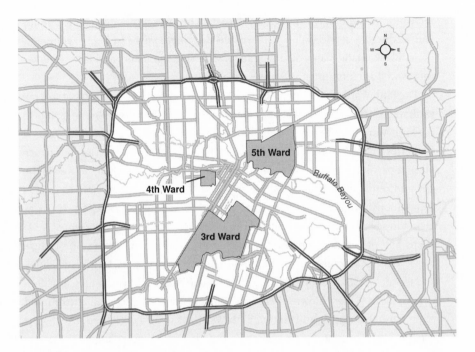

Houston's Third, Fourth, and Fifth wards

Third Ward became a densely populated tenement district for poorly educated, restless, and frequently violent rural migrants from East Texas and South Louisiana. Shotgun houses filled many of the blocks south of downtown. Along the Dowling Avenue business street, a new entertainment district appeared. Black-owned businesses lined Dowling Street and its intersecting streets—grocery and clothing stores, medical and law offices, funeral homes, storefront Pentecostal and Sanctified Baptist churches, two movie houses, a radio station, and dozens of pawn shops, music stores, bars, taverns, honky-tonks, and nightclubs, including the famed Eldorado Ballroom, the socially prestigious Club Ebony, and notorious Shady's Place.

At the southern end of the Third Ward, middle-class blacks formed a neighborhood of their own where they controlled Houston's black civic organizations, the most prominent lodge halls, Jack Yates High School, the black public library, a hospital, several Methodist churches, the NAACP, and Texas Southern University. The paper of record for black Houston, the *Informer*, accepted advertising from the honky-tonks and nightclubs along Dowling Street, which kept readers informed of black Houston's raucous and raunchy nightlife. In the *Informer*, middle-class education and uplift coexisted with working-class entertainment and recreation. On the religion page, Pentecostal churches announced their Sunday and Wednesday services alongside middle-class Methodist and Baptist congregations. Black retailers appealed to readers with skin-lighteners and fine china tea sets as well as chitterlings and pickled pig feet and tails.[95]

The Fifth Ward, on the city's northeast quadrant, which included Houston's rail yards and ship channel, underwent even more dramatic change. New migrants to the Fifth Ward found employment on the city's docks, railroads, factories, and oil refineries. In the South, only Birmingham offered black males such an abundance of good-paying, blue-collar jobs. Many Fifth Ward males had recently arrived in the city and remained single, spending much of their earnings on clothes, female companionship, and entertainment. Lyons Avenue rivaled Dowling Street as Houston's black main street. Lyons Avenue featured the usual assortment of retail shops and professional offices, funeral homes, storefront churches, the Deluxe Movie Theater, dozens of dives, bail bond agencies, flop houses, the Crystal Hotel, and two of the South's top black nightclubs—the Bronze Peacock and Club Matinee. In nearby Frenchtown, the Silver Slipper offered zydeco and rhythm and blues dance bands. Nightlife in the Fifth Ward was largely unpoliced. During the war, the Lyons Avenue strip earned the reputation as the most dangerous place in Houston. Locals called the blocks along Jensen and Lyons avenues "Bloody Alley" and "Pearl Harbor." In the clubs and dives of Lyons Avenue and along Dowling Street, young Houston African Americans fashioned a gritty, urban culture around heavy drinking, drugs, sex, and Texas blues.[96]

On Dowling Street in the Third Ward, Samuel "Lightnin' " Hopkins reigned as the king of Houston blues. Hopkins reshaped the sorrowful, country blues of "Blind Lemon" Jefferson and Huddie "Leadbelly" Ledbetter into a lively urban music.[97] A master bluesman, Lightnin' Hopkins never abandoned his simple upbringing or his Third Ward neighbors. In the 1950s, after he had become a rhythm and blues legend, he rarely left the Third Ward except to take a city bus to play a Lyons Avenue gig. Record producer Chris Strachwitz first heard Hopkins on a Los Angeles radio station. Hoping to sign him for Arhoolie Records, Strachwitz searched in vain for Hopkins in the black clubs of South Central L.A. In 1959 Strachwitz received a postcard from his close friend and fellow record producer Sam Charters: "I found Lightnin' Hopkins. He lives in Houston, Texas." When Strachwitz met Hopkins, "He was singing a low-down blues about how his shoulder was aching, and how he could hardly get to the job tonight.... It was like how I would imagine ... a griot in Africa. He was simply the community poet who would tell people what they liked to hear. And he would argue with the women in front of him, 'Whoa, woman, you in the red dress?' And then he would just go in this

Blues musicians at Silver Slipper in Houston's Fifth Ward (Will Scott)

musical tirade about her, and she would yell back at him! . . . I thought, 'this is the nastiest down-home blues I have ever heard.' And that's all I wanted to hear."[98]

Born in 1911 in Centerville, Texas, Hopkins moved to Houston shortly after World War I. A musical prodigy, as a young boy Hopkins had jammed with Blind Lemon Jefferson. Trained on the acoustic guitar, Hopkins adopted Jefferson's fingerpicking style, conversational lyrics, and preference for solo performances. Rural migrants from East Texas and South Louisiana, who flooded Houston's Third and Fifth wards in the 1940s, found Hopkins's music comfortingly familiar even as its tempo and content addressed city life. Easily recognized, the lanky and handsome Hopkins, with a cigarette dangling from the side of his mouth, a warm, toothy smile, dark sunglasses, and his jauntily cocked fedora, became a Houston landmark. As a solo musician, who carried his guitar with him, Hopkins's danceable blues and friendly repartee perfectly suited the seedy dives and small clubs along Dowling and Lyons. For little more than tips and drinks, any club or bar in town could afford Lightnin' Hopkins. Shady's Place on Simmons Street, just off Dowling, often featured Hopkins. Shady's "come as you are" dress code and Hopkins's fondness for down and dirty blues, drew working-class blacks. Seating about two hundred hard-drinking and lively dancing patrons, Shady's gave many Houston entertainers their first break. Hopkins's enormous popularity and his generosity toward young musicians ensured that young Texas rhythm and blues musicians stayed in touch with the blues, giving electrified Texas blues its distinct grittiness.[99]

Rhythm and blues producer and historian Arnold Shaw described the blues as "trouble music" and urban blues as "adjustment song."[100] The blues that Lightnin' Hopkins played were both. Inspired by Huddie Ledbetter as well as Blind Lemon Jefferson, Hopkins recounted in his plaintive "Tom Moore Blues" and "Bud Russell Blues" the "slavery times" on Tom Moore's Brazo Bottoms plantation and the brutality of warden Bud Russell's Texas state prison. In "Tom Moore Blues," Hopkins explained that when told "my wife is dead," the "meanest man I ever seen" told Lightin', "I may let you bury that woman some lunch time." These grim ballads matched up with the "trouble music" of any Texas or Delta bluesman. When Hopkins played "Penitentiary Blues," "Cotton Field Blues," and "Black and Evil Blues," his Third Ward listeners remembered the harsh, rural South from which they had escaped.

Cashing in on the wartime popularity of Hopkins and other Texas bluesmen, in 1945 Don Robey opened the Bronze Peacock in the Fifth Ward. An upscale restaurant and club, the Bronze Peacock placed Houston at the center of postwar rhythm and blues. During the war, Houston's electrified blues musicians played for its newly arrived and gainfully employed rural black migrants. Along the strips of Lyons and Dowling, on Thursday, Friday, Saturday, Sunday, and Monday nights, scores of bars and clubs booked solo musicians or small bands to entertain their hard-drinking, harder dancing, looking-for-a-good-time patrons. During World War II, Houston musicians abandoned the twelve-bar blues structure in favor of the more lively and danceable eight- and sixteen-bar structure of popular music. Inspired by Louis Jordan's jump blues and Charlie Christian's jazz guitar, black club bands adopted the electric guitar and bass, the tenor saxophone, and drums. Female musicians and singers dressed in formal, usually strapless, dresses with elaborate hairdos, while the men dressed in brightly colored, hand-tailored, double-breasted suits with long tails and baggy legs and sleeves. These black Houston show bands shouted and clowned while their audiences danced and yelled wildly.[101]

Don Robey's Bronze Peacock became Houston's premier black nightclub. An upscale, white tablecloth club, the Bronze Peacock catered to Houston's black upper and middle classes and musically knowledgeable whites. Robey's longtime assistant, Evelyn Johnson, explained, "We had the finest food and chefs. We couldn't sell anything to drink, but people could bring their own bottle. We sold set-ups and they could drink until midnight. Then we had to pick up everything."[102] The Bronze Peacock booked the region's established musicians, such as Lightnin' Hopkins and T-Bone Walker, and introduced up-and-coming stars such as "Gatemouth" Brown.[103]

In 1949 *Billboard* magazine changed its category for black music from "race records" to the less offensive term "rhythm & blues." Audiences and musicians applied the term to the new, up-tempo dance music that had emerged in black clubs during the war. Not content with owning Houston's most important night-club, in 1949 Robey took advantage of the moment to form an independent rhythm and blues recording company that operated out of his Peacock Music Store on Lyons Avenue. Peacock Records produced gospel and rhythm and blues. Its first hit, "Our Father," by the Five Blind Boys of Mississippi, established Peacock's reputation in the rapidly growing rhythm and blues market. In addition to gospel groups, such as the Five Blind Boys, the Dixie Hummingbirds, and the Bells of Joy, Peacock recorded Bronze Peacock house musicians, who included jump blues singer "Gatemouth" Brown. In 1952 Robey acquired Duke Records of Memphis, bringing to Peacock rhythm and blues stars Big Mama Thornton, Bobby Blue Bland, and Johnny Ace. The Peacock-Duke 1953 release of Big Mama Thorntons's "Hound Dog" marked the unacknowledged beginning of rock and roll. At its height, Peacock Records was a rhythm and blues powerhouse with more than a hundred musicians under contract and another hundred studio musicians.

On the lookout for new opportunities, in 1950 Robey organized the Buffalo Booking Company that Evelyn Johnson ran from 1950 to 1967. Through perfor-mances at the Bronze Peacock, the recordings of Peacock-Duke, and the booking gigs of Buffalo Booking, Robey and Johnson dominated the southern rhythm and blues circuit through the mid-1960s. Between Robey's clubs and record enter-prises, the Dowling and Lyons strips, and Houston's two rhythm and blues radio stations, KCOH and KYOK, Houston emerged as the rhythm and blues center of East Texas, Oklahoma, Arkansas, and Louisiana. Dowling and Lyons offered na-tional venues for aspiring rhythm and blues musicians, agents, photographers, costume designers and tailors, music stores, and disk jockeys. In the early 1960s, Houston's moment in the rhythm and blues sun passed. Rock and roll stole much of its audience and many of its artists. Desegregation ended the protected status Third and Fifth Ward clubs enjoyed among blacks during the Jim Crow era. All that remained was Lightin' Hopkins.[104]

DIXIE FAREWELL

During World War II, thousands of rural blacks had flocked to Houston. Other thousands of Texans looked farther west to California. The most likely to leave Texas were the young and poor, many from Houston's impoverished Third, Fourth, and Fifth wards and the Brazos River Bottoms of East Texas. Black mi-grants carried to the West Coast Houston's Sanctified Baptist and Pentecostal

A classic shotgun house in Houston's Third Ward (Will Scott)

Christianity, the cultural uplift and political consciousness of the Third Ward's middle class, the Creole ways of Frenchtown, the honky-tonk world of Houston's black nightlife, and the Dew Drop Inns of rural East Texas. They also bore with them a Texas toughness and proclivity to violence. Following the Japanese attack on Pearl Harbor, Los Angeles became the West Coast center of the Pacific Theater. Southern California's aircraft factories, shipyards, and the military-training bases beckoned to young and hopeful black Texans. Some, like T-Bone Walker, drove west on U.S. Highway 66, while others, like future dance choreographer Alvin Ailey and his mother, traveled to Los Angeles on the Southern Pacific Railroad. Whether they came by car or train, in California black Texans found a new world.

Alvin Ailey made this clear. A child of a single mother who had survived the Depression by picking cotton in the Brazos River Valley, Ailey's East Texas childhood colored his later dance compositions. "I'm talking about living with aunts, cousins, and grandparents, and not truly belonging anywhere. . . . My mother and I rented a house with no furniture." In his hometown of Rogers, "There were mostly mills, filling stations, and schools. There was a black school, all run down, at the bottom of the hill." In nearby Cameron, at age nine, Ailey remembered "a procession of people, all in white, going down to the lake. The minister was baptizing everybody as the choir sang 'Wade in the Water.'" He recalled his mother coming home one evening after being beaten up and raped by four white men; he watched movies in the black-only balconies of the small-town movie house; and when his family ran out of food, to staunch his hunger he ate "Texas clay." In the evenings, Ailey's mother hung out at the local roadhouse where "the women wore bright, flashy, red dresses. The men carried big knives called Texas Specials and did a lot of fighting. . . . Many of the same people who went to the Dew Drop Inn on Saturday night went to church on Sunday morning . . . . Musicians like Sonny Boy Williamson, Blind Lemon Jefferson, and Big Boy Crudup were among those who would come to Sunday barbecues and play music while everybody danced."[105] Ailey's only memory of his father was as a Texas cowboy, who "used to chase the Ku Klux Klan on horses."[106]

In 1942, fed up with Texas and wanting more for her son, Lulu Ailey boarded a Southern Pacific train to Los Angeles. After finding a job in an airplane factory, she sent home for her son. Ailey recounted his arrival: "The war was on when I arrived in Los Angeles and was met by my mother. I found a city that was completely wrapped up in the war."[107] Ailey, his mother, T-Bone Walker, and other black Texans found a new life in Southern California, and like other American immigrants and migrants, they carried to the City of Angels the ways of their families back home. Ailey and Walker both understood and cherished their Texas roots. Neither, however, fully understood that those roots extended to West Africa. Even so, like other children of the African diaspora, these black Texans pursued their quest for freedom and autonomy guided by their ancestors' West African ways. Los Angeles offered them opportunities unmatched anywhere else. In return, they helped make Los Angles the most musically dynamic city in the world.[108]

CALIFORNIA DREAMING

• 9 •

South Central LA

Los Angeles stands apart from other American cities. The customary American definitions of race and class, even gender, never applied in what Californians call their "Southland." Nowhere else in North America has the dream of material prosperity and individual freedom been more fully realized. For black Americans, who had suffered the indignities of racial prejudice and southern apartheid, Los Angeles became the land of dreams. Before the 1920s, however, few African Americans even knew that Los Angeles existed and even fewer could afford the train fare to go there. Moreover, Los Angeles, unlike the northern cities of New York, Pittsburgh, and Chicago, offered little employment for unskilled laborers from the rural South.

Before World War I, Los Angeles served as the western terminus of the Texas and Pacific Railroad and the transportation hub and port of entry for Southern California, a region built around agricultural and retirement communities, not manufacturing and commerce. Mexican, Chinese, and Japanese workers filled the region's relatively few unskilled menial and agricultural jobs.[1] Only middle-class African Americans could afford the train fare to Los Angeles, where numerous lower middle-class jobs in retailing and service industries were available. These aspiring middle-class African Americans, from cities across the nation, found Southern California a far better place for African Americans than anywhere else in the United States. In the City of Angels, educated African Americans shared in the bounty of the West and did not find entry into the middle class closed.

This had been true since the city's founding in 1780 as a Spanish pueblo, Señora la Reina de los Angeles (Our Lady Queen of the Angels), a name that residents quickly shortened to Los Angeles. The city's forty-four first families included Native Americans, Spaniards, Mexicans, and African Americans. In 1848, during the Mexican War, the United States occupied California. American annexation led to an influx of African Americans brought in by southern slave-holders. In 1850, when the United States admitted California to the Union as a free state, the California Supreme Court declared all slaves in California free, the first public emancipation of slaves since the early decades of the republic. During the Civil War, most white southerners abandoned California to fight for the Confederacy. This left Los Angeles in the hands of pro-Lincoln Republicans, who, following the war, eagerly enforced the newly ratified Fourteenth and Fifteenth Amendments to the U.S. Constitution that extended citizenship and the vote to African Americans. By 1880, African Americans in Los Angeles had formed a Methodist church and two Baptist churches and started a black newspaper, all clustered near the Union Railroad Terminal at Central Avenue and First Street. In 1900 two thousand African Americans lived in Los Angeles. In 1920 the number reached 15,000, out of a total population of half a million—the largest concentration of African Americans west of Houston.[2]

Virtually all lived in "South Central," a six-block-wide neighborhood of residences, small businesses, and warehouses that paralleled the rail line that ran from downtown Los Angeles to the port of San Pedro, ten miles south. Along the first ten blocks of Central Avenue, African Americans pursued a variety of occupations. They drove wagons, cleaned homes, clerked in retail stores, owned barber and beauty shops, ran restaurants, operated a hotel, managed a livery stable, taught music, and worked as conductors and cleaning crews for the Pullman cars that operated out of the nearby Union Railroad Terminal. Drawn from across the country, most pre–World War I Los Angeles African Americans had attended high school, a number had earned college degrees, several practiced law and medicine, and about 40 percent owned their own homes. Lower middle class in income, they conducted themselves in classic Old Settler fashion.[3]

Before World War I, several race papers served South Central, including the *Liberator*, the *New Age*, and the *Eagle*. In 1914 the editor of the *Liberator* died. In 1915 the editor of the *New Age* left Los Angeles and sold his paper to a white-owned newspaper chain. The *Eagle* also faced extinction. In 1912 the founder of the paper, John Neimore, died and left the struggling paper to his young assistant Charlotta Spear, who recruited Joe Bass, an experienced newspaper man, to help her run the paper. Soon after, Spear married Bass. Together, they reorganized the *Eagle* and moved it into new quarters at 814 Central Avenue. For the next seventy-five years, the *California Eagle* portrayed itself as the voice of black Los Angeles.[4]

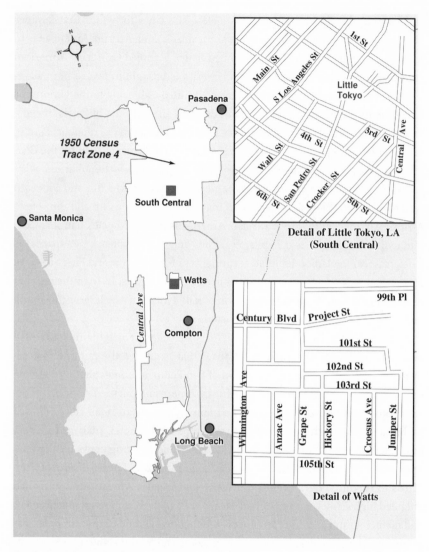

South Central Los Angeles

Under Spear and Bass, the *Eagle* became the advocate of black, middle-class Los Angeles and the most important black newspaper in the West.

In 1913, at Spear's urging, the Los Angeles chapter of the National Association for the Advancement of Colored People invited the editor of *Crisis* magazine, W. E. B. Du Bois, to Los Angeles. Impressed by the parade of cars that met him at Union Station and the racially mixed audience of 2,300 that warmly greeted his speech in a local theater, Du Bois noted that, even though Los Angeles shops refused to allow African American women to try on clothing before purchase and denied blacks access to select hotels and restaurants, "the better class of people, colored and white, can and do meet each other" in a spirit of "cooperation and good will." Los Angeles Negroes, declared Du Bois, "are without a doubt the most beautifully housed group of colored people in the United States." Spurred by such flattery, the *California Eagle*'s readers set about making Los Angeles the nation's premier middle-class black community.[5]

SOUTH CENTRAL

With the onset of World War I, most African American migrants went to cities in the Northeast and Midwest, not to the West. But following World War I, a steady stream flowed westward. Because of its warm climate and substantial black community, most black migrants to the West chose Los Angeles. Yet the increase in the city's black population failed to keep pace with Los Angeles's white population. In 1940 Los Angeles, along with San Francisco, San Diego, and Seattle, remained the whitest major cities in the United States. In 1940 blacks made up only 5 percent of the residents of Los Angeles. Even so, South Central boasted the wealthiest and best-educated black community in the United States.[6]

Until 1940, South Central remained a racially mixed neighborhood. Blacks made up about a third of the households. Most of the city's black children attended the racially mixed Jefferson High School and its middle and elementary feeder schools as members of a racial minority. Before World War II, about a third of the black residents of South Central owned their own homes, most modest, one-story, brightly painted California bungalows with yards filled with rose bushes and orange, grapefruit, and avocado trees. The neighborhood supported numerous black churches, several black sororities and fraternities, Masonic and Elk lodges, several black nightclubs, funeral homes, burial societies, and insurance companies. Still, it was not a black neighborhood. While South Central maintained one all-black fire company, it had no all-black schools and no black slum. Below the high school level, its schools employed black faculty who taught white and black children, and black and white police officers patrolled its streets. Whites and blacks lived in close proximity to one another. They rarely mixed socially, however, almost never intermarried, and 95 percent of the city's African Americans remained in the fifty-block area bounded on the east by Alameda Avenue, on the west by Main Street, on the north by First Street, and on the south by Twenty-first Street. Racial differences and prejudice existed. Pre–World War II Los Angeles was a city in which whites enjoyed enormous advantages over Afri-

Waiters on the Southern Pacific at LA's Union Station, 1945 (Shades of L.A. Archives, Los Angeles Public Library)

can, Hispanic, and Asian Americans. Compared to the remainder of urban America, however, Los Angeles seemed a racial Shangri-la.[7]

Before World War II, Los Angeles avoided much of the racial violence that plagued the remainder of the nation. Until the completion of U.S. Highway 66 in the late 1920s, the Texas Pacific and Southern Pacific railroad offered the only practical entry into Los Angeles from the East. The expensive, two-day train ride from the East placed Los Angeles out of reach for the South's rural poor. Before completion of Highway 66, African American migrants hailed from southern cities, especially Texas, as well as established black communities in New York, Philadelphia, Chicago, and Saint Louis. More than three-quarters had lived in cities before coming to Los Angeles. Whether northern or southern, most Los Angeles African Americans before 1940 were middle class and city born. They fit in and adjusted easily to Southern California middle-class life. From across the South and North, Los Angeles beckoned to young and ambitious, often college-educated, African Americans, who in South Central organized their own businesses or entered the professions. For African Americans, the New Negro dream began when they arrived at Union Station in downtown LA.[8]

Los Angeles blacks made downtown LA, south of Wilshire Boulevard, their home. Indeed, Central Avenue provided Los Angeles much of its urban density, although, it resembled a face-to-face town more than a large, impersonal city. Before 1940, Main Street divided Los Angeles along class lines. Middle-class whites lived west of Main in what was called "West LA." Working-class whites, Hispanics, Asian Americans, and African Americans lived east of Main in "East LA." High housing prices and deed restrictions kept West LA almost exclusively middle class and white. In East LA, African, Asian, and Hispanic Americans lived alongside working-class whites. To the east, rail yards and the Los Angeles River sealed off the racially mixed and working-class Central Avenue from the city's more distant, all-white communities. This created a narrow band of working-class neighborhoods along Central Avenue, twelve to fifteen blocks wide, that ran south toward Long Beach. In 1920 the South Central neighborhood reached Twentieth Street. In 1930 it extended to Forty-fifth Street, and by 1940 South Central extended to 103rd Street and Watts.[9]

The narrow, South Central strip paralleled the Alameda Corridor, the warehouse and manufacturing district that lined the South Pacific's rail tracks from downtown to the port of San Pedro. Linked by the Red Car Trolley Line, which ran up and down Central Avenue, South Central was the most densely populated neighborhood in Los Angeles. Squeezed together on small house lots, South Central brought together recent immigrants from Europe—Russian Jews, Italians, and Poles—and Americans of Japanese, Chinese, Philippine, Mexican, and African ancestry. Like the working-class neighborhoods of eastern cities, South Central exhibited a rich ethnic and racial mix. Buddhists, Catholics, Jews, and Protestants lived, worshiped, shopped, played, and learned together. South Central's grocers and eateries sold an enormous array of ethnic foods and dishes while its residents performed most of Los Angeles's menial and skilled work. About half the residents described themselves to 1940 census takers as white and a third as black.[10]

In the 1920s the South Central business district extended about ten blocks south of downtown Los Angeles. In the business section, residents lived in second- and third-story walk-ups. Central Avenue teemed with people and enterprise. Almost anything could be bought there. With a modest investment, anyone could start up a business and thrive, buy an unpretentious home, and claim a share of the American dream, or just hang out.[11] No other American city offered African Americans as much. Nearly one-third owned their homes.[12] After graduating from Jefferson High School, their children could enroll at the Los Angeles branch of the University of California or the University of Southern California.

Women could choose between twenty different black women's clubs, men could join the black YMCA, the Elks, or the Masons, and anyone could use the Booker T. Washington community building, browse in Spikes Record Store for the latest, best-selling "race" record, attend live performances by black touring companies, or subscribe to the *California Eagle*.

South Central African Americans worshiped at the First African Methodist Episcopal, the Colored Methodist Episcopal, the Second Baptist, Mount Zion Baptist, Saint Phillips Episcopal, the People's Independent, the First Holiness, and a dozen other racially mixed or black churches. They could buy clothing at any store on the street, take music and dance lessons from a variety of teachers, and one day a week swim at the municipal pool. Most impressively, beginning in 1918, the voters of the Seventy-fourth District of the state assembly, which included South Central, elected Frederick Roberts to the California statehouse as California's first black state assembly representative—even though only one-fifth of South Central voters were black.[13]

For the next sixteen years, the voters of the Seventy-fourth District reelected Roberts to the state legislature. Roberts's success pointed up an important aspect of Southern California's racial politics. Since statehood, California had been a secure Republican state whose politics had been forged during the Civil War. South Central blacks, like most other African American electors, voted solidly Republican until the 1930s. In California, Africans Americans belonged to the political establishment and had been among its founding members in the 1850s. The Republican Party had opposed slavery and, after emancipation, defended the rights of blacks to American citizenship, including the right to vote. For California Republicans, black citizenship was the "new birth of freedom" that Abraham Lincoln had hallowed at Gettysburg. For many of the Seventy-fourth District's white voters, the election of Frederick Roberts affirmed their democratic ideals.[14]

The city's most important newspaper, the *Los Angeles Times*, endorsed Roberts over his white opponents. The *Times* editorial declared, "The man of color no doubt was the strongest candidate in his assembly district."[15] *Times* editor, General Harrison Gray Otis was a virulent opponent of organized labor but courageously defended the principal of racial equality. When southern editors sharply criticized Theodore Roosevelt for inviting Booker T. Washington to lunch in the White House, Otis described such attacks as unreasonable, unjust, and preposterous. "As to the fearful danger of miscegenation . . . we might suggest that some white women—even southern women—might do much worse than have Booker T. Washington for a spouse."[16] In 1909 Otis celebrated the hundredth anniversary of Lincoln's birth with a special edition of the *Times* that recounted the history of

African Americans in Los Angeles.[17] For black migrants, who had fled the South, Otis, the *Los Angeles Times,* and the California Republican Party had made good on the promises of emancipation. California was different.

Key to California's difference was the absence of stark black and white polarities. In the remainder of the country, the term race conjured the image of black and white. In California, race had first meant red and white, followed by brown and white, then yellow and white, and finally, in the mid-twentieth century, black and white. Since the Mexican War in 1848, white "Anglos" had dominated Los Angeles life. Although a white man's city, the sheer variety of nonwhites clouded the lens of white racism. Of the city's racial minorities, African Americans seemed the most "Anglo." God-fearing Protestants, duly registered Republicans, and staunchly middle class, African Americans even enjoyed special constitutional protection. Compared to Native Americans, Mexican Americans, Jews, and Asians, African Americans seemed familiar and benign, especially when so few lived in Los Angeles, and these relatively few behaved reassuringly middle class. They seemed white men in black skins. The presence of several racial minorities in Los Angeles defused appeals to white racism, making racism unfocused and less effective. Still, Los Angeles blacks kept racial issues in sight. As editors of the racially defined *California Eagle,* Charlotta Spear and her husband Joe Bass, voiced the concerns of Los Angeles's black middle class.[18]

Spear and Bass described themselves as "race people" and the *California Eagle* as a "race paper."[19] In the first decades of the twentieth century, African Americans applied the term "race" to those blacks who identified with other African Americans and who supported the cause of all African Americans. Race people saw themselves as standing as one with "their race." They did not try "to pass" as whites, nor did they seek the approval of whites. In response to white racism and racial segregation, race-conscious African Americans joined black social clubs, patronized black businesses, worshiped in black churches, married other black individuals, subscribed to black magazines and newspapers, and for all intents and purposes lived their lives within the confines of their black communities. In most cities, this meant living in neighborhoods that whites had designated as "colored," often black ghettos on "the other side of the tracks."[20] In the decades before World War II, no such racially defined ghetto existed in Los Angeles. While virtually all of the city's African Americans lived in South Central, until the 1940s blacks made up only a minority of the households in the neighborhood, rarely more than a third of the families on any single block. At the same time, many members of the Los Angeles black middle class imagined themselves citizens of a racially defined black community that the *California Eagle* jealously guarded.[21]

Like so many other educated African Americans in the early twentieth century, Spear and Bass embraced the self-help ideas of Booker T. Washington as well as W. E. B. Du Bois's belief in the racial responsibilities of "the better class." As editors of Los Angeles's most important race paper, they advocated racial solidarity, self-reliance, and racial uplift. In every weekly issue of the *California Eagle*, they extolled the virtues of education, hard work, Christian morality, good manners, community service, Republican politics, and racial progress. Spear and Bass accepted advertising from white businesses, but most of their income derived from black advertisers, black subscribers, and their printing business. Politically and financially independent, the *California Eagle* served as the paper of record for black South Central.[22]

Joe Bass brought to the *California Eagle* a wealth of newspaper experience. With Spear, he published a paper that, in format and quality of print, compared favorably with any other black weekly of the time. The editors approved only well-written and meticulously proofed articles. The *Eagle* looked and read very much like the *Los Angeles Times*. It rarely published political cartoons but always included one to two pages on local church activities and two society pages that recounted the latest activities of black Greek-letter sororities and fraternities, the Louisiana and Texas Clubs, local marriages and deaths, the doings of the community's high profile personalities, and school activities. Each issue of the *Eagle* included several pages of sports news that reported the wins and losses of UCLA and USC, kept track of national sports events as well as black athletes and teams, and published frequent articles on Jefferson High School teams and athletes. Each edition included feature stories on black entertainment personalities and shows, especially live performances playing at Central Avenue clubs and theaters. Even a casual reader quickly discovered that South Central offered its African American residents a rich, varied, even uplifting life. On a given day, residents might see a Shriners' Parade, attend a Duke Ellington concert, view *Shuffle A' Long* at the Lincoln Theatre, listen to a symphonic performance directed by local composer William Grant Still, or meet a black film star on the street or in a club. The paper honored and promoted its local black valedictorians, athletes, and high-profile personalities.[23]

In each issue of the *California Eagle*, local realtors purchased nearly two pages of advertising, outstripping the combined advertising expenditures of department stores, entertainment, and grocery stores. South Central realtors offered property in newly opened subdivisions in Watts and Compton to the south, previously owned bungalows and cottages along and just off Central Avenue, apartments and houses to rent, and newly built two- and three-bedroom homes to own "with all the latest features," including carports, indoor plumbing, hot water, electricity, and gas heating. South Central automobile dealers and garages insisted that no true Californian could be without a car. Beauty shops and cosmetic companies offered a variety of hair straighteners, pomades, perfumes, and skin lighteners, while retailers paraded the latest fashions and appliances. Most telling, the classified ads offered hundreds of jobs for men and women as porters, chauffeurs, domestic help, clerks, plumbers, trolley drivers, Pullman conductors, masons, nurses, teachers, police officers, waiters, and office and construction workers. When Los Angeles boomed, it turned to South Central for its labor. These fully employed workers spent much of their income in South Central, fueling the community's economy.[24]

Idyllic as life in South Central might appear, the *California Eagle* never let its readers forget that they lived in a larger world in which African Americans faced enormous injustices and indecencies. Its front page, in bold, large headlines, invariably drew readers' attention to the latest racial atrocity or triumph, whether a lynching in Alabama, the desegregation of a theater in Chicago, or the election of a black alderman in Saint Louis. Each week, it pointed out that whites continued to persecute blacks and that each day, through fortitude and courage, African Americans slowly vanquished their racial foes. On an adjoining front-page column, in equally bold type, the editors reported important national or international events such as wars, natural disasters, economic concerns, or a critical election. Just below the headlined stories, also in large, bold type, the *Eagle* recounted, in sensational detail, a local murder or the sexual misconduct of South Central's sporting underworld.

To a disinterested *Eagle* reader, South Central resembled almost any other middle-class, urban American community. The *Eagle's* concern for education, church, social uplift, sports, society doings, fashion, and décor conformed to the interests and activities of other middle-class American newspapers. Its readers lived in similar houses, adopted similar fashions, read similar books, drove similar cars, attended the same movies, danced to jazz music, worshiped in similar ways at similar churches, prepared their food in similar fashions, raised their children similarly, shared similar aspirations, and voted Republican. The differences were that, on the whole, the black readers of the *California Eagle* earned less money and were employed in more menial work than most middle-class white Americans, and *Eagle* readers lived in a racially mixed community. Finally, however, Los Angeles severely limited African Americans' place of residence, professional ambitions, and leisure venues, due solely to the color of their skin.

The culminating moment for South Central's New Negro middle class came in

One of America's best: Jefferson High School, Los Angeles, July 17, 1939, by Federal Writers' Project (Security Pacific Collection, Los Angeles Public Library)

1928, a year before the stock market crash. Since the late nineteenth century, the African American business district functioned as a poor relation to Los Angeles's white downtown, just to its north and west. South Central lay near city hall and Union Station and adjoined the downtown skid row district to its west. Blacks shared the north end of South Central with Los Angeles's other minorities and working classes. African Americans occupied an important place in South Central's public life, but they could not claim it as their own. It was shared civic space. In 1928 several events occurred that shifted the center of South Central black life southward toward Watts.[25]

After World War I, South Central's growth relied heavily on black migrants. As South Central edged southward, it also became more African American and more distant from the downtown. Marking the first stage of the southward shift, in December 1927 John Somerville, a prominent, black South Central dentist, political activist, and founder of the Los Angeles chapter of the NAACP, announced his plan to build a 150-room luxury hotel at the corner of Forty-first and Central Avenue that would cater to black patrons.[26] Five stories high, constructed of stone and brick in a Spanish-colonial style then popular in Los Angeles, the Hotel Somerville offered spacious and modern rooms, a beauty salon, barbershop, drugstore, shoeshine stands, and a real estate office. Wrought iron steps and the mezzanine balcony framed the hotel restaurant that lay just off the two-story lobby that was paved with colorful Spanish tiles. The menu offered a variety of seafood and meat entrées prepared by a chef. Somerville explained that the new hotel would make black guests "feel happy that they did not have to wait for white people to wear off the newness." The *California Eagle* described the Hotel Somerville as the "beauty spot of Los Angeles" while W. E. B. Du Bois called it "a jewel done with loving hands." The Somerville opened two weeks before it hosted the first NAACP national convention held in Los Angeles.[27]

For two years, Somerville and other South Central black leaders had courted the NAACP. The local chapter had even sponsored a presentation of Du Bois's epic drama *The Star of Ethiopia* to ingratiate itself to the general secretary. More concretely, Somerville had promised to build his hotel specifically to accommodate the convention. On June 27, at the downtown Philharmonic Hall, Los Angeles mayor George Cryer welcomed the 3,500 NAACP convention guests to Los Angeles. Du Bois gave the keynote address. Work sessions took place all over Los Angeles County from Pasadena in the northeast foothills to the beaches of Santa Monica in the southwest. No other American city had made the NAACP feel so welcome or as important. At the end of the afternoon sessions, conventioneers retreated to South Central and their gracious rooms at the Hotel Somerville. When Du Bois and his followers departed, Somerville provided office space on the hotel's ground floor for the Los Angeles NAACP chapter.[28]

Soon after, across the street from the Hotel Somerville, black businessmen Claude Hudson and E. B. Liddell built the Hudson-Liddell Medical Building. Black Los Angeles architect Paul Williams designed the building in the Spanish colonial style. The same year, several black nightclubs—the Apex Club, the Club Memo, and the Downbeat Club—opened next to and across the street from the hotel. Also in 1928, William Nickerson completed the new headquarters of Golden State Insurance Company on the corner opposite the Somerville, at 4111 Central Avenue, to accommodate his 150 employees. Chartered in 1925, Golden State was the largest black-owned business in California, the flagship company of South Central. Nickerson also chose a black architect and contractor as well as the Spanish colonial style.

On the eve of the stock market crash, South Central's black community shed its hand-me-down image and asserted its arrival as a prosperous, even glamorous, addition to modern Los Angeles. Anyone who traveled down Central Avenue to Forty-first Street saw that Los Angeles's black middle class had arrived in full Spanish colonial glory, certified by Du Bois himself. No other black community in the United States had accomplished more than South Central. They had built a New Negro heaven in California's Southland, around values and institutions borrowed from Old Settler communities in Pittsburgh, Chicago, and other cities in the East, South, and Midwest.

FROM LALA TO WEST COAST JAZZ

Even in such a New Negro heaven as South Central, temptation lurked just around the corner. South Central, like all cities, served as a haven for a wide variety of people. Each minority contained factions whose members could barely tolerate each other's presence. So too, America's black metropolises suffered enormous inner tensions between their poorest and wealthiest residents, be-tween their high-church Episcopalians and their boisterously egalitarian Pen-tecostals, between city-born, educated Old Settlers and rural, poorly educated southern migrants. As troubling as such divisions were, they paled in significance to the conflict between Du Bois's "better class" of New Negroes and the "sporting class" denizens of the black underworld. Unlike white middle-class communities, the black middle class lacked the power and authority to police its streets and to rid its communities of undesirables.[29] South Central's better class acquired homes, secured good jobs, and sent their children to some of the best public schools in the city. They provided their families firm religious and moral guidance and offered personal examples of what a New Negro should be. But they did not control South Central.[30]

Outside South Central's well-kept, well-run, and racially diverse schools, just down the street from its imposing churches, and up and down the bustling sidewalks and streets of Central Avenue, the agents of destruction and disorder shamelessly displayed their wares and services. Tolerated and even protected by police on the beat and authorities in city hall, drug dealers, prostitutes, bootleg-gers, gamblers, and pimps freely plied their trades along Central Avenue and its side streets.[31] A black middle-class heaven, South Central was also Los Angeles's primary red-light district. As an imagined community, dominated by a racial minority, who exercised no political control over its geographic boundaries and no police power, South Central's black middle class futilely distanced itself and its families from South Central's illicit sporting life. The price of failure, as each week the *California Eagle* made dramatically clear in searing, front-page head-lines, was death, shame, impoverishment, and loss of middle-class respectability and social status.

Like the alluring prostitute who sauntered down Central Avenue, the neighborhood's sporting life often proved irresistible even to its black middle class. For those who lived outside the neighborhood, Central Avenue's fame derived from its legendary nightlife, not its striving black middle class. By the early 1920s, Central Avenue, like Harlem and Chicago's Stroll, emerged as a premier, national venue for jazz and other black entertainment. Billing themselves as Harlem West, Central Avenue clubs borrowed the names of famous Harlem and Chicago nightspots such as the Cotton Club and Club Alabam; their bands played songs that had debuted in Chicago and New York; and their partygoers emulated Harlem and Bronzeville fashions and dances, including the Charleston, the Lindy Hop, and the Stride. Big name Midwest and East Coast jazz bands regularly stayed in Los Angeles for extended engagements at South Central clubs or, like Ellington, to perform in Hollywood movies.[32]

No other place treated black musicians more hospitably. On Central Avenue, black entertainers played to packed houses of racially mixed audiences. Black entertainers could dine in virtually any restaurant in the city, visit anywhere that they chose, and stay at the fashionable Somerville. In racially mixed South Central, they faced little discrimination, and their audiences feted them as royalty. Gerald Wilson, trumpeter in the Jimmie Lunceford Orchestra, recalled his reception by a boisterous crowd when the band disembarked from its train at Union Station. Their admirers paraded Wilson and the other members of the band down Central Avenue in open convertibles to the Hotel Somerville. "I made up my mind that day," explained Wilson, "I was going to live in Los Angeles."[33] Like Wilson, many other eastern jazzmen, once in Los Angeles, chose to remain despite lucrative jobs in big-name, national bands. Even the high-powered Duke Ellington Orchestra lost its lead vocalist, Ivey Anderson, to Los Angeles, where she opened her famous Chicken Shack restaurant.

Jazz had arrived on Central Avenue just before World War I, directly from New Orleans. In 1908 bassist Bill Johnson and his New Orleans band played what jazz historians believe was jazz at the Red Feather Tavern. Ernest Coycault and Oliver "Dink" Johnson arrived from New Orleans soon after. In 1914 Freddie Keppard and George Baquet joined Coycault and Johnson to form the Original Creole Band, which jazz historians credit with the first use of the term jazz.[34] The Original Creole Band ushered in Los Angeles's jazz age. In 1917 Jelly Roll Morton moved from New Orleans to Los Angeles for a five-year stay. In addition to his club appearances, Morton ran his "Pacific Coast Line," a string of light-skinned prostitutes, out of the Cadillac Café on Central Avenue near Fifth Street. In 1922 "Kid" Ory replaced Morton at the Cadillac, continuing the club's New Orleans connection.[35]

Between the wars, "Papa Mutt" Carey directed the most important New Orleans band in Los Angeles. Mutt favored Louisiana musicians. Drummer Lee Young, Lester's younger brother, recounted attending an audition at Carey's club at Pico Boulevard and Georgia Street on the West Side:

> He was from Louisiana. My dad was from Louisiana. For some reason, the people from Louisiana are very, clannish, very, very clannish. . . . He [Papa Mutt] said, "Who is your dad"
>
> "My dad's Billy Young."
>
> "You got the job."
>
> Then Papa Mutt ended up hiring my sister as female vocalist.[36]

By 1940 nearly a hundred New Orleans musicians had migrated to Los Angeles, making it the most important northern outpost of New Orleans jazz.

Creole jazz musicians, "lalas" as they called themselves, were the most conspicuous element of a much larger cohort of New Orleans migrants to Los Angeles. Black Creoles settled around Leimert Park, on the West Side between Crenshaw Boulevard and Vernon Avenue.[37] In 1945 the *Los Angeles Times* estimated that fifteen thousand black Creoles lived in Los Angeles, the largest contingent outside New Orleans itself. Of the major northern cities that attracted black migrants, Los Angeles was the most southern and the most like New Orleans.[38] It boasted a warm climate, and the city's relaxed, easygoing ways appealed to Louisiana Creoles. Fletcher Smith, who played banjo at the Club Alabam, explained the appeal of Los Angeles, "It's more casual out here, you know. See New York is stiff. People are stiff in New York, you know. People out here swing. . . .They are casual . . . that makes it comfortable."[39] Creoles also found the multiracial mix of South Central comfortably reminiscent of New Orleans. Moreover, the Spanish-Catholic heritage of Los Angeles paralleled the French-Spanish Catholicism of New Orleans.[40]

After World War II, Los Angeles's black Creoles invited Clifton Chenier and zydeco to the West Coast. Much as had occurred in Houston, Louisiana zydeco bands played regular engagements in the city's Catholic recreational centers to raise money and popularize their music. By 1960 the West Coast zydeco circuit led to the formation of a number of West Coast zydeco bands and singers, such as Queen Ida, who played and sang blues-based zydeco as well as old-time Francophone lala dance music. Zydeco not only made Los Angeles and Oakland important musical centers but also sustained the black Creole culture that accompanied New Orleans jazz.[41]

From the start, Louisiana Creoles dealt easily with Central Avenue's sporting

life. Like the French Quarter, in Los Angeles Creoles worked in the clubs, patronized the bars, served gumbo in South Central restaurants, and played New
Orleans jazz. Steeped in the Afro-French Catholicism of New Orleans, Los Angeles Creoles did not rigidly separate the sacred from the profane. Creoles also
had a different sense of racial consciousness than other African Americans. De-
scended from *gens de couleur libres*, black Creoles were often quite light-skinned.
Proud of their African ancestry, they were equally proud of their Native American,
Spanish, and French ancestry. A people of mixed race and culture, Louisiana
Creoles thrived in the complex ethnic and racial caldron of South Central. Neither
race nor assimilation threatened a people who took immense pride in their own
diversity. Not being a race people, Creoles worked easily with white club owners,
booking agents, and mixed-race audiences. Trained in New Orleans jazz, they
helped other more racially conscious black musicians to play in a manner that
appealed to whites. As Catholics, the Creoles attended religious services that
lacked much of the loud music and ecstatic behavior characteristic of black Sanctified and Pentecostal churches, making them more like their white neighbors and
less like other southern blacks.[42]

After World War I, South Central's black musicians formed the Negro Musicians' Union Local 767 of the American Federation of Labor. Located near Seventeenth Street on Central Avenue, Local 767 anchored South Central's first entertainment district, which included the Lincoln Theatre, a group of clubs between
Eleventh and Fourteenth streets, the Rosebud Theatre, the Clark Hotel, the Blue-
bird Inn, the Quality Café, Lyons Hotel, and Spikes Record Shop. During the day,
musicians hung out at Local 767 and, across the street, in Spikes Record Shop,
the primary booking agent for Los Angeles black bands in the 1920s.[43] Reb and
Johnnie Spikes arrived from Texas following the war. Their "Major and Minor
Orchestra" quickly became one of South Central's most popular bands and their
record shop, on Twelfth and Central, acted as the clearinghouse for Los Angeles
jazz. They sold the latest records and became the "go-between" for South Central
bands and Hollywood film studios. In 1921, the Spikes recorded "Kid" Ory on
their Sunshine label, which marked the beginning of the independent record
industry in Los Angeles.[44]

In the twenties, jazz saxophonist Marshall Royal worked in the taxi-dance
clubs where he earned fifty dollars a week to play for female taxi dancers. For fifty
cents a song, the girls danced with customers on Friday and Saturday nights.
Marshall and friends also transported illegal Canadian whiskey to Los Angeles
clubs. "There was a big flat part of sand near San Juan Capistrano," Marshall
explained. "These boats . . . with this liquor on them . . . put them on floats . . . .

The high tide would bring the floats onto the beach. Then you would pick up the bootleg whiskey, put it in your car, and bring it back to Los Angeles."[45]

The Hotel Somerville (renamed the Dunbar in 1933) became the fulcrum of South Central's upscale entertainment. Couples met at the Somerville, dined in its restaurant, met local celebrities, and visited nearby clubs. The Apex stood next door and the Downbeat, the Memo, and the Last Word were just across the street. Ivey Anderson's Chicken Shack beckoned a few blocks to the south, three blocks from Dynamite Jackson's Club Araby and the Savoy Theatre. When the Golden State Insurance Company built its headquarters across the street from the Somerville, it attracted even more businesses and residents to the Forty-second Street area.[46] Two blocks east stood Thomas Jefferson High School, between Alameda and Hooper avenues. Jefferson High students studied jazz in their music classes only a short walking distance from Central Avenue's vibrant jazz scene.

Marshall Royal arrived in Los Angeles in 1918 as a young boy with his father. Marshall's parents were educated and formally trained musicians, and each claimed a "Caucasian grand-father." His mother's father, David Walton, founded the David Walton School, the first school for blacks in Denison, Texas. The Walton School trained nearly a dozen major jazz musicians, several of whom migrated to Los Angeles. Marshall's parents "were perfect, as far as perfect can be." His father had brought him to Los Angeles because "at the time it was known as the land of the free, where segregation wasn't too tough . . . . He told me as long as I lived to never go back down South."[47] Marshall, a childhood neighbor of the famed Jefferson High School music instructor Sam Browne, recalled Browne escorting him to kindergarten, looking out for him in middle school, and being his friend at Jefferson High School.

Until the 1930s, the Los Angeles School Board prohibited nonwhites from teaching at the high school level. Before Sam Browne's appointment, the Jefferson High white faculty offered a rigorous music program but did not include jazz. "When I went to school it was mandatory that you take some form of music," explained Marshall. "The California school system had one of the highest ratings in the United States." Marshall took classes in keyboard harmony and four more semesters of harmony in which he learned to write scores and compose. To prepare for his music classes, he also took private lessons on Saturdays and during the summers. Marshall's father had brought him out to California because it gave him an "opportunity," and at Jefferson High, he was treated like all the other students. "There wasn't a whole lot of variation between the different nationalities," he explained. "They were all in the same room, and they got along very well. Very mixed. When I went to Jefferson, there were about 20 percent blacks, 5 percent Español, 2 percent Japanese, Italians would be 25 percent, the Jewish people would be 20 percent, and the rest would be regular Caucasians."[48]

Few institutions in the 1930s played a larger role in the training of young West Coast jazz musicians than Jefferson High School, and no one at Jefferson played a more important part than Sam Browne. Born in Los Angeles, Browne studied music with a local, classically trained music teacher, attended Jefferson High School, and graduated with honors from the University of Southern California. In 1936 Jefferson High School hired Browne, its first African American faculty member. Until the 1950s, Browne taught classes on harmony, counterpoint, and reading and organized the Jefferson swing band The Democrats.[49] Texas-born jazz pianist and composer Horace Tapscott recalled, "When I was in junior high school, Mr. Browne would come over and recruit for his band at Jefferson. . . . But coming to Jeff, it was something. There was a lot of activity. Anything you wanted to get into was available on campus . . . .There were no gates, no fences, no locks, no graffiti . . . .There were a lot of opera singers that went over to Europe to work that studied under Samuel Browne . . . Jefferson was a proud school. Everybody wanted to do their best."[50]

After classes, Browne often took band members to Central Avenue clubs to meet the musicians and watch them work. He also invited top jazz musicians and others to his classes at Jefferson and to band practice. His guests included Lester Young and Sonny Criss as well as Lionel Hampton, Nat King Cole, Ethel Waters, Paul Robeson, opera singer Marian Anderson, symphonic composer William Grant Still, and W. E. B. Du Bois. "I didn't bring jazz in: it was already there," explained Browne. "I just met it head-on and I put my arms around it. I salvaged it because it was here to stay. . . . I personally had a classical background and was trained in European music." Browne devoted his whole life to teaching music.[51]

Browne ensured that South Central students received the best music education available, classical and jazz. He also introduced them to the rich musical resources of the Los Angeles area that included Arnold Schoenberg and other European modernists at UCLA and USC. Jefferson graduates, regardless of their academic interest, understood and appreciated a broad range of Western music. Browne rigorously trained the few truly talented and musically passionate in composition, reading, and performance. These students included concert performers, opera singers, and jazz musicians, such as Marshall Royal's brother Ernie and the great bebop saxophonist Dexter Gordon. A remarkable number went on to distinguished careers in music. Browne's imprint on the city's jazz musicians was profound. In interview after interview, his former students confirmed the thoroughness of their musical education at Jefferson.[52]

Legendary music teacher Sam Browne dressed for work, Los Angeles, 1925
(Shades of L.A. Archives, Los Angeles Public Library)

Learning jazz at Jefferson under Sam Browne, however, was different than
picking it up in New Orleans's French Quarter. At Jefferson, Browne taught jazz
formally and systematically. Instruction included music history, theory, and composition, and his students learned to play using proper conservatory techniques.
Browne used jazz as a carrot to introduce his students to the European symphonic
tradition. As he explained, he did not teach jazz because he loved it; rather, he

Paradise Club in Watts, 1950 (Shades of L.A. Archives, Los Angeles Public Library)

"salvaged it, because it was here to stay." Browne taught a gentrified form of jazz, divorced almost entirely from southern blues and sporting life raunchiness. At Jefferson High School, under Sam Browne's tutelage, jazz swung, but genteelly.[53]

In the 1930s the refinement of Los Angeles jazz had only started. Despite the repeal of prohibition in 1933, Central Avenue remained the unchallenged center of Los Angeles nightlife until the late 1940s. The Club Alabam drew white patrons from across Los Angeles County and movie celebrities from Hollywood and Beverly Hills, including industrialist Howard Hughes and actress Ava Gardner. At its peak, Club Alabam employed more than a hundred servers, band members, dancers, bartenders, and kitchen help. In the 1930s, several Central Avenue–based orchestras toured nationally. These included Marshall Royal's and Lee and Lester Young's bands and the Nat King Cole Trio. Major national swing bands, led by Cab Calloway, Count Basie, Chick Webb, Jimmie Lunceford, and Duke Ellington, played frequently on Central Avenue.

In 1936 the arrival of Nat King Cole solidified Los Angeles's claim as a major jazz city. Central Avenue provided other Los Angeles–area clubs and film studios with black musicians, dancers, vocalists, and comedians. In Culver City, Frank Sebastian ran the most famous black club outside South Central, the whites-only Cotton Club, which often featured Louis Armstrong backed by Les Hite's Orchestra. The heavy infusion of New Orleans jazz, Sam Browne's formal training of young jazz players, and the employment of Central Avenue musicians in Hollywood and white clubs on Sunset Strip and in Culver City, combined with Central Avenue's appeal to white patrons, produced a West Coast jazz that exhibited only minimal blues content and that relied heavily on romantic lyrics and technical virtuosity. Central Avenue jazz became so genteel that by 1940, the city's newly arrived southern migrants shunned South Central's integrated jazz clubs in favor of all-black, rhythm and blues joints, ushering in a new era in South Central.[54]

THE WHIRLWIND

Compared to other black communities, South Central fared well during the depression. In 1940 about one-third of its residents still owned their homes in contrast to 15 percent in other northern black communities.[55] Still, with unemployment on the rise, in 1932, for the first time, South Central blacks voted Democratic. The first sign of economic distress had occurred in 1931, when the federal government rounded up thousands of Mexican Americans in South Central. In response, the *California Eagle* focused on its "buy black" campaign that encouraged African Americans "to take care of their own."[56]

In a similar vein of racial self-help, Father Divine's Harlem-based Peace Movement opened an independent Los Angeles branch for South Central's growing number of poor. The Divine Mission set up soup kitchens and boardinghouses and published a newspaper, the *Spoken Word*. In the early 1930s, local numbers czar, Lucius Lomax, acquired the Hotel Somerville to save it from foreclosure and renamed it the Dunbar, after the black poet Paul Lawrence Dunbar. Then, in 1934, to the consternation of the *California Eagle* and South Central's better class, the Divine Peace Mission purchased the Dunbar and converted it into a worship center, dining hall, and dormitory for its members.[57]

The sudden appearance of the Peace Mission reflected the changes in South Central during the Depression. The population of South Central barely increased during the 1930s. The arrival of poor black migrants from the South, largely from Texas, Oklahoma, and Louisiana, offset the federal government's deportation of thousands of South Central's Mexican residents. In 1930 blacks made up about one-third of South Central's population. In 1940 they accounted for nearly two-thirds. According to the Census Bureau, the neighborhood remained uncrowded; its housing stock above average; its schools superior; its crime-rate minimal; and, compared to other black communities, it continued to prosper, although South

Central's poor had increased in number and percentage. For the first time, South Central attracted more poor, uneducated, and rural blacks than educated, middle-class New Negroes.[58]

In the 1920s U.S. Route 66 replaced the Texas Pacific and Southern Pacific railroad as the primary avenue of migration to Los Angeles, accelerating the "southernization" of Los Angeles. The new migrants gravitated to the Peace Mission and to dozens of storefront Holiness, Pentecostal, and Sanctified Baptist churches that sprang up all over South Central. These lower-class churches challenged the dominance of South Central's middle-class black Baptist and Methodist churches, much as the New Deal challenged the district's Republicans and rhythm and blues challenged jazz.[59]

In the 1930s the federal government took over many functions traditionally overseen by churches and private charities. In providing emergency food, shelter, and employment to the needy, the New Deal pushed aside traditional elites, who included South Central's black Republican establishment. In the 1934 Democratic primary election, Augustus Hawkins defeated five other black Democratic contenders for the state assembly seat, setting up a black against black contest in the general election. Born in Louisiana, Hawkins had attended Jefferson High School and then UCLA. He led a cohort of young black South Central UCLA graduates who identified with the New Deal and the Democratic Party. The new generation of black leaders aligned itself with the district's increasingly southern and poor blacks. In a close vote, Hawkins won the election to represent the newly renumbered Sixty-second District. In 1934 the Democrats also gained control of Los Angeles city government.[60] South Central's switch from Republican to Democratic foreshadowed more profound change. In December 1941 Congress declared war on Japan. Wartime mobilization ended the Depression and opened the floodgates of southern migration to California. The wartime economic boom drew tens of thousands of poor, southern blacks to South Central, drawing the curtain on South Central's black middle-class world.

The Japanese attack on Pearl Harbor led directly to the wartime incarceration of nearly 120,000 Japanese American citizens. The federal government rounded up Japanese Americans from throughout the western states. Eighty-five percent, however, came from California and about one-half of these came from Little Tokyo in South Central. In the winter of 1942, the Roosevelt administration forcefully removed all Japanese American residents in Little Tokyo, destroying the largest Japanese American community in the United States. In less than a month, the federal government identified and shipped in railroad cars between sixty thousand to eighty thousand residents of Little Tokyo to internment camps

Japanese internment, Union Station, Los Angeles, 1942 (Herald Examiner Collection, Los Angeles Public Library)

in the Sierra Madres. California state and local officials, including Governor Culbert Olson, state attorney general Earl Warren, Los Angeles mayor Fletcher Bowron, and the Los Angeles board of county supervisors all endorsed Japanese American internment. In most of the West, internment meant the removal of only several families from the local community or a few thousand in cities such as Seattle, Portland, and San Francisco. In Los Angeles, overnight, it completely emptied the city's most populous neighborhood, momentarily transforming the northern end of South Central into a ghost town.[61]

Within weeks of the internment of South Central's Japanese Americans, the federal, state, and city governments relocated homeless, black residents of South Central into the vacated housing and businesses of Little Tokyo. The departure of South Central's Japanese Americans relieved the neighborhood's wartime housing shortage. It also marked the formation of Los Angeles's all-black ghetto. In 1942, South Central became the first predominantly black community on the West Coast. Wartime prosperity masked the change from middle-class respectability to impoverished ghetto. After 1945, South Central became steadily blacker, poorer, and more violent—a trajectory that led directly, in the summer of 1965, to the Watts riot, when South Central became the symbol of everything wrong in American life, a travesty of the California dream.

During World War II, however, life in South Central had never been better.

World War II remade Los Angeles from an important West Coast city into a world metropolis. In 1940 a million and a half people lived in the city of Los Angeles. In 1950, according to the U.S. Census Bureau, two million people lived in the city, a 25 percent increase. In 1940 about 100,000 newly arrived African Americans called Los Angeles home. In 1950 more than 200,000 black migrants lived in Los Angeles, almost all in South Central. In 1940 African Americans constituted one in twenty Los Angeles residents. In 1950 they constituted one in ten.

South Central's emergence as a black metropolis coincided with the acceleration of black migration to the West. In 1940 about 170,000 African Americans lived in the Mountain West and along the Pacific Coast. In 1950 the number had tripled to more than a half million. At the same time, the overall population of the western states increased about 40 percent from 14 million to just over 20 million. The population of California increased 54 percent from nearly 7 million people to about 10.5 million. World War II gave birth to the modern West, and nowhere else was the change as dramatic as in South Central.[62]

In 1937 not a single mile of freeway existed in Los Angeles County. Still, it ranked as the third-largest manufacturing city in the United States. The extension of the Southern Pacific Railroad in 1880 to Los Angeles and the building of the Port of San Pedro at Long Beach before World War I assured the city's preeminence as the port of entry and primary shipping center for the American Southwest. In 1939 LA ranked first in the nation in the manufacture of aircraft, oil equipment, motion pictures, food, and sportswear. Aircraft makers alone employed more than fifteen thousand workers in Los Angeles. Major eastern manufacturers, such as Firestone, R.C.A. Victor, and Bethlehem Steel, built their West Coast headquarters in Los Angeles. In 1940 Los Angeles eclipsed San Francisco as the nation's largest western city. Early on, black migrants had sensed Los Angeles's bright future. Since World War I, nearly half of the African Americans who moved to the West chose Los Angeles. World War II enhanced Los Angeles's status as the preeminent city in the West as well as the primary western terminus of the Great Migration.[63]

With war imminent, in 1941 employment in Los Angeles aircraft factories soared to more than 120,000 workers and employment in shipbuilding rose from 1,000 in 1939 to 22,000 in 1941. Much of this growth derived from federal spending as Los Angeles became the largest defense-manufacturing region in the nation and, after Pearl Harbor, the primary military port for the Pacific Theater. The Long Beach Naval Base served as homeport for the world's largest naval fleet. The army, navy, and air force built numerous training camps and research and development centers in the Los Angeles area, swelling the region's employment rolls. In all, between 1941 and 1943, the city added more than half a million jobs. Los Angeles offered depression-weary Americans not only unprecedented employment opportunities but also pay scales, health, and retirement benefits that ranked near the nation's top. Southerners, black and white, earned nearly twice as much as they would have working at the same job in the South. For southerners, the warm, dry Southern California climate enhanced Los Angeles's appeal. By the end of the war, poorly educated, rural, devoutly religious, and racially defined southerners had replaced midwesterners as Los Angeles's primary migrants.[64]

Because of the conscription of young males by the military and the booming defense industries, jobs went begging in Los Angeles. Desperate for workers, Los Angeles employers actively recruited women and blacks. Female employment in the aircraft industry grew from 143 in 1941 to 65,000 in 1943. In the shipyards, black employment increased from a few hundred in 1941 to 7,000 in 1944. By the end of the war, African Americans constituted nearly 15 percent of Los Angeles shipbuilders, 11 percent of its steelworkers, and 7 percent of its aircraft employees. Except for the aircraft industry, located in the suburbs far away from South Central, these percentages exceeded the percentage of blacks in the city's population. These were the best industrial jobs in the nation for African Americans. In 1949 the median income for blacks in California exceeded $1,500 compared to $1,100 nationally, and only $750 in the South. On average, southern states spent less than $10 to educate each black child compared to $67 in Los Angeles. For southern African Americans, who had moved to California, World War II must have seemed as important as their ancestors' emancipation from slavery.[65]

Until the 1930s, South Central had attracted migrants from throughout the United States. Most came from cities, many from the North, and, on the whole, these early migrants were well educated. In 1940 a third of the black households in South Central still owned their own homes, the same percentage as whites in Los Angeles. In the 1940s, about two-thirds of the city's black migrants arrived from Texas, Oklahoma, and Louisiana. Census takers categorized 75 percent of these migrants as unskilled, with only a grade-school education or less. During the 1940s, each month, about six thousand unskilled, poorly educated, and often rural blacks arrived in South Central to join family or friends in ever more congested housing. Facing rising demand, landlords subdivided single-family homes to accommodate several families; many families took in boarders or newly arrived family members; and the federal government built public housing.[66]

In the 1920s many white homeowners in the all-white neighborhoods bordering Central Avenue had inserted restricted covenants into their deeds that pro-

Selling Texas watermelons in South Central (Peter Rutkoff)

hibited sale to African, Asian, and Mexican Americans. By the mid-1930s, these restrictions limited black residency to the South Central corridor. With the departure of Mexican laborers during the Depression, Japanese Americans in 1942, and working-class whites during the war, South Central became a virtually all-black neighborhood and Jefferson High School and Jordan High School, in Watts, all-black high schools. Dozens of Sanctified Baptist, Holiness, and Pentecostal churches moved into empty Central Avenue storefronts. Food markets advertised pork barbecue, fried chicken, okra, yams, black-eyed peas, fatback, and "Texas" watermelons. Barbershops and beauty shops promised to straighten customers' hair and fix it in the latest style. Blues blared out the doors of juke joints and bars, while theaters and dance halls featured swing bands, light-skinned chorus girls, comedy acts, and bawdy vaudeville shows. Along Central Avenue, a rich mixture of sounds and smells greeted southern migrants—collard greens, rhythm and blues, street preachers, and venders, all suffused with the warm cacophony of East Texas and Louisiana accents.[67]

On adjacent blocks, the remnants of South Central's middle class tenaciously hung on in their palatial Baptist and Methodist edifices north of Forty-second Street, at the offices of the Urban League and NAACP, on the social pages of the *California Eagle,* in the Masonic and Elks lodge halls, and at the Golden State

Mutual Life Insurance Company. Wartime Central Avenue exhibited great class diversity. During World War II, a full spectrum of African Americans lived along Central Avenue, the rich and the poor, the educated and uneducated, the religious and the profane, southern as well as northern. During World War II, like Harlem, Pittsburgh, and Chicago, South Central embraced all segments of black America. Crowded and boisterous, South Central, for another decade, remained a complex black community, not a dumping ground for the benighted poor of Los Angeles.

In the 1940s much changed for South Central's black middle class. No longer members of a largely middle-class black community, they nonetheless retained their leadership of black South Central. The hardening of residential segregation after World War I had forced South Central's middle-class blacks to stand by their race and remain in South Central. During World War II the wartime sense of racial brotherhood minimized class differences. As a race people, until the end of World War II South Central's black middle class avoided assimilation into white, middle-class Los Angeles.[68]

The give-and-take between South Central's urban middle class and its rural poor was only part of the story. In South Central, young African Americans struggled to assert their identities apart from their parents as well as from white youth, who looked down on them as country bumpkins and racial inferiors. Los Angeles offered young African Americans much—education, plentiful jobs, attractive and safe neighborhoods, and opportunities unavailable in the South or even in the Northeast and Midwest. Still, at every turn, white Los Angelinos made them feel inferior. Many young blacks concluded that no matter what they did, finally, whites would always consider them members of a racially defined underclass, at best "a colored people." Deciding not to compete in a contest that they could not win, they embraced their blackness and stood apart, indifferent to white opinion. Unable to become acceptable in white terms, they became "cool."[69]

From the beginning of the Great Migration, young blacks had used the freedom of northern cities to express their cultural style. In the South, to have done so would have invited white hostility and even violence. In Harlem and elsewhere in the North, young black men and women could wear whatever clothes they wished, fashion their hair in whatever style struck their whim, dance and sing music of their choice, and speak their own hip lingo—choices that freed them from white and parental judgment. Rather than walk down the street, they sauntered; rather than dress according to the latest downtown styles, they concocted their own wardrobes and hairdos. "Stylin'" set young urban blacks apart and enabled them to shed the trappings of inferiority. In their own eyes and in their peers', they were cool, cool as Joe Louis, Cab Calloway, or a Texas cowboy.[70]

In the late 1930s young black males in Harlem started to wear "zoot suits." Jazz musicians, such as Cab Calloway, picked up on the style, certifying its *hipness*. The style spread quickly to other northern black communities and even appeared in some southern cities. The zoot suit went well beyond dressing to "the nines." The ensemble began with a broad-brimmed felt hat, turned up in the rear, and snapped down smartly at the front, with a creased crown and a wide colorful band, with the added dash of a feather. The coat, however, was the definitive garment. Wedge-shaped, the jacket sported broad, padded-shoulders that tapered at the waist with a skirt that sometimes reached to the knees. Most were double breasted, and some belted across the rear waistline. Hipsters considered bright, loud colors especially cool. Usually the wearer bought oversize pants which he had cut down to specifications. Classic zoot suit pants included wide pleats, baggy legs, and tapered cuffs. Zoot-suiters preferred patent leather shoes with raised heels and pointed toes, shirts in colors that either jarringly contrasted with the suit or matched it exactly. Ties were broad and bright. Dressed "to kill," zoot-suiters costumed themselves as soon as they got off work or out of school. Properly attired, they swaggered down the street with an equally coolly attired "chick" or just hung out together on the corners of black neighborhoods.[71]

Los Angeles, as in so much else, offered a West Coast variation. Because of wartime labor needs, in 1942 the federal government instituted its Bracero Program, which invited thousands of Mexican farm laborers into the United States. Once in the United States, many *bracero* workers left the fields for San Antonio, Fort Worth, Dallas, and Los Angeles to secure jobs in war plants or as urban laborers. In Los Angeles, *braceros* suffered the same racial discrimination that blacks faced. Like blacks, they confronted restricted covenants that forced them to live in the predominantly black neighborhoods of South Central. Mexican children attended public schools with black children, and Central Avenue served as the downtown for both groups, especially its nightclubs, bars, strip clubs, and bordellos. Young Mexican males, known as p*achucos*, quickly adopted the draped zoot suit, with its pegged pants. Young Mexican females, called *pachuquitas* also borrowed their styles from young, black females or "chicks"—short skirts, long hair, see-through blouses, heavy makeup and perfume, fishnet stockings, and high heels. If anything, the young black and Mexican women of South Central swaggered with even more exaggerated gaits than their male cohorts, strutting down the streets of South Central with a lit cigarette dangling from the corner of their mouths or between their fingers.[72]

The styling of young zoot-suiters and their chicks served two interrelated purposes—one cultural and the other political. As in Harlem, styling in South

Central asserted the individual's indifference, if not contempt, for white middle-class culture that the black middle class seemed to slavishly emulate. Lower-class black and Hispanic youths conformed to their own dress code, their own slang, and their own moral code. Styling declared their cultural declaration of independence from whites, from the country ways of the rural South, from Mexico, from the black middle class. Their urban styling asserted their superiority, their coolness. White became stodgy. Black and brown became cool; chicks and *pachuquitas* hot. In the language of Madison Avenue advertisers, zoot-suiters and chicks exemplified "the modern city." During World War II, like jazz musicians before them, young urban blacks infused the African American notion of cool into American urban culture. Cool, hip, and citified became interchangeable terms. The youth of America's Bronzevilles set the stage for postwar American youth.[73]

World War II and the conscription of young males catapulted zoot-suiters into the political arena. In the first years of the war, local, all-white draft boards systematically disqualified many blacks and Hispanics on either educational or medical grounds. Almost no Hispanic youths volunteered. Very few blacks volunteered because of the reputation of the American military services for racial discrimination during the First World War. The few colored youths who served in the military found themselves excluded from combat, relegated to kitchen and latrine duty, burial details, transportation, and other menial labor. Moreover, a high percentage of Hispanic and black youths never registered for the draft.[74] This resulted in a much higher percentage of colored youths evading military service than white youths. In white eyes, after Pearl Harbor these "draft dodgers" shamelessly flaunted their lack of patriotism in their zoot suits, accompanied by their stylishly attired chicks. In Los Angeles, with its large naval and air bases and dozens of military training camps, the contrast between young white men in their military uniforms and clipped haircuts and the city's young colored men in their zoot suits and carefully coiffed hair, accompanied by hot-looking chicks, became too much to bear.[75]

On June 3, 1943, a group of white sailors, on leave from the Long Beach Naval Station, attacked a group of Hispanic males, beat them, and then stripped off their zoot-suits, leaving them on the street in their underpants, their girlfriends agasp. At first, military authorities and Los Angeles police looked the other way and even applauded what they saw as the patriotism of the assault of white sailors on colored draft dodgers. Tellingly, the police arrested only the zoot-suited black and Hispanic victims, not the uniformed white rioters. The *California Eagle* reported that the Los Angeles County Board of Supervisors had taken the absurd position of outlawing zoot suits as a wartime necessity. According to the reasoning of zoot-suit critics, the War Department placed strategic items on a rationing list, including cloth. By using excessive material, draft-dodging zoot-suiters violated the spirit, if not the letter, of the law. Authorities asked Central Avenue shop owners to remove zoot suits from their windows.[76]

The riots continued unabated, largely because neither the police nor the military acted. Night after night, white soldiers and sailors drove to Central Avenue and hunted for colored zoot-suiters. When questioned by reporters, many of the white rioters complained that when they had approached Hispanic and black women for companionship, their zoot-suited escorts attacked them and drove them off. Black and *pachuco* males resented the presumption that "their" women would choose whites over them. Service uniforms and zoot suits became signifiers of contending racial groups, and Central Avenue, its clubs and its women, the spoils of racial warfare. After nearly a week of escalating riots, military authorities ordered all enlisted personnel to remain on base. By June 13, the riots ended. Central Avenue merchants, facing police hostility, removed zoot suits from their shelves. To no avail, *pachuco* and black males simply bought extra-large-size suits and took them home where their families cut them down and tailored them into fashionable zoot suits. Within a year, Central Avenue clothing shops, again, prominently advertised zoot suits in the *California Eagle*. Perhaps, because black chick and *pachuquita* styles required little cloth, neither the Los Angeles County Supervisors nor the white sailors asked them to forgo their stylish dress.[77]

The zoot-suit riots, much like the relocation of Japanese Americans, revealed the racial divisions and inequities that American wartime authorities tried to cover over. In the United States, even in Southern California, race determined the rights of citizenship. Young blacks and Hispanics, having left behind the servile worlds of their parents, refused to bow to white values or political authorities. In South Central, and other black, urban centers, they dressed according to their own taste and expected respect. When white soldiers and sailors tried to put them in their place and take command of South Central, black and Hispanic youth fought back, refusing to become "good colored people."

Seemingly an unimportant and local disturbance, the Los Angeles zoot-suit riots, drew the first battle lines of nation's postwar racial struggles. During World War II, in the nation's sequestered, black metropolises, a new generation of African and Hispanic Americans matured. Determined to govern their lives, free from racial harassment, they rejected white standards of behavior, whether from white authorities or middle-class blacks. Instead, they stood their ground even when threatened by violence. For the duration of the war, the racial tensions in Los Angeles remained muted. But when peace returned and the wartime boom ended, the children of black migrants looked to themselves for validation.

STORMY MONDAY

In surveys conducted by the army at the end of the war, more than half of southern black inductees indicated that military service had advanced their education, and well over half said that they did not intend to return to the South after their discharge.[78] Such attitudes fed the continued movement of blacks from rural areas to cities and from the South to the North. The war also accelerated the shift of the nation's population westward, especially black Americans. Everyone who had served in the Pacific Theater embarked from the West Coast and most from Los Angeles. The large number of military training bases in Southern California meant that even many of the individuals who served in the European Theater received their training near Los Angeles. Black service personnel became familiar with the laid-back, easygoing ways of Southern Californians, the mild, southern-like climate, and the still comparatively liberal Los Angeles racial attitudes. Black service personnel also took note of the region's burgeoning defense industry and the dynamic and prosperous black community of South Central that combined southern ambience with northern prosperity. Determined to share in the good life that Southern California offered, black service personnel brought to Los Angeles their wartime experience and their veterans' benefits.[79]

Like postwar America, demobilization was not colorblind. During the war, Los Angeles defense contractors had employed tens of thousands of black workers, male and female. For nearly all, it was the best job they had ever held. Most shipyards, the primary employer of black industrial workers, closed after 1945, throwing thousands of African Americans out of work. The Los Angeles economy, however, quickly shifted gears. The postwar boom in housing created thousands of construction jobs, and the aircraft industry remained intact, now building private commercial aircraft rather than military planes. In 1950 one-third of African American workers found work in either government, public transportation, or communication. Almost all of these jobs required a distant commute from South Central. Black women suffered a serious decline of income. During the war, many had earned good wages in the shipyards and airplane factories. At the end of hostilities, employers discharged nearly all of these women. In an increasingly tight, postwar job market, most black women found employment only as domestic help or other low-paid menial labor.[80]

Compared to the rest of the country, however, Los Angeles offered African Americans an attractive life. Homeownership in South Central remained high. At least one member of most families enjoyed gainful employment. Migrants continued to pour in from the South. In 1950 more than 200,000 African Americans lived in South Central, about 9 percent of the city's population. During the war, most of the region's labor unions had repealed their whites-only membership clauses, and in most areas of the economy, for the first time, African Americans moved up the employment ladder to lower-level management positions. Geographically, the black community expanded southward to include Watts and westward into West Jefferson and Crenshaw Avenue. Central Avenue also continued to thrive. Its theaters and clubs joined Sunset Strip and Hollywood as primary entertainment districts, and South Central musicians played in clubs across the city from Santa Monica and Venus Beach on the west side to Pasadena in the east and Long Beach to the south. The renamed University of California, Los Angeles (UCLA), welcomed black students and became the college of choice for university-bound Jefferson and Jordan High School graduates. This had the unintended effect of moving young, ambitious blacks out of South Central into the mainstream of Los Angeles life, a result that benefited them but drained South Central of its most talented children.[81]

Paradoxically, postwar South Central's most serious problem derived from its relative prosperity and attractiveness. From 1940 to 1950, the community's black population more than doubled, from 98,000 to 212,000. The movement of blacks into Watts to the south and to West Jefferson to the west absorbed some of the increase. Both of these communities consisted largely of low-density, suburban homes. These bungalow, owner-occupied communities extended to black families many of the amenities of Southern California life, but they offered little to the thousands of poor migrants who arrived every month from Texas and Louisiana, individuals who were qualified for only for menial, unskilled labor and who could afford only low-cost housing.[82]

World War II masked the change that had occurred in South Central. Each Saturday issue of the *California Eagle* recorded the prosperity and celebrated the good times. The LA police's heavy-handed and racially targeted response to the zoot-suit rioters failed to dampen the high spirits of wartime South Central. With the end of the war, South Central faced increasingly sober prospects. The return of Japanese Americans forced the eviction of hundreds of black families and drove up rents. At the same time, the navy closed its shipyards at Long Beach and the air force canceled orders for military planes. Thousands of South Central residents found themselves without work and were often forced to compete for employment with recently discharged service men and women. All along Central Avenue, from Little Tokyo to Watts, businesses and clubs closed, the unemployed hung out on street corners, and panhandlers begged for food and lodging.[83]

Much of the change in South Central had begun during the war. By 1945 South Central's middle class no longer set the community's standards. South Central's wartime sense of racial brotherhood had only masked class differences. The members of South Central's middle class saw themselves as the agents of racial uplift and refinement. When they distanced themselves from southern diets, blues, and Sanctified Christianity and ridiculed the speech and country ways of southern migrants, they viewed these as not racial but social and cultural issues. Migrants resented such judgments as examples of class snobbery and racial betrayal. They found South Central's prestigious churches cold and formal, its music stilted, its social clubs and fraternities snooty, the public school teachers condescending, the women prudish, its men aloof, its children quiet and standoffish, and its police brutish. Having grown up in the Jim Crow South, migrants harbored few illusions about being accepted as equals by white Los Angeles. South Central's new migrants broke bread with their middle-class racial brothers and sisters, but on their own terms.[84]

The change manifested itself in South Central's music. In the 1930s several Chicago composers and singers, including Thomas Dorsey and Mahalia Jackson, had crafted and popularized a blues-derived gospel music that appealed to southern migrants. After the war, the most successful gospel groups, such as Chicago's Soul Stirrers, appeared on Sunday radio programs, cut records, published sheet music, and toured nationally. They also organized gospel choirs in mainline black churches throughout the country, including South Central. By the 1940s, blues-based gospel choirs were mainstays in most old-line churches that sought to attract southern migrants.[85] In 1940 South Central's most prestigious black churches—People's Independent Church, Progressive Baptist, Zion Hill Baptist, Bethel Church of Christ, Phillips Colored Methodist, and First AME Church—all sponsored large gospel choirs. A few choirs even performed on weekly radio programs and undertook their own national tours. In the 1940s the St. Paul Baptist choir Echoes of Eden, led by Earl Hines, became Los Angeles's premier gospel choir, and in 1947 Hines began a national radio program. By the late 1940s, gospel directors and their lead vocalists were stars in the emerging Los Angeles constellation of media celebrities, keeping South Central's older, black churches vibrant.[86]

Indeed, by 1950 the reputation of South Central's black churches depended as much on their gospel choirs as their ministers. Both, however, responded to the expectations of their increasingly southern membership. After 1940, nearly all

South Central churches offered more music than preaching. Ministers improvised, preaching rather than reading prepared sermons. Congregants responded to the minister extemporaneously with "Amen preacher," "Praise Jesus," and "Hallelujah," much as they had done in Oklahoma, Louisiana, and Texas. The greatest growth in church membership, however, took place in South Central's exuberant Pentecostal-Holiness and Sanctified Baptist churches.[87]

A few of South Central's Holiness and Pentecostal congregations traced their origins to the pre–World War I Azusa Street Revivals and conducted themselves like other establishment, South Central black churches. Southern migrants, however, preferred newly formed Pentecostal churches, founded by other migrants. During the war, small, often storefront, Holiness and Sanctified Baptist churches sprouted up throughout South Central. Many affiliated with national church organizations, such as the Church of God in Christ, but most resembled start-up family businesses owned and directed by the minister and his wife. Much more southern than South Central's older churches, even with their gospel choirs, the services of these newly formed Holiness and Sanctified churches often lasted six or more hours, sustained by almost unrelenting music and shouting. Typically, the churches featured choirs, a pianist, an organist, and a small band with an electric guitar, a saxophone, and a drum set. Those who attended the Sanctified Baptist church of recent Texas migrant Vida Lee would have heard her husband, guitarist "T-Bone" Walker, play a religious version of his Texas blues.

T-Bone Walker was born in 1910 and grew up in Dallas. His mother and her family played a variety of musical instruments. They taught young Thibeaux (T-Bone) to play the guitar, the mandolin, the banjo, and piano as well as to dance and sing. A close family friend, "Blind Lemon" Jefferson regularly ate Sunday dinner at the Walker home, and, as a boy, Thibeaux walked the bluesman to Central Avenue (Dallas) where Jefferson played for handouts. Personable and outgoing, as an adolescent Thibeaux toured with a medicine show and played in regional swing bands as a guitarist and tap dancer. When Bill "Bojangles" Robinson appeared in Dallas, Thibeaux danced on the stage with him. Walker turned down several offers to join national swing bands, preferring to stay with his own band in Dallas so that he could live with his mother. In 1935, at age twenty-five, now called "T-Bone," Walker handed over his Dallas band to his close friend, jazz guitarist Charlie Christian, and left for Los Angeles.[88]

In South Central, T-Bone Walker found an effervescent and diverse music community. Central Avenue clubs featured Nat King Cole, Lou Hite's swing band, and touring national bands that included Duke Ellington and Benny Goodman. Both whites and blacks patronized Central Avenue clubs, and most males brought female dates. The most successful clubs featured large dance bands of ten to fifteen musicians, a dance line of six to eight light-skinned dancers, a comedian, and singers. Small clubs offered ballad-style singers accompanied by a pianist or a small combo with a guitar, saxophone, and drums. Catering to couples and racially mixed audiences, these clubs featured easy-listening jazz and mellow crooners throughout the evening. In contrast, after-hour clubs, which opened after the regular shows closed, around two o'clock in the morning, played to younger and largely black audiences, who expected an upbeat boogie-woogie piano, electric guitars, and honking jazz horns. South Central band director Johnny Otis explained, " 'T-Bone' Walker, Charles Brown, Lowell Fulson, Ray Charles was on the West Coast—all these things together became the California influence.... California was made up of black people from many places, the church was part of our heritage, gospel music and even some Caribbean input—West Indian sisters and brothers—and New York."[89]

During the war, in South Central's after-hours clubs, blues musicians played an upbeat dance music soon to be called rhythm and blues. Influenced by Louis Jordan's New York City jump blues, swing jazz, Texas blues, and gospel music, T-Bone Walker found his audience in South Central. On his first gig, T-Bone played at Little Harlem three nights a week for $11 and shared the "kitty" with three other band members. Walker and Charlie Christian had pioneered the electric guitar in Dallas—Walker in blues and Christian in jazz. Walker's electrified blues guitar attracted southerners to Little Harlem. On Central Avenue, T-Bone Walker reworked the country blues of Blind Lemon Jefferson and Lightnin' Hopkins into an electrified, urban dance-music. Like Christian, Walker played in a riff style that fluidly, even lyrically, combined notes, a trait that distinguished the Texas blues and jazz from Delta blues. A versatile musician, in 1939, Walker toured with Lou Hite's swing band and accepted an extended engagement at Joe Louis's Rhumboogie Club in Chicago. But he always came back to Los Angeles, his adopted home, where he lived in Watts, with his wife and mother.[90]

Walker loved music, especially the blues. He also loved to entertain. In wartime Los Angeles, he directed his entertainment to southern migrants like himself, who had left the South in search of opportunity. Racially conscious, Walker and his southern audiences found in South Central a world apart, but not impoverished and not without hope. Los Angeles whites exhibited strong racial prejudices, but the city had been built around opportunity and hope, not slavery and racial hegemony. In Little Harlem and other Central Avenue clubs, southern blacks celebrated the good times that they found in Los Angeles and turned their backs on the bad times of Jim Crow. Walker's synthesis of sophisticated jazz with the earthy tones of Texas blues appealed to his audiences who wanted music with a dance-able rhythm, a nightclub ballad singing style, and a show-time attitude. A master guitarist, T-Bone played the electric guitar behind his back while doing splits to the applause of his audience.[91] He sang in a strong, clear voice with sympathetic lyrics, many about fickle, two-timing women. Always meticulously groomed, Walker strutted on the stage in iridescent suits, white polished shoes, and a warm smile, backed by a tenor and alto sax, a piano, a trumpet, and a drum set with cymbals. He celebrated the good times. Reflecting his family's religious commitments, he also warned men against messing with married women, too much drinking, and gambling—all problems that he shared with his male listeners.[92]

In 1940 Walker recorded "They Call it Stormy Monday," his best-known and best-selling song. Because of the wartime shortage of shellac, Black and White, a Los Angeles independent label, did not release "Stormy Monday" until 1946. Its release announced the musical changes that had occurred in South Central's after-hour clubs during the war. To avoid confusion with Billy Eckstine's earlier "Stormy Monday," Walker named his song "They Call It Stormy Monday, but Tuesday's Just as Bad." For listeners, the next song line, "Wednesday's worse and Thursday's also sad" said it all. "Stormy Monday" recounted the repetitious, workaday drudgery that every person in Little Harlem had endured until the end of the week arrived:

> The Eagle flies on Friday, and Saturday I go out to play;
> Sunday I go to church, then I kneel down and pray.

Then, it began all over, another "Stormy Monday, but Tuesday's just as bad."[93]

Rhythm and blues captured the mood of wartime migrants to South Central. The area's phenomenal wartime success, however, rested on the accumulated wealth and entrepreneurial talent of South Central Old Settlers. In 1930 Los Angeles claimed more black-owned businesses than any other black community in the nation, more than the second- and third-ranked communities combined. The South Central black middle class was better educated and wealthier than all other black middle classes, including the larger and longer established black elites of Atlanta, Washington, D.C., Harlem, Pittsburgh, and Chicago. Until World War II, black recording artists had relied on major labels to record and promote their music, and these companies distributed their "race record lists" exclusively to black markets.

In contrast, South Central recording producers, like Black and White, formed independent labels that featured the new gospel music and rhythm and blues. Los Angeles independents marketed to both whites and blacks. At the end of the war,

Los Angeles "indies," with their exclusive lists of gospel and rhythm and blues artists, became the fastest-growing segment of the recording industry. South Central independents—Specialty Records, Exclusive Records, Black and White Records, Modern Music, Aladdin, and Modern Records—dominated the new market, making LA the center of postwar popular music. To promote new releases, the independents courted LA jukebox distributors, small retailers, and, beginning in 1943, Los Angeles disc jockeys at KPAS, KXLA, and KFVD.[94]

Beginning with "Stormy Monday," white Los Angeles youth learned to listen and dance to Central Avenue rhythm and blues music, compliments of Los Angeles's booming independent record studios and the city's youth-oriented radio stations. At Jordan High School in Watts, rhythm and bluesman "Big Jay" McNeely, along with jazzmen Charles Mingus and the Woodman brothers, studied under Charles Reece, a friend of Jefferson High School's Sam Browne. Big Jay described the impact of southern migrants on the local musicians.

> You hear somebody from down South, like out of Texas, Fort Worth, and Dallas, man who can play!... Heavy cats come out of Texas.... See you have the blues from down South, the regular blues, the Muddy Waters blues, all the Cajun music, and all the types of blues ... played in little holes-in-the-wall.... When the whites come along, they just took what we did and put guitars and voice on top of it. They called it rock 'n' roll.[95]

Unlike the zoot-suit craze, white Los Angeles youths quickly claimed rhythm and blues as their own—renamed "rock 'n' roll." Even as black rhythm and blues musicians, producers, and clubs lived the California dream, they revolutionized American popular music.[96]

OUT OF THE FRYING PAN

In 1950 Central Avenue still served as the commercial and civic core of a dynamic and thriving black community. By 1965 it had become a tragic example of rampant urban decay, plagued by abandoned storefronts, burned-out buildings, impoverished and homeless street people, drug dealers, prostitutes, and other criminals who lived off the poor. In 1950 Jefferson High School and Jordan High School stood as proud monuments to rising black expectations. In 1965 only a handful of their graduates went on to UCLA or any of the city's other colleges and universities. In 1965 Jefferson and Jordan faculty focused almost exclusively on retention rates, not academic excellence. Yet the 1960 federal census reported unprecedented, even phenomenal, upward mobility among Los Angeles African

Americans. The disjunction of these incontrovertible facts makes the story of postwar black Los Angeles especially important, perhaps as important as the civil rights movement in the South.[97]

On May 3, 1948, a unanimous United States Supreme Court declared, in *Shelley v. Kraemer*, that the enforcement by state courts of restrictive covenants based on race denied property owners "the equal protection of the law guaranteed by the Fourteenth Amendment." In *Shelley v. Kraemer* white property owners in Missouri argued that the title of the property in question prohibited its owner from selling that property to or allowing its use by "people of the Negro or Mongolian Race." The Supreme Court ruled that such clauses abridged the property rights of the deed owner and violated the Fifth Amendment prohibition that no person shall "be deprived of life, liberty, or property." In addition, the enforcement of restrictive covenants by state courts amounted to "state action" that violated the Fourteen Amendment that prohibited any state from denying the "privileges and immunities of citizens of the United States."[98]

Brought by the NAACP and argued by attorney Thurgood Marshall, in 1948 *Shelley v. Kraemer* destroyed the last vestige of legally sanctioned segregation in Los Angeles. Since the Civil War, California blacks had voted and served on juries. In the 1930s, the Los Angeles branch of the NAACP had forced Los Angeles to desegregate the city's public high school faculties and its public beaches and pools and to remove seating restrictions on public transportation. In a community dominated by owner-occupant homeowners, *Shelly v. Kraemer* overshadowed these earlier civil rights gains. In Los Angeles, *Shelly v. Kraemer* carried more weight than the court's 1954 *Brown v. Board of Education* decision that desegregated public education, a constitutional issue never in dispute in California. In *Shelly v. Kraemer*, the Supreme Court struck down the legal barriers that separated black South Central from white Los Angeles. After 1948, African Americans no longer found themselves restricted to the narrow Alameda–Central Avenue corridor.[99]

In 1956 a survey of Los Angeles black families indicated that 84 percent wished to purchase a home in a white neighborhood. Many South Central black families fulfilled their wish. In 1960 virtually all census districts in Los Angeles contained at least one black household. Most white neighborhoods, however, remained racially intact with a 95 percent or higher rate of white residency. Black middle-class neighborhoods also remained racially homogeneous. On the heels of *Shelley v. Kraemer*, black middle-class homeowners in South Central purchased homes in the previously all-white or largely white neighborhoods near South Central. These included Watts and Compton to the south, West Jefferson and Leimert Park to the west, and Baldwin-Hills and West Adams to the northwest.

Most whites in these neighborhoods sold their homes to blacks and moved to nearly all-white neighborhoods. After 1950, black Los Angeles spread southward, westward, and northward. To the northwest, Baldwin Hills and West Adams became predominantly upper-class black communities, while West Jefferson and Leimert Park attracted black middle-class families, as did Compton and Watts.[100]

As a consequence, in the 1950s blacks dominated most of central Los Angeles, but the rigid east-west racial boundary disappeared. In Los Angeles, except for South Central, almost everyone had some white and black neighbors. In terms of social class, however, the old east-west line of demarcation remained intact. The poor of Los Angeles, most of whom happened to be black, lived to the east of Main Street and south of Wilshire Boulevard. Downtown, middle-class families, most of whom were also black, lived to the west of Main Street, north of Wilshire Boulevard, or in Watts and Compton to the south. On the West Side in the 1950s, Crenshaw Avenue replaced Central Avenue as the center of black, middle-class life. Free of nightclubs, honky-tonks, strip joints, and boisterous street life, a large community of black Creoles had made Crenshaw their home. While Crenshaw Avenue was black and proud, it was also quiet and respectable.[101]

In the 1950s no one confused Crenshaw with Central Avenue. Desperate for housing, poor black migrants continued to flock to South Central. Now, however, it contained almost no whites and few middle-class blacks. Crime increased, businesses failed or relocated, and the housing stock deteriorated. While federal housing authorities refused to grant loans on any property whose deeds contained restricted covenants, they rarely approved government-subsidized, low-interest loans in the South Central area. From 1950 to 1954, the Federal Housing Authority (FHA) granted 125,000 loans in Los Angeles but only 3,000 to non-whites. Ten percent of the population received only 2.5 percent of the federal loans. The problem went beyond the federal government. In the 1930s the FHA had developed color-coded maps to designate high- and low-risk lending areas. Red included high-density housing, mixed with manufacturing. Green indicated low-density housing free of commercial and industrial activity. On metropolitan maps, central cities became red zones and suburbs green. After the war, the FHA ceased using its green- and red-lining to determine federal loan eligibility. Private lenders, however, adopted the federal system, leading them to red-line most inner-city neighborhoods, which, like South Central, were also black and poor. After the war, the neighborhoods that most needed financial assistance received the least, both from the federal government and from private banks. Inadvertently, federal and local governments aided and abetted residential segregation by imposing an indirect residential tax on the nation's urban poor.[102]

Public housing in LA: Jordan Downs in Watts (Will Scott)

Governmental authorities inflicted another unintentional blow to South Central. Following World War II, federal and state governments concluded that private landlords, by themselves, could never meet the need in Los Angeles for low-income housing. Determined to provide all residents of Los Angeles with decent housing, the city authorized the construction of three large public housing projects—Nickerson Gardens, Jordan Downs, and Imperial Courts. When the city looked for possible sites, middle-class whites and blacks opposed construction of public housing in their neighborhoods. Unwilling to relocate the city's poor into more affluent, politically powerful neighborhoods, Los Angeles built all three projects in or near Watts.[103]

Pastoral as they might appear, Jordan Downs, Nickerson Gardens, and Imperial Courts radically changed Watts. The nearly three thousand family units, which housed more than ten thousand people, now set the tone of once rural Watts. By law, only low-income families qualified for public housing. Low income also usually meant poorly educated. In Los Angeles that also meant newly arrived, southern, and black. At the very time that the most ambitious and successful residents in Watts were moving to West Jefferson, Compton, and West Adams, the city placed in the middle of Watts ten thousand low-income and needy people, many unemployable. Others were single, working mothers, who depended on others to look after their children. The overwhelming majority of public housing residents were school-age children or younger. Overnight, Watts lost much of its remaining middle class. Its black poor were left to take care of themselves with the help of frazzled welfare workers, police, and schoolteachers. In concentrating its poor in Watts, Los Angeles exacerbated South Central's postwar problems. For many in Los Angeles, whether black or white, suburban flight had become a moral imperative.[104]

South Central's black musicians followed the lead of its middle class. Before 1950, Central Avenue jazz had bound together black Los Angelinos. When founded, the musicians Local 47 of the Los Angeles American Federation of Labor excluded black musicians. In response, in the 1920s Central Avenue black musicians formed their own local, Number 767, with offices at Eighteenth and Central Avenue. "The musicians local," explained jazzman Marshall Royal, "was one of the places where you could go and find your peers. We'd go down there and play pinochle or talk and be friendly. It was not quite a hangout, but it was a good meeting place for a lot of the fellows." Local 767 set rates and maintained a registry for the city's black musicians. A neighborhood institution, Local 767 arranged the music and entertainment for local black functions and engagements throughout the city as well as the film studios in Hollywood and Culver City. On Labor Day, every year, its members led the Central Avenue parade. After the war, Local 767 also supplied musicians for white clubs.[105]

By most accounts, Local 767 maintained a friendly, working relationship with Local 47, but the larger, white local secured the most lucrative jobs in the city and treated 767 as a poor relation. Many South Central black musicians preferred their own local even if it meant fewer and lower-paying jobs. In 1953, facing mounting pressures from the national federation, members of Local 767 agreed to meet with members of Local 47 to work out a merger. Local 767 disappeared. Its office on Central Avenue closed. All Local 767 members became members of Local 47. Most members of the new, consolidated Local 47 were white, most of its officers were also white, and at first, its old officers discriminated against black musicians when assigning jobs. Within a couple of years, however, according to most accounts, jobs became integrated, officers included both black and white members, and union staff administered job assignments fairly. By 1960, Local 47 had become a fully integrated union and a model of racial cooperation. The consolidation of Local 767 with Local 47, however, deprived South Central of one of its most important institutions. In the 1950s, at every turn, South Central's wealth and talent moved up and out.[106]

EASY RAWLINS'S WATTS

Before World War II, Watts was predominantly white and working class. Located between downtown Los Angeles and the port of San Pedro in Long Beach, Watts straddled the Alameda Corridor. Most Watts males found employment in the ten-mile-long, four-block-wide Alameda manufacturing and warehouse district. In 1927 Los Angeles had annexed Watts to increase the number of white voters in the South Central state assembly district. The strategy worked only a short time. World War II drew thousands of southern migrants to Los Angeles. Many secured jobs in the Alameda Corridor and housing in Watts. Served by the Pacific Electric's Red Car Trolley Line, Watts retained its suburban character through the 1940s. The Red Car Line offered easy and inexpensive transportation for laborers and domestic workers, while Watts's large house lots and open-spaces enabled rural migrants to raise vegetables and fruit as well as goats, cows, pigs, and chickens. For recreation, Watts families could visit Leak's Lake or the Plantation Club on Central Avenue. Jazz musician William Woodman recalled growing up in prewar Watts: "It was a showcase for talent . . . a place of entertainment, a melting pot for all races."[107]

In 1946 blacks in Watts outnumbered whites by two to one—twenty thousand to ten thousand. With the closing of the Long Beach shipyards at the end of the war, unemployment rose to nearly 14 percent. Still, nearly half the residents of Watts owned their own homes, which gave the community its suburban, middle-class character. This changed in 1953 with the construction of the Nickerson Gardens and Jordan Downs housing projects in Watts and the nearby Imperial Gardens. By 1960, homeownership in Watts had dropped to 28 percent. Public housing drew to Watts the city's poor and unemployed. It also continued to attract newly arrived southern migrants. By 1960, 85 percent of the residents of Watts were black. Because of gerrymandering, in 1960 Watts elected no public official to represent it, either to the state assembly or to Los Angeles's city council. In 1961 the Red Car Trolley Line ended service to Watts, making it difficult for residents to shop outside the neighborhood or to commute to jobs in other parts of Los Angeles. Like the remainder of Los Angeles, residents of Watts became dependent on the automobile and were bounded by the freeway system. Still, with all its problems, unemployment in Watts rose only 1 percent between 1950 and 1960, from 13.5 to 14.5 percent.[108]

In 1960 a majority of Watts's residents came from outside Los Angeles, most born in the South. They attended Sanctified churches, and they listened and danced to rhythm and blues. Men dressed in jeans and boots and sported wide-

Before the decline: Watts, 1930 (Security Pacific Collection, Los Angeles Public Library)

brimmed Stetsons; women wore tight-fitting dresses, high-heel shoes, and elaborate hairstyles. Many mothers bore their children out of wedlock, and its residents often settled personal disputes violently, drank heavily, and distilled their own whiskey. Almost exclusively African American, the residents of Watts spoke with Texas twangs and Louisiana drawls, and ate pork and chicken barbeque, fried chicken, collard greens, sweet potatoes, and black-eyed peas. They drank their beer cold out of longneck bottles, sold "Texas Watermelons" from the backs of pickup trucks, and drove big cars with loud radios and prominent fishtail fins. Few registered to vote because few elected officials courted their vote or sought their favor. Most cared little about education, and they treated middle-class ways with indifference, if not contempt.[109]

Watts stood apart from the prevailing, middle-class values and outlook of the remainder of Southern California. As the western terminus of the southern black migration, Watts resembled the South more than California. By 1950, anyone from the Cotton Belt of the South would have found themselves at home in Watts.

Even the police behaved as they did in the Jim Crow South. As in the South, the residents of Watts danced to their own rhythm, worshiped in their own fashion, and step by begrudging step, assimilated to middle-class California life, all the while singing the blues and praising the Holy Ghost. In 1990 Walter Mosley published *Devil in a Blue Dress*, the first in his series of "Easy Rawlins" detective novels that charted the travails and ecstasy of Watts from 1946 to the riot of 1965.[110]

Unlike most other commentators on Watts, Mosley wrote as an insider, a member of the Watts community, who told its stories in its own terms. Mosley understood the transient, transitional nature of postwar Watts. World War II and public housing had destroyed Watts as a middle-class community. In its place, Watts became a migrant way station for southern blacks in quest of the California dream. It served as a step on the ladder of upward mobility. After 1953, few realized their dreams in Watts itself.[111]

Born in Los Angeles in 1952, Mosley left the year following the 1965 riot, at the age of thirteen. Having gone to college in the East, in 1986 he moved to New York City where he began his "Easy Rawlins" chronicle of postwar Watts. In 1990 Mosley's *Devil in a Blue Dress* established him as a best-selling detective writer.[112] The protagonist of the book, Easy Rawlins, was a World War II veteran and private detective, who pursued justice in postwar Watts, a responsibility that the LA Police Department shirked. Easy and his friend Mouse Alexander had met in Houston's Fifth Ward, and both had family in Louisiana. Tired of Houston, in the early fifties Rawlins and Mouse left for Los Angeles. Easy explained, "Home meant that everybody already knew what you could do and if you did the slightest little thing different they'd laugh you right down into a hole . . . . There were all kind of ways out. You could get married, get drunk, get next to somebody's wife. You could take a shotgun and eat it for a midnight snack." Young and restless, Easy moved to California: "In California the sun shone three hundred and more days in the year. In California you could work until you dropped. And when you got up, there was another job waiting for you."[113] Determined to take part in the California dream, at his first opportunity Rawlins secured a mortgage to a small house in Watts. "The thought of paying my mortgage reminded me of my front yard and the shade of fruit trees in the summer heat. I felt I was just as good as a white man."[114]

Like other southern migrants, Rawlins embraced Southern California. Even when he prepared his food, California seeped in. He explained, "Then I chopped tomatoes, Bermuda onions, and little green pepper together with ripe avocados to make a light relish-like salad. I laced it with lime and a touch of cayenne."[115]

Determined to make good, Rawlins purchased several rental properties in Watts, worked as the head custodian at Sojourner Truth Junior High, and free-lanced as an unlicensed private detective. Like other Los Angelinos, Rawlins rushed from one job to another, driven by the clock. He often felt guilty for not giving his time freely to others. " 'Okay now, Mrs. Grant. See ya later.' Another time I would have offered to come by and see after her now and then. But my working life kept me away from the everyday country kind of living that I had known in Texas and Louisiana. It bothered me . . . but I had chosen my path."[116] Rawlins observed, "Looking out the window is different in Los Angeles than it is in Houston. No matter where you live in a Southern city (even a wild and violent place like Fifth Ward, Houston) you see almost everybody you know by just looking out your window. Every day is a parade of relatives and old friends."[117] Consciously conflicted, Rawlins explained his torn loyalties, "I always tried to speak proper English in my life, the kind of English they taught in school, but I found over the years that I could only truly express myself in the natural, 'uneducated' dialect of my upbringing."[118]

In times of stress and exhaustion, the pull of home invariably won out. "California was like heaven for the Southern Negro," explained Rawlins. "People told stories of how you could eat fruit right off the trees and get enough work to retire one day. The stories were true for the most part but the truth wasn't like the dream. Life was still hard in L.A. and if you worked every day, you still found yourself on the bottom. But being on the bottom didn't feel too bad if you could come to John's now and then and remember how it felt back home in Texas, dreaming about California."[119] According to Rawlins, "Bone Street was local history. A crooked spine down the center of Watts' jazz heyday, it was four long and jagged blocks. West of Central Avenue and north of 103d Street. . . . Bones, as it was called, was a center for late-night blues, and whiskey so strong that it could grow hairs on the glass it was served in . . . and the women were still there. But their clothes didn't fit right anymore. All the promise after the war had drained away and a new generation was asking 'Where's ours?' "[120] Rawlins "went over to the bar and ordered two ales. It looked like half of Houston was there."[121]

Other aspects of LA also reminded Rawlins of the South. In the 1960s, he explained, "Black men couldn't take a leisurely drive in white Los Angeles without having the cops wanting to know what was going on . . . . I was back, suddenly, in the Deep South."[122] But Watts was not Houston, and the people who had come from Houston behaved differently in Los Angeles. Facing what he saw as a racist, arbitrary, brutal police force, no different than what he had known in Houston, Easy Rawlins and other southern migrants responded by "standing tall and making a difference." He described himself as "an important, intelligent man, but he was afraid."[123] In Watts, Rawlins realized the California dream. Like Alvin Ailey's mother, Rawlins left Texas for Los Angeles. Like Ailey, Walter Mosley built his art around his mother's southern culture.[124]

But as Mosley made clear in his novels, Easy Rawlins represented only one part of postwar Watts. For every Easy Rawlins who climbed out of Watts into the American middle class, another migrant died of violence or drugs. Easy Rawlins's best friend, Mouse Alexander, exemplified the violent, self-destructive side of Watts that manifested itself in the 1965 riot. In background and age, Easy and Mouse were indistinguishable, but their response to Watts could not have been more different. Easy owned a home, established a business, built a stable family that included an adopted child, and looked out for others. Mouse lived alone, moved from one woman to another, and cared only about himself and Easy. He took what he wanted, often violently.[125]

In 1965, fed up with the arbitrary harassment and brutality of the LA police, much like Mouse, Watts responded violently. Unlike the vast majority of other Los Angeles blacks, most Watts rioters were newly arrived and southern born. Poorly educated and underemployed, the black youth of Watts understood the difference between Houston and Los Angeles. In Houston, angry as blacks might become, they knew that the police would carry out summary white justice. Only by staying in their designated place would the police leave them alone. In their near-lawless wards, blacks took care of themselves. In Los Angeles, migrants saw middle-class blacks treated by whites as if they were white, and they knew blacks on the West Side who lived in well-governed, peaceful neighborhoods. They were aware that the Los Angeles Police Department employed blacks, and some even served as officers, such as the city's future mayor, Tom Bradley. Migrants also understood that the LAPD represented itself to the world at large as a professional, nonracist organization, charged with fair and equal enforcement of the law. In Watts, they expected justice and respect.[126]

On August 11, 1965, in downtown Watts, a white police officer stopped a black youth, Ronald Frye, and ticketed him for driving under the influence of alcohol. Frye's mother came to her son's defense and attacked the officer. Quickly, a crowd of angry bystanders formed and taunted the officer. He called for backup, and the police arrested Frye and his mother, who were taken to the downtown lockup. Infuriated, the mob attacked the police remaining on the scene. For the next four days, an estimated ten thousand rioters controlled Watts, challenging the police and burning white-owned businesses along 103rd Street. When the violence ended, thirty-four persons had been killed, and another one thousand seriously injured. The riots destroyed an estimated $40 million worth of commercial property, and the police arrested more than three thousand people.[127] In the "hot summer" of 1965, when race riots broke out in dozens of other American cities, none approached the violence and the number of deaths of the Watts riot.[128]

According to the Los Angeles police, less than 3 percent of the residents of Watts had participated in the riots. Most, like Easy Rawlins, preferred a nonviolent approach to their grievances. And, like Rawlins, most Watts residents had assimilated to middle-class Los Angeles in their own way and at their own pace. Conversely, white Southern Californians had adopted many of the ways of Watts, including its blues-based music, Sanctified Christianity, and lusty, too often violent conduct. On the road to their Southern California dream, poor southern blacks cast off their slavish deference to white authority and assumed the rights of American citizenship. Confident of their rights, like other Texans, like Mouse Alexander, when treated wrongly, many responded violently.[129]

Deeply troubled by the Watts riots and the damage that the community had inflicted on itself, Walter Mosley addressed the riot in his Easy Rawlins novel, *Little Scarlet*. Rawlins observed, "On Avalon and Central and Hooper the burned buildings outnumbered the ones still intact. There was at least one torched car hunkered down at the curb on almost every block. Debris was strewn along the sidewalks and streets. Smoke still rose here and there from the wreckage."[130] In retrospect, Mosley realized that, however tragic, the 1965 riot was not an aberration. It was part and parcel of southern blacks' legacy of slavery, segregation, and migration. "This is a tough place, Ada," explained Rawlins. "You got working men and women all fenced in together, brooding about what they see and what they can't have. Almost every one of them works for a white man. Every child is brought up thinking that only white people make things, rule countries, and have history. They all come from the South. They all come from racism so bad they don't even know what it's like to walk around with your head held high. They get nervous when the police drive by. They get angry when their children are dragged off in chains. Almost every black man, woman, and child you know feels that anger."[131]

The McCone Commission, formed by Governor Edmund Brown after the riots, devoted two-thirds of its report to delineating the economic problems that faced black youth in Watts, the need for government job programs, improved schools, public housing, and the ending of racial discrimination in hiring and housing. It appended a fifteen-page photo-essay chosen from pictures taken by news organizations during the riots. The photo-essay of the riot included pictures of disciplined columns of white, national guard in full-battle regalia, buildings on fire, seized guns, overturned and burned automobiles, black children looting a liquor store, the burned wreckage of a Watts retail store guarded by armed, white soldiers, and a final photo of a white soldier, in stylish sunglasses with fixed bayonet, standing guard behind a building with a fire company, in the background, extinguishing a fire.[132]

Almost unanimously, however, the residents of Watts disagreed with the commission's main conclusion that the Los Angeles Police Department enforced the law without racial bias. In interview after interview, as the McCone Commission acknowledged, the residents of Watts pointed their fingers directly at the Los Angeles Police Department. They testified that the LAPD treated nonwhites differently than whites.[133] If the police found blacks in predominantly white neighborhoods, they stopped and questioned, even harassed them. Arrests for minor offenses were much higher in Watts than elsewhere in Los Angeles, and according to the McCone Commission, even though blacks made up less than 14 percent of the Los Angeles population, one-half the inmates in the city jail were black. More disturbing, virtually everyone interviewed from Watts recounted a story of a friend or relative who had suffered police abuse, often brutality, and, in some cases, death. Tragically, the most racially enlightened city in the nation tolerated a police department that Watts residents ranked with those in Birmingham, Detroit, and Johannesburg. During the Watts riot, the LAPD and the California National Guard had inflicted, by far, the most deaths during an urban riot by any law enforcement organization in the nation.[134]

Watts remains the most powerful image of black Los Angeles. It conjures up police brutality, economic deprivation, a dysfunctional welfare system, the despair and hopelessness of inner-city life, especially for black youths, and in the 1980s, the home of "'gangsta' rap."[135] This image originated in the 1965 Watts riot, but it had begun with World War II. The war changed Los Angeles. It also changed Watts, but in profoundly different ways. Before the war, except for their color, residents of Watts looked and behaved like the rest of Los Angeles. Beginning with Pearl Harbor, Watts and other South Central neighborhoods became blacker, less middle class, poorer, and quite southern. Fewer of its residents were Methodist and more were Pentecostal. It lost its middle class and its skilled, unionized workers. Its nightclubs employed many more rhythm and blues than jazz musicians, and its churches featured gospel blues rather than choral hymns. Walking down Central Avenue, visitors were as likely to be accosted by gamblers and pimps as by preachers and social workers. From a suburb in Beverly Hills, Santa Monica, Pasadena, or even West Jefferson and Crenshaw Avenue, South Central appeared to have fallen into irreparable decay. It had become a racial ghetto and a social slum.

Poor migrants from the South, like Easy Rawlins, saw South Central differently. For the disenfranchised poor, South Central was the gateway to the Promised Land of upward mobility, economic security, and political and legal equality. In Watts, the dispossessed of the South found sanctuary, fellow travelers, comfortable and familiar surroundings, and opportunity. They also confronted a hostile police. Tellingly, of the 3,438 adults arrested during the 1965 Watts riot, 2,057 had been born in the South.[136]

ONLY IN LA

Following the riot, for the next fifteen years almost no new businesses opened in Watts and few of the burned-out businesses reopened. Middle-class homeowners, like Easy Rawlins and Alvin Ailey, left in despair, making Watts and neighboring Compton even more ghettoized. In 1992, when Los Angeles again erupted into violence over the brutal, videotaped police beating of Rodney King, most observers shook their heads at what they saw as a replay of the 1965 Watts riot. In thirty years, seemingly, nothing had changed in East LA or in the LAPD. The Rodney King riot, however, was much larger. It resulted in 16,000 arrests compared to only about 3,000 in 1965, billions of dollars in damages compared to only fifty million earlier, and fifty-two deaths compared to thirty-four in the Watts riot. The land of plenty seemed cursed. But for those who looked closely, after 1965 a profound change had occurred in Watts.[137]

Most rioters in 1992 were Hispanic, not black.[138] The Rodney King riot was a Hispanic, not an African American riot, just as Watts, and indeed all of South Central LA, was no longer African American, but Hispanic. One of the most important social revolutions in the turbulent social history of Los Angeles had taken place in the two decades following the Watts riot. In 1965 Congress enacted the Hart-Cellar Immigration Act that liberalized immigration restrictions against Hispanics and Asians. Asians and Hispanics poured into Los Angeles. At the same time, economic prosperity and enforcement of federal civil rights in the South brought to a close the African American migration out of the South. According to the 2000 federal census, Los Angeles had changed from a predominantly white community with a large and rapidly growing African American minority, to a Hispanic-Asian community, with a large but dwindling white and black minority. While numerous and growing in number, newly arrived Hispanics were the poorest ethnic group in Los Angeles. Recent Mexican and other Latin American immigrants filled the city's lowest-paid and most-menial jobs. They also occupied the poorest neighborhoods in Los Angeles and filled the city's public housing complexes, including those in Watts.[139]

Hispanic children performed poorly in school, dropped out early, and failed to learn "proper" English. They also committed most of the city's crimes, and many of its children were born out of wedlock. Watts continued to suffer from drug and alcohol abuse as well as personal and domestic violence. The predominantly black police officers, who patrolled Watts, enforced the department's long-term, tough-love policy of containment, harassment, and random brutality. Most of Watts's Holiness and Sanctified Baptist churches now bore Spanish names and conducted their services in Spanish, as did the neighborhood's newly organized Catholic churches. Store signs bore Spanish names and advertisements of small, family-owned restaurants that featured enchiladas rather than barbecue and fried chicken Its young people continued to dress in bright, attention-grabbing styles and colors, but with a decided Hispanic flare. Even Watts's infamous "gangsta rap" came in Hispanic versions.[140]

After 1945, Watts ceased being a middle-class community. Instead, it became a migrant and then an immigrant way station. The memoirs of Watts's jazz men, collected by UCLA in the 1990s, make that clear. When they grew up, before World War II, Watts offered them a wonderful, near-middle-class life. Racially diverse, it boasted good schools, suffered little crime, and most of its children were born in Los Angeles and aspired to attend UCLA. After the war, Los Angeles built most of the city's public housing projects in or near Watts. The crime rate escalated, illegitimacy soared, and schools deteriorated. Sanctified Baptist and Holiness churches replaced staid, middle-class congregations, and barbecue shacks and blues joints proliferated. Southerners replaced Californians, and the LAPD treated Watts as a foreign, territorial possession, filled with intractable aliens, alien both to William Parker and to his black, West Side protégé Tom Bradley. Social scientists wrung their hands at the neighborhood's dysfunctional families, the violence and crime, its drug addiction and prostitution, its abysmal schools. Legendary Jefferson High School music teacher Sam Browne observed, "In the late fifties. I could see it in my classes. I could see it all around me. I could see it in the student body. I could see it in what I had to work with, their waning interests and waning motivation. So I said, 'Well, it's time to make a change. It's time to move on to some other ground.' "[141] Judged from such a middle-class perspective, Watts and South Central seemed embarrassing social failures, grist for reformers' mills, nearly as dismal as the Lower East Side immigrant slums in nineteenth-century New York.[142]

Mississippi-born jazz man Gerald Wilson offered a different take. "Don't cry for South Central. We got what we wanted." So did tens of thousands of other southern blacks. In South Central, southern migrants found a home and a neighborhood full of friendly, even familiar faces. But it was not the South, and it was not a community. Migrants came to South Central as their first stop on their way to middle-class America. Many migrants remained and died in South Central. Most did not, and almost all their children left, acquiring a home in West Los Angeles or even in the regions' distant "Inland Empire." So rapid was the in- and out-migration that from year to year residents on a single block or in a single public housing unit in Watts might completely change, even students in a school class might be entirely different from one year to the next. Teachers came and went, social workers turned over quickly, police transferred out at the first opportunity, ministers organized churches and then moved them to West Jefferson or West Adams, businesses opened and closed in rapid succession, and Walter Mosley went off to college in Vermont and Alvin Ailey to New York's Upper West Side.[143]

From day to day, little remained the same except the poverty, the violence, the crime, the newness of the migrants, and their restless, ruthless energy. As fast as migrants arrived, older settlers left. Until 1970, black arrivals from the South outnumbered black departures, making it difficult to grasp the amazing success that South Central migrants achieved. Understandably, public attention focused on South Central's failures, the large number of individuals who had succumbed to drugs, alcohol, prostitution, crime, and depression. The federal census of 1990 and 2000 revealed another South Central. By 2000, 90 percent of the more than quarter of a million black southern migrants who came to South Central after World War II had left, many to middle-class neighborhoods such as West Adams, others for jobs out of Los Angeles and California, and even more back to the South, taking with them the wealth and the education acquired in South Central.[144]

Even more strikingly than in New York or Pittsburgh or Chicago, the story of the migration to Los Angeles revealed the meaning of the Great Migration. After World War I, black southerners created economically self-sufficient, politically vibrant, and culturally rich neighborhoods in the cities of the North and West. Working-class and "down-home" cities within cities—Harlem, Bronzeville, the Hill, and South Central—offered African Americans social and cultural way stations on their journey out of the South. But, as Los Angeles dramatically demonstrated, the Great Migration was never just to a place. Rather, it had always been the American middle-class dream, a destination that most African Americans, thankfully, have now reached.[145]

CIRCLE UNBROKEN

•10•

Three Stories and a Conclusion

The Great Migration began in earnest with World War I. During World War II, black migration out of the South peaked and sustained that level through the 1950s. At the end of the 1960s migration slowed dramatically, and by the 1980s it had ended. It is impossible to know precisely how many African Americans left the South to live in the North and West. Census data indicate only who answered the census taker's knock. Many migrants came and left between census years. According to the census, more than three million black southerners left the South after 1910 to take up long-term residence in the cities of the North and West. At least as many rural blacks moved to southern cities. Very likely, another three to four million left the South, lived in the North for several years, and either returned to the South or moved to another northern or western city.[1]

Before the twentieth century, virtually all African Americans lived in the South. Most were uneducated, disenfranchised, rural sharecroppers or farm tenants. By 2000, almost all African Americans lived in cities and half of these outside the South. A majority had earned high school degrees, about one in ten had graduated from college, and almost none earned their livings in agriculture. This was also true of rural, white southerners. In the twentieth century, the transformation of southern farming, from labor-intensive peasant agriculture to highly mechanized commercial farming, affected all agricultural workers. Like other southern migrants who left the impoverished, southern countryside, the lives of African Americans fundamentally changed. They found opportunities for themselves and their children unimaginable to their parents and grandparents. In the twentieth century, African Americans acquired formal education, gainful employment, civil rights, and political access, even power. None of this came easy. At every step, they confronted opposition.

By the end of the Great Migration, African Americans bore a dual legacy. They dominated American popular music and high profile intercollegiate and professional sports. African Americans influenced American dress, food, and language. A large, black middle class prospered, claiming the rewards made possible by improved education and economic opportunity. At the same time, many African Americans remained poor and uneducated, isolated in America's desolate inner cities where public school systems had imploded and legitimate employment was nonexistent. Today, millions of the children and grandchildren of southern migrants confront futures as dismal as their sharecropping and slave ancestors. While large in number and highly visible, even so they represent a minority of African Americans. The black population of Pittsburgh's Hill District, for example, had been fifty thousand in 1958. By 2000 only fifteen thousand, mostly poor and underemployed African Americans, remained. Yet, as in slavery and in the Jim Crow South, even in the bleakest inner city ward, African Americans find solace and joy in their West African–rooted religion and music.

METAMORPHOSIS

In 1923 Houston artist John Biggers was born in Gastonia, North Carolina, the son of Cora and Paul Biggers, themselves the children of slaves. Educated at a missionary-run school, John Biggers's father taught school, repaired shoes, and served as a Baptist minister. At age thirteen, John's father died; his mother took a job at a nursing home; and John and his brother enrolled in Lincoln Academy, a boarding school run by the American Missionary Society for Negro boys. A star student, John made the honor roll at Lincoln every semester and in 1941 entered Hampton Institute in Virginia, the model for Booker T. Washington's Tuskegee Institute. Hampton's motto was "head, hand, and heart." Not wanting to become a cobbler or a minister, John enrolled in art classes taught by Victor Lowenfield, a Holocaust survivor from Nazi Germany. A socialist, Lowenfield taught his students to paint in a social realist style popular in the 1930s. At Lowenfield's urging, young Biggers painted portraits of "suffering" southern blacks.[2]

In 1949 Biggers accepted a faculty appointment at Texas Southern University in Houston's Third Ward. As chairman of the Texas Southern art department, Biggers encouraged his students to paint "their communities," by which he meant black Texas. In the early fifties, Biggers received the Neiman Marcus Prize for the best drawing by a Houston artist. When the Houston Fine Arts Museum realized Biggers was black, it canceled his reception, allowing him only to view the exhibit privately. In 1951 Biggers accepted a commission to paint a large mural for the Third Ward's Blue Triangle Colored YWCA entitled, "Contributions of Negro Women to American life and Education." The "Negro Women" mural stood solidly in the American Scene painting tradition of suffering but noble subjects.[3] Except for their clothing and skin color, the women could have easily been oppressed but noble women anywhere in the world. Only in color were the women African American.[4]

In 1957 John Biggers accepted a UNESCO fellowship to study in Dahomey (Benin after 1960) and the newly independent nation of Ghana—the West African ancestral lands of many African Americans. Overwhelmed by the richness and vitality of West Africa, Biggers reacted to everything—the colorful umbrellas, the exquisitely woven cloth, the water, women's combs, ceremonial masks, village dances, and the vibrant tropical colors, especially the reds and blues. Everywhere he looked he saw faces that he had grown up with in North Carolina. He met basket makers, drummers, dancers, skilled net makers, singers, and even young people who respected their elders. Most of all, he encountered a sculptural tradition that drew on the symbols of West African culture.

On his return in 1962, Biggers published *Ananse*, an artistic reflection on his experience in Ghana.[5] "Ananse is the spider," wrote Biggers. "He [God] taught him architecture, the structure of dwellings, and the structure of life and society. . . . [H]is web stands for the sun, its rays, and the sun personifies God."[6] Biggers explained how in Ghana, a shared culture connected everything. Everyone had a place and a function, and everyone looked out for one another. *Ananse* contained about eighty drawings that included a Fanti boat, a fishing village, yams, a potter, children, market scenes, women dancers, a parade, Yoruba masks, and priests. While Biggers used cultural symbols, he depicted them in a social realist style. His West African works differed from his earlier art only in cultural details and the absence of victims. He presented Ghanaians in traditional clothing, a people who lived composed and dignified lives within village communities that they controlled. For African Americans, who lived in Houston's Third Ward, Biggers's West African drawings could just as well have been of Martians. His drawings failed to connect the Third Ward to West Africa. His trip to West Africa had changed him but not his art.[7]

Fifteen years after his return from Ghana, Biggers attended a traveling exhibition of African sculpture and carvings called *Art of the Dogan*, at the Houston Museum of Fine Arts. The Dogan exhibit transformed Biggers's art. Immediately after studying the Dogan sculptures, he began an ambitious mural, "Family Unity," for the newly constructed Texas Southern Student Union. The mural included a panel entitled *Metamorphosis: Birth and Rebirth*. This panel was as much about Biggers as about African Americans. Adopting the symbolism of the Dogan, Biggers addressed African American issues through highly stylized, West

African symbols. Students, who ascended the stairway that overlooked the mural, expressed a sense of spiritual fulfillment.[8]

At age fifty, everything that Biggers painted seemed fresh, powerful, and relevant. He no longer painted scenes of striving but victimized African Americans or of noble but traditional Ghanaians. Instead, Biggers underpinned Houston's Third Ward with its ancient West African heritage. His art helped his students and other Third Ward African American residents to understand who they were, where they had come from, and the richness of their past. Biggers's artistic transformation allowed African Americans, who had not visited Ghana, to share his experience. His mural enabled others to see beyond the details of their all-too-familiar and mundane lives. By transforming their vision, he opened the possibility for them to transform their lives. Like the circle, mask, and drums of Ghana, Biggers's art was magical.

Metamorphosis was only the beginning. In the next fifteen years, Bigger painted the most powerful works of his career. He evolved from being a good, hardworking, earnest artist into a great twentieth-century painter. His symbolic *Upper Room* (1984), *Wheel in Wheel* (1986), and *Climbing High Mountains* (1886) connected ancient West Africa to African America. From 1986 to 1989, he completed a series of Texas paintings that infused well-known vernacular objects and events, such as patchwork quilts, Sanctified spirituals, full-immersion baptism, and shotgun houses, with West African images and symbols. Biggers gave these everyday African American things new meaning and value.

Biggers's 1987 paintings of Houston shotgun houses made this clear. On the porch of each of three shotgun houses in *Shotguns, Third Ward,* a black woman stood barefoot. Adorned with a West African hairdo and dress, each of the three female figures held a net and each wore a cowrie shell necklace and earrings. Biggers separated the shacks from the viewer by a modern railroad track that stretched across the bottom of the canvas. Behind the three shotguns, as far as the eye could see, stood rows and rows of other shotguns, over which flew five white doves. Biggers composed a companion painting, *Shotguns, Fourth Ward,* in a similar manner with a railroad track across the bottom of the painting. The front row of *Fourth Ward,* however, featured five black women, not in West African costume, but in simple cotton housedresses common among African American women in Houston. Beside each woman sat a laundry basket that held a familiar washboard and a water jug.

Each of the five priestess-like but American figures bore in their arms a dollhouse-size white shotgun or praise house. In this set of paintings, Biggers meshed West Africa with Houston's Third and Fourth wards and the North Carolina of his

John Biggers's Houston: Third Ward yard art, 2002 (Will Scott)

parents. He made it visually impossible to separate one painting from the other or to understand one without the other. Biggers explained, "I told myself, hey, I've got to show this whole community as it is with women on the porches. . . . It came to me . . . you're painting shotgun blocks, their own special concept, all the houses of the past, all the houses of the future, just let it roll."[9] Art historian Robert Farris Thompson described Biggers's remarkable set of shotgun paintings as "American Kongo." Thompson argued that Biggers had imagined "a new America" that pushed "up from the depths of its architecture, plural and rich, at the dawn of a universal nation."[10]

HOLY SPIRIT REVIVAL

Goodwill AME in Mount Pleasant, South Carolina, is quite likely the oldest, independent black church in the South. Its historian, Janette Gaillard Lee, traced its origins to the last decades of slavery. In 1830 a Low Country mapmaker labeled it "Independent Church." In 1881 the Goodwill congregation purchased eighteen acres from the Gregory family, giving the congregation legal title to land it had worshiped on for a half century. Until the 1930s, Goodwill's Gullah congregants had buried their dead in unmarked graves near their homes on plantation land purchased after the Civil War. In response to state burial regulations, between 1931 and 1979 Goodwill families buried their dead in the cemetery of Olive Branch AME, located to the south on the Old Georgetown Road, or in Mount Pleasant's Ocean Grove Cemetery. In 1979, when Goodwill replaced its white, log chapel with a white cement-block sanctuary, it included a cemetery. According to Lee, at local funerals until the 1960s, Gullah families passed infants across the bodies of the dead, placed coins in coffins, sang spirituals at gravesites, and blanketed graves with sun-bleached conch shells as well as broken personal items of the deceased. As in Mount Pleasant's Oak Grove Cemetery, they buried their dead facing east. Since the 1960s, Lee reported that many of the older Gullah practices had disappeared.[11]

A historian of the Mount Pleasant sweet-grass basket makers dates the disappearance of Gullah burial practices to a revival at Goodwill AME that took place from 1959 to 1960.[12] After the revival, many young congregants at Goodwill found its services overly formal and staid. They lacked the personal warmth and emotional intensity of earlier times. They thought that the services at Goodwill resembled AME services in Charleston and Mount Pleasant. Several revivalists left Goodwill to meet in the home of Marie Rivers for prayer meetings. The meetings attracted enough people for Rivers to form a new church, the Garden of Prayer Pentecostal-Holiness Church. Because the Memphis-based, Pentecostal Church, the Church of God in Christ, did not allow female ministers, Rivers affiliated with a Harlem-based Pentecostal church. The new Pentecostal church found itself the object of local ridicule for speaking in tongues, Holy Spirit healing, loud shouting during the service, boisterous music, and full-immersion baptisms. Critics called congregants "Holy Rollers" and "Tongue Rollers." Many Goodwill basket makers joined the Garden of Prayer, including Alfred Jefferson, then training to become a veterinarian, who had received his ministerial training at a Pentecostal seminary in Thompsonville, New York. Today, the Garden of Prayer occupies a modern, air-conditioned church on U.S. Highway 17. It serves a congregation of more than two hundred, prosperous and educated families, most of them nearby residents of Hamlin community and many descendants of Gullah slaves.[13]

When Bishop Rivers retired, Alfred Jefferson became the bishop of Garden of Prayer. The services conducted by Bishop Jefferson were intense. A service in the summer of 2001 began when a small group of women formed at the front of the church to sing a cappella an old Gullah spiritual.[14] Alerted, worshipers filed in, many women dressed in white and the male church elders in suits and ties. The all-black congregation stood and clapped rhythmically to a drum cadence. Shortly after, the organ joined the drum at which point the church elders and the robed choir took their places at the front of the sanctuary. When the music paused, a male elder read from the Bible. A female elder followed him and announced upcoming events. Led by the organist, the music quickened and Bishop Jefferson arrived. At the front of the church, Jefferson led the congregation in a rousing song, accompanied by the drum, a guitar, a piano, the organ, the robed choir, and the congregation, standing, swaying, clapping.

Jefferson welcomed his congregation. The elders instructed everyone to walk to the front of the sanctuary and place their offering in a large, sweet-grass basket. When everyone returned to their seats, the bishop asked visitors to stand, introduce themselves, and identify their home church. Several were white. The bishop began his sermon by reading a passage from the Bible. At first, he spoke in a quiet, conversational tone. About half way through, his voice became more intense and chantlike. The organist and drummer softly joined in as, one by one, the congregation stood, raised their arms, swayed from side to side in unison, praised Jesus, and acknowledged the presence of the Holy Spirit. As the emotional level rose, individual members spoke in tongues, a few started to shake, and one or two fell into a trance and were eased to the floor by an elder. Between the sermon, the music, the choir's clapping and singing, and the participation of the congregation, the service assumed a hypnotic state that swept over everyone.

Sensing the departure of the Holy Spirit, Jefferson lowered his voice and slowed his cadence. The musicians and choir followed his lead and lowered their intensity. One by one, worshipers resumed their seats, exhausted. In a quiet voice, Jefferson offered a prayer and thanked the Holy Spirit. In the after-wash of ecstasy, worshipers looked around and smiled at one another. The bishop praised the congregation and asked those present to shake hands and hug one another in an embrace of Christian love. With warmth, visitors hugged and were hugged as each praised Jesus and thanked the Holy Spirit. After the bishop ended the service, he waited at the door, with his wife, to greet the congregants individually as they left. For all who attended, the three-hour long service at the Garden of Prayer was the most important event of their week. Renewed, everyone, it seemed, looked forward to the new week with joy and resolution, purged of their frustrations and anger, filled with happiness and love. The Pentecostal term, "amazing grace," seemed apt.

In an interview, Jefferson explained that Garden of Prayer sponsored community outreach programs to feed the poor, to counsel married couples, and to work with those who suffered from alcohol or drug addiction as well as a prison outreach program. To an outside observer, several things stood out—the apparent prosperity and well-being of the church's members and their generosity to the church. It was not simply spiritual but also socially active and deeply rooted in the Hamlin community. Compared to their parents, the congregants had prospered in the post–Jim Crow Carolina Low Country. And compared to Friendship AME, its mother church, services at the Garden of Prayer were lively and informal. It offered music that would have brought audiences at the Apollo Theater to their feet. Most of all, church members believed that the Holy Spirit directly intervened

Getting the spirit, healing service, Ho, Ghana, 2007 (Peter Rutkoff)

in their lives. Without the Holy Spirit's vibrant presence, few would have come to the Garden of Prayer. Worshipers believed fervently that the Holy Spirit not only possessed them but spoke in tongues through them, and at times it healed them of their troubles and medical disorders. Church members embraced the magical powers of the Holy Spirit. West African in ancestry and proud of their Gullah heritage, nonetheless this modern, Low Country Pentecostal congregation sustained an unrelenting crusade against root doctors, Satan, and black magic. Members also maintained a praise house. They sewed sweet-grass baskets, wove traditional cast nets, and made quilts in the West African way. They buried their dead facing east. They painted the trim on their houses in blue or green to ward off "haunts." They celebrated Watch Night on December 31, and they ate Hoppin' John, yams, and collard greens on New Year's Day.

From the perspective of Charleston, these churches seem rural and traditional, a holdover from slavery. From the perspective of the Hamlin community, they are proponents of a modern, reform Christianity that directly involves itself in the personal lives of its members and the world in which they live and work. While they embrace the spiritualism of West African religion, they reject those aspects of West African and Gullah culture that they consider self-destructive and pagan. The Garden of Prayer emphasizes sexual chastity and the sanctity of marriage, and it rejects the use of drugs and alcohol and all forms of spiteful behavior, including black magic. Much like the eighteenth- and nineteenth-century Great

Awakenings, the twentieth-century Pentecostal Revival reinvigorated southern Protestantism even as it transformed and modernized it. Within Christianity, Pentecostalism, more than any other church, addresses the problems and concerns of the urban poor, and many, like the Garden of Prayer, do so without regard to race, gender, or social class. With antecedents in slavery, Pentecostalism looks at the world from the viewpoint of the poor, disenfranchised, and dispossessed. As important as Pentecostalism has become in the United States, it has been even more important in the West Indies, Brazil, Korea, and Ghana. Globally, for many, Pentecostalism is God's way.[15]

WEST AFRICAN PENTECOST

On June 22, 2007, in a remote rural village in Ghana, a Presbyterian minister conducted an open-air church service. Dressed in a purple shirt with a bleached, white collar, like the other Presbyterian ministers of the region, he was West African. Ethnically Ewe, his skin glistened in the sunlight. The German-based, Evangelical Presbyterian Church, of which he is a member, has provided ministerial training to this region of Ghana for more than a century. Bremen village, located about five miles from Ho, the regional capital of the Volta region, supports an agricultural demonstration farm and the small outdoor chapel. This year, the staff at Ho Farms taught local farmers how to cultivate snails. An American philanthropist and food-agriculturalist recommended these protein-rich animals as part of an initiative to train Ghanaian farmers in sustainable agriculture. Americans present at the service were also Presbyterian, residents of a prosperous farming region in Ohio famed for its equally flourishing Amish community.

Ho Farms, the sole employer in Bremen village, is a compound of a half-dozen buildings. Some serve as dormitories, others rabbit hutches, and some as barns for farm machinery and implements. It has also become a cultural center for residents of the nearby provincial city of Ho. On this late June day, at least a hundred Ghanaians gathered on Ho Farms to attend the outdoor service. They dressed eclectically. Some wore Ewe-inspired kente cloth, others sported American t-shirts that read "Kerry for President" or "THE Ohio State University," and others mixed and matched traditional with modern clothing. The congregants sat out-of-doors on wooden, folding-chairs scattered over an apron of stone pebbles. The sacred space, a circle cleared from the encroaching brush, was framed by a dozen tall trees that leaned toward the center of the circle, creating a natural canopy, an arbor. In pre-Christian times, the clearing had also served as a sacred meeting ground.[16]

The wooden chairs fanned out informally across the clearing. Some congregants faced the front of the clearing, some sat in small clusters with their chairs pulled up to face one other, and some situated themselves randomly. The ceremony was, at first, simple and calm. Congregants moved to the front of the clearing while several men touched the shoulders of worshipers gently. As the ritual proceeded, it gained in complexity and intensity. Simultaneously, many movements took place, all part of a larger pattern. The initial calm was only a prelude. The worship, itself, was in constant motion.

A single male drummer sat in the middle of the congregation. He played a *djembe*, a traditional Ewe ceremonial drum, tucked between his knees. His hands flew. They were so fast that it looked and sounded like several drummers playing at once. As he played, a group of six, sometimes eight, women danced. They swayed below the waist, held their arms at right angles from their torsos with their hands forehead high, and they tilted their heads first one way and then the next.

A lone woman danced, holding a tambourine. She followed the lead of the drummer by using her hands and her thighs to embellish the drumbeats. Two more female dancers appeared, one with gourds, *shekeres*, and another with a brass bell. They formed a percussion chorus. They all danced as they played— except for the drummer who remained seated, still the only male in the midst of the swirling female dancers. The dancers moved counterclockwise, from right to left. Following the drumbeat, they did not change speed or intensity. Then suddenly, one of the women raised a white handkerchief above her head and swirled it around and around. A smile spread across her face as her eyes shone. She moved in a tight circle in the center of the ring of women, who danced around her.

One of the women dancers detached herself from the group and moved to a line of plastic lawn chairs that lined the edge of the brush-arbor church. A black magic-marker identified the chairs as belonging to the EPCSR (Evangelical Presbyterian Church), on which several other women sat. One by one, they rose and stood in front of the purple-shirted priest, who had been joined by two other men, one of whom wore a white clerical shirt and collar. The third man dressed in a rumpled, bluish-purple blazer. Together, the three moved from chair to chair and placed their hands on the foreheads of the supplicants who stood before them.

This Presbyterian remnant of German imperial rule had become Africanized. The Ewe of Ho had woven a traditional West African healing ritual into a European Protestant service. In the healing service, the celebrants performed a ring shout, danced to a polyrhythmic West African drummer, and laid on priestly hands. This took place out-of-doors, in a brush arbor, itself situated on a traditional Ewe sacred ground. *Ashe*, the "power to make things happen," worked in

Bluesman Robert Junior Lockwood, musical heir to Robert Johnson, and Peter Rutkoff, Helena, Arkansas (Peter Rutkoff)

Ghana, reinvigorating German Presbyterianism as witnessed by Presbyterians from Ohio, who at home listen to Scottish bagpipes, Amish hymns, country and western music, and rap. Delta bluesman Robert Johnson would have recognized the brush arbor at Bremen village as a magical crossroads.

A NEW BIRTH OF FREEDOM

In New York, Pittsburgh, Chicago, and Los Angeles, African American migrants from the Carolina Low Country, Alabama's Mineral District, the Mississippi Delta, and Houston's black wards challenged and overcame racial discrimination in politics, the workplace, and housing. In their northern, inner-city communities, migrants built lives inspired by the communities they had left in the South. They also changed. Through their votes, southern migrants secured power in the Democratic Party, through their labor most gained economic security, and many, but not all, shed the shackles of poverty and public assistance. Until the 1970s, however, institutional and cultural segregation sheltered African Americans in the North from their white neighbors. The emergence of an autonomous African American urban culture "behind the veil" of segregation enabled African Americans, of all

A touch of "soul" on 125th Street billboard in Harlem (Will Scott)

social classes, to participate as members of these inner-city communities. In the cities of the North and West, the culture of the Great Migration altered American life.

After 1970, many African Americans turned their backs on the racially segregated, inner-city world that for decades had nurtured and confined them. Access to higher education and to economic opportunity allowed them to reject racial segregation, even as they held firm to their southern and West African heritage. Safe in the North, African American migrants and their children used their hard-won power to reconstruct the Jim Crow South. They demanded that the South dismantle its century-old system of racial apartheid and end racial violence. Because of their efforts in the South, black students gained access to the same public education available to white students, African Americans freely exercised their constitutional rights, and black workers demanded that employers hire and promote on merit, not race. By the 1980s, a large and prosperous African American middle class had reaped the benefits of the Great Migration and the civil rights movement. The newly influential black middle class, like John Biggers and Bishop Jefferson, also fostered a renewed appreciation for African American and West African culture, allowing all African Americans to take pride in their West African ancestry and culture.

In the half century after World War I, African American migrants changed the racial composition of American cities, shifted national power away from white southerners, and reconfigured American culture. By 1980 the white, sexually repressive, and class-ridden Victorian world of Woodrow Wilson had all but disappeared, a relic of another time. The arrival of African Americans from the rural and culturally isolated South into the nation's centers of culture and power set in motion changes that altered American life. African Americans in the North forced European Americans to reimagine American culture as well as American democracy.

Today, much of the global appeal of American popular culture, religion, and democracy is a consequence of the African American migration to American cities. Having confronted their racial biases and ethnic prejudices, today Americans have begun to remove the racial qualifications that have marred American democracy since its origins. The twentieth-century flowering of African American culture and African American enfranchisement outside the South forced all Americans to reconsider the nation's ideals and unequivocally to reaffirm human freedom and equality. For nearly four centuries, a white male country, today the United States aspires to universal human equality and liberty. No longer for "whites only," because of the Great Migration Americans can dream and "fly away" home to a more humane future.

NOTES

CHAPTER 1: OUT OF AFRICA: WEST AFRICAN ORIGINS

1. Rev. R. H. Strong, *In Africa's Forest and Jungle: Of Six Years among the Yorubans* (New York, 1899), 20, 21, 23.

2. Robert Farris Thomson, *Flash of the Spirit: African and Afro-American Art and Philosophy* (New York, 1984).

3. Robert Farris Thompson, "West African Art and Dance" (Kenyon College, Fall 2001). See also the catalog *Le Geste Kongo* that Thompson curated at the Musée Dapper, Paris, 2002–2003. The authors thank Thompson for his notification of the exhibit that they subsequently attended.

4. R. G. Armstrong, "African Religion and Cultural Renewal," *Orta* 9 (1998). See also H. Abrahamsson, *The Origin of Death: Studies in African Mythology* (Uppsala, 1951).

5. Steven Barbosa, *The Door of No Return* (New York, 1994); Maria Diedrich, Henry Louis Gates, and Carl Pedersen, eds., *Black Imagination and the Middle Passage* (New York, 1999).

6. Melville Herskovits, *The Myth of the Negro Past* (Boston, 1990); Sterling Stuckey, *Slave Culture: Nationalist Theory and the Foundations of Black America* (New York, 1987); Sylvia Frey and Betty Wood, *Come Shouting to Zion: African American Protestantism in the American South and the British Caribbean* (Chapel Hill, N.C., 1998); Albert Raboteau, *Slave Religion: The "Invisible Institution" in the Antebellum South* (New York, 1978); Mechal Sobel, *The World They Made Together: Black and White Values in Eighteenth-Century Virginia* (Princeton, 1987); John Thornton, *Africa and Africans in the Making of the Atlantic World, 1400–1680* (New York, 1998); Ira Berlin, *Many Thousands Gone: The First Two Centuries of Slavery in North America* (Cambridge, Mass., 1998); Michael Gomez, *Exchanging Our Country Marks: The Transformation of African Identities in the Colonial and Antebellum Souths* (Chapel Hill, N.C., 1998); Lawrence Levine, *Black Culture and Black Consciousness: Afro-American Folk Thought from Slavery to Freedom* (New York, 1977).

7. Joseph Holloway, *Africanisms in American Culture* (Bloomington, Ind., 2005), and John Michael Vlach, *The Afro-American Tradition in Decorative Arts* (Cleveland, Ohio, 1978).

8. Vlach.

9. Interview with Divine Gbagbo and Francis Dzormeku, Ho, Ghana, June 27, 2006.

10. Interview with Preston Smith, Tutwiler, Mississippi, October 2001.

11. Joyce Coakley, *Sweetgrass Baskets and the Gullah Tradition* (Mount Pleasant, S.C., 2006).

12. Interview with William Lowry, Chicago, March, 2002.

13. Paul Lawrence Dunbar, *The Collected Poetry of Paul Lawrence Dunbar*, ed. Joanne M. Braxton (Charlottesville, Va., 1993).

14. See Howard Sacks and Judy Sacks, *Way Up North in Dixie* (Champaign, Ill., 1995).

15. Ladislas Sagy, *The Masks of Black Africa* (New York, 1975), and Laurie Meyer, *Black African Masks, Sculpture, and Jewelry* (Paris, 1973).

16. Robert Farris Thompson, "An Aesthetic of the Cool," in Gena Dagel Caponi, ed., *Signifyin(g), Sanctifyin', & Slam Dunking* (Amherst, Mass., 1999).

17. Interview with Dickson Asase, Ho, Ghana, June 29, 2007. See also R. B. Fisher, *West African Religious Traditions: Focus on the Akan of Ghana* (Los Angeles, Calif., 1998).

18. See, for example, Samuel Floyd, *The Power of Black Music* (New York, 1995); Stuckey.

19. Asase interview, Ho, Ghana, June 29, 2007. Stuckey.

20. Stuckey; A. Adegbite, "The Drum and Its Role in Yoruba Religion," *Journal of Religion in Africa* 18 (1988).

21. Jaqui Malone, *Steppin' on the Blues* (Urbana, Ill., 1996), 27.

22. Gena Davis Caponi, "The Case for an African American Aesthetic," in Caponi, *Signifyin'*, 11. See also John Blacking, *How Musical Is Man?* (Seattle, Wash., 1973).

23. Raboteau; Frey and Wood.

24. See Albert Murray, *Stompin' the Blues* (New York, 1976).

25. John Blacking, "Songs, Dances, Mimes, and Symbolism," *African Studies* 28, no. 1 (1969).

26. Michael T. Coolen, "Senegambian Influences on Afro-American Musical Culture," *Black Music Research Journal* 11, no. 2 (1991); "All Night Long," Junior (David) Kimbrough, *All Night Long*, Fat Possum Records, 1995. We spent a day (and night) with Kenny Kimbrough, the drummer-nephew of Junior Kimbrough, at their juke joint in Holly Springs, Mississippi, only six months before fire destroyed the structure in 2000.

27. Holloway. The wealth and depth of Holloway's neo-Herskovitsian perspective complements the powerful influences of Thompson and Stuckey on our work in *Fly Away*.

28. Philip Curtin, *The Atlantic Slave Trade: A Census* (Madison, 1969).

29. Berlin, *Many Thousands Gone*.

CHAPTER 2: NEW AFRICA: SOUTH CAROLINA LOW COUNTRY

1. Shailagh Murray, "A Family Tree Rooted in American Soil," *Washington Post*, October 2, 2008, p. C01 (washingtonpost.com).

2. Peter Wood, *Black Majority: Negroes in Colonial South Carolina from 1670 to the Stono Rebellion* (New York, 1974); Donald Dodd and Wynelle Dodd, *Historical Statistics of the South, 1790–1970* (Tuscaloosa, 1973); George Devlin, *South Carolina and Black Migration, 1865–1940* (New York, 1989).

3. South Carolina Writers' Project, *South Carolina: A Guide to the Palmetto State* (New York, 1941), 8–22.

4. Alexander S. Salley Jr., ed., *Narratives of Early Carolina, 1650–1707* (New York, 1911).

5. M. Eugene Sirmans, *Colonial South Carolina: A Political History, 1663–1763* (Chapel Hill, N.C., 1966); Richard S. Dunn, *Sugar and Slavery: The Rise of the Planter Class in the*

English West Indies, 1624–1713 (New York, 1972) and "The English Sugar Islands and the Founding of South Carolina," *South Carolina History and Genealogical Magazine* 72 (1971); Daniel C. Littlefield, *Rice and Slaves: Ethnicity and the Slave Trade in Colonial South Carolina* (Urbana, Ill., 1991); Verner W. Crane, *The Southern Frontier, 1670–1732* (Ann Arbor, 1956). Judith A. Carney, in *Black Rice: The African Origins of Rice Cultivation in the Americas* (Cambridge, Mass., 2001), makes a compelling argument in favor of the African origins and meanings of Low Country rice.

6. Carney.

7. Wesley Frank Craven, *The Southern Colonies in the Seventeenth Century* (Baton Rouge, 1949), 310–360; Peter A. Coclanis, *The Shadow of a Dream: Economic Life and Death in the South Carolina Low Country, 1670–1920* (New York, 1989), 3–111; Lewis C. Gray, *History of Agriculture in the Southern United States to 1860* (New York: 1969 [1933]), 1:277–293; A. S. Salley Jr., "The Introduction of Rice Culture into South Carolina," *Bulletin of the Historical Commission of South Carolina,* no. 6 (Columbia, S.C, 1919).

8. Philip D. Morgan, *Slave Counterpoint: Black Culture in the Eighteenth-Century Chesapeake & Lowcountry* (Chapel Hill, N.C., 1998).

9. Wim Klooster and Alfred Padula, *The Atlantic World: Essays on Slavery, Migration, and Imagination* (Upper Saddle River, N.J., 2005). The book also contains a good bibliography on Atlantic slave trade and its impact.

10. Ibid. and Littlefield.

11. Michael A. Gomez, *Exchanging Our Country Marks: The Transformation of African Identities in the Colonial and Antebellum South* (Chapel Hill, N.C., 1998), 1–37; Philip D. Curtin, *Atlantic Slave Trade: A Census* (Madison, Wis. 1969); John Thornton, *Africa and Africans in the Making of the Atlantic World, 1400–1800,* 2d ed. (Cambridge, 1998); Herbert S. Klein, *The Atlantic Slave Trade* (Cambridge, 2000).

12. Sterling Stuckey, *Slave Culture: Nationalist Theory and the Foundations of Black America* (New York, 1987); Joseph E. Holloway, ed., *Africanisms in American Culture* (Bloomington, Ind., 2005), 18–38.

13. Gomez, 154–185; Paul E. Lovejoy, "Trans-Atlantic Transformations: The Origins and Identity of Africans in the Americas," in Klooster and Padula.

14. Wood, *Black Majority,* 63–166.

15. Edward Ball, *Slaves in the Family* (New York, 1998), 88–109; Wood, *Black Majority,* 95–130.

16. Charles Joyner, *Down by the Riverside: A South Carolina Slave Community* (Urbana, Ill., 1984), 1–89, 196–124; Stuckey, 3–97.

17. Ira Berlin, *Many Thousands Gone: The First Two Centuries of Slavery in North America* (Cambridge, Mass., 1998), 15–28, 64–76, 142–176.

18. Gomez; Albert Raboteau, *Canaan Land: A Religious History of African Americans* (New York, 2001); Peter H. Wood, *Strange New Land: Africans in Colonial America* (New York, 2003).

19. Ira Berlin, "From Creole to African: Atlantic Creoles and the Origins of African-American Society in Mainland North America," *William and Mary Quarterly,* 3rd ser., 53 (1996).

20. Gomez, 14–153; Stuckey, 3–97; Robert Raboteau, *Slave Religion: The "Invisible" Institution in the Antebellum South* (New York, 1978), 3–94.

21. United States, Works Progress Administration, *Slave Narratives: From the Federal Writers Project; South Carolina*, 2 (Washington, D.C., 1936–1938); Savannah Unit, Georgia Writers' Project, *Drums and Shadows: Survival Studies among the Georgia Coastal Negroes* (Athens, 1986 [1940c]). While colony and later state boundaries separated the slaves and African Americans of the Carolina and Georgia Low Country, they are culturally indistinguishable. All came largely from present-day Sierra Leone and Angola, and all speak the same Gullah language and share a common culture. In Georgia, such African Americans are called "Geechees," meaning "rice-eaters," and in Carolina, "Gullah." The Gullah cultural region runs along the coast from Jacksonville, North Carolina (near the South Carolina–North Carolina state line) to Jacksonville, Florida. See Joseph A. Opala, *The Gullah*, a pamphlet published by the National Park Service (2000).

22. Lorenzo D. Turner, *Africanisms in the Gullah Dialect* (Chicago, 1949); Margaret Washington Creel, *"A Peculiar People": Slave Religion and Community—Culture among the Gullahs* (New York, 1988); William S. Pollitzer, *The Gullah People and Their African Heritage* (Athens, 1999); Mary A. Twining and Keith E. Baird, eds., *Sea Island Roots: African Presence in the Carolinas and Georgia* (Trenton, N.J., 1991); Joyner.

23. Floyd White, St. Simons Island, in Georgia WPA, *Drums and Shadows*, 185; Malcolm Bell Jr., *Major Butler's Legacy* (Athens, 1987), 132; William D. Piersen, *Black Yankees: The Development of an Afro-American Subculture in Eighteenth Century New England* (Amherst, Mass., 1988), 75; Gomez, 115–121.

24. Pricilla McCullough, Darien, Georgia, in Georgia WPA, *Drums and Shadows*, 154.

25. Mose Brown, Tin City, in ibid., 18.

26. Because the interviewers were not Gullah speakers, they failed to accurately record what they had heard and, instead, translated it into "broken" English. Our translations record the meaning a non-Gullah speaker would have heard. Jack Tatnall, Wilmington Island, in ibid., 108; Wallace Quarterman, Darien, in ibid., 150–151. See also note 2 in chapter 8.

27. Shad Hall, Sapelo Island, in ibid., 169.

28. Floyd White, St. Simons Island, ibid., 185.

29. John S. Bassett, *Slavery in the State of North Carolina* (Baltimore, 1899), 92–93.

30. Sterling Stuckey, in *Slave Culture*, identifies the "ring shout" as the central ritual of African American slave culture, the source of ritual identity, religious behavior, music, and dance. According to Stuckey, expressions of the ring shout lay at the center of North American African civilization. Also see a similar argument in R. Raboteau, 43–94, and Cheryl Sanders, *Saints in Exile: The Holiness-Pentecostal Experience in African American Religion and Culture* (New York, 1996). Sanders ties the ring shout, healing, "speaking in tongues," and other West African religious ways to Pentecostalism.

31. Creel; Gomez, 114–292.

32. Edward King, *The Great South: A Record of Journeys* (Hartford, Conn., 1875), quoted in Joyner, 196.

33. Fredrika Bremer, *The Homes of the New World: Impressions of America* (New York, 1853), 1:394.

34. Ibid., 371.

35. Turner, 256.

36. Joyner, 196–224.

37. Ian F. Hancock, "A Provisional Comparison of the English-Based Atlantic Creoles," *Sierra Leone Language Review* 8 (1969).

38. P. E. H. Hair, "Sierra Leone Items in the Gullah Dialect of American English," *Sierra Leone Language Review* 4 (1965). See Holloway's essay, "What Africa Has Given America," in Holloway, *Africanism*, 39–64, for a summary of the linguistic research on Gullah.

39. Jerome S. Handler and JoAnn Jacoby, "Slave Names and Naming in Barbados, 1650–1830," *William and Mary Quarterly*, 3rd ser., 53 (1996).

40. Joseph A. Opala, *The Gullah: Rice Slavery, and the Sierra Leone-American Connection* (Washington, D.C., 1987).

41. William Faulkner's "The Past Is Not Dead. In Fact, It's Not Even Past," in *Requiem for a Nun* (New York, 1951), views this West African notion as "Southern."

42. Joyner, 195–224; Creel.

43. Henry William Ravenel, "Recollections of Southern Plantation Life," *Yale Review* 25 (1935).

44. Ibid., 770–777.

45. WPA, *Slave Narratives: South Carolina*, 2:11.

46. Ibid., p. 117; John Blassingame, *The Slave Community: Plantation Life in the Antebellum South* (New York, 1979), 49–148.

47. Georgia WPA, *Drums and Shadows*, 149–150.

48. Jeffrey R. Young, "Ideology and Death on a Savannah River Rice Plantation, 1833–1867: Paternalism amidst 'a Good Supply of Disease and Pain,' " *Journal of Southern History* 59 (1993); T. J. Woofter Jr., *Black Yeomanry: Life in St. Helena Island* (New York, 1930); Pollitzer.

49. Quoted in Creel, 282–283.

50. Quoted in ibid., 180–181.

51. Kenneth Little, "Political Function of the Poro," part I, *Africa: Journal of the African Institute* 35 (1965); part II, 36 (1966).

52. Charles Lyell, *A Second Visit to the United States of North America* (New York, 1855), 1: 270.

53. Bremer, 1:261–305, 330–397; Miss Forten, "Life on the Sea Islands," *Atlantic Monthly* 13 (1864); H. G. Spaulding, "Under the Palmetto," *Continental Monthly* 4 (1863); Edward L. Pierce, "The Freedmen of Port Royal," *Atlantic Monthly*, 12 (1863); Elizabeth Ware Pearson, *Letters from Port Royal, 1862–1868* (Boston, 1906); Laura Towne, *Letters and Diary of Laura M. Towne: Written from the Sea Islands of South Carolina, 1862–1884* (New York, 1912). Also see Sterling Stuckey's essay on the ring shout in *Slave Culture*.

54. Mary Maxwell, Possum Point, in Georgia WPA, *Drums and Shadows*, 143.

55. Elaine Nichols, ed., *The Last Miles of the War: African-American Homegoing Traditions* (Columbia, S.C., 1989).

56. Maxwell, in Georgia WPA, *Drums and Shadows*, 141.

57. Ibid., 92, 112, 113, 122, 125, 156, 177, 180, 184, 185.

58. William Ravanel, "Recollections of Southern Plantation Life," *Yale Review* 25 (Sum-

mer 1936); Yvonne Chireau, "Conjure and Christianity in the Nineteenth-Century: Religious Elements in African American Magic," *Religion and American Culture* 7 (1997).

59. William Francis Allen, Charles Pickard Ware, and Lucy McKim Garrison, comps., *Slave Songs of the United States* (New York, 1867); the introduction discusses the spirituals as they were sung on Saint Helena Island, South Carolina. Miles Mark Fisher, *Negro Slave Songs in the United States* (Ithaca, N.Y., 1953); Lydia Parrish, *Slave Songs of the Georgia Sea Islands* (Hatboro, Pa., 1965); Thomas Wentworth Higginson, "Negro Spirituals," *Atlantic Monthly* 21 (1867): 666–694; *Hymns for the Use of the Methodist Episcopal Church* (Cincinnati, 1870).

60. Creel, 276–302.

61. Harvey Cox, *Fire from Heaven: The Rise of Pentecostal Spiritualism and the Reshaping of Religion in the Twenty-first Century* (Reading, Mass., 1995), and Sanders, *Saints in Exile*.

62. Mamie Fields, *Lemon Swamp and Other Places: A Carolina Memoir* (New York, 1983), 244–247.

63. Bremer, 1:264.

64. George C. Rogers Jr., *Charleston in the Age of the Pinkneys* (Columbia, S.C., 1969).

65. Bremer, 1:265.

66. Bernard Powers, *Black Charlestonians: A Social History, 1822–1885* (Fayetteville, Ark., 1994), 9–35; Kenneth Greenberg, *Masters and Statesmen: The Political Culture of American Slavery* (Baltimore, 1985) and *Honor and Slavery: Lies, Duels, Noses, Masks, Dressing as Women, Gifts, Strangers, Humanitarians* (Princeton, N.J., 1996); Bertram Wyatt Brown, *Southern Honor: Ethics and Behavior in the Old South* (New York, 1982).

67. Greenberg, *Masters and Statesmen* and *Honor and Slavery*.

68. Powers, 9–35.

69. Walter J. Fraser Jr., *Charleston! Charleston! The History of a Southern City* (Columbia, S.C., 1989), 169–246; Robert N. Rosen, *A Short History of Charleston* (Columbia, S.C., 1992), 67–106; Lionel H. Kennedy, "Sentence on Denmark Vesey," in *Charged with an Attempt to Raise an Insurrection in the State of South Carolina: Preceded by an Introduction and Narrative; and, in an Appendix, A Report of the Trials of Four White Persons on Indictments for Attempting to Excite the Slaves in Insurrection* (Charleston, 1822); Michael P. Johnson, "Denmark Vesey and His Co-conspirators," *William and Mary Quarterly,* 3rd ser., 58 (2001); Douglas R. Egerton, "Forgetting Denmark Vesey: Or, Oliver Stone Meets Richard Wade," ibid.; Michael P. Johnson, "Reading Evidence," *William and Mary Quarterly,* 3rd ser., 59 (2002).

70. *Report of the Trials.*

71. Daniel Alexander Payne, *Recollections of Seventy Years* (Nashville, Tenn., 1888).

72. *United States Census, 1850* (Washington, D.C., 1851).

73. Vivian Conger, "The Widow's Might: Colonial Widows in Charleston, Baltimore, and Boston" (Ph.D. diss., Cornell University, 1998).

74. Michael P. Johnson and James L. Roark, eds., *No Chariot Let Down: Charleston's Free People of Color on the Eve of the Civil War* (New York, 1984) and *Black Masters: A Free Family of Color in the Old South* (New York, 1984); Powers, 36–72.

75. Powers, 36–72.

76. Robert Carse, *Department of the South: Hilton Head Island in the Civil War* (Hilton Head Island, S.C., 2002).

77. Joel Williamson, *After Slavery: The Negro in South Carolina during Reconstruction, 1861–1877* (Chapel Hill, N.C., 1965), 64–95.

78. Charles B. Fox, *Record of the Service of the Fifty-fifth Regiment of Massachusetts Volunteer Infantry* (Cambridge, Mass., 1868), 57.

79. Ibid., 58.

80. *Charleston Daily Courier,* March 22, 1865, quoted in Powers, 69.

81. Powers, 9–70.

82. Ibid., chap. 3.

83. George Tindall, *South Carolina Negroes, 1877–1900* (Columbia, S.C., 1952), 15–91, 291–302; Francis Butler Simkins, *Pitchfork Ben Tillman: South Carolinan* (Baton Rouge, 1944).

84. Tindall, 233–259.

85. Charles S. Johnson, ed., *Statistical Atlas of Southern Counties: Listing and Analysis of Socio-Economic Indices of 1104 Southern Counties* (Chapel Hill, N.C., 1941), 194–204.

86. Devlin, 59–108.

87. U.S. Census, *United States Census, South Carolina: Beaufort, Georgetown, Colleton, and Charleston Counties* (Washington, D.C., 1941).

88. Charleston, South Carolina, Freedmen's Bureau Papers, National Archives, Washington, D.C; Peggy G. Harris and Patrick M. Horan, " 'The Low Country Advantage' for African-Americans in Georgia, 1880–1930," *Journal of Interdisciplinary History* 28 (1997).

89. Williamson, 33–58.

90. Woofter.

91. Willie Lee Rose, *Rehearsal for Reconstruction: The Port Royal Experiment* (New York, 1967); Williamson, 54–63.

92. R. N. Scott et al., eds., *War of the Rebellion: A Compilation of the Official Records of the Union and Confederate Armies* (Washington, D.C., 1880–1891), ser.1, XLVII, part 2, pp. 60–62.

93. Williamson, 62–95; Towne; and Pearson.

94. One of the rare examples is the plat for the Hamlin Gullah community, drawn up in 1881. Elizabeth Hamlin McConnell, Mount Pleasant, South Carolina.

95. Information about these negotiated settlements is drawn from oral accounts, census records, and sample title searches in the Registry of Mesne Conveyances for Charleston County. Interviews with Janette Gailliard Lee, Hamlin Road, November 6, 2000; Sharon Crews, Bee Hive, October 23, 2000; Thomasina Stokes-Marshall, Snowden, October 27, 2000; Alfaii Sanders, South Santee, November 7, 2000; Pearl Lewis, Snowden, October 28, 2000; Elizabeth Mazyck, Six Mile, November 8, 2000; William Mitchell, Six Mile, October 25, 2000; Fred Scott Jr., Indigo Wharf, October 25, 2000. All informants, except Alfaii Sanders, are residents of Christ Church Parish, which lies east of Charleston. Sanders lives in St. James Parish on the Santee River. The Hamlin family papers contain a survey of the subdivision for Hamlin community. Elizabeth Hamlin McConnell, Mount Pleasant, South Carolina. See note 94.

96. *United States Census, South Carolina*, Charleston County, Christ Church Parish, 1880, 1890, 1900.

97. Ibid. and Johnson, 195–204.

98. *United States Census, South Carolina*, Charleston County, Christ Church Parish, 1880, 1890, and 1900.

99. The authors conducted title searches in the Charleston Register of Mesne Conveyances (RMC) on lots randomly chosen from Remley's Point, Green Hill, Snowden, Bee Hive, and Lincolnville. In almost all instances, no deeds were registered before 1890, and most were recorded after World War I. The RMC records indicated that in the late 1860s and 1870s many owners of Christ Church Parish plantations created "subdivisions" of two hundred to three hundred acres of ten- to twenty-acre lots, but the RMC has no record of the conveyance of deeds to the black owners whose property titles entered the county registry after 1890. In the interviews, cited in note 95, informants explained their understanding of the conveyance to Gullah owners based on oral tradition and family stories.

100. Mary Twining and Keith E. Baird, "Sea Island Culture: Matrix of the African American Family," Maidele Agbassegbe Demerson, "Family Life on Wadmalaw Island," and Mary Twining, "Time Is Like a River: The World View of the Sea Island People," all in Twining and Baird; Patricia Jones-Jackson, *When Roots Die: Endangered Traditions on the Sea Islands* (Athens, 1987), 5–33. During recent hearings on the conflict between Low Country developers, Gullah "heirs' property" was a central concern. See transcripts, United States Park Service, "Gullah Hearings: Charleston Country" (2000), available at the Charles Pinckney Historical Center, Mount Pleasant, South Carolina. A recent out-of- court settlement between heirs of land in the Ten Mile community and a developer delineates the complexity of the issue. The details of dispute, including a detailed, four-generation family genealogy that goes back to the original freedman titleholder, are in legal papers of attorney Fred Scott Jr., Mount Pleasant, South Carolina.

101. For a recent statement of the Gullah position, see Marquetta L. Goodwine, ed., *Igbo Landing: Gullah Roots of African American Culture* (Atlanta, 1998).

102. The Low Country "growing houses" appear to be the prototype of African American rural houses throughout the South, as discussed in John Michael Vlach, *Back of the Big House* (Chapel Hill, N.C., 1993), and Richard Westmacott, *African American Gardens and Yards in the Rural South* (Knoxville, Tenn., 1992). Venni Deas-Moore has identified the special character of the Low Country "growing house." Moore lives in McClellanville, South Carolina. Examples are still extant throughout the Low Country and in the photography collections of the Avery Center at the College of Charleston, the Charleston Museum, and the South Carolina Library at the University of South Caroliniana at Columbia. The WPA photographs on South Carolina in the Library of Congress also contain a number of Low Country "growing houses."

103. Creel; Georgia WPA, *Drums and Shadows*; Clyde Vernon Kiser, *Sea Island to City: A Study of St. Helena Islanders in Harlem and Other Urban Centers* (New York, 1932), 58–116; Guy Carawan and Candie Carawan, eds., *Ain't You Got a Right to the Tree of Life? The People of Johns Island, South Carolina* (New York, 1966).

104. Thomas Wentworth Higginson, *Army Life in a Black Regiment* (Boston, 1870), 17–18.

105. Creel; William E. Montgomery, *Under Their Own Vine and Fig Tree: The African-*

American Church in the South, 1865–1900 (Baton Rouge, 1993), 253–352; C. Eric Lincoln and Lawrence H. Mamiya, *The Black Church in the African American Experience* (Durham, N.C., 1990), 20–75; R. Raboteau, 95–322; Walter F. Pitts, *Old Ship of Zion: The Afro-Baptist Ritual in the Diaspora* (New York, 1993); Sanders; Zora Neale Hurston, *The Sanctified Church* (Berkeley, Calf., 1981).

106. Virtually all AME and black Baptists churches organized in the Low Country before 1900 include the Masonic emblem on their cornerstones. William H. Grimshaw, *Official History of Freemasonry among the Colored People in North America* (New York, 1903), 67–83, 263–264; David G. Hackett, "The Prince Hall Masons and the African American Church: The Labors of Grand Master and Bishop James Walker, 1831–1918," *Church History* 69 (2000). See discussion of secret societies in Creel, 55–57, 181–182, 288–292; Kenneth Little, *The Mende of Sierra Leone* (London, 1951); Little, "The Poro Society as Arbiter of Culture," *African Studies* 7 (1948); George W. Harley, "Notes on the Poro in Liberia," *Papers of the Peabody Museum of American Archaeology and Ethnology* 19 (1941).

107. Joyce Coakley, "'Seeking' at Boon Hall Plantation," unpublished paper, Hamlin community, South Carolina, n.d.

108. James A. Holmes Jr. and Richard Allen Leonard, *African Methodism in South Carolina* (Tappan, N.Y., 1987), 25–43, 119–145.

109. Lee interview.

110. Title of Goodwill, AME, in Charleston County Register of Mesme Conveyances (RMC); map of Boone Hall, Laurel Hill, and Parker's Island, Christ Church (1926), in estate plat in RMC; plat of Six Mile subdivision of Boon Hall (1873), in estate plat in RMC.

111. RMC.

112. Sanders.

113. Lincoln and Mamiya, *Black Church*, 11–75.

114. Payne, 252–257, 236–239.

115. Georgia WPA, *Drums and Shadows*; WPA, *Slave Narratives: South Carolina*, vol. 2.

116. Lee interview.

117. Nichols, 10–55; WPA, *Slave Narratives: South Carolina*; Georgia WPA, *Drums and Shadows*. Observations of authors (October 2000) of the following African America cemeteries in Charleston, Christ Church, and St. James parishes: Goodwill AME, Ocean Grove, Unity and Friendship Society, Humane and Friendship Society, Brotherly Association, Brown Fellowship, Monrovia, Long Point Missionary Baptist, Olive Branch AME, New Hope Missionary Baptist, Greater Zion AME, First Sewee Baptist, Union AME, Mount Nebo AME, and South Santee Cemetery.

118. May A. Waring, "Mortuary Customs and Beliefs of South Carolina Negroes," *Journal of American Folk-Lore* 7 (1894): 318–319; Spaulding, 188–203; Lee interview; and interview with Alphonso Brown, Charleston, November 10, 2000.

119. Georgia WPA, *Drums and Shadows*, and WPA, *Slave Narratives: South Carolina*, vol. 2. Also see Melville Herskovits, *Dahomey: An Ancient West African Kingdom* (Evanston, Ill., 1958), 2 vols.; Melville Herskovits and William R. Bascom, *Continuity and Change in African Cultures* (Chicago, 1959); Robert Farris Thompson, "African Influence on the Art of the United States," in Armstead L. Robinson et al., *Black Studies in the University* (New Haven, Conn. 1969), 122–170; Robert Farris Thompson, *Flash of the Spirit: African and Afro-Ameri-*

can Art and Philosophy (New York, 1984); Theophus H. Smith, *Conjuring Culture: Biblical Formations of Black America* (New York, 1994); Joseph M. Murphy, *Working the Spirit: Ceremonies of the African Diaspora* (Boston, 1980); Hurston; Sanders; Yvonne Chireau, "Conjure and Christianity," *Religion in American Society* 7 (1997).

120. Roger Pinckney, *Blue Roots: African American Folk Magic of the Gullah People* (St. Paul, Minn., 1998); Creel, Georgia WPA, *Drums and Shadows*; John Bennett, *The Doctor to the Dead* (New York, 1946); Interview with Dr. James Ward, Mount Pleasant, October 25, 2000; Genevieve Chandler, collector, *Coming Through: Voices of South Carolina Gullah Community from WPA Oral Histories*, ed. Kincaid Mills, Genevieve C. Peterkin, and Aaron McCollough (Columbia, S.C., 2008).

121. William Wiggins and H. Douglas DeNatale, eds, *Jubilation! African American Celebrations in the Southwest* (Columbia, S.C., 1993), 7–67; Guy Carawan, "Christmas Eve Watch on Johns Island," in Twining and Baird, 103–106.

122. Interviews with Damon Fordham, Mount Pleasant, November 5, 2000; Brown; Kamille Johnson, Atlanta, January 15, 2001; Ward.

123. Interviews with Lee and Mayzick.

124. Twining, "Baskets and Quilts: Women in Sea Island Arts and Crafts," in Twining and Baird, 129–140; John Michael Vlach, *The Afro-American Tradition in Decorative Arts* (Cleveland, 1979), 43–67; Jacqueline Tobin and Raymond Dobard, *Hidden in Plain View* (New York, 1999); Maud Southwell Wahlman and John Scully, "Aesthetic Principles in Afro-American Quilts," in William Ferris, ed., *Afro-American Folk Arts and Crafts* (Jackson, Miss., 1983), 79–98; Thompson, 194–224; Ward interview.

125. Karen Hell, *The Carolina Rice Kitchen: The African Connection* (Columbia, S.C., 1992). Interview with Daniel Dent, Wadamalaw Island, Charleston, 1983, in Jones-Jackson, 153–155.

126. A basket maker herself and a member of the Hamlin community near Boon Hall, Joyce Coakley, in *Sweetgrass Baskets and the Gullah Tradition* (Mount Pleasant, 2006), studied the basket makers, the flower women, and their community. For an historical-anthropological study, see Dale Rosengarten's *Row upon Row: Sea Grass Baskets of the South Carolina Lowcountry* (Columbia, S.C., 1987); Twining, "Baskets and Quilts"; Vlach, *Afro-American Tradition*, 7–19; Interviews at various times with Janette Gailliard Lee (Hamlin Road); Elizabeth Mazyck (Six Mile); Mazie Lee Coaxum (Phillips); Mary and Jessie Bennet (Phillips); Joyce Coakley (Hamlin); and Joseph Foreman (North Charleston).

127. John Michael Vlach, *Charleston Blacksmith: The Work of Philip Simmons* (Athens, Ga., 1981).

128. John Meffert, Sherman Pyatt, et al., *Charleston, South Carolina: Black America Series* (Charleston, 2000), 57–72; Powers, 160–188.

129. Census Bureau, *United States Census, South Carolina, Charleston, 1860* (Washington, D.C., 1861); *United States Census, South Carolina, Charleston, 1900* (Washington, D.C., 1901).

130. Field.

131. Wiggins and DeNatale.

132. Andrew Karhl ("Black Recreation Areas in Jim Crow South," unpublished paper, Indiana University, 2007) is completing a book that looks at these facilities across the

South; Marsha Phelts, *An American Beach for African Americans* (Gainesville, 1997), completed a similar study in Florida. Herb Frazier, at the *Charleston Post and Courier*, has written several articles on Low Country, black recreational facilities. Also see Meffert and Pyatt; Jack McCray, *Charleston Jazz* (Charleston, 2007).

133. Albert Raboteau addressed this issue in "The Debate" between black sociologist Franklin Frazer and anthropologist Melville Herskovits occasioned by the publication of Herskovits's *The Myth of the Negro Past* (Boston, 1958). See R. Raboteau, 48–55. For details of Charleston, see Meffert and Pyatt; Rosen, 133–154; Fraser, 323–393; McCray; Coakley, Field, 1–82; Esau Jenkins Papers, Avery Center, Charleston, South Carolina; James R. Logan Scrapbook Collection, Avery Center; Septima Clark Papers, Avery Center; Mamie Garvin Fields Papers, Avery Center; Lois Sims, "Profiles of African American Females in the Low Country of South Carolina," Avery Center. Interviews with Lois Sims, Charleston, October 24, 2000; Richard Brewer Jr., Charleston, October 26, 2000; Thomas McFall, Charleston, October 25, 2000; Damon Fordham, Charleston, November 5, 2000.

134. Dubose Heyward, *Porgy* (New York, 1925) and *Mamba's Daughters* (New York, 1929); Julia Peterkin, *Green Thursday* (New York, 1924), *Black April* (Indianapolis, 1927), *Scarlet Sister Mary* (Indianapolis, 1928), and *Bright Skin* (Indianapolis, 1932); Peterkin and Doris Ulmann, *Roll Jordan Roll* (Indianapolis, 1933); Ambrose E. Gonzales, *The Black Border: Gullah Stories of the Carolina Coast* (Gretna, La., 1922); Harlan Greene, *Mr. Skylark* (Athens, Ga., 2001); Martha R. Severens, *The Charleston Renaissance* (Spartanburg, S.C., 1998): James M. Hutchison, *Dubose Heyward: A Charleston Gentleman and the World of Porgy and Bess* (Jackson, Miss., 2000).

135. Powers, 245–254.

136. Interview with Joyce Coakley, Mount Pleasant, April 2008.

137. Ibid.

138. Observations of Donna H. Scott (July 1998), Gambier, Ohio. Interviews with Mitchell; Fordham; Lee.

139. The cemeteries lay between Simmons and Royal Avenues, abutting McCant's Drive, on the south edge of old Mount Pleasant.

140. Avery Normal Institute Papers, Avery Center; Edmund L. Drago, *Initiative Paternalism and Race Relations: Charleston's Avery Normal Institute* (Athens, Ga., 1990); Meffert and Pyatt, *Charleston*, 47–56; Powers, *Black Charlestonians*, 160–188; I. A. Newby, *Black Carolinians* (Columbia, S.C., 1973), 82–114; Fields, *Lemon Swamp*, 83–140, 204–222. Interviews with Sims; Brewer; McFall; Brown.

141. Jenkins Orphanage Papers, Avery Center; SC ETV, *The Jenkins Orphanage Band: Viewers Guild* (Columbia, S.C., 1970); Edward Ball, *The Sweet Hell Inside* (New York, 2001).

142. Ball.

143. James P. Johnson, "Conversations," in Martin Williams, ed., *Jazz Panorama* (New York, 1962). Also see John Strausbaugh, "Cradle for Serious Grooving," Weekend Explorer, *New York Times*, February 1, 2008.

144. McCray.

145. John Chilton, *A Jazz Nursery: The Story of the Jenkins' Orphanage Bands of Charleston, South Carolina* (London, 1980); SC ETV, Video, *Jenkins Orphanage Band* (1970); Ball, 227–324; http://northbysouth.kenyon.edu/1998/charlestonharlem.

146. Newby, 27–184.

147. Devlin, 1–82; Edward Ayers, *Southern Crossing: A History of the American South* (New York, 1995), 25–70.

148. See Devlin, 383–386, table 6.

149. Coclanis, 111–158; Rosen, 133–154; Fraser, 323–393.

150. Devlin, 137–377 and tables 1 and 5, 379, 383–386.

151. Ibid., 142–218; I. A. Hanby, *Black Carolinians: A History of Blacks in South Carolina from 1895–1968* (Columbia, S.C., 1973), 185–193.

152. *Charleston News and Courier*, May 11, 1919; *New York Times*, May 12, 1919; Devlin, 23–236.

153. *New and Courier*, September 15, 1936; August 1, 1938; July 24, 1950; *Charleston City Directory* (1903); William Fleetwood, *Tidecraft: Boats of South Carolina, Georgia, and Northern Florida* (Tybee Island, Ga., 1995); Fields, 13–14.

CHAPTER 3: NEGRO CAPITAL OF THE WORLD: HARLEM

1. Claude McKay, *Harlem: Negro Metropolis* (New York, 1940), 15–16.

2. W. E. B. Du Bois, *Souls of Black Folk* (Chicago, 1903).

3. Jervis Anderson, *This Was Harlem: A Cultural Portrait* (New York, 1982).

4. James Weldon Johnson, *Black Manhattan* (New York, 1930).

5. William B. Scott and Peter M. Rutkoff, *New York Modern: The Arts and the City* (Baltimore, 1999), 133–162.

6. For historical details of the *New York Age* and the *Amsterdam News*, see Rodland E. Wolsely, *The Black Press, USA* (Ames, Iowa, 1971).

7. Willard B. Gatewood, *Aristocrats of Color: The Black Elite, 1880–1920* (Bloomington, Ind., 1990); Lawrence Otis Graham, *Our Kind of People: Inside America's Black Upper Class* (New York, 1999).

8. John Hope Franklin, *From Slavery to Freedom: A History of African Americans* (New York, 1994), 45–476; David Levering Lewis, *When Harlem was in Vogue* (New York, 1982), 3–24; Anderson, 101–109; David Kennedy, *Over Here: The First World War and American Society* (New York, 1980), 29–30.

9. Kennedy, 156–163, 281–284.

10. Franklin, 477–497.

11. Emmett J. Scott, *Negro Migration during the War* (New York, 1920); Gilbert Osofsky, *Harlem: The Making of a Ghetto; Negro New York, 1890–1930* (New York, 1966).

12. Lewis, 89–118.

13. Alain Locke, ed., *The New Negro: An Interpretation* (New York, 1925).

14. Lewis, 50–239.

15. Ibid., 25–118.

16. Ibid., 89–155.

17. Eileen Southern, *The Music of Black Americans* (New York, 1983); Samuel A. Floyd Jr., ed., *Black Music in the Harlem Renaissance* (Westport, Conn., 1990); Jon Michael Spencer, *The New Negroes and Their Music: The Success of the Harlem Renaissance* (Knoxville, 1997).

18. Samuel Charters and Leonard Kunstadt, *Jazz: A History of the New York Scene* (New York, 1962), 165–175; James Weldon Johnson, *Black Manhattan* (New York, 1930); Kathy J. Ogren, *The Jazz Revolution: Twenties, America, and the Meaning of Jazz* (New York, 1989).

19. Charters and Kunstadt, 165–183; John Edward Hasse, *Beyond Category: The Life and Genius of Duke Ellington* (New York, 1993), 34–60; Walter Allen, *Hendersonia: The Music of Fletcher Henderson and His Musicians* (Highland Park, N.J., 1973); Gunther Schuller, *Early Jazz: Its Roots and Musical Development* (New York, 1968); Martin Williams, *The Jazz Tradition* (New York, 1983).

20. Scott and Rutkoff, 155–162.

21. Ibid.

22. Garvin Bushell, with Mark Tucker, *Jazz from the Beginning* (Ann Arbor, 1988), 19.

23. Clyde Vernon Kiser, *Sea Island to City: A Study of St. Helena Islanders in Harlem and Other Urban Centers* (New York, 1932), 145–173; *Charleston (S.C.) News and Courier*, September 15, 1936; August 1, 1938; July 24, 1950; William Allen, Charles Pickard Ware, and Lucy McKim Garrrison, comps., *Slave Songs of the United States* (Bedford, Mass., 1995).

24. Anderson, 59–136.

25. New York Urban League, *Twenty-four Hundred Negro Families in Harlem* (New York, 1927).

26. Ralph Ellison, *Invisible Man* (New York, 1952), 228–231.

27. Ibid., 235–236.

28. Garvin Bushell, "Jazz in the Twenties," in Martin Williams, ed., *Jazz Panorama* (New York, 1962), 82.

29. Charles E. Hall, ed., *Negroes in the United States, 1920–1930* (Washington, D.C., 1933), 23 and 29.

30. Kiser, 117–144.

31. U.S. Census Bureau, *1920 United States Census: New York City, Manhattan* (Washington, D.C., 1921), enumeration districts 1330 and 1344.

32. Charles Barnes, *The Longshoremen* (New York, 1915), 9, 16, 48, 73, 81–2, 115–116, 133. Bruce Nelson, *Divided We Stand: American Workers and the Struggle for Black Equality* (Princeton, N.J., 2001), 12–56, 86–98; Calvin Winslow, "On the Waterfront: Black, Italian, and Irish in the New York Harbor Strike of 1919," in John Rule and Robert Malcolson, eds., *Protest and Survival: The Historical Experience: Essays for E. P. Thompson* (London, 1993), 355–393; Calvin Winslow, *Waterfront Workers: New Perspectives on Race and Class* (Urbana, Ill., 1998); Bruce Nelson, *Workers on the Waterfront: Seamen, Longshoremen, and Unions in the 1930s* (Urbana, Ill., 1988); Eric Arnesen, *Waterfront Workers of New Orleans: 1863–1923* (New York, 1991); Vernon H. Jensen, *Hiring of Dock Workers and Employment Practices in the Ports of New York, Liverpool, London, Rotterdam, and Marseilles* (Cambridge, Mass., 1964).

33. James P. Johnson, "Conversations with James P. Johnson," in Williams. Also see Strausbaugh, "Cradle for Grooving," *New York Times*, February 8, 2008.

34. Johnson, 49–50; Bushell, *Jazz from the Beginning*, 28. Johnson's most popular music is recorded in *James P. Johnson*, Olympic Records.

35. U.S. Bureau, *Manhattan Census, 1920*; U.S. Census Bureau, *Manhattan Census, 1930* (Washington, D.C., 1931); U.S. Census Bureau, *Manhattan Census, 1940* (Washington, D.C., 1941); Jesse Carney Smith and Carrell Peterson Horton, eds., *Historical Statistics of Black*

America (New York, 1995); Ira Rosenwaike, *Population History of New York City* (Syracuse, 1972), 103–104, 141.

36. Bushell, *Jazz from the Beginning*, 29.

37. U.S. Census Bureau, *Manhattan Census*, 1940, 1950, 1960; Rosenwaike, 103–104, 141.

38. Frank Byrd, comp., "32 Negro Market Songs of Harlem," typescript, New York Public Library, 1934.

39. Writers' Program, New York, N.Y., "History of Negroes in New York: Research Studies," 1936–1940, (typescript, Schomburg Library, New York); Karen Hess, *The Carolina Rice Kitchen: The African Connection* (Columbia, S.C., 1992); John Henrick Clarke, *Harlem: A Community in Transition* (New York, 1969).

40. Kiser, 18–57, 191–215, 235–264.

41. Ibid., 18–57, 191–215, 235–264; Writers' Program, "History of Negroes in New York"; Interviews with Sharon Crew, Bee Hive, Christ Church Parish, Charleston, South Carolina, October 2000; Janette Gailliard Lee, Ten Mile, Christ Church Parish, Charleston, South Carolina, October 2000; Rev. Alice Franklin, 27 East 53nd Street, Brooklyn, N.Y., March 2001.

42. "Snowden," "Phillips," "Beehive," "Ten Mile," "Greenhill," and Remley Point," in *Realty Atlas: Charleston County, South Carolina*, 26th ed. (Riverside, Calif., 2000).

43. A remarkable example of this can be found in the work of the Saint Helena Island Gullah painter, Sam Doyle whose "St. Helena paintings" contain a large number of Harlem images, including the Apollo Theater. Red Piano Gallery, Saint Helena Island, South Carolina, January 2001.

44. Father Divine, *New Day*, December 12, 1940, 18; Jill Watts, *God, Harlem U.S.A.: The Father Divine Story* (Berkeley, 1992), 11–24.

45. Watts, 25–41.

46. McKay, 35–36; Ruth Boaz, "My Thirty Years with Father Divine," *Ebony* 20 (May 1965); *World Herald*, 1936–1937; Gains S. Reid, "Who Is Father Divine?" 14–24, 44–91, Schomburg Library, New York; Robert Weisbrot, *Father Divine and the Struggle for Racial Equality* (Urbana, 1883), 12–22; Watts, 43–69.

47. Watts, 82–166; Weisbrot, 61–119.

48. Ibid.

49. Clinton V. Black, *The History of Jamaica* (Essex, Eng., 1983); Irma Watkins-Owens, *Blood Relations: Caribbean Immigrants and the Harlem Community, 1900–1930* (Bloomington, Ind., 1996); Calvin Holder, "The Causes and Composition of West Indian Immigration to New York City, 1900–1952," *Afro-Americans in New York Life and History* 2, no. 1 (1977).

50. Martha Beckwith, *Black Roadways: A Study of Jamaican Folklife* (New York, 1969 [1929]); Leonard Barrett, *The Sun and the Drum: African Roots in Jamaican Folk Tradition* (Kingston, Jamaica, 1976); Edward Brathwaite, *The Folk Culture of the Slaves in Jamaica* (London, 1981).

51. Diane J. Austin-Broos, *Jamaican Genesis: Religion and the Politics of Moral Orders* (Chicago, 1997), 4–43; George Eaton Simpson, *Religious Cults of the Caribbean: Trinidad, Jamaica, and Haiti* (Rio Piedras, Puerto Rico, 1980), 157–228; Malcolm J. C. Calley, *God's People: West Indian Pentecostal Sects in England* (London, 1965), 72–95; William Wedenoja,

"Modernization and the Pentecostal Movement in Jamaica," in Stephen Glazier, ed., *Perspectives on Pentecostalism: Case Studies for the Caribbean and Latin America* (New York, 1980), 27–48; Ira Berlin, "From Creole to African: Atlantic Creoles and the Origins of American Society in Mainland North America," *William and Mary Quarterly*, 3rd ser., 53 (1996); David Eltis, "Identity and Migration: The Atlantic in Comparative Perspective," and Paul E. Lovejoy, "Trans-Atlantic Transformation: Origins and Identity of Africans in the Americas," both in Wim Klooster and Alfred Padula, eds., *The Atlantic World: Essays in Slavery, Migration, and Imagination* (Upper Saddle River, N.J., 2005).

52. Joseph G. Moore, "Religion of Jamaican Negroes: A Study of Afro-Jamaican Acculturation" (Ph.D. diss., Northwestern University, 1954); Braithwaite, 7; Beckwith, 55–65; Barrett, 15–17.

53. Braithwaite,9–16; Beckwith, 70–112; Barrett, 12.

54. Watkins-Owens; Ira de Augustine Reid, *The Negro Immigrant, His Background, Characteristics, and Social Adjustment, 1899–1937* (New York, 1939); R. B. LePage, *Jamaican Creole* (New York, 1960), 99–101, 117–120; Beryl L. Bailey, *Jamaican Creole Syntax* (Cambridge, 1966), xiii and 5–6; Philip D. Curtin, *Two Jamaicas: The Role of Ideas in a Tropical Colony, 1830–1865* (Cambridge, Mass., 1955).

55. Austin-Broos, 26–32.

56. U.S. Census Bureau, *Manhattan, 1920*; Philip Kasinitz, *Caribbean New York* (Ithaca, N.Y., 1992), 25, 41; Watkins-Owens.

57. I. Reid, 81–150: Barrington Dunbar, "Factors in Cultural Backgrounds of the British West Indian Negro and the American Southern Negro That Conditioned Their Adjustments to Harlem" (M.A. thesis, Columbia University, 1936), 22; F. Donnie Forde, *Caribbean Americans in New York City, 1895–1975* (Charleston, S.C., 2002).

58. I. Reid, McKay, 143–177; Dunbar.

59. U.S. Census Bureau, *Manhattan Census, 1920*; Kasinitz, 25, 41; Calvin Holder, "The Rise of the West Indian Politician in New York City, 1919–1959," *Afro-Americans in New York Life and History* 4, no. 1, (1981).

60. Austin-Broos, 25–28.

61. Ibid.

62. Ibid., 39–169.

63. Marcus Garvey, *Philosophy and Opinions of Marcus Garvey*, comp. Amy Jacques Garvey (London, 1967–1977), 2:41.

64. *Messenger*, January 1923, 126.

65. *Messenger*, March 1923, 638.

66. Randall K. Burkett, "Religious Dimensions of the Universal Negro Improvement Association of African Americans," *Afro-Americans in New York Life and History* (Buffalo, N.Y.), no. 2 (1977): 167–182; Rupert Lewis and Patrick Bryan, eds., *Garvey: His Work and Impact* (Trenton, N.J., 1991); Rupert Lewis and Maureen Warner-Lewis, eds., *Garvey: Africa, Europe, the Americas* (Kingston, Jamaica, 1986).

67. Greater New York Federation of Churches, *The Negro Churches of Manhattan* (New York, 1930); Church History Committee, "History of the St. John's Baptist Church, 448 West 152d Street: 1918–1988," 1988, typescript, Schomburg Library, New York; Bethel, A.M.E, "History of Bethel AME Church," typescript, 1959, archives, Bethel, AME, New

York; Community Council of Greater New York, Bureau of Community Statistical Services, *Manhattan Communities, Central and East Harlem*, vol. 2 (New York, 1955).

68. Interview with Olive Adams, West 121st Street, Harlem, April 2001; Interview with Alice Franklin, 52nd Street, Brooklyn, N.Y., March 2001; Milton C. Sernett, *Bound for the Promised Land: African American Religion and the Great Migration* (Durham, N.C., 1977), 131–135, 181–191; C. Eric Lincoln and Lawrence H. Mamiya, *The Black Church and the African American Experience* (Durham, N.C., 1990), 115–163, 309–345; Ray Allen, *Singing in the Spirit: African American Sacred Quartets in New York City* (Philadelphia, 1991); Clarence Taylor, *The Black Churches of Brooklyn* (New York, 1994).

69. Anderson, 20–24, 104–105, 254–261; Allon Schoener, ed., *Harlem on My Mind: Cultural Capital of Black America, 1900–1968* (New York, 1968), 17–168; Rev. Jessica Kendall Ingram, "Women's Day Sermon," March 25, 2001, Bethel, AME, 54–60 West 132nd Street, Harlem, N.Y.

70. Julia Kirk Blackwelder, *Styling Jim Crow: African American Beauty Training during Jim Crow* (College Station, Tex., 2003).

71. Roi Ottley, *New World A-Coming* (New York, 1968); James Baldwin, *Go Tell It on the Mountain* (New York, 1953); R. Allen, *Singing in the Spirit*; Harlem Development Corporation, *A Profile of the Harlem Area* (New York, 1973); Black Theology Project (1976–1987), typescript, Schomburg Center for Research in Black Culture, New York; Protestant Council of the City of New York, *Harlem-Upper Manhattan Church and Community Study* (New York, 1962); Clarke; U.S. Census Bureau, *The Social and Economic Status of the Black Population of the United States*, prepared by Nampeo D. R. McKenney (Washington D.C.: U.S. Government Printing Office, 1974).

72. Anderson; Cheryl Greenberg, *Or Does it Explode? Black Harlem in the Great Depression* (New York, 1991).

73. Richard Sasuly, "Vito Macantonio: The People's Politician," in Harvey Goldberg, ed., *American Radicals: Some Problems and Personalities* (New York, 1957), 145–162.

74. Peter Paris, *Black Religious Leaders: Conflict in Unity* (Louisville, Ky., 1991), 145–183.

75. Anderson, 337–341.

76. Ted Fox, *Showtime at the Apollo* (New York, 1983), 1–66.

77. Ibid., 66–213.

78. Ibid., 109–111.

79. Smith and Horton, 2:1627.

80. Scott and Rutkoff, 260–288.

81. Dizzy Gillespie, with Al Fraser, *To Be, or Not to Bop: Memoirs* (Garden City, N.Y., 1979), 15–31.

82. Ibid., 32, 151, 223–224.

83. Ibid., 294, 318–320, 485.

84. Richard J. Powell, *Homecoming: The Art and Life of William H. Johnson* (Washington, D.C., 1991), 1–8.

85. Ibid., 123–216.

86. Ibid., 34; Peter T. Nesbett and Michelle DuBois, *Over the Line: The Art and Life of Jacob Lawrence* (Seattle, 2000).

87. Interview with Jacob Lawrence, by Caroll Green, October 26, 1968, Archives of American Art, Smithsonian Institution, Washington, D.C.

88. Ibid., 11.

89. Nesbett and DuBois.

90. Quoted in Alvin Ailey, with Peter Bailey, *Revelations: The Autobiography of Alvin Ailey* (New York, 1995), 5.

91. Jennifer Dunning, *Alvin Ailey: A Life in Dance* (New York, 1996), 23.

92. Ailey, 31–43.

93. Ibid., 57–93.

94. Alvin Ailey, *An Evening with the Alvin Ailey American Dance Company,* video recording, produced and directed by Thomas Grim, Danmarks Radio Arts, Chicago, 1986.

95. Ibid.

96. Arnold Shaw, *Honkers and Shouters: The Golden Years of Rhythm and Blues* (New York, 1978), 57–139.

97. Interview, 1977, in Shaw, 66. Louis Jordan, *Jiving with Jordan,* Proper Records, Kent, England, 2002, includes the Tympany Five's complete 1940s recordings, more than a hundred altogether.

98. Quoted in Shaw, 63; John Chilton, *Let the Good Times Roll: The Story of Louis Jordan and His Music* (Ann Arbor, 1997); David Ake, *Jazz Cultures* (Berkeley, 2002), 42–61.

99. Quoted in Shaw, 64.

100. Quoted in ibid.

101. James Brown, with Bruce Tucker, *James Brown: Father of Soul* (New York, 1986).

102. Ibid., 18.

103. Ibid., 101.

104. Ibid., 143.

105. See Roger Abrahams, *Deep Down in the Jungle: Negro Narrative Folklore from the Streets of Philadelphia* (Chicago, 1970).

CHAPTER 4: MULES AND MEN: BIRMINGHAM

1. WPA, *Slave Narratives: Alabama and Indiana Narratives,* vol. 5 (St. Clair Shores, Mich., 1976), 39.

2. Writers' Project, Works Progress Administration, *Alabama: A Guide to the Deep South* (New York, 1941), 150–177.

3. Brenda McCallum, "Songs of Work, Songs of Worship: Sanctifying Black Unionism," *New York Folklore* 14, nos. 1–2 (Winter–Spring 1988): 10.

4. WPA, *Alabama: A Guide to the Deep South,* 167.

5. Marjorie Longenecker White, *The Birmingham District: An Industrial History and Guide,* Birmingham Historical Society and Junior League (Birmingham, Ala., 1981), 41.

6. W. David Lewis, *Sloss Furnace and the Rise of the Birmingham District* (Tuscaloosa, Ala., 1994), 58.

7. White, 33–45.

8. Phillip Taft Research Files on Alabama Labor History, Department of Archives and

Manuscripts, Birmingham Public Library. See also Charles Johnson, *Patterns of Negro Segregation* (New York, 1943).

9. *Slave Narratives*, 5:62.

10. "Like It Ain't Never Passed: Remembering Life in Sloss Quarters," Sloss Oral History Project, Sloss Furnaces National Historic Landmark, Sloss Furnace, Birmingham, Ala., 2005.

11. *Slave Narratives*, 5:21.

12. Lewis, 83.

13. Henry M. McKiren Jr., *Iron and Steel: Class, Race, and Community in Birmingham, Alabama, 1875–1970* (Chapel Hill, N.C., 1995), 25.

14. Ibid., 44.

15. Ibid, 25–44.

16. Bobby M. Wilson, *America's Johannesburg,: Industrialization and Racial Transformation in Birmingham* (Oxford, 2000), 57.

17. Wilson, 57–86.

18. Daniel Letwin, *The Challenge of Interracial Unionism: Alabama's Coal Miners, 1878–1921* (Chapel Hill, N.C., 1998), 18.

19. Wilson, 93.

20. White, 48.

21. Paul Hemphill, *Leaving Birmingham: Notes of a Native Son* (New York, 1993), 21.

22. Letwin, 19.

23. Lewis, 186.

24. McKiren, 115–124.

25. Ibid., 118.

26. Letwin, 29.

27. Wilson, 20–88.

28. James Say Brown Jr., ed., *Up before Daylight* (Tuscaloosa, Ala., 1982), 77.

29. Geraldine Moore, *Behind the Ebony Mask* (Birmingham, Ala., 1961), 12.

30. Ibid., 12–13.

31. McKiren, 58.

32. Lynne Feldman, *A Sense of Place* (Tuscaloosa, Ala., 1999), 91.

33. Peter Rutkoff, class notes, Kenyon College, 2001.

34. Feldman, 107.

35. Ibid., 9.

36. Wilson Fallin Jr., *The African American Church in Birmingham, Alabama, 1815–1963* (New York, 1997), 79.

37. Wilson, 171.

38. Ibid., 130.

39. *Birmingham Reporter*, July 24, 1920.

40. Feldman, 21.

41. Lewis, 290. In 1901 U.S. Steel and Morgan had purchased Carnegie Steel and added fourteen additional companies to create an industrial empire that controlled one thousand miles of track and 112 steam ships and produced half the coke and pig iron in America.

42. Richard A. Straw, "The Collapse of Biracial Unionism: The Alabama Coal Strike of 1908," *Alabama Historical Quarterly* 37, no. 2 (Summer 1975).

43. Letwin, 151.

44. Ibid., 152. See also, *We Shall Overcome*, film, narrated by Harry Belafonte, California Newsreel, 1998.

45. White, 102.

46. Ibid., 103.

47. Fairfield Chamber of Commerce, *Fairfield: Past Present and Future* (Fairfield, Ala., 1985).

48. White, 106–107.

49. Joe Brooks, tape 1.

50. Deborah E. McDowell, *Leaving Pipe Shop: Memories of Kin* (New York, 1998), 51.

51. Wilson, 50–88.

52. Ibid., 91.

53. Robin D. G. Kelley, *Hammer and Hoe: Alabama Communists during the Depression* (Chapel Hill, N.C., 1990).

54. "KU," 12, Sloss Oral History Project.

55. Clarence Dean, April 12, 1985, 9, Sloss Oral History Project.

56. Lewis, 90.

57. Wilson, 193.

58. Lewis, 286.

59. McKiren, 116.

60. White, 157.

61. *ACIPCO News* may be found at the Birmingham Public Library and at the Public Affairs office of ACIPCO, North Sixteenth Street, Birmingham, Ala.

62. *Birmingham Reporter*, April 22, 1928.

63. *ACIPCO News*, August, 1930.

64. "Like It Ain't Never Passed," 8, Sloss Oral History.

65. *ACIPCO News*, August, 1919.

66. Christopher Dean Fullerton, *Every Other Sunday* (Birmingham, Ala., 1999), 41.

67. Ibid.

68. Barry Brooks, producer, *Every Other Sunday*, CD ROM, interviews with players of the Birmingham Black Barons.

69. Interview with Rev. William Greason, Birmingham, Alabama, January 2005.

70. Peter Filichia, *Professional Baseball Franchises from the Abbeville Athletics to the Zanesville Indians* (New York, 1993).

71. Fullerton, 69.

72. Ibid., 72.

73. *Birmingham Reporter*, July 14, 1919.

74. *Birmingham Reporter*, August 19, 1919. There are no official rosters of black industrial team players. Historians depend on local newspapers for data, sometimes unreliable, always "local." The real names of many players have been lost, and we have only the nicknames used by fans and the press.

75. *Birmingham Reporter*, March 20, 1920.

76. *Birmingham Reporter,* August 27, 1920.

77. William Peterson, *Only the Ball Was White* (Englewood, N.J., 1970). See also Peter Rutkoff, *Shadow Ball: A Novel of Baseball and Chicago* (Jefferson, N.C., 2001).

78. John B. Holway, *Blackball Stars: Negro League Pioneers* (New York, 1988), 266.

79. *Birmingham Reporter,* April 30, 1925.

80. Fullerton, 92.

81. *Defender,* May 11, 1929.

82. Leroy Satchel Paige, as told to Hal Lebovitz, *Pitchin' Man: Satchel Paige's Own Story* (Westport, Conn., 1992). See also the "Satchel Paige" file at the National Baseball Hall of Fame Museum and Library, Cooperstown, New York.

83. Greason interview.

84. Ibid.

85. *Birmingham Reporter,* April 23, 1927.

86. Greason interview.

87. Ibid.

88. Fullerton, 57.

89. Greason interview.

90. *Birmingham Reporter,* June 11, 1927.

91. Willie Mays and Charles Einstein, *My Life in Baseball* (New York, 1966), 21. The Barons lost to the Cleveland Buckeyes in the 1948 Negro Leagues World Series, the same year that the Cleveland Indians of the white major leagues won their last World Series.

92. Peterson, 23–75.

93. Feldman, 40.

94. Interview with Frank "Doc" Adams, Birmingham, Alabama, January 2005.

95. Feldman, 41.

96. Interview with Sallye Davis, 1981, "Birmingfield Papers," Birmingham Public Library.

97. Adams interview.

98. Ibid.

99. Feldman, 130.

100. Arthur H. Parker, *A Dream That Came True: The Autobiography of Arthur Harold Parker,* (n.d.), 6, Parker File, Birmingham Public Library.

101. Ibid., 11.

102. Feldman, 121.

103. Ibid., 116.

104. Ibid.

105. Feldman, 128.

106. Horace Mann Boyd, *Negro Education in Alabama* (Tuscaloosa, Ala., 1969); Michael Keith Honey, *Black Workers Remember: An Oral History of Segregation, Unionism, and the Freedom Struggle* (Berkeley, 1999), 70.

107. Rosa Washington, in Honey, 70.

108. Stone Johnson, in ibid., 33.

109. Feldman, 132.

110. Larry Ragan, *True Tales of Birmingham* (Birmingham, Ala., 1992), 40.

111. Feldman, 172.

112. "Tuxedo Junction" file, Birmingham Public Library.

113. Jonathan McKinley Calkins, "The Birmingham Jazz Tradition: The Role and Contributions of African-Americans" (M.A. thesis, University of Pittsburgh, 1982), 42–44.

114. Ibid., 45.

115. C. Marzetta Bolivar, Swing Lowe (New York, 2001), 33, 125.

116. Ibid., 79.

117. Ibid., 130.

118. Adams interview.

119. Parker, 60.

120. Christian Science Monitor, n.d., 1930.

121. Birmingham News, February 17, 1970. Industrial, renamed Parker High School in 1940, grew to approximately 3,600 students at the height of segregation in the region.

122. Interview with Alona Cunningham, Birmingham, Alabama, 2005.

123. Industrial High School Record, January 1936. The authors are grateful to the guidance department of Parker High School for allowing them access to the files of school newspapers. The school plans to donate them to the Civil Rights Museum in Birmingham.

124. Industrial High School Record, April 30, 1935.

125. Bolivar, 29, 38.

126. Calkins, 60, 64.

127. Ibid., 74.

128. Adams interview.

129. Ibid.

130. Bolivar, 42.

131. Alabama State had been Alabama State Normal School, near Huntsville, Alabama, and renamed. W. C. Handy taught there briefly, as did W. G. Still, father of composer William Grant Still.

132. Bolivar, 52.

133. Adams interview.

134. Bolivar, 97.

135. Adams Interview.

136. Bolivar, 78.

137. Calkins, 110.

138. Gunther Schuller, The Swing Era: The Development of Jazz, 1930–1945 (New York, 1989), 410.

139. Birmingham News, July 25, 1980.

140. Sammy Lowe as quoted in Bolivar, 77.

141. Birmingham News, May 10, 1972.

142. Doug Seroff, "Gospel Quartet Singing," in Stephen H. Martin, ed., Alabama Folklife: Collected Essays, Alabama Folklife Association (Birmingham, Ala., 1989), 57. This section owes much of its information to the lifelong tradition of Doug Seroff's gospel scholarship. We are grateful to him for his help and work.

143. Ibid., 60.

144. "Tuxedo Junction" file, Birmingham Public Library.

145. Fallin, 82.

146. "Quartet Trainers in the Birmingham Style," Notes from the "Sterling Jubilee Singers," New World Records, 80513.

147. Doug Seroff, liner notes, *Birmingham Quartet Anthology*, Clanka-Lanka Records, 1980. This remarkable reunion concert in Birmingham of the still-singing groups from the 1920s and 1930s offers a window into a vanished world of gospel quartet music.

148. Ibid.

149. McCallum, 11.

150. Seroff, *Birmingham Quartet Anthology*.

151. "Quartet Trainers."

152. Ray Funk, "Birmingham Quartets Celebrate the Union Movement," in *Spirit of Steel: Music of the Miners Railroads and Mills of the Birmingham District*, Sloss Furnace Historical Landmark publication (Birmingham, Ala., 1999), 11.

153. Ray Allen, *Singing in the Spirit: African American Sacred Quartets in New York* (Philadelphia, Pa., 1991), 2.

154. Seroff.

155. Nell Irvin Painter, *The Narrative of Hosea Hudson: His Life as a Negro Communist in the South* (Cambridge, Mass., 1979). See also, Kelley.

156. McCallum, 20.

157. Seroff.

158. Ibid.

159. Alan Young, *Woke Me Up This Morning: Black Gospel Singers and the Gospel Life* (Oxford, Miss., 1997).

160. "The Exodus of Negroes from the Southern States," in U.S. Department of Labor, Division of Negro Economics, *Negro Migration, 1916–1917* (Washington, D.C., 1919), 63.

161. Ibid., 64–65.

162. Ibid.

163. Emmett J. Scott, "More Letters of Negro Migrants, 1916–1918," *Journal of Negro History* 4, no. 4 (October 1919).

164. Ibid.

165. Interview with Charlie Harrell, 3, Sloss Oral History.

166. Wilson, 90.

CHAPTER 5: BLUES PIANOS AND TRICKY BASEBALLS: PITTSBURGH

1. J Ernest Wright, *The WPA History of the Negro in Pittsburgh*, ed. Lawrence Glasco (Pittsburgh, 2004), 25.

2. Rob Ruck, *Sandlot Seasons: Black Sport in Pittsburgh* (Pittsburgh, 1987). This is the best single source for sport in general and baseball in particular for Pittsburgh.

3. Wright, 54–57.

4. Ibid., 61.

5. Andrew Buni, *Robert L. Vann of the Pittsburgh Courier* (Pittsburgh, 1974), 24. See also Laurence Glasco, "High Culture and Black America: Pittsburgh Pennsylvania, 1900–1920" (unpublished paper, University of Pittsburg, 1997. The authors are grateful to Pro-

fessor Glasco for permission to read from his work. See also Jacqueline Welch Wolfe, "The Changing Pattern of Residence of the Negro in Pittsburgh, with Emphasis on the Period 1930–1960" (M.A. thesis, University of Pittsburgh, 1962).

6. Buni, 22.

7. Ibid., 26.

8. Ibid., 21.

9. Wright, 271–275.

10. Ibid., 295.

11. Glasco, "High Culture," 15.

12. Wright, 280–295.

13. Buni, 42.

14. Glasco, "High Culture," 13.

15. Ruck, 125.

16. *Pittsburgh Courier*, February 24, 1962. See also Ruck, 128.

17. Ruck, 129–131.

18. Margaret F. Byington, *Homestead: The Households of a Mill Town* (Pittsburgh, 1974), 17. This was one of the separately published volumes of the survey done between 1908 and 1912 by a team of Progressive urban reformers whose own agenda included the Americanization of foreign workers.

19. Peter Gottlieb, *Making Their Own Way: Southern Blacks' Migration to Pittsburgh, 1916–1930* (Urbana, Ill., 1997), 73.

20. Ibid., 73.

21. Lawrence Glasco, "Double Burden: The Black Experience in Pittsburgh," in Samuel P. Hays, ed., *City at the Point* (Pittsburgh, 1989), 81.

22. Gottlieb, *Making Their Own Way*, 198–202.

23. Dennis Dickerson, *"Out of the Crucible": Black Steel Workers in Western Pennsylvania* (Albany, N.Y., 1986), 65.

24. Ibid., 20.

25. John Bodnar, Michael Weber, and Roger Simon, *Lives of Their Own: Blacks, Italians, and Poles in Pittsburgh, 1900–1960* (Urbana, Ill., 1983), 74. The Hill contained half the black churches in Pittsburgh.

26. Wright, 313.

27. Ibid., 314.

28. Glasco, "High Culture," 25.

29. Ibid., 13.

30. John Bodnar, Michael Weber, and Roger Simon, "Migration, Kinship, and Urban Adjustment: Blacks and Poles in Pittsburgh, 1900–1930," *Journal of American History* 26, no. 3 (December 1979). See also Joe Darden "The Effect of World War I on Black Occupational and Residential Segregation: The Case of Pittsburgh," *Journal of Black Studies* 18, no. 3 (March 1988).

31. Bodner, Weber, and Simon, *Lives of Their Own*, 71.

32. Buni, 82.

33. *Pittsburgh Courier*, February 24, 1962.

34. Demographic numbers wobble a bit, but these figures derive from a number of

sources, including Gottlieb, *Making Their Own Way*, 41; "The Exodus of Negroes from the Southern States," in the United States Department of Demographics, Division of Negro Economics publication, *Negro Migration in 1916–1917* (Washington, D.C., 1919); Peter Gottlieb, "Migration and Jobs: The New Black Workers in Pittsburgh 1916–1930," in Joe Trotter and Eric Ledell Smith, eds., *African Americans in Pennsylvania* (State College, Pa., 1997), 272; Joe Trotter, "Reflections on the Great Migration to Western Pennsylvania," *Pittsburgh History* (Winter 1995–1996); and Abraham Epstein, *The Negro Migrant in Pittsburgh* (repr., New York, 1969).

35. Bodnar, Simon, and Weber, *Lives of Their Own*, 186–188.

36. Epstein, 24–25.

37. Gottlieb, *Making Their Own Way*, 27.

38. Epstein, 24.

39. Ibid., 31.

40. Arthur Edmunds, *Daybreakers: The Story of the Urban League of Pittsburgh* (Pittsburgh, 1983), 28–41.

41. Gottlieb, *Making Their Own Way*, 70.

42. Trotter, 156.

43. Gottlieb, *Making Their Own Way*, 158.

44. Glasco, "Double Burden," 77.

45. Ibid., 78.

46. Wolfe, 2–26; Wright, 26.

47. Bodnar, Simon, and Weber, *Lives of Their Own*, 122.

48. Wright, 25.

49. Ibid., 287–292.

50. Ruck, 27.

51. Edmunds, 45.

52. *Who's Who in Colored America* (1927), 213.

53. Interview with Hampton Johnson, Washington, D.C., April 20, 2005. Earl Johnson's son, Hampton provided much of the information about his father, as did Samuel Black of the Western Pennsylvania Historical Society, Pittsburgh (WPHS).

54. *Pittsburgh Courier*, June 19 and July 9, 1924.

55. Johnson interview.

56. See the entire run of the *Westinghouse Electric News*, WPHS.

57. Ruck, iv–xii.

58. *Homestead Daily Messenger*, July 11, 1922.

59. Interview with Parker and Ware, 1981, Black Pittsburgh Baseball Oral History Collection (BPBB), Library of the University of Pittsburgh. These are the 1981 interviews that Rob Ruck conducted for his comprehensive book, *Sandlot Seasons*.

60. Interview with F. F. Moody, BPBB.

61. Interview with C. Hughes, BPBB.

62. Don Rosogin, *Invisible Men: Life in Baseball's Negro Leagues* (Lincoln, Neb., 1993), 13.

63. *Homestead Daily Messenger*, August 22, 1925.

64. Rosogin, 75.

65. James Banks, *The Pittsburgh Crawfords: The Lives and Times of Baseballs Most Exciting Team* (Dubuque, Iowa, 1991), 74.

66. *Pittsburgh Courier*, March 29, 1930.

67. Ruck, 172.

68. Ibid., 17.

69. *Pittsburgh Courier*, August 26, 1921.

70. *Pittsburgh American*, September 15, 1922; Dorsey scrapbooks, WPHS.

71. *Pittsburgh American*, September 22, 1922; Dorsey scrapbooks, WPHS.

72. Edmunds, 98.

73. *Pittsburgh Courier*, June 4, 1927; April 6, 1929; April 25, 1931.

74. *Pittsburgh Courier*, June 24, 1930.

75. Interview with C. Clark, BPBB.

76. Interview with B. Harris, BPBB.

77. William Brashler, *Josh Gibson: A Life in the Negro Leagues* (New York, 1978), 58–59.

78. Moody interview.

79. Brashler, 59; Rosogin, 45.

80. Ruck, 148.

81. Ibid., 164. This followed a bizarre episode in 1937, when many of the Crawford players jumped ship and went to play for Rafael Trujillo, the dictator of the Dominican Republic, who had determined to buy the pennant in his own country's baseball league.

82. Interview with Robert Lavelle, Pittsburgh, March 10, 2005.

83. Lavelle interview. See also, Interview with James Stewart, BPBB.

84. Lavelle interview.

85. Interview with Art Rooney, BPBB.

86. Interview with Parker Ware, BPBB.

87. Interview with Elijah Miller, October 30, 2004, tape, WPHS.

88. Lavelle interview.

89. Interview with Levi Williams, Pittsburgh, March 10, 2005.

90. Brent Kelley, "Harold Tinker," in *Voices from the Negro Leagues* (Jefferson, N.C., 1998), 16.

91. Interview Levi Miller, Pittsburgh, March 15, 2005.

92. Banks, 54.

93. Miller interview. See also Banks 101.

94. Robert Peterson, *Only the Ball Was White* (New York, 1992), 144.

95. Interview with Larry Doby, Cleveland, February 2000. Doby and Paige roomed together in Cleveland in 1948.

96. Rosogin, 24.

97. Interview with John Watkins and Levi Williams, Pittsburgh, March 10, 2005. Gibson died of a brain tumor, but his peers and neighbors attributed his demise to being passed by in favor of Jackie Robinson as the first black to sign to play in the Major Leagues.

98. Banks, 113.

99. Rosogin, 52.

100. Ibid., 45.

101. John Holloway, *Blackball Stars: Negro League Pioneers* (New York, 1992), 12.

102. Rosogin, 56.

103. John Holloway, *Everything about the Negro Leagues* (Westport, Conn., 2001), 264. See also Rosogin, 56.

104. Rosogin, 73.

105. Brashler, 28–31.

106. *Sporting News,* August 15, 1952, and "The Fabulous Satchel Paige," *Colliers,* October 1953. Both courtesy of the National Baseball Hall of Fame and Library, Cooperstown, N.Y.

107. Rosogin, *Invisible Men,* 98.

108. Interview with Eddie Garvin, proprietor of Eddies Spaghetti House, Pittsburgh, March 2000.

109. August Wilson, *The Piano Lesson* (New York, 1990), act II, scene 5, 106.

110. Interview with Harold Lee, July 3, 1997, African American Jazz Preservation Society of Pittsburgh (AAJPSP) Oral History Project, UE/Labor Archives, University of Pittsburgh.

111. Wright, 244.

112. David Hajdu, *Lush Life: A Biography of Billy Strayhorn* (New York, 1999), 13.

113. *The House,* documentary film, WQED, TV Pittsburgh, 2005.

114. Hajdu, 14.

115. Interview with Adolph Doug Cook, August 22, 1997, AAJPSP.

116. Interview with Dr. Nelson Harrison, Pittsburgh, March 10, 2005. Harrison, a working jazz musician, also teaches psychology, the discipline of his doctorate.

117. Interview with Jerome and Alice Eisner, Pittsburgh, March 18, 2005.

118. Harrison interview.

119. Glasco, "High Culture and Black America," 42.

120. *The House,* WQED.

121. Wright, 286. Here, a mulatto bought drinks for a buck.

122. Harrison interview.

123. Interview with Joe Kennedy Jr., interview, September 1998, AAJPSP.

124. Interview with George Thompson, December 3, 1997, AAJPSP.

125. Interview with Robin Webster, September 25, 1997, AAJPSP.

126. Interview with Charles Austin, August 2, 1995, AAJPSP.

127. Hajdu, 10.

128. Listen, for example, to *Earl "Fatha" Hines,* Epic LN 3501, liner notes by Charles Edward Smith.

129. Gunther Schiller, *The Swing Era* (New York, 1999), 23.

130. Ibid., 25–50.

131. Tammy L. Kernodle, *Soul on Soul: The Life and Music of Mary Lou Williams* (Boston, 2004), 25.

132. Mary Lou Williams, Oral History, June 26, 1973, Institute of Jazz Research, Rutgers University, Newark, New Jersey.

133. Ibid.

134. Kernodle, 59.

135. Mary Lou Williams, *Mary Lou Williams, 1927–1940*, Classics Chronological, CD 630.

136. Linda Dahl, *Morning Glory: A Biography of Mary Lou Williams* (New York, 1999), 31.

137. Hajdu, 39; Jerome and Alice Eisner interview.

138. Billy Strayhorn, *Lush Life*, Red Baron Records, CD AK52760, liner notes by Stanley Dance.

139. Hajdu, 49.

140. From the Mary Lou Williams autobiography first printed in the jazz journal, *Melody Maker* (1954), reprinted in Robert Gottlieb, ed., *Reading Jazz* (New York, 1999), 106.

141. Interview with Joe Negri, Pittsburgh, March 18, 2005.

142. Jerome and Alice Eisner interview.

143. Peter Wainright, "Erroll Garner, Early Biographical Data," *Journal of the Erroll Garner Club* 2, no.2 (April 1992).

144. This is the Jamal legend, true, but only part of the story. Harrison interview.

145. Interview with Pete Henderson, March 8, 1997, AAJPSP.

146. Negri interview. Negri, a white guitar player, witnessed the moment. He gained a second career as Handy Man Negri on *Mr. Roger's Neighborhood*, created and broadcast in Pittsburgh.

147. Harrison interview.

148. Negri interview.

149. Interview with A. Jamal, in French, "Ahmad Jamal: 1974, un célèbre meconnu," *Jazz Magazine* (www.Jazzmagazine.com), 1974, translated by the authors. This is the best source about the details of Jamal's life we have located.

150. Nat Hentoff, *Hear Me Talkin' to Ya: The Story of Jazz* (New York, 1955). Cited in liner notes to *Ahmad Jamal: The Legendary OKEH & Epic Recordings*, Epic CD EK 93580. On the peel-off label, Davis is quoted: "All of my inspirations come from Ahmad Jamal."

151. Jamal interview.

152. Ibid.

153. Harrison interview.

154. *Ahmad Jamal: The Legendary OKEH and Epic Recordings*.

CHAPTER 6: WALKIN' EGYPT: MISSISSIPPI DELTA

1. St. Clair Drake and Horace Cayton, *Black Metropolis* (Chicago, 1970).

2. J. H. Dillard, *Negro Migration, 1916–1917* (Washington, D.C., 1919), 18.

3. Ibid.

4. Neil McMillan, *Dark Journey: Black Mississippians in the Age of Jim Crow* (Urbana, Ill., 1989), 119.

5. See James Grossman, *Land of Hope: Chicago, Black Southerners, and the Great Migration* (Chicago, 1989), 3. For statistics by county in the south, see Richard Forstall, *Population of States and Counties of the United States: 1790–1990*, Department of Commerce, U.S. Bureau of the Census (Washington, D.C., 1996), and the remarkable compilation by Lewis Jones, *Statistical Atlas of the Southern States, 1900–1930* (Nashville, Tenn., 1940).

6. Dillard, *Negro Migration*, 18.

7. Carol Marks, *So Long—We're Good and Gone: The Great Black Migration* (Bloom-

ington, Ind., 1989), 65. Marks also sees a greater proportion of relatively skilled migrants leaving during this period.

8. Grossman.

9. McMillan, 45.

10. Ibid., 265.

11. All testimony cited from Federal Writers Project of the Works Progress Administration for the State of Mississippi, *The American Slave: A Composite Autobiography*, vol. 7, *Oklahoma and Mississippi Narratives* (1941; repr., Westport, Conn., 1972).

12. Vincent Harding, "Religion and Resistance among Antebellum Slaves," in Timothy Fulop and Albert J. Raboteau, eds., *African-American Religion: Interpretive Essays in History and Culture* (New York, 1977), 118.

13. Robert Farris Thompson, *Flash of the Spirit: African and Afro-American Art and Philosophy* (New York, 1984), 47, 79.

14. Ibid., 93.

15. Theophus H. Smith, *Conjuring Culture: Biblical Formations of Black America* (New York, 1994). See also Thompson, *Flash of the Spirit*; Samuel A. Floyd, *The Power of Black Music* (New York, 1995); Albert J. Raboteau, *Slave Religion: The "Invisible Institution" in the Antebellum South* (New York, 2004).

16. Emphasis added.

17. WPA, *Oklahoma and Mississippi Narratives*.

18. Harding, 122.

19. William Francis Allen, Charles Ware, and Lucy McKim Garrison, *Slave Songs of the United States, 1867* (New York, 1952), xiii.

20. Lydia Parrish, *Slave Songs of the Georgia Sea Islands* (New York, 1942), 18.

21. Walter Pitts Jr., *Old Ship of Zion: The Afro-Baptist Ritual in the African Diaspora* (New York), 1993.

22. "In a Cloud," cited in Lawrence Levine, "Slave Songs and Slave Consciousness," in Fulop and Raboteau, *African-American Religion*; "I was twelve years old," in WPA, *Oklahoma and Mississippi Narratives*, 1.

23. Miles M. Fisher, *Negro Slave Songs in the United States* (Secaucus, N.J., 1998), 90.

24. Federal Writers Project, *Mississippi: The WPA Guide to the Magnolia State* (Oxford, Miss., 2009), 23.

25. Lawrence Levine, *Black Culture and Black Consciousness* (New York, 1978), 38.

26. Fred Chisenhall and Margaret McKee, *Beale Black and Blue* (Baton Rouge, La., 1981), 28.

27. Thomasina Neely, "Relief, Ritual and Performance in a Black Pentecostal Church: The Musical Heritage of the Church of God in Christ" (Ph.D. diss., University of Indiana, 1993), 69.

28. Horace Clayton Boyer, *How Sweet the Sound: The Golden Age of Gospel* (Washington, D.C., 1995), 15.

29. Paul Oliver, *Songsters and Saints* (New York, 1984), 171.

30. Neely, 166.

31. *Memphis Gospel, 1927–1929*, Document Records, DOCD-5072.

32. Oliver, 185.

33. Richard Wright, *Black Boy* (New York, 1945).

34. Mississippi Delta Chapter, Daughters of the American Revolution, Florence Stillers, Regent, *History of Bolivar County, Mississippi* (Clarksdale, Miss., 1948), 2–4.

35. Ruby Sheppard Hicks, *The Song of the Delta* (Jackson, Miss., 1976), 4.

36. See James Cobb, *The Most Southern Place on Earth: The Mississippi Delta and the Roots of Regional Identity* (New York, 1994). This is the best single treatment of the Delta.

37. Charles S. Aiken, *The Cotton Plantation South since the Civil War* (Baltimore, 1998), 60.

38. McMillan, 50–95.

39. Interview with Jerry Ricks, Helena, Arkansas, October 2001. Ricks introduced the author to Mississippi John in 1966.

40. Cobb, 297.

41. Ibid., 99.

42. John C. Willis, *Forgotten Time: The Yazoo Mississippi Delta after the Civil War* (Charlottesville, Va., 2000), 48.

43. Ibid., 5.

44. See Cobb and Aiken, for full discussions of the "furnish" and the "settle."

45. Interview with Joe Rice Dockery, December 13, 1979, transcript, Mississippi Department of Archives and History, Jackson, Mississippi.

46. Willis, 117.

47. Janet Sharp Herman, *The Pursuit of a Dream* (New York, 1981), 221.

48. Interview with Milburne Crowe, Mound Bayou, October 2001.

49. Herman, 170–190.

50. Ibid., 50.

51. Ibid., 188.

52. First Baptist Church of Mound Bayou, *First Baptist Gospel Newsletter,* Fall edition, 2000, author's collection; Interview with First Baptist Gospel Choir, Mound Bayou, Miss., February 2001.

53. Jones. Bolivar County had 8 reported lynchings between 1900 and 1930. Interview with Norva Lee Harris, retired nurse, Mound Bayou, Mississippi, October 2000.

54. Interview with Preston Holms, retired postmaster, Mound Bayou, Mississippi, October 2000.

55. Telephone interview with Milburn Crowe, Mound Bayou, Mississippi, February 2001.

56. David Beito, "Black Fraternal Hospitals," in *From Mutual Aid to the Welfare State* (Chapel Hill, N.C., 1999). The story of this facility remains fascinating. Directed by a recruited Fisk-Meharry Medical School surgeon, Doctor Theodore Roosevelt Mason Howard, Taborian opened in 1942 at the cost of $100,000 raised from subscribers statewide. Annual dues of $8.40 brought burial payments of $200.00 and thirty-one days of hospitalization. Eventually Howard and Smith became rivals, and Howard opened another hospital, a community swimming pool, a 1,600-acre plantation, and an insurance company. In 1954 Howard moved into political organizing, spearheaded voter registration drives in Mound Bayou, and hired the young Medgar Evers to work in his insurance company. Finally, following his attempt to locate witnesses in the Till case, which produced

death threats, Howard left the Delta in 1956 for Chicago, where he opened a medical practice on the South Side.

57. Telephone interview with Norva Lee Harris, Mound Bayou, Mississippi, January 2001.

58. Kay Hivley and Albert E. Brumley Jr., *I'll Fly Away: The Life Story of Alfred Brumley* (Branson, Mo., 1990), 44.

59. Interview with Rev. Willie Morganfield, Clarksdale, Mississippi, February 2001.

60. Letter to Dorothy Horstman, January 10, 1973, http//members nbei.com. Bob Dylan accompanied Carolyn Hester on "I'll Fly Away," September 29, 1961.

61. Gwendolyn Sims Warren, *Ev'ry Time I feel the Spirit* (New York, 1997), 139.

62. Harris interview.

63. Gayle Dean Wardlow, *Chasin' the Devil's Music* (San Francisco, Calif., 1988), 102–104. Wardlow and his editor Edward Komura have worked to find the documents that reconcile the often-contradictory gaps between life and legend of the dozens of Delta blues players. White may have shot but not killed someone, and may have been sentenced for two or three years and not life, but the Wardlow-Komura evidence is convincing in his case.

64. Two recent histories of Parchman, David Oshinsky, *"Worse than Slavery": Parchman Farm and the Ordeal of Jim Crow Justice* (New York, 1996), and William Banks Taylor, *Down on Parchman Farm* (Columbus, Ohio, 1999), provide much of the information in this section.

65. Hortense Powdermaker, *After Freedom: A Cultural Study of the Deep South* (New York, 1940).

66. Oshinsky and Taylor.

67. Oshinsky, 133.

68. Interview with Joe Rice Dockery, December 1, 1979, transcript, Mississippi Department of Archives and History.

69. Oshinsky, 220.

70. Ibid., 224.

71. Taylor, 9.

72. Interview with Fred Storey, Parchman, Mississippi, February 2001.

73. Oshinsky, 141.

74. Taylor, 59.

75. Jeff Todd Titon, *Early Down Home Blues* (Chapel Hill, N.C., 1977), 25. "Oh, Kate's up the river, Stack-O'Lee's in the ben'" was one of the fragments that W. C. Handy reported hearing in 1903.

76. Oshinsky, 220.

77. Muddy Waters, "Flood," as quoted in Cobb, 297.

78. John M. Barry, *Rising Tide: The Great Mississippi Flood of 1927 and How it Changed America* (New York, 1997). See also Cobb and McMillan.

79. *Memphis Gospel (1927–1929)*, Document Records, DOCD-5072.

80. Titon, 210. Titon provides examples of "down-home" blues released before 1926, but he also shows that sales of classic blues reached their apex in 1927.

81. "High Water Everywhere" (part 1), *Charlie Patton: Complete Recorded Works in*

Chronological Order, Volume 2—Late November/Early December, 1929, Document Records, DOCD-5010.

82. Barry, 312.

83. Ibid.

84. McMillan, 148.

85. Barry, 334.

86. "High Water Everywhere" (part 2), *Charlie Patton,* vol. 2.

87. Interview with Paul Oscher, Los Angeles, January 2001; Robert Springer, *Authentic Blues* (New York, 1999). See also David Evens, *Big Road Blues* (Berkeley, 1982), and Paul Oliver, *Blues Fell This Morning* (New York, 1960).

88. Owenby, 115–118.

89. Leroy Carr, "How Long, How Long Blues," JSP Records, 2008.

90. Robert Johnson, "Terraplane Blues," in *The Complete Recordings of Robert Johnson,* Sony, 1990.

91. Charlie Patton, "Pony Blues," in *Charlie Patton Pony Blues,* Proper Records, 2004.

92. Oscher interview.

93. Son House, "Preaching the Blues," in Son House, *Preachin' the Blues,* Catfish Records, 2000.

94. Jon Michael Spencer, *Blues and Evil* (Knoxville, Tenn., 1993), 11.

95. Levine, *Black Culture, Black Consciousness,* 237.

96. The discussion of Robert Johnson's "new" technique owes itself to the learned study by Edward Komara, *The Road to Robert Johnson,* which Mr. Komara provided in proof form to the authors.

97. Spencer, 64.

98. Madge Baucom, *Clarksdale—The Wonder City of the Delta,* Clarksdale Chamber of Commerce, n.d., Carnegie Free Library, Clarksdale, Mississippi.

99. Samuel G. Adams, "Changing Negro Life in the Delta" (M.A. thesis, Fisk University, 1947). Adams was a member of the Lomax "team" that studied the Delta. Much of the material he collected was used by Lomax to document his work on the origins of the blues.

100. Ibid., 14.

101. Ted Owenby, *American Dreams in Mississippi* (Chapel Hill, N.C., 1999), 64–72.

102. Abe Isaacson, who moved to Clarksdale in 1914, quoted in *History of Clarksdale and Coahoma County,* n.d., Clarksdale Public Library, 109.

103. Adams, 11; Alan Lomax, *The Land Where the Blues Began* (New York, 2002), 37. Lomax did not get the quote right. It may be found in the *History of Clarksdale and Coahoma County.*

104. Lewis Jones, Memorandum to Alan Lomax and Charles S. Johnson, "Field Trip to Coahoma County," Division of Folklife, Library of Congress, Washington, D.C.

105. Sandra Tooze, *Muddy Waters: The Mojo Man* (Chicago, 1996), 37.

106. Ibid., 20–24. Statistics on the Rosenwald Schools may be found in Jones.

107. Owenby, 64–72.

108. Aiken, 111.

109. Morganfield interview.

110. Lomax, 72.

111. Tooze, 26–33.

112. Roxy David LePue, "Muddy Waters Library of Congress Field Recordings: An Analysis of His Early Repertoire" (M.A. thesis, University of Memphis, 1998).

113. Muddy Waters, "I Be's Troubled," in *The Complete Plantation Recordings*, Chess, 1993.

114. Gerhard Kubik, *Africa and the Blues* (Jackson, Miss., 1999), 9–16, 59–92.

115. Charles Joyner, *Down by the Riverside* (Urbana, Ill., 1985), 200–201. See also J. L. Dillard, *Black English: Its History and Usage in the United States* (New York, 1972).

116. Dillard, *Negro Migration*, 16.

117. McMillan, 261.

118. Marcus Jones, *Black Migration in the United States with Emphasis on Selected Central Cities* (Saratoga, Calif., 1980), 47.

CHAPTER 7: BRONZEVILLE'S PINKSTER KINGS: SOUTH SIDE CHICAGO

1. Dominic A. Pacyga and Ellen Skerrett, *Chicago: A City of Neighborhoods* (Chicago, 1986), 1.

2. The list of books on the Great Migration and the history of the South Side begins with the excellent James Grossman, *Land of Hope: Chicago, Black Southerners and the Great Migration* (Chicago, 1989); it includes as well, Arnold D. Hirsch, *Making the Second Ghetto: Race and Housing in Chicago, 1940–1960* (New York, 1983); Thomas Lee Philpott, *The Slum and the Ghetto: Neighborhood Deterioration and Middle Class Reform, Chicago, 1880–1939* (New York, 1978); Milton Sernett, *Bound for the Promised Land: African American Religion and the Great Migration* (Durham, N.C., 1997); Carole Marks, *Farewell—We're Good and Gone: The Great Black Migration* (Bloomington, Ind., 1989); Joe William Trotter, ed., *The Great Migration in Historical Perspective* (Bloomington, Ind., 1991); Nicolas Leman, *The Promised Land: The Great Black Migration and How it Changed America* (New York, 1991); and Allan Spear, *Black Chicago: The Making of a Negro Ghetto* (Chicago, 1967). Finally, see the classic *Black Metropolis*, by St. Clair Drake and Horace Cayton, whose research notes may be found at the Vivian Harsh Collection of the Carter Woodson Library, a branch of the Chicago Public Library system.

3. William Tuttle, *Race Riot: Chicago and the Red Summer of 1919* (Champaign, Ill., 1996).

4. Grossman.

5. Interview with Joan Snowden, February 3, 1938, Illinois Writers Project, WPA, Vivian Harsh Collection, Carter Woodson Library, Chicago. In the 1930s, the WPA-sponsored Illinois Writers Project interviewed dozens of Old Settlers. Many of the interviews, usually conducted by white graduate students at the University of Chicago, remain unexamined. The WPA materials along with the "Survey of Negro Life in Chicago," compiled in the 1920s, provided a snapshot of Old Settler life and attitudes during the first generation of the Great Migration.

6. Ibid.

7. Interview with Gertrude Davis, January 18, 1937, Illinois Writers Project, Harsh Collection.

8. Interview with Bell Harper Graves Fountain, February 15, 1937, Illinois Writers Project, Harsh Collection.

9. Roi T. Ottley, *The Lonely Warrior: The Life and Times of Robert S. Abbott* (Chicago, 1955), 25–32.

10. Ibid., 126.

11. See Adam Green, *The Rising Tide of Youth* (New York, 2001).

12. *The Survey of Negro Life in Chicago*, published by the Intercollegiate Club, Chicago, Harsh Collection. Also known as *The Wonderbook*.

13. Pamphlet, *Negro Jobs and Occupations in Chicago, 1910–1930*, Harsh Collection, 195–196.

14. Ibid., 219.

15. *Survey of Negro Life*, 180.

16. Grossman, 149–150.

17. *Survey of Negro Life*, 185.

18. Davarian Baldwin, *Chicago's New Negroes* (Chapel Hill, N.C., 2007).

19. See the "Black Metropolis Historic District" planning report submitted to the Chicago Historical and Architectural Landmarks Commission, March 7, 1984, Harsh Collection.

20. Philpott, 185.

21. Gwendolyn Brooks, "A Song in the Front Yard," from *A Street in Bronzeville*, reprinted in *Blacks* (Chicago, 1987).

22. Philpott, 196.

23. Ibid., 179.

24. *Survey of Negro Life*, 85. See also Jontyle Theresa Robinson and Wendy Greenhouse, *The Art of Archibald Motley* (Chicago, 1991). See also Amy M. Mooney, "Representing Race: Disjunctures in the Work of Archibald J. Motley, Jr.," in *African Americans in Art: Selections from the Art Institute of Chicago* (Chicago, 1999).

25. Interview with Archibald Motley Jr., by Dennis Barrie, Chicago, January 23, 1978, p. 26, Archives of American Art, Chicago Historical Society.

26. Ibid., 25.

27. William Howland Kenney, *Chicago Jazz: A Cultural History, 1904–1930* (New York, 1993), 14–23. Kenney quotes "head rags" from the *Defender*. The actual description of The Stroll is taken from several of Motley's paintings, especially *Black Belt* (1934), *Barbecue* (1934) and *Bronzeville at Night* (1949).

28. Kenny, 56–60.

29. Archibald Motley Jr., "Sketchbook," 27, Motley Papers, Chicago Historical Society.

30. See Wallace Best, *Passionately Human, No Less Divine* (Princeton, N.J., 2005). The authors thank Best for his suggestions early on in their research.

31. Sernett, 119–157.

32. "The Negro in Illinois," 1941, Illinois Writers Project, Harsh Collection.

33. "History of Progressive Baptist Church," *Progressive Baptist 50th Anniversary Program* (Chicago, 1969), collection of the authors.

34. Vatel Elbert Daniel, "Ritual in Chicago's South Side Churches for Negroes" (Ph.D. diss., University of Chicago, 1940), 83.

35. Robert L. Sutherland, "An Analysis of Negro Churches in Chicago" (Ph.D. diss., Divinity School, University of Chicago, 1930); Daniel, 15.

36. Daniel, 124.

37. "The Negro in Chicago," 1940, Illinois Writers Project, Harsh Collection, Carter Woodson Library, courtesy of Michael Flug, Curator.

38. "Annual Report of Cosmopolitan Community Church," 1964, Joyner Papers, Harsh Collection.

39. Horace Clarence Boyer, How Sweet the Sound: The Golden Age of Gospel (Washington, D.C., 1995), 79.

40. Wallace Best and Michael Flug, "Smith, Lucy Madden," in Rima Lunin Schultz and Adele Hast, eds., Women Building Chicago, 1790–1990: A Biographical Dictionary (Bloomington, Ind., 2001), 814–817. The authors thank Best and Flug for providing them with the text.

41. Sernett, 119–157.

42. The Pentecostal Ensign, February 1936, Collier Papers, Harsh Collection.

43. Best and Flug, 6.

44. Boyer, How Sweet the Sound, 38.

45. Mahalia Jackson, with Evan McLeod Wylie, Movin' On Up (New York, 1966), 32–33.

46. Thomasina Neeley, "Relief, Ritual, and Performance in a Black Pentecostal Church" (Ph.D. diss., University of Indiana, 1993),164–165.

47. Boyer, 78–79.

48. Critic Robert Anderson, quoted Anthony Heilbut, liner notes to The Great Gospel Women, Shanachie 6004.

49. Mellonee V. Burnim, "Conflict and Controversy in Black Religious Music," in Victor Smythe and Howard Dotson, eds., African American Religion: Research Problems and Resources for the 1990s (New York, 1992), 82.

50. Ibid., 90.

51. Alan Young, Woke Me Up This Morning (Jackson, Miss., 1991), 9.

52. Timothy Kalil, "The Role of the Great Migration of African Americans to Chicago in the Development of Traditional Black Gospel Piano by Thomas A. Dorsey, circa 1930" (Ph.D. diss., Kent State University, 1993), 39.

53. Herbert Morrison Smith, "Three Negro Preachers in Chicago" (M.A. thesis, University of Chicago, 1935), 7.

54. Boyer, 42. See also William Thomas Dargan, "Congregational Church Songs in a Black Holiness Church: A Musical and Textural Analysis" (Ph.D. diss., Wesleyan University, 1994), 13.

55. Cynthia Dawn Stephens, "The Origins of Gospel Piano: People, Events and Circumstances" (D.M.A. diss., University of Washington, 1987), 13.

56. Michael W. Harris, The Rise of the Gospel Blues: The Music of Thomas Andrew Dorsey and the Urban Church, (New York, 1993), 180.

57. Kalil, 83.

58. See Angela Davis, Blues Legacies and Black Feminism (New York, 1998).

59. Harris, 75.

60. Quoted in Mellonee V. Burnim, "Religious Music," *Garland Encyclopedia of World Music*, (New York, 2001), 631. See also, Mellonee V. Burnim, "The Black Gospel Tradition: A Complex of Ideology, Aesthetic, and Behavior," *Western Journal of Black Studies* 12, no. 2 (1988).

61. Harris, 125.

62. Anthony Heilbut, *The Gospel Sound: Good News and Bad Times* (New York, 1971; rev. ed., 1997), 31.

63. Boyer, 85.

64. Heilbut, 65.

65. Horace Boyer, *Roberta Martin: Innovator of Modern Gospel Music* (Washington, D.C., 1992).

66. *Defender*, August 23, 1933.

67. See William D. Peterson, *Black Yankees: The Development of an Afro-American Subculture in Eighteenth Century New England* (Amherst, Mass., 1988); Joseph P. Reidy, "Negro Election Day and Black Community Life in New England, 1750–1860," *Marxist Perspectives* 1, no. 3 (Fall 1978): 102–117; Shane White, "Pinkster: Afro Dutch Syncretization in New York City and the Hudson Valley," *Journal of American Folklore* 102, no. 403 (January–March, 1989): 68–76.

68. *Defender*, August 23, 1933.

69. *Defender* writer Earl Calloway wrote on August 12, 2000, of the first parade taking place in 1929 and moving down Michigan Avenue. There is no record of the year or route in the *Defender* until 1930.

70. Willard Motley, "Sister and Brother," *Defender*, September 26, 1922. "My first published story," Motley wrote in his scrapbook, Willard Motley Papers, Northern Illinois University Rare Books Collection, DeKalb, Illinois. The authors thank Professor Craig Abbott of NIU for locating the story in the collection.

71. *New York Sun*, July 17, 1930, reported on Motley's thirteen-day bicycle trip from Chicago to New York that summer, where he would await his "brother" painter Archibald Motley's return from Paris. The 1930 date also underscores the year of the First Bud Billiken Day and parade. The authors thank Archie Motley for disclosing this information.

72. Daniel Mark Epstein, *Nat King Cole* (New York, 1999), 29.

73. Grossman, 145.

74. *Defender*, August 17, 1929.

75. *Defender*, August 26, 1933. Abbott, sadly, had been forced to purchase the Rolls through the intermediary of a white friend to circumvent the dealer's unwillingness to "dilute" the car's value by selling to an African American. Roi Ottley, *The Lonely Warrior* (Chicago, 1955), 223.

76. *Defender*, August 23, 1933.

77. Epstein, 33.

78. *Defender*, August, 18, 1934.

79. Interview with William Lowry, Gambier, Ohio, May 25, 2001.

80. Mechal Sobel, *"Trabelin" On* (Princeton, N.J., 1988).

81. David W. Blight, *Race and Reunion: The Civil War in American Memory* (Cambridge,

Mass., 2004), 65. See also Bernard Powers Jr., *Black Charlestonians: A Social History, 1822–1865* (Fayetteville, Ark.,1994).

82. William Wiggins and Douglas DeNatale, eds., *Jubilation!: African American Celebrations* (Columbia, S.C., 1993), 64. See also John Meffert and Sherman Pyatt, *Charleston South Carolina* Avery Center (Charleston, S.C., 2007), 40.

83. Robert F. Thompson, *Four Moments of the Sun: The Kongo in the New World* (London, 1951). Interview, Gambier, Ohio, November 2001.

84. Wiggins, 75.

85. Ibid., 77.

86. Video, Channel 9, Chicago, August 12, 1971 (Chicago Historical Society) clearly shows the stylized, back-and-forth, ring shout–derived dance motion of marching black participants in the parade. The ensemble of multiple marching bands and the accompanying clapping of the crowds made for a polyrhythmic African musical experience. When William Lowry, who attended his first Bud Billiken Day parade in 1942, viewed the 1971 tape, he reported that the tape showed "exactly" the same parade as the one he had participated in. "Even the float from Pekin Cleaners. I'll be darned." Interview with William Lowry, Gambier, Ohio, May 25, 2001. See also Geneviève Fabre, "African American Commemorative Celebrations in the Nineteenth Century," in Geneviève Fabre and Robert O'Meally, *History and Memory in African American Culture* (New York, 1994), 72.

87. Karen Dalton and Peter Wood, *Winslow Homer's Images of Blacks: The Reconstruction and Civil War Years* (Austin, 1990), 101.

88. Reidy, 108.

89. Shane White and Graham White, *Stylin': African American Expressive Culture from Its Beginnings to the Zoot Suit* (Ithaca, N.Y., 2001), 92–93.

90. White and White, 97.

91. Susan Herbst, *Politics at the Margins* (New York, 1994), 71.

92. Olivia Mahoney, *Douglas/Grand Boulevard: A Chicago Neighborhood* (Chicago, 2001), 89.

93. Herbst, 73.

94. *Defender*, October 27, 1934.

95. *Defender*, June 22 and 29, 1935.

96. *Defender*, May 7, 1935.

97. Herbst estimates that the *Defender*'s circulation had dropped considerably from its high of 200,000 copies per week in 1925.

98. *Defender*, August 17, 1935.

99. *Defender*, September 14, 1935.

100. Lowry interview.

101. *Defender*, July 9, 1938.

102. *Defender*, August 7, 1940. Featured on the society page, light-skinned women dominated the ten finalists of 1940. Winner Miriam Ali would compete in the Miss Bronze America contest later in the month at the American Negro Exposition.

103. Interview with Dempsey Travis, Chicago, April 20, 2001.

104. See Victor Turner, *Dramas, Fields and Metaphors: Symbolic Action in Human Society* (Ithaca, N.Y., 1974), 30.

105. Roger Biles, " 'Big Red in Bronzeville': Mayor Ed Kelly Reels in the Black Vote," in Rosemary K. Adams, *A Wild Kind of Boldness* (Chicago, 1998), 410–415.

106. Interview with Ko-Ko Taylor, Chicago, March 2001.

107. Interview with Prentiss Brown, Greenville Club, Chicago, March 2001.

108. Ibid.

109. Lowry interview.

110. "Remembering 47th Street," *Chicago Stories*, WTTE Chicago, May, 2001.

111. Nicholas L. Lehman, *Promised Land: The Great Black Migration and How It Changed America* (New York, 1992), 70–74.

112. Interview with Prentiss Brown and Mary Wiley, Greenville Club, Chicago, March 2001.

113. Daniel Wolff, *You Send Me: The Life and Times of Sam Cooke* (New York, 1995), 48.

114. Heilbut, xxix.

115. Boyer, 31.

116. Ibid., 95–97.

117. Ibid., 97.

118. Wolff, 83.

119. Heilbut, 75.

120. Wolff, 64.

121. Robert Palmer, *Deep Blues* (New York, 1981), 35.

122. Ibid., 24 and 34. See also Wolff, 12.

123. Wolff, 19.

124. Ibid., 37–42.

125. *Sam Cooke: With the Soul Stirrers*, Specialty Records, CD SPDC-7009-2.

126. Boyer, 196.

127. Interview with Bill Branch, Evanston, Illinois, March 2001.

128. Rowe, *Chicago Blues*, 78. See Nadine Cohodas, *Spinning Blues into Gold* (New York, 2000), 7–34.

129. Sandra Toze, *Muddy Waters: The Mojo Man* (Chicago, 1996), 59–82.

130. Robert Gordon, *Can't Be Satisfied: The Life and Times of Muddy Waters* (Boston, 2002), 93.

131. Palmer, 143.

132. Brown interview.

133. Sebastian Danchin, *Earl Hooker, Blues Master* (Jackson, Miss., 2001), 23.

134. Palmer, 96. See also, Robert Farris Thompson's discussion of Niski charms in *Flash of the Spirit: African and Afro-American Art and Philosophy* (New York, 1983).

135. Mike Rowe, *Chicago Blues: The City and the Music* (New York, 1975), 80.

136. Toze, 79.

137. Richard Okoar, a Nigerian ethnomusicologist, in private communication with the authors.

138. Palmer, 96.

139. Branch interview.

140. Willie Dixon with Don Snowden, *I Am the Blues* (New York, 1989), 2.

141. Dixon, 7.

142. Rowe, 138.

143. Charles Sawyer, *The Arrival of B. B. King* (New York, 1980) 63.

144. Taylor interview.

145. Ibid.

146. Ibid.

147. Rowe, 172.

148. Adam Green, *Selling the Race* (Chicago, 2007). The authors thank Professor Green for sharing the manuscript with them prior to publication.

149. See *Chicago Politics Ward by Ward,* n.d., Chicago Historical Society, and the collection of *Local Community Fact Books (1934, 1960, 1980),* Chicago Historical Society.

150. *Chicago Politics Ward by Ward,* 83. See also Charles R. Branham, "The Transformation of Black Political Leadership in Chicago, 1864–1942" (Ph.D. diss., University of Chicago, 1981).

151. Lehman, 74–75.

152. Ibid., 71.

153. *Defender,* May 23, 1962.

154. *Chicago Sun-Times,* June 27, 1955.

155. "This Is Your Life Reverend T. E. Brown," Progressive Baptist Program, 1978; Interview with Rev. Dr. Christopher Bullock, Chicago, April 2001.

156. Interview with Ann Smith, Chicago, April 2001.

157. *Defender,* March 18–24, 1961.

158. Smith interview.

159. *Chicago Sun-Times,* September 13, 1957.

160. *Defender,* March 18–24, 1961.

161. Ibid.

162. Florence Hamlish Levinsohn, *Harold Washington: A Political Biography* (Chicago, 1983).

CHAPTER 8: DIXIE SPECIAL: HOUSTON

1. Walter Johnson, *Soul by Soul: Life Inside the Antebellum Slave Market* (Cambridge, Mass., 1999); Alrutheus A. Taylor, "The Movement of Negroes from the East to the Gulf States from 1830 to 1850," *Journal of Negro History* 3 (1923): 367–383.

2. United States, Works Progress Administration, *Slave Narratives from the Federal Writers Project, 1936–1938, Texas* (Washington, D.C., 1941), vols. 3 and 4. In quoting from the narratives in this chapter, we have not reproduced the "black dialect" used by the interviewers, who were not trained linguists. Instead, we have "translated" the accounts into what we believe the interviewees intended to say. That is, we have not corrected syntax such as "ain't," double negatives, or singular pronouns in reference to plural subjects characteristic of black English, but we have not reproduced the misspellings of the interrogators such as "massa" for master, "bud" for bird, or "dawg" for dog because such misspellings exist only in the transcripts of the interviewers, not the oral statements of the informants. It is likely that most slaves' speech conformed to Gullah language patterns, but rather than compound earlier errors, we simply translated the meaning, not the sounds of the interviews.

3. Michael A. Gomez, *Exchanging Our Country Marks: The Transformation of African Identities in the Colonial and Antebellum South* (Chapel Hill, N.C., 1998); Ira Berlin, "From Creole to African: Atlantic Creoles and the Origins of American-American Society in Mainland North America," *William and Mary Quarterly*, 3rd ser., 53 (1996): 251–288.

4. U.S. Census Bureau, *United States Census, Texas* (Washington, D.C., 1861).

5. William Adams, in *Texas Narratives*, vol. 3, part 1, 1–10.

6. Madison Bruin, in *Texas Narratives*, vol. 3, part 1, 170.

7. Wash Wilson, in *Texas Narratives*, vol. 3, part 2, 195–200.

8. Ibid.

9. Ibid.

10. Charley Mitchell, in *Texas Narratives*, vol. 4, part 3, 113.

11. Richard Caruthers, in *Texas Narratives.*, vol. 3, part 1, 199.

12. Ellen Payne, in *Texas Narratives*, vol. 4, part 3, 179.

13. Lorenz Ezell, in *Texas Narratives*, vol. 3, part 2, 32. For other conjure and hoodoo statements, see *Texas Narratives*, vol. 3, part 1, 5–8, 43–44, 137–142, 217–218, 244–245, 282; vol. 3, part 2, 2, 209, 219; vol. 4, part 2, 36–38, 44, 86, 136–137; vol. 4, part 3, 96, 149–150.

14. Randolph B. Campbell, *Gone to Texas: A History of the Lone Star State* (Austin, 2003), 26–206.

15. James Cape, in *Texas Narratives*, vol. 3, part 1, 195.

16. Martin Jackson, in *Texas Narratives*, vol. 3, part 2, 192.

17. Amos Lincoln, in *Texas Narratives*, vol. 4, part 3, 17.

18. Tom Mills, in *Texas Narratives*, vol. 4, part 3, 88–107.

19. Trudier Harris, " 'The Yellow Rose of Texas': A Different Cultural View," *Callaloo* 20 (1997).

20. Francis Edward Abernethy and Carolyn Fiedler Satterwhite, eds., *Juneteenth Texas* (Denton, Tex., 1996).

21. Ibid., 106–112; Campbell, 268–289.

22. Lawrence C. Goodwyn, "Populist Dreams and Negro Rights: East Texas as a Case Study," *American Historical Review* 76 (1971).

23. Campbell, 268–289.

24. Dudley Taylor Cornish, *The Sable Arm: Black Troops in the Union Army, 1861–1865* (Lawrence, Kans., 1987).

25. Quoted in Quintard Taylor, *In Search of the Racial Frontier* (New York, 1998), 167.

26. Frank N. Schubert, *On the Trail of the Buffalo Soldier: Biographies of African Americans in the U.S. Army, 1866–1917* (Wilmington, Del., 1995).

27. *Texas Narratives*, vol. 4, part 2, 190–210.

28. Howard Beeth and Cary D. Wentz, eds., *Black Dixie: Afro-Texan History and Culture in Houston* (College Station, Tex., 1992), 14–21; "Brief History of the Fourth Ward," *Houston Metropolitan* (1991): 28–33, 59; James M. SoRelle, "Darker Side of Heaven" (Ph.D. diss., Kent State University, 1980), 48–49; U.S. Census Bureau, *United States Census*, 1870, 1880, 1910, Texas (Washington, D.C., 1871, 1881, 1911).

29. U.S. Census Bureau, *United States Census*, 1870.

30. William H. Wiggins Jr., "Juneteenth: A Red Spot Day on the Texas Calendar," in Abernathy and Satterwhite, *Juneteenth Texas*, 237–254.

31. William H. Wiggins Jr., "From Galveston to Washington: Charting Juneteenth's Freedom Trail," in William H. Wiggins Jr. and Douglas DeNatale, eds., *Jubilation!: African American Celebrations in the Southeast* (Columbia, S.C., 1994), 61–67; SoRelle, "Founders Park: Brief History of the Fourth Ward," *Houston Metropolitan* (1991): 28–33, 59; "Freedmen's Town Historical District," Texas Historical Commission, Austin, Texas; "Juneteenth," *Houston Chronicle,* July 21, 1975; Lorenzo Thomas, "Texas Tradition: Juneteenth," *Blazon Magazine,* June 1983, 6–7.

32. David G. McComb, *Houston: The Bayou City* (Austin, 1969), 3–166.

33. *Texas Narratives.*

34. SoRelle, 3–75.

35. Beeth and D. Wintz, 87–102.

36. William H. Grimshaw, *Official History of Freemasonry among the Colored People in North America* (New York, 1903), 67–83, 263–264.

37. Henry Faulk, recorder, "Black Baptist Services" (1940), Folklore Center Archives, Barker Texas History Center, University of Texas, Austin.

38. Walter F. Pitts Jr., *Old Ship of Zion: The Afro-Baptist Ritual in the African Diaspora* (New York, 1993). Also see Melville Herskovits, *Myth of the Negro Past* (Boston, 1958); Victor Turner, *The Ritual Process: Structure and Antistructure* (Ithaca, N.Y., 1977); Robert Farris Thompson, *Flash of the Spirit: African and Afro-American Art and Philosophy* (New York, 1983).

39. Walter F. Pitts Jr., "Like a Tree Planted by the Water: The Musical Cycle in the African-American Baptist Ritual," *Journal of American Folklore* 104 (1991).

40. This account by Pitts conforms to the authors' experiences at dozens of other "Sanctified" services in Houston and throughout the South and North.

41. Cheryl Sanders in *Saints in Exile: The Holiness-Pentecostal Experience in African American Religion and Culture* (New York, 1996) provides a similar account and explanation of black Pentecostalism.

42. Walter F. Pitts Jr., "'Keep the Fire Burning': Language and Ritual in the Afro-Baptist Church," *Journal of the American Academy of Religion* 56 (1988): 77–97.

43. Harvey Cox, *Fire From Heaven: The Rise of Pentecostal Spirituality and the Reshaping of Religion in the Twenty-first Century* (Reading, Mass., 1995).

44. Sanders, 3–27; Joe Creech, "Visions of Glory: The Place of the Azusa Street Revival in Pentecostal History," *Church History* 65 (1996): 405–424.

45. Douglas J. Nelson, "For Such a Time as This: The Story of Bishop William J. Seymour and the Azusa Street Revival" (Ph.D. diss., University of Birmingham, England, 1981).

46. Ibid.

47. Quoted in Iain MacRobert, T*he Black Roots and White Racism of Early Pentecostalism in the USA* (London, 1988), 54.

48. Aldolfo C. Valdez, "Tongues and Healing at the Azusa Street Revival," in Colleen McDannell, ed., *Religions of the United States in Practice* vol. 2 (Princeton, N.J., 2001), 221.

49. Nelson.

50. MacRobert, 48–59.

51. David Daniels, "The Cultural Renewal of Slave Religion: Charles Price Jones and

the Emergence of the Holiness Movement in Mississippi" (Ph.D. diss., Union Theological Seminary, 1992).

52. Sanders, 3–34.

53. Ibid., 35–48.

54. [Emmett J. Scott], *Red Book of Houston* (Houston, 1910). Copy in Texas Southern University Library, Houston.

55. Texas Historical Commission, *Freedmen's Town Historical District, Houston, Texas* (Austin, 1984).

56. Robert E. Ziegler, "The Working Man in Houston, Texas, 1865–1915" (Ph.D. diss., Texas Tech University, 1972), 85–97, 164–171.

57. David McComb, *Houston: The Bayou City* (Austin, 1969); Campbell.

58. Garnal L. Christian, *Black Soldiers in Jim Crow Texas, 1899–1917* (College Station, Tex., 1995), 69–91; Steven A. Reich, "Soldiers of Democracy: Black Texans and the Fight for Citizenship," *Journal of American History* 82 (1996).

59. Ann J. Lane, *The Brownsville Affair: National Crisis and Black Reaction* (Port Washington, N.Y., 1971); John D. Weaver, *The Brownsville Raid* (New York, 1970); Taylor, *In Search of the Racial Frontier*, 177–179; Marvin Fletcher, *The Black Soldier and Officer in the United States Army, 1891–1917* (Columbia, S.C., 1974).

60. Robert Haynes, *Night of Violence: The Houston Riot of 1917* (Baton Rouge, 1976), 8–46.

61. Ibid., 47–170; Edgar A. Schuler, "The Houston Race Riot, 1917," *Journal of Negro History* 29 (1944).

62. Taylor, *In Search of the Racial Frontier*, 179–181; Haynes, *Night of Violence*, 171–323.

63. Jay D. Edwards, "The Origins of Creole Architecture," *Winterthur Portfolio* 29 (1994).

64. Patricia Smith Prather, "Frenchtown," *Houston Chronicle*, September 15, 1986.

65. John Minton, "Houston Creoles and Zydeco: The Emergence of an African American Urban Popular Style," *American Music* 14 (1996).

66. Marie Lee Phelps, "Visit to Frenchtown," *Houston Post*, May 22, 1955; David Kaplan, "Houston's Creole Quarter," *Houston Post*, March 19, 1989; James Robinson, "Fifth Ward Redevelopment Starts Next Week," *Houston Chronicle*, August 1, 1991; "Frenchtown," *Houston Chronicle*, February 23, 1992.

67. Daniel H. Usner Jr., *Indians, Settlers, and Slaves in a Frontier Exchange Economy: The Lower Mississippi Valley before 1783* (Chapel Hill, N.C., 1992).

68. Alice Dunbar-Nelson, "People of Color in Louisiana," *Journal of Negro History* 1 (1916): 361–376; Arnold R. Hirsch and Joseph Logsdon, eds., *Creole New Orleans: Race and Americanization* (Baton Rouge, 1992); Rebecca J. Scott, "Defining the Boundaries of Freedom in the World of Cane: Cuba, Brazil, and Louisiana after Emancipation," *American Historical Review* 99 (1994): 70–102; Ira Berlin, "From Creole to African: Atlantic Creoles and the Origins of African-American Society in Mainland North America," *William and Mary Quarterly*, 3d ser., 53 (1996).

69. Thomas N. Ingersoll, "The Slave Trade and the Ethnic Diversity of Louisiana's Slave Community," in Charles Vincent, ed., *The Louisiana Purchase Bicentennial Series in Louisiana History*, vol. 9 (Lafayette, La., 1999), 61–77; Marie Lee Phelps, "Visit to Frenchtown," *Houston Post*, May 22, 1955.

70. Thomas Marc Fiehrer, "The African Presence in Colonial Louisiana: An Essay on the Continuity of Caribbean Culture," in Vincent, 82–106; Romeo B. Garrett, "African Survivals in American Culture," *Journal of Negro History* 51(1966): 239–245; J. A. Harrison, "The Creole Patois of Louisiana," *American Journal of Philology* 3(1882); Marcia Gaudet, "Bouki, the Hyena, in Louisiana and African Tales," *Journal of American Folklore* 105 (1992).

71. Fredrika Bremer, *The Homes of the New World* (New York, 1854), 200–237.

72. Thompson; Yvonne Chireau, "Conjure and Christianity in the Nineteenth Century: Religious Elements in African American Magic," *Religion and American Culture* 7 (1997): 225–246.

73. Fiehrer, 82–106; Jeffrey E. Anderson, *Conjure in African American Society* (Baton Rouge, 2005); Robert Tallant, *Voodoo in New Orleans* (Greta, La., 1946).

74. Thompson, 161–192.

75. Elizabeth McAlister, "The Rite of Baptism in Haitian Vodou," in McDannell, 362–371, quotation on 367.

76. Thompson, 161–192.

77. Authors' observance in New Orleans, Houston, and Charleston.

78. Bill Minutaglio, "Voodoo [in Houston]," in "Texas Magazine," *Houston Chronicle,* May 2, 1982.

79. Michael Tisserand, *The Kingdom of Zydeco* (New York, 1998), quotation on 29.

80. Rick Koster, *Louisiana Music* (Cambridge, Mass., 2002).

81. Some African musicians also embraced the accordion, adapting it to traditional African music. Examples can be heard in the music of Boubacar Traoré from Mali and Régis Gizavo from Madagascar: *Songs and Music: Boubacar Traoré,* Label Bleu (1998) and Boubacar Traoré, "Kanou," on *Mali,* Putumayo (2005).

82. Minton, 480–526.

83. Carl A. Brasseaux, Keith P. Fontenot, and Claude F. Oubre, *Creoles of Color in the Bayou Country* (Jackson, Miss., 1994); Shane K. Bernard, *Swamp Pop: Cajun and Creole Rhythm and Blues* (Jackson, Miss., 1996).

84. Tisserand, 50–51.

85. Michael Doucet, "Amede Ardoin's Blues: An Introduction" and Jared Snyder, "Amede's Recordings," in liner notes and French and English lyrics for *The Roots of Zydeco: Amede Aroin: I'm Never Coming Back,* reissue of 1930–1934, New Orleans, San Antonio, and New York recordings, Arthoolie Productions (1995).

86. From liner notes in *Roots of Zydeco,* 62–79.

87. Minton, 480–526.

88. Roger Wood and James Fraher, *Texas Zydeco* (Austin, 2006).

89. Phelps.

90. Clifton Chenier, *Louisiana Blues and Zydeco,* Arhoolie Records (1990). Also see liner notes.

91. Quoted in Minton, 507.

92. Tisserand, 137–138, 247–268; Wood and Fraher, 166–173.

93. U.S. Department of Commerce, "Population and Housing: Houston, Texas," *United States Census,* 1940 and 1950 (Washington, D.C., 1941, 1951). These reports provide data on income, employment, housing, and education for each of the enumeration dis-

tricts. Conclusions based on sampling of predominantly black enumeration districts in the old Third, Fourth, and Fifth Wards.

94. United States Census, *Census of Population and Housing*, 1940 and 1950.

95. *Informer*, 1940–1950.

96. Robert Bullard, *Invisible Houston: The Black Experience in Boom and Bust* (College Station, Tex.,1987).

97. Arnold Shaw, *Honkers and Shouters: The Golden Age of Rhythm and Blues* (New York, 1928), 57–89.

98. Quotes taken from interviews conducted or quoted by Roger Wood, *Down in Houston: Bayou City Blues* (Austin, 2003), 13–16.

99. Shaw, 113–123.

100. Ibid., xvi.

101. Ibid., 57–89.

102. Interview quoted in Alan Govenar, *The Early Years of Rhythm and Blues* (Houston, 1990), 5.

103. Wood, 187–230.

104. Ibid.; Govenar.

105. Alvin Ailey, with A. Peter Bailey, *Revelations: The Autobiography of Alvin Ailey* (New York, 1995), 17–19.

106. Ibid., 27.

107. Ibid., 31.

108. Michael Theodore Coolen, "The Fodet: A Senegambian Origin for the Blues," *Black Prospective in Music* 1 (1982).

CHAPTER 9: CALIFORNIA DREAMING: SOUTH CENTRAL LA

1. Douglas Flamming, *Bound for Freedom: Black Los Angeles in Jim Crow America* (Los Angeles, 2005), 1–17.

2. Ibid., 17–190.

3. Ibid.

4. *California Eagle*, published weekly from its editorial offices on Central Avenue.

5. W. E. B. Du Bois, "Colored California," *Crisis* 6 (August 1913); Flamming, 92–125.

6. Lawrence B. deGraaf and Quintard Taylor, eds., *Seeking El Dorado: African Americans in California* (Seattle, 2001).

7. Lawrence B. deGraaf, "Negro Migration to Los Angeles, 1930 to 1950" (Ph.D. diss. University of California, Los Angeles, 1962).

8. DeGraaf and Taylor.

9. Bette Yarbrough Cox, *Central Avenue: Its Rise and Fall, 1890–1955* (Los Angeles, 1993). Cox has complied a rich and veritable published archive or "family scrapbook" of South Central's middle class. Her collection includes photographs, poetry, oral history, maps, and a chronology.

10. U.S. Census Bureau, Fourteenth Census of the United States, 1920, *Population* (Washington, D.C., 1921); Flaming, 60–91.

11. Cox, *Central Avenue*, 5–22.

12. U.S. Census, 1920, *Population*.

13. Flamming, 159–189.

14. Ibid., 35–59.

15. *Los Angeles Times*, September 28 and November 5, 1918.

16. *Los Angeles Times*, October 21, 1901.

17. *Los Angeles Times*, February 12, 1909.

18. Raphael J. Sonenshein, *Politics in Black and White: Race and Power in Los Angeles* (Princeton, N.J., 1993), 21–36.

19. Flamming, 24–27, describes the "race" identity of Bass and others.

20. Ibid.

21. Cox, *Central Avenue*.

22. Flamming, 17–35, tells the story of the *California Eagle*.

23. *California Eagle* 1919–1929.

24. *California Eagle*, classified pages.

25. Cox, *Central Avenue*, 25–38.

26. Flamming, 283–294.

27. *California Eagle*, June 29, July 5, and July 12, 1928.

28. *California Eagle*, June 22 and 29, 1928.

29. St. Clair Drake and Horace R. Cayton, *Black Metropolis: A Study of Negro Life in a Northern City* (Chicago, 1945), 27–29, 564–657.

30. Cox, *Central Avenue*.

31. Tom Reed, *Black Music History of Los Angeles* (Los Angeles, 1970). Reed's study documents the sporting life of South Central, including numerous photographs.

32. Jacqueline Cogdell DjeDje and Eddie S. Meadows, eds., *California Soul: Music of African Americans in the West* (Los Angeles, 1998), 28–60; Clora Bryant et al., eds., *Central Avenue Sounds: Jazz in Los Angeles* (Los Angeles, 1998), 1–88.

33. Interview with Gerald Wilson, Special Collections, UCLA, Los Angeles, 1995.

34. Lawrence Gushee, "New Orleans-Area Music on the West Coast, 1908–1925," *Black Music Research Journal* 9 (1989).

35. Ibid., 1–18.

36. Interview with Lee Young, Special Collections, UCLA, 1996.

37. www.leimertparkmovie.com.

38. Lynell George, " 'Whose Your People': LA to LA—The Creolization of Los Angeles," in *No Crystal Stair: African Americans in the City of Angels* (New York, 1992), 220–243.

39. Interview with Fletcher Smith, Special Collections, UCLA, 1995.

40. Carl Brasseaux, Keith P. Founenot, and Claude F. Oubre, *Creoles of Color in the Bayou Country* (Jackson, 1994).

41. Michael Tisserand, *Kingdom of Zydeco* (New Orleans, 1980).

42. Brasseaux, Founenot, and Oubre.

43. Interview with Marshall Royal, Special Collections, UCLA, 1996; Young and Smith interviews.

44. Bette Yarbrough Cox, "Evolution of Black Music in Los Angeles, 1890–1955," in deGraaf and Taylor, 250–269.

45. Royal interview.

46. Cox, "Evolution of Black Music in Los Angeles."

47. Royal interview.

48. Ibid.

49. Interview with Samuel Browne, in Cox, *Central Avenue*, 97–112.

50. Interview with Horace Tapscott, in Bryant et al., 282–310.

51. Browne interview.

52. See oral interviews of Central Avenue jazz musicians available in Special Collections Library, UCLA.

53. Royal, Tapscott, and Young interviews.

54. Ralph Eastman, " 'Pitchin' Up a Boogie': African American Musicians, Nightlife, and Music Venues in Los Angeles, 1930–1945," in DjeDje and Meadows, 79–103.

55. U. S. Census Bureau, Sixteenth Census of the United States, 1940, *Housing*, Los Angeles, Block Statistics (Washington, D.C., 1941), 5; Los Angeles County Housing Authority, *Real Property Inventory and Low Income Housing Area Survey of a Portion of Los Angeles County, California, 1939–40* (Los Angeles, 1941); deGraaf.

56. Flamming, 299.

57. Ibid., 304–305.

58. U. S. Census Bureau, *United States Census, 1940, California* (Washington, D.C., 1941).

59. Ibid., 296–330.

60. Interview with Augustus Hawkins, Special Collections, UCLA, 1995; Flamming, 315–319.

61. Morton Grodzins, *Americans Betrayed: Politics and the Japanese Evacuation* (Chicago, 1949); Roger Daniels, *Concentration Camps: North America Japanese in the United States and Canada during World War II* (Malabar, Fla.,1971); David O'Brien and Stephen Fugita, *The Japanese American Experience* (Bloomington, Ind., 1984).

62. U.S. Census Bureau, *United States, 1940, California*; U.S. Census Bureau, Seventeenth Census of the United States, *1950, California* (Washington, D.C., 1951); California Department of Industrial Relations, "Negro Californians" (Sacramento, 1963); U.S. Census Bureau, United States Census: 1940, "California," in *Housing Census Report* (Washington, D.C., 1941), V, part 100; U.S. Census Bureau, United States Census: 1950, "Los Angeles Block Statistics," in *Housing Census Report* (Washington, D.C., 1951), V, part 100.

63. Roger W. Lotchin, "California Cities and the Hurricane of Change: World War II in San Francisco, Los Angeles, and San Diego Metropolitan Areas," *Pacific Historical Review* 63 (1994); Arthur Verge, "The Impact of the Second World War on Los Angeles," *Pacific Historical Review* 63 (1994); Gerald Nash, *The American West Transformed: The Impact of the Second World War* (Bloomington, Ind., 1985), 56–74.

64. Lotchin; Verge.

65. Lawrence deGraaf, "Negro Migration to Los Angeles, 1930–1950" (Ph.D. diss., UCLA, 1962), 79–180; Keith Collins, *Black Los Angeles: The Maturing of the Ghetto, 1940–1950* (Saratoga, Calif., 1980), 5–25; Josh Sides, *LA City Limits: African American Los Angeles from the Great Depression to the Present* (Los Angeles, 2003), 12–90.

66. DeGraaf, "Negro Migration"; Cox, *Central Avenue*, 59–90; Flamming, 331–365.

67. Sides, 38–57; Lawrence B. deGraaf, introduction to deGraaf and Taylor, 3–30.

68. *California Eagle*, 1941–1945.

69. Shane White and Graham White, *Stylin': African American Expressive Culture from Its Beginnings to the Zoot Suit* (Ithaca, N.Y., 1998); Katrina Hazzard-Gordon, *Jookin: The Rise of Social Dance Formations in African American Culture* (Philadelphia, 1990).

70. Bruce Tyler, "Black Jive and White Repression," *Journal of Ethnic Studies* 16 (1989): 32–66; Kobena Mercer, "Black Hair/Style Politics," *New Formations* 3 (1987).

71. Steve Chibnall, "Whistle and Zoot," *History Workshop Journal* 20 (1985); Stuart Cosgrove, "Zoot-Suit and Style Warfare," *History Workshop Journal* 18 (1984).

72. Douglas Henry Daniels, "Los Angeles Zoot: Race 'Riot,' the Pachuco, and Black Music Culture," *Journal of African American History* 87 (2002); Roger Waldinger and Mehdi Bozorgmehr, eds., *Ethnic Los Angeles* (New York, 1996), 10.

73. Robin D. G. Kelley, "Riddle of the Zoot," in *Race Rebels: Culture, Politics, and the Black Working Class* (New York,1994), 161–181, 275–281.

74. George Flynn, "Selective Service and American Blacks during World War II," *Journal of Negro History* 69 (1984).

75. Daniels.

76. Mauricio Mazon, *The Zoot-Suit Riots* (Austin, 1984); *California Eagle*, June, 1943.

77. K. Collins, 28.

78. John Modell, Marc Goulden, and Sigurdur Magnusson, "World War II in the Lives of Black Americans: Some Findings and Interpretations," *Journal of American History* 76 (1989).

79. DeGraaf, "Negro Migration to Los Angeles."

80. U.S. Census Bureau, *United States Census*, 1950; U. S. Census Bureau, "Los Angeles Block Statistics: 1950, Negro Californians: Population, Employment, Income, Education"; Sides, 37–98.

81. Sides, 57–102.

82. U.S. Census Bureau, *United States Census*, 1950, "Los Angeles."

83. *California Eagle*, September 1945–September 1946.

84. Walter Mosley's "Easy Rawlins" novels describe the life of southern migrants in South Central. Mosley grew up in South Central and his parents came to Los Angeles from Louisiana and Texas shortly after the war. See *Gone Fishing* (Baltimore, 1997). Also see Rosina Becerra, "Folk Medicine Use: Diverse Populations in a Metropolitan Area," *Social Work in Health Care*, 21 (1995).

85. Cox, "Evolution of Black Music in Los Angeles, 1890–1955," 250–269; Jacqueline Cogdell DjeDje, "Gospel Music in the Los Angeles Black Community: A Historical Overview," *Black Music Research Journal* 9 (Spring 1989): 35–79; Jacqueline Cogdell DjeDje, "Los Angeles Composers of African American Gospel Music: The First Generations," *American Music* 11 (Winter 1993).

86. DjeDje, "Gospel Music in the Los Angeles Black Community."

87. Jacqueline Cogdell DjeDje, "California Black Gospel Music Tradition," in DjeDje and Meadows, 124–177.

88. Interview with T-Bone Walker, by Jim O'Neal and Amy van Singel, Chicago, September 30, 1972, published in *Living Blues* 11 (Spring 1973).

89. Interview with Johnny Otis, by Willie R. Collins, quoted in DjeDje and Meadows, 216.

90. Helen Oakley Dance, *Stormy Monday: The "T-Bone" Walker Story* (Baton Rouge, 1987).

91. Arnold Shaw, *Honkers and Shouters: The Golden Years of Rhythm & Blues* (New York, 1978), 89–271; Dance.

92. "T-Bone" Walker, *The Complete Imperial Recordings, 1950–1954*, liner notes by Pete Welding, EMI Records (1991).

93. "T-Bone" Walker, *The Very Best of "T-Bone" Walker: The Classic Black and White and Imperial Recordings, 1949–1954*, EMI Records (2000).

94. Ralph Eastman, "Central Avenue Blues: The Making of Los Angeles Rhythm & Blues," *Black Music Research Journal* 9 (Spring 1989): 19–33.

95. Interview with Cecel McNeely, Special Collections, UCLA, 1993.

96. Kwaaku Person-Lynn, "Insider Perspectives on the American Afrikan Popular Music Industry and Black Radio," in DjeDje and Meadows, 179–197; Shaw, parts 1, 2, and 3.

97. Paul Bullock, ed., *Watts: The Aftermath* (New York, 1969); Patricia Rae Adler, "Watts: From Suburb to Black Ghetto" (Ph.D. diss., University of Southern California, 1977); Paul Langham Robinson, "Class and Place within the Los Angeles African American Community, 1940–1990" (Ph.D. diss., University of Southern California, 2001); Robert Fogelson, *The Fragmented Metropolis: Los Angeles, 1850–1930* (Cambridge, 1967); Lawrence B. deGraaf, "City of Black Angels," *Pacific Historical Review* 39 (1970): 323–352; Flamming; Sides; Sonenshein; Mike Davis, *City of Quartz* (New York, 1992); Christopher Rand, *Los Angeles: The Ultimate City* (New York, 1967).

98. *Shelley v. Kraemer*, 334, *U.S. [S.C.] Report* (Washington, D.C., 1949), 1–23.

99. Sides, 95–130.

100. Ibid., 95; deGraaf, "Negro Migration to Los Angeles"; K. Collins.

101. Robinson.

102. Sides, 95–130; Kenneth T. Jackson, *Crabgrass Frontier: The Suburbanization of the United States* (New York, 1985), 172–230.

103. Adler, 236–293: Sides, 114–118.

104. Ibid.

105. Royal interview; Horace Tapscott, *Musical and Soul Journey* (Durham, N.C., 2001), 27–33.

106. Bryant et al., 385–397.

107. Interview with William Woodson, Special Collections, UCLA, 1995.

108. Adler; K. Collins.

109. See Walter Mosley, *Devil in a Blue Dress* (New York, 1990); *Black Betty* (New York, 1994); *A Little Yellow Dog* (New York, 1996); *The White Butterfly* (New York, 1992); and *Bad Boy Brawly Brown* (New York, 2002).

110. Mosley, *Devil in a Blue Dress*.

111. Ibid.

112. Ibid.; Eastman, "Pitchin' Up a Boogie," 79–103; Person-Lynn, 179–197.

113. Mosley, *Black Betty*, 31.

114. Mosley, *Devil in a Blue Dress*, 53.

115. Mosley, *A Little Yellow Dog*, 214.

116. Ibid., 299.

117. Mosley, *Devil in a Blue Dress*, 94.

118. Ibid., 54.

119. Ibid., 72.

120. Mosley, *The White Butterfly*, 62.

121. Mosley, *Devil in a Blue Dress*, 74.

122. Mosley, *A Little Yellow Dog*, 64 and 208.

123. Mosley, *Bad Boy Brawly Brown*.

124. Walter Mosley, *Walter Mosley.com*.

125. Mosley, *Devil in a Blue Dress*.

126. Gerald Horne, *Fire This Time: The Watts Uprising and the 1960s* (Charlottesville, Va., 1995).

127. *Los Angeles Times*, August 12–16, 1965.

128. Governor's Commission on the Los Angeles Riots, *Violence in the City: An End or a Beginning* (Los Angeles, December 2, 1965).

129. Walter Mosley's *Little Scarlet* (New York, 2004) probes the causes and motives of the 1965 Watts riot that Mosley witnessed.

130. Ibid., 53.

131. Ibid., 83–84.

132. Ibid., 38.

133. Paul Bullock, ed., *Watts: The Aftermath; An Inside View of the Ghetto by the People of Watts* (New York, 1969).

134. Ibid.; Lynell George, *No Crystal Stair: African Americans in the City of Los Angeles* (New York, 1992); Horne; Mark Baldassare, ed., *The Los Angeles Riots* (San Francisco, 1994).

135. Robin D. G. Kelley, "Kickin' Reality, Kickin' Ballistics: 'Gansta Rap' and Postindustrial Los Angeles," in *Race Rebels*, 183–227, 282–294.

136. Lawrence B. deGraaf, "African-American Suburbanization in California, 1960–1990," in deGraaf and Taylor, 3–69, 407–428. For arrest statistics during the riot and profile of those arrested, see McCone Report, 24, cited above in note 28.

137. Baldassare.

138. Ibid.; *Los Angeles Times*, April 29–June 4, 1992.

139. U. S. Census Bureau, *United States Census, 2000, Population and Housing, Los Angeles and Long Beach, California* (Washington, D.C., 2001).

140. Raul Homero Villa and George J. Sanchez, "Los Angeles Studies and the Future of Urban Culture," 499–405; Greg Hise, "Border City: Race and Social Distance in Los Angeles," 545–559; Dana Cuff, "The Figure of the Neighbor: Los Angeles Past and Present," 559–582, all in *American Quarterly*, 56 (2004), which focuses on Los Angeles. Also see William A. V. Clark and Sarah A. Blue, "Race, Class, and Segregation Patterns in U.S. Immigrant Gateway Cities," *Urban Affairs Review* 39 (2004): 667–689; Curtis C. Roseman and Seong Woo Lee, "Linked and Independent African American Migration from Los Angeles," *Professional Geographer* 50 (1998): 204–214; Moses Rischin, "Immigration, Migration, and Minorities in California: A Reassessment," *Pacific Historical Review* 41(1972); Sides, chap. 6 and 209–216, maps of black housing patterns in Los Angeles from 1930 to

1980; Peter Morrison and Ira S. Lowry, "A Riot of Color: The Demographic Setting," in Baldassare, 19–46.

141. Interview with Sam Browne, in Cox, *Central Avenue*,109.

142. See recommendations in McCone Report.

143. Waldinger and Bozorgmehr.

144. Baldassare. In addition see *American Quarterly* 56 (2004, dedicated to Los Angeles, and the last chapter in Sides. Also Patricia Hall and Steven Ruggles, " 'Restless in the Midst of Prosperity': New Evidence on the Internal Migration of Americans, 1850–2000," *Journal of American History* 91 (2004); James Johnson, "Black Flight to the South," *Society* 24 (1987); Rischin.

145. James N. Gregory, *The Southern Diaspora: How the Great Migrations of Black and White Southerners Transformed America* (Chapel Hill, N.C., 2005), 81–112, 321–328; U.S. Census Bureau (Washington, D.C., 2001), "Home Ownership by Race"; U.S. Census Bureau (Washington, D.C., 2007), "Current Population Survey, 2006 Annual Social and Economic Supplement," Education by Race and Income by Race.

CHAPTER 10: CIRCLE UNBROKEN: THREE STORIES AND A CONCLUSION

1. James N. Gregory, *The Southern Diaspora: How the Great Migrations of Black and White Southerners Transformed America* (Chapel Hill, N.C., 2005), 321–328.

2. Alvia Wardlaw, "Metamorphosis: The Life of John Biggers," in Wardlaw, ed., *The Art of John Biggers: View from the Upper Room* (Houston, 1995), 16–75; Alvia Wardlaw, "John Biggers—Artist, Traditional Folkways of the Black Community," in Francis Edward Abernethy, ed., *Juneteenth Texas: Essays in African-American Folklore* (Denton, Tex., 1996),209–222.

3. John Biggers and Carroll Simms, *Black Art in Houston: The Texas Southern University Experience* (College Station, Tex., 1978).

4. John Biggers, *John Biggers: My America; The 1940s and 1950s—Paintings, Sculptures, & Drawings* (New York, 2004).

5. John Biggers, *Ananse: The Web of Life in Africa* (Austin 1962).

6. Ibid., title page.

7. Wardlaw, "Metamorphosis," 16–75; Biggers and Simms.

8. Christine McConnell, dir., *Kindred Spirits: Contemporary African American Artists* (film, 1992).

9. Interview with Biggers by Robert Farris Thompson, quoted in Wardlaw, *Art of John Biggers*, 110.

10. Robert Farris Thompson, "John Biggers's Shotguns of 1987: An American Classic," in Wardlaw, *Art of John Biggers*, 111.

11. Interview with Janette Gailliard Lee, Hamlin community, South Carolina, November 6, 2000.

12. Interview with Joyce Coakley, Hamlin community, South Carolina, July, 2002.

13. Joyce V. Coakley, *Sweetgrass Baskets and the Gullah Tradition* (Mount Pleasant, S.C., 2006), 89–96.

14. Service, Garden of Prayer Pentecostal Church, Mount Pleasant, June 2001.

15. Harvey G. Cox, *Fire from Heaven: The Rise of Pentecostal Spirituality and the Reshaping of Religion in the Twenty-first Century* (Reading, Mass., 1995); Cheryl J. Sanders, *Saints in Exile: The Holiness-Pentecostal Experience in African American Religion and Culture* (New York, 1996); Albert J. Raboteau, *Slave Religion: The "Invisible Institution" in the Antebellum South* (New York, 1978); David Lehmann, *Struggle for the Spirit: Religious Transformation and Popular Culture in Brazil and Latin America* (Oxford, 1996); Stephen D. Glazier, ed., *Perspectives on Pentecostalism: Case Studies from the Caribbean and Latin America* (Washington, D.C., 1980); Allan H. Anderson and Walter Hollenweger, eds., *Pentecostals after a Century: Global Perspectives on a Movement in Transition* (Sheffield, 1999); Brigit Meyer, "Praise the Lord: Popular Cinema and Pentecostal Style in Ghana's New Public Sphere," *Ethnologist* 31 (2004).

16. Interview with Divine Gbagbo, Wooster, Ohio, March 4, 2008.

INDEX